empowered™

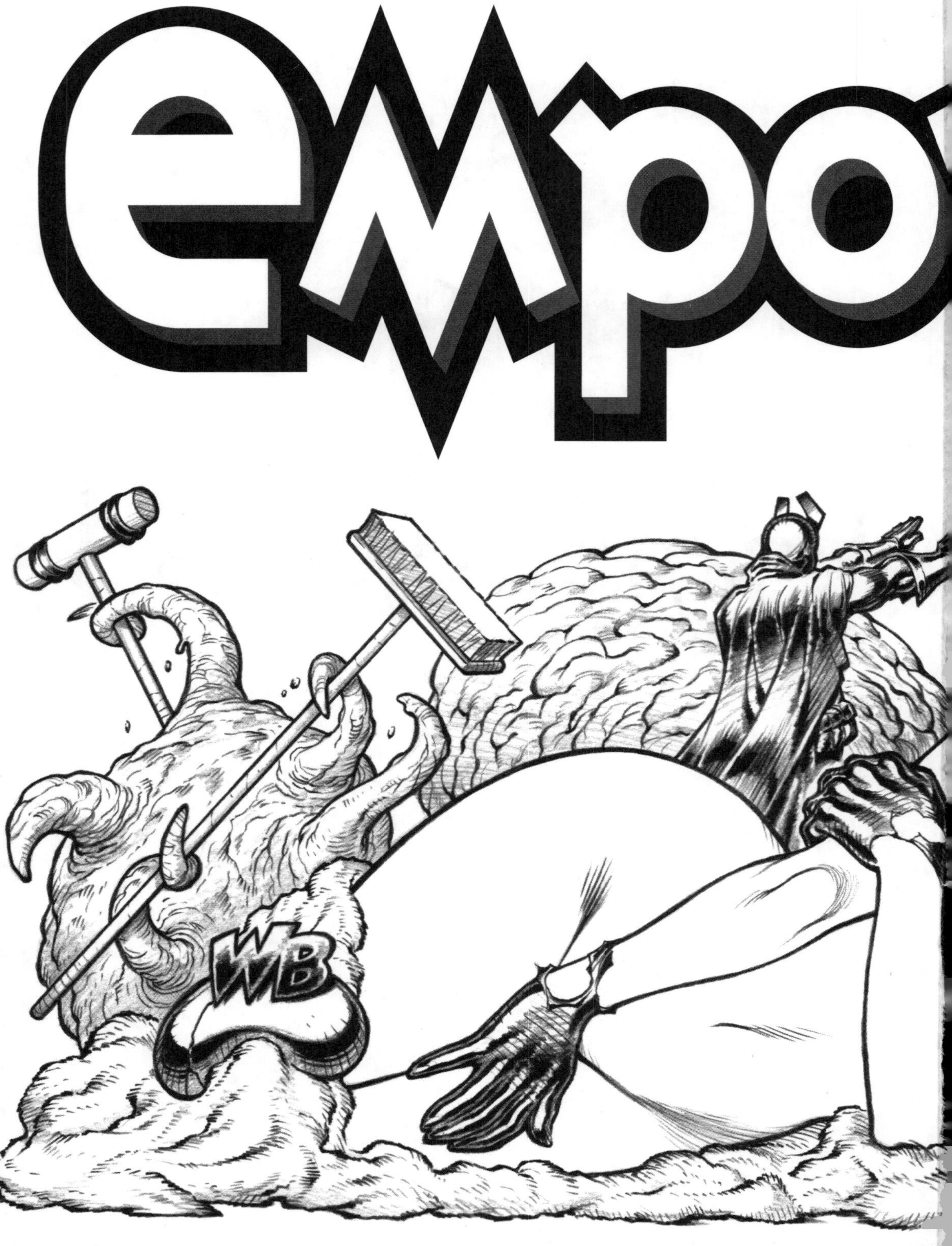
empo
WB

wered™

volume 4

by ADAM WARREN

cover colors by LEE DUHIG for GURUeFX

empowered logo by EUGENE WANG

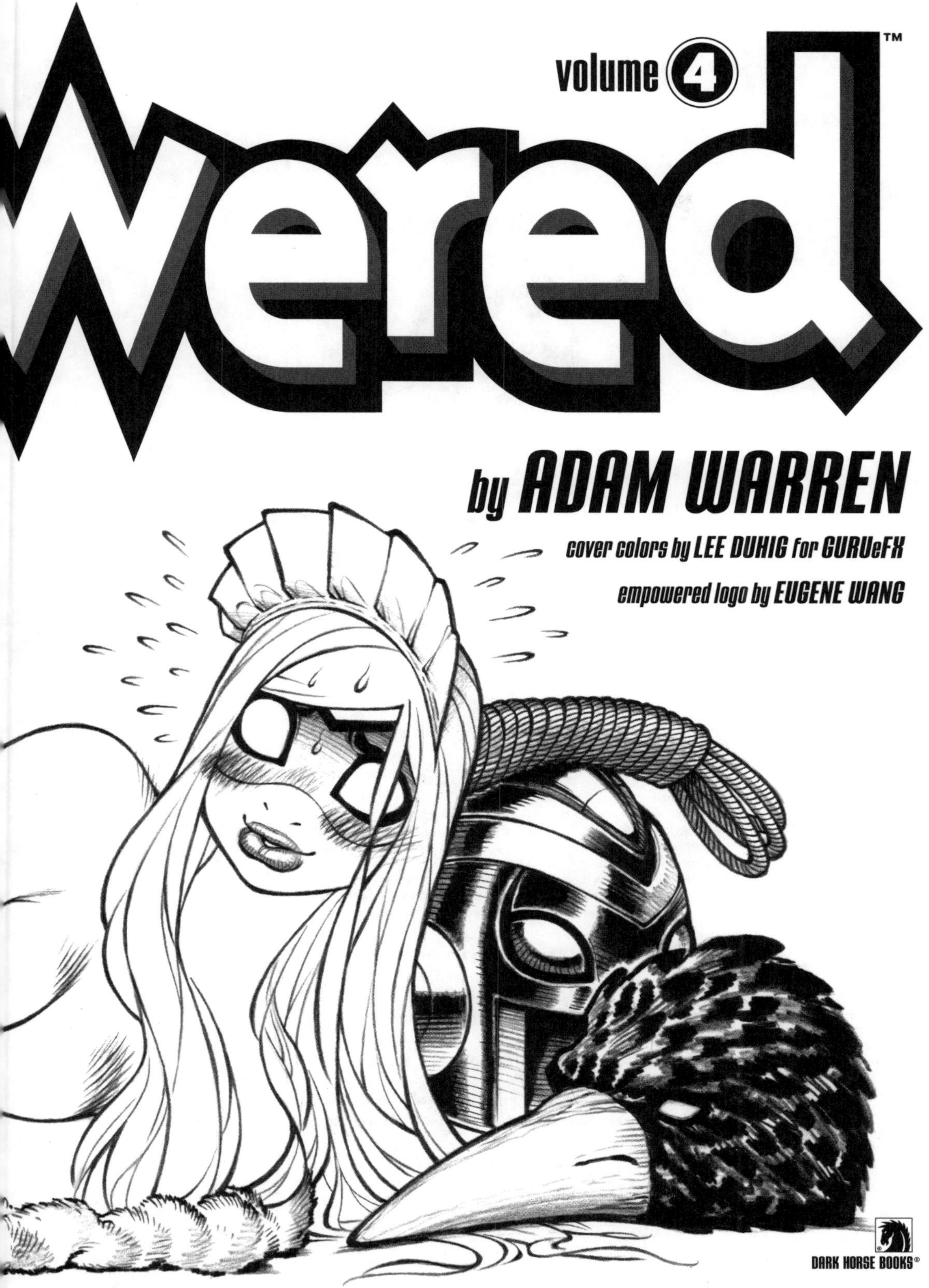

DARK HORSE BOOKS®

publisher
Mike Richardson

editor
Chris Warner

designer
Josh Elliott

art director
Lia Ribacchi

EMPOWERED VOLUME 4

Dark Horse Books
A division of Dark Horse Comics, Inc.
10956 SE Main Street
Milwaukie, OR 97222

darkhorse.com

To find a comics shop in your area, call the Comic Shop
Locator Service toll-free at 1-888-266-4226

First edition: October 2008
ISBN 978-1-59307-994-9

3 5 7 9 10 8 6 4 2

Printed in the United States of America

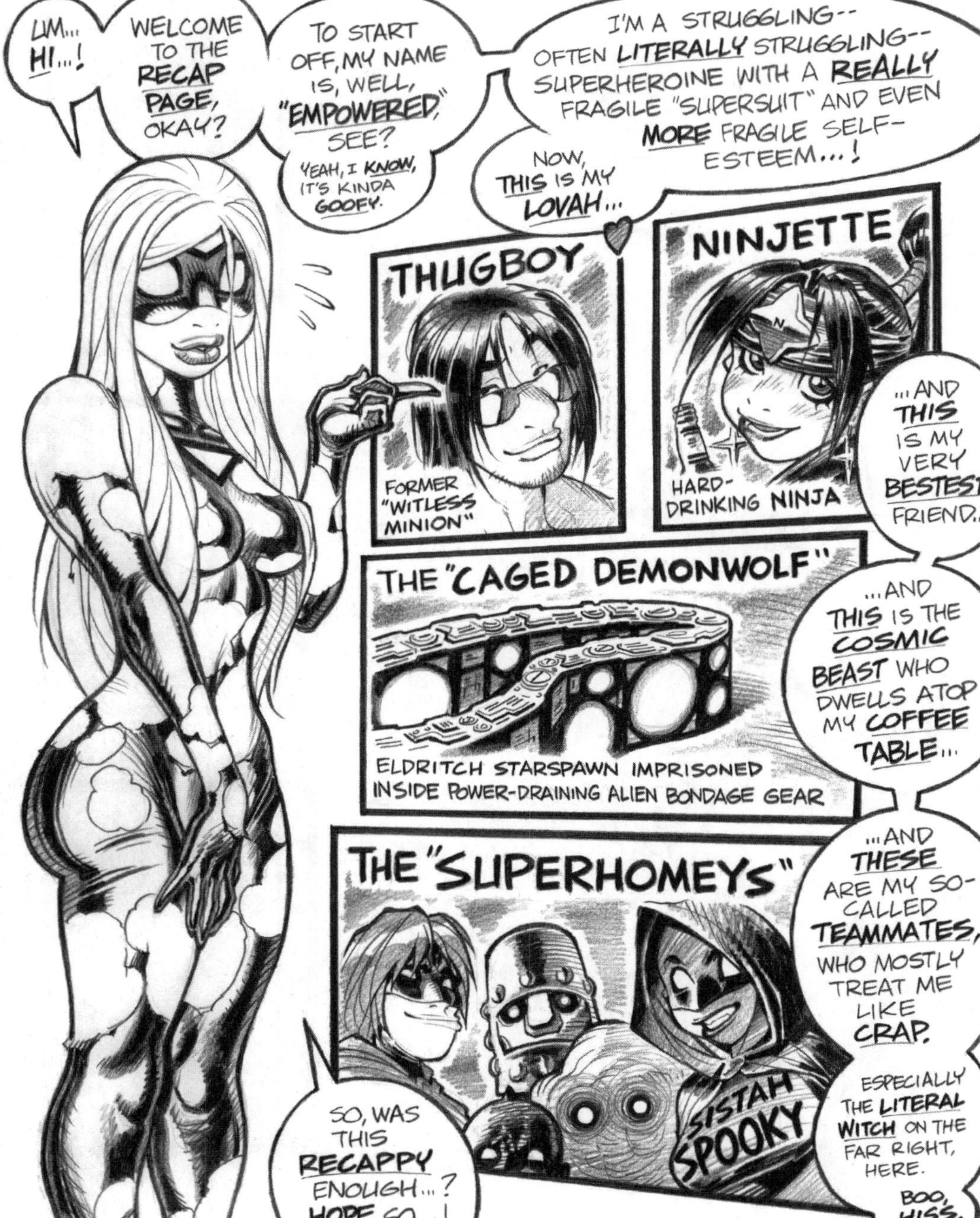
UM... HI...!
WELCOME TO THE RECAP PAGE, OKAY?
TO START OFF, MY NAME IS, WELL, "EMPOWERED," SEE?
YEAH, I KNOW, IT'S KINDA GOOFY.
I'M A STRUGGLING-- OFTEN LITERALLY STRUGGLING-- SUPERHEROINE WITH A REALLY FRAGILE "SUPERSUIT" AND EVEN MORE FRAGILE SELF-ESTEEM...!
NOW, THIS IS MY LOVAH...
THUGBOY
FORMER "WITLESS MINION"
NINJETTE
HARD-DRINKING NINJA
...AND THIS IS MY VERY BESTEST FRIEND...
THE "CAGED DEMONWOLF"
ELDRITCH STARSPAWN IMPRISONED INSIDE POWER-DRAINING ALIEN BONDAGE GEAR
...AND THIS IS THE COSMIC BEAST WHO DWELLS ATOP MY COFFEE TABLE...
THE "SUPERHOMEYS"
SISTAH SPOOKY
...AND THESE ARE MY SO-CALLED TEAMMATES, WHO MOSTLY TREAT ME LIKE CRAP.
ESPECIALLY THE LITERAL WITCH ON THE FAR RIGHT, HERE.
BOO, HISS.
SO, WAS THIS RECAPPY ENOUGH...? HOPE SO...!

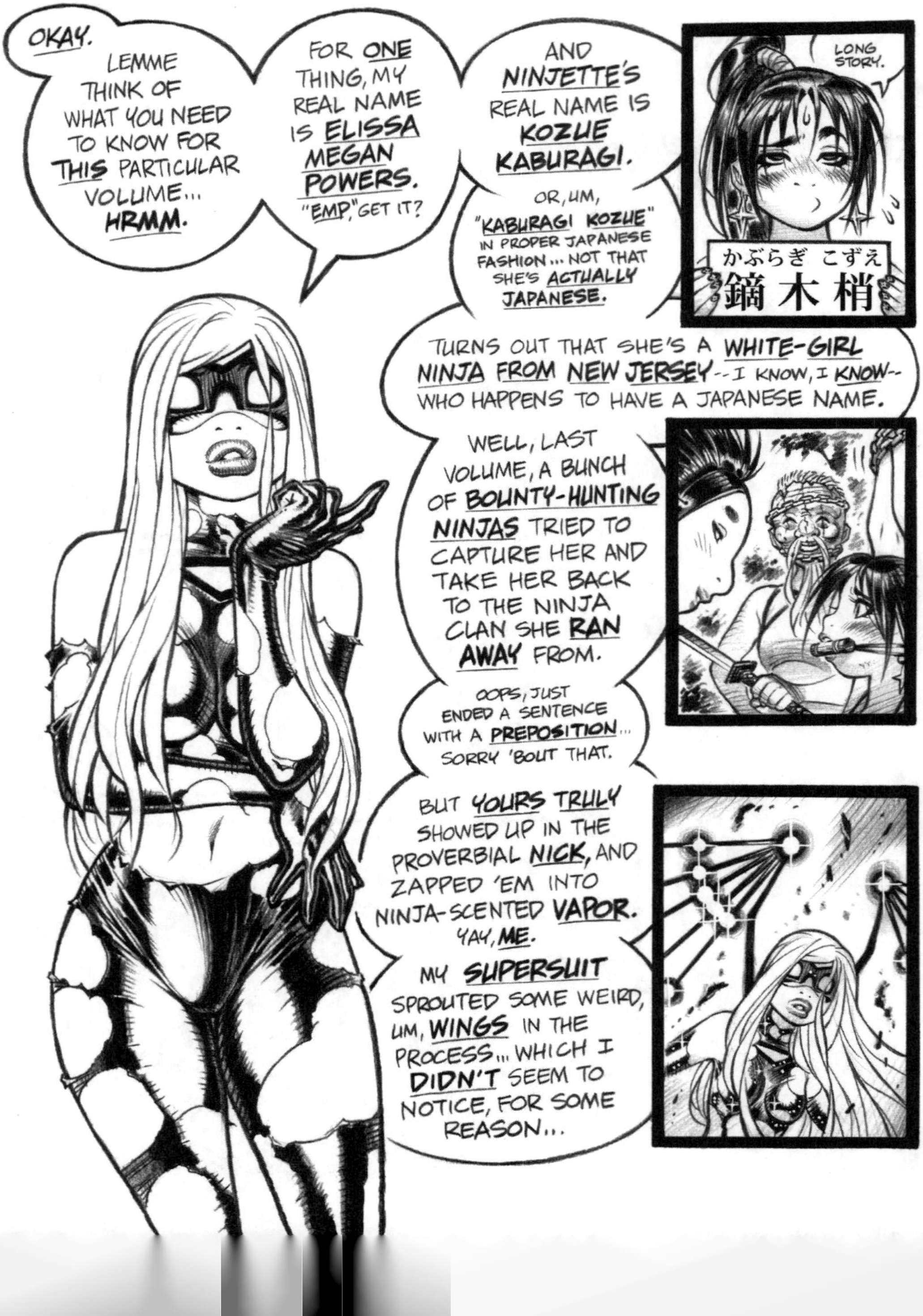
OKAY. LEMME THINK OF WHAT YOU NEED TO KNOW FOR THIS PARTICULAR VOLUME... HRMM.
FOR ONE THING, MY REAL NAME IS ELISSA MEGAN POWERS. "EMP," GET IT?
AND NINJETTE'S REAL NAME IS KOZUE KABURAGI.
OR, UM, "KABURAGI KOZUE" IN PROPER JAPANESE FASHION... NOT THAT SHE'S ACTUALLY JAPANESE.
LONG STORY.
かぶらぎ こずえ
鏑木梢
TURNS OUT THAT SHE'S A WHITE-GIRL NINJA FROM NEW JERSEY--I KNOW, I KNOW--WHO HAPPENS TO HAVE A JAPANESE NAME.
WELL, LAST VOLUME, A BUNCH OF BOUNTY-HUNTING NINJAS TRIED TO CAPTURE HER AND TAKE HER BACK TO THE NINJA CLAN SHE RAN AWAY FROM.
OOPS, JUST ENDED A SENTENCE WITH A PREPOSITION... SORRY 'BOUT THAT.
BUT YOURS TRULY SHOWED UP IN THE PROVERBIAL NICK, AND ZAPPED 'EM INTO NINJA-SCENTED VAPOR. YAY, ME.
MY SUPERSUIT SPROUTED SOME WEIRD, UM, WINGS IN THE PROCESS... WHICH I DIDN'T SEEM TO NOTICE, FOR SOME REASON...

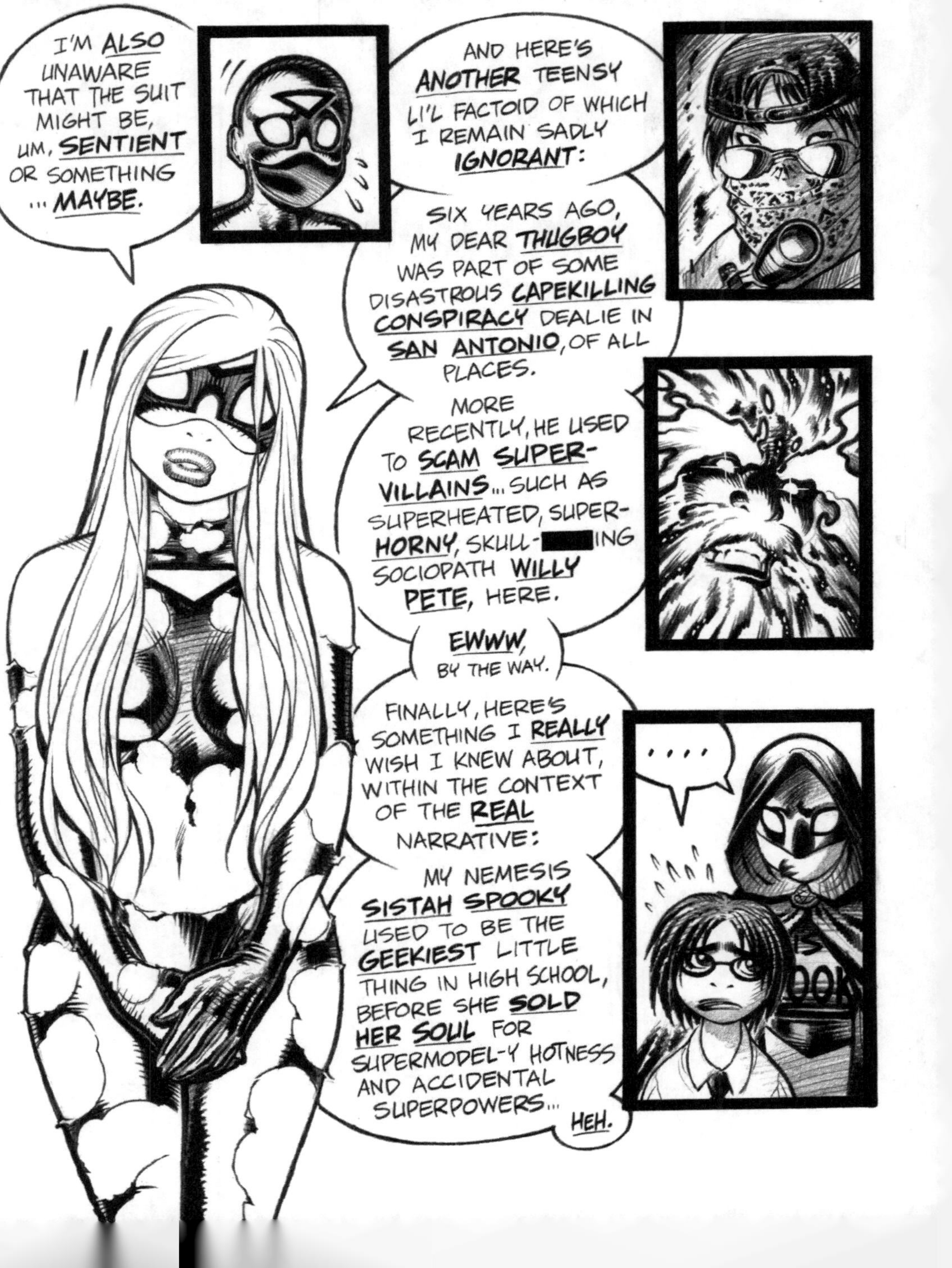
I'M ALSO UNAWARE THAT THE SUIT MIGHT BE, UM, SENTIENT OR SOMETHING ... MAYBE.
AND HERE'S ANOTHER TEENSY LI'L FACTOID OF WHICH I REMAIN SADLY IGNORANT:
SIX YEARS AGO, MY DEAR THUGBOY WAS PART OF SOME DISASTROUS CAPEKILLING CONSPIRACY DEALIE IN SAN ANTONIO, OF ALL PLACES.
MORE RECENTLY, HE USED TO SCAM SUPER-VILLAINS... SUCH AS SUPERHEATED, SUPER-HORNY, SKULL-[redacted]ING SOCIOPATH WILLY PETE, HERE.
EWWW, BY THE WAY.
FINALLY, HERE'S SOMETHING I REALLY WISH I KNEW ABOUT, WITHIN THE CONTEXT OF THE REAL NARRATIVE:
MY NEMESIS SISTAH SPOOKY USED TO BE THE GEEKIEST LITTLE THING IN HIGH SCHOOL, BEFORE SHE SOLD HER SOUL FOR SUPERMODEL-Y HOTNESS AND ACCIDENTAL SUPERPOWERS... HEH.
....

Empowered™

Who da Übermensch?

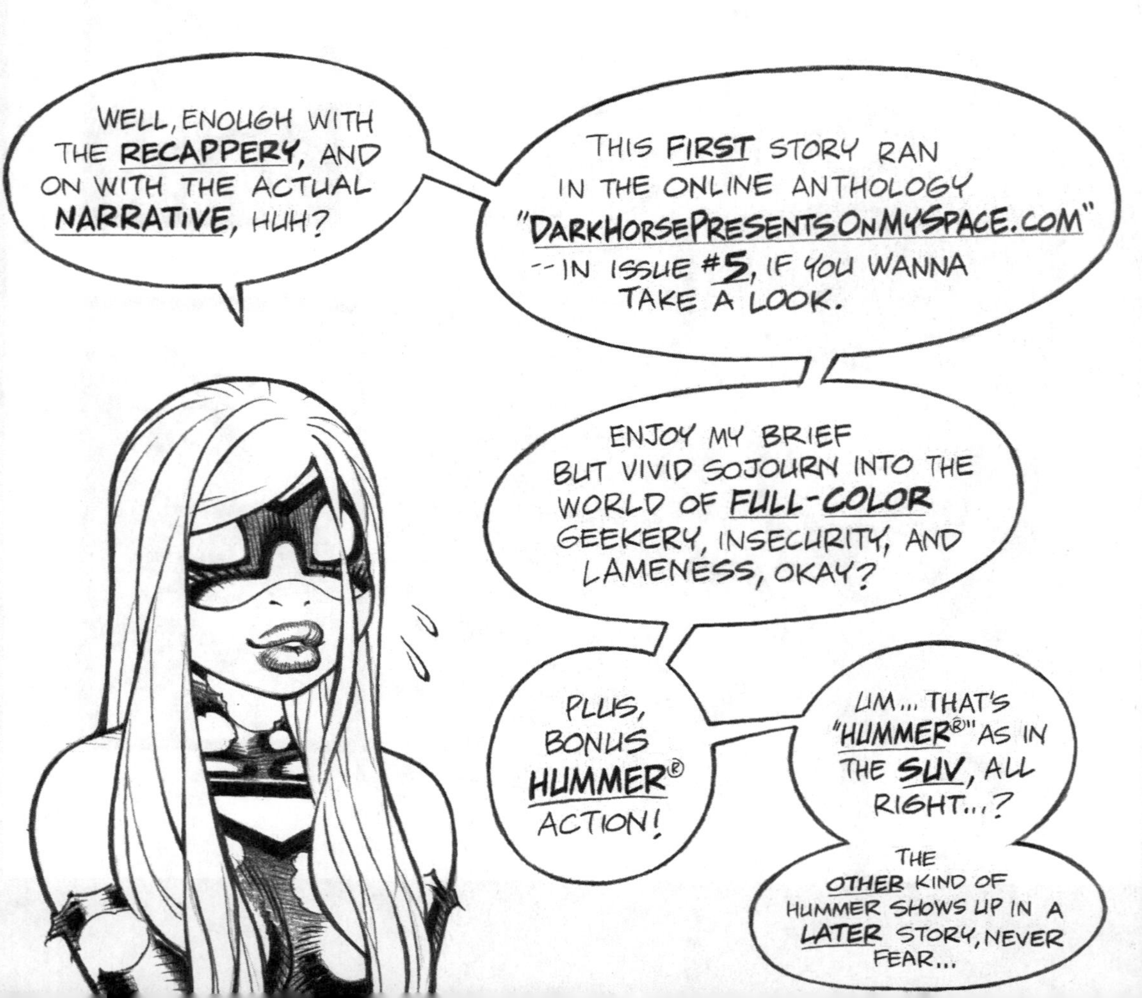
WELL, ENOUGH WITH THE RECAPPERY, AND ON WITH THE ACTUAL NARRATIVE, HUH?
THIS FIRST STORY RAN IN THE ONLINE ANTHOLOGY "DARKHORSEPRESENTSONMYSPACE.COM" --IN ISSUE #5, IF YOU WANNA TAKE A LOOK.
ENJOY MY BRIEF BUT VIVID SOJOURN INTO THE WORLD OF FULL-COLOR GEEKERY, INSECURITY, AND LAMENESS, OKAY?
PLUS, BONUS HUMMER® ACTION!
UM... THAT'S "HUMMER®" AS IN THE SUV, ALL RIGHT...?
THE OTHER KIND OF HUMMER SHOWS UP IN A LATER STORY, NEVER FEAR...

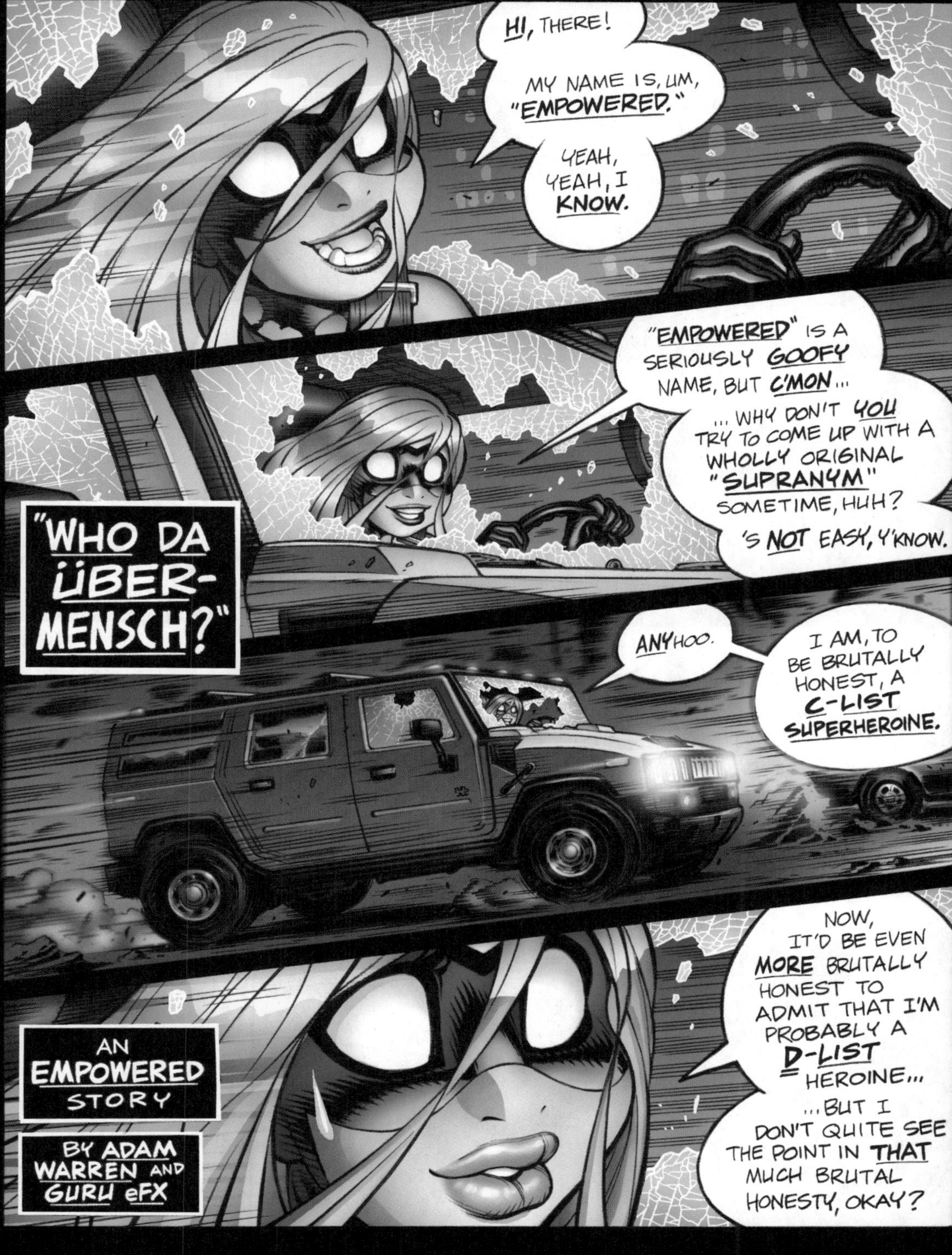
HI, THERE!
MY NAME IS, UM, "EMPOWERED."
YEAH, YEAH, I KNOW.
"WHO DA ÜBER-MENSCH?"
"EMPOWERED" IS A SERIOUSLY GOOFY NAME, BUT C'MON...
...WHY DON'T YOU TRY TO COME UP WITH A WHOLLY ORIGINAL "SUPRANYM" SOMETIME, HUH?
'S NOT EASY, Y'KNOW.
ANYHOO.
I AM, TO BE BRUTALLY HONEST, A C-LIST SUPERHEROINE.
AN EMPOWERED STORY
BY ADAM WARREN AND GURU eFX
NOW, IT'D BE EVEN MORE BRUTALLY HONEST TO ADMIT THAT I'M PROBABLY A D-LIST HEROINE...
...BUT I DON'T QUITE SEE THE POINT IN THAT MUCH BRUTAL HONESTY, OKAY?

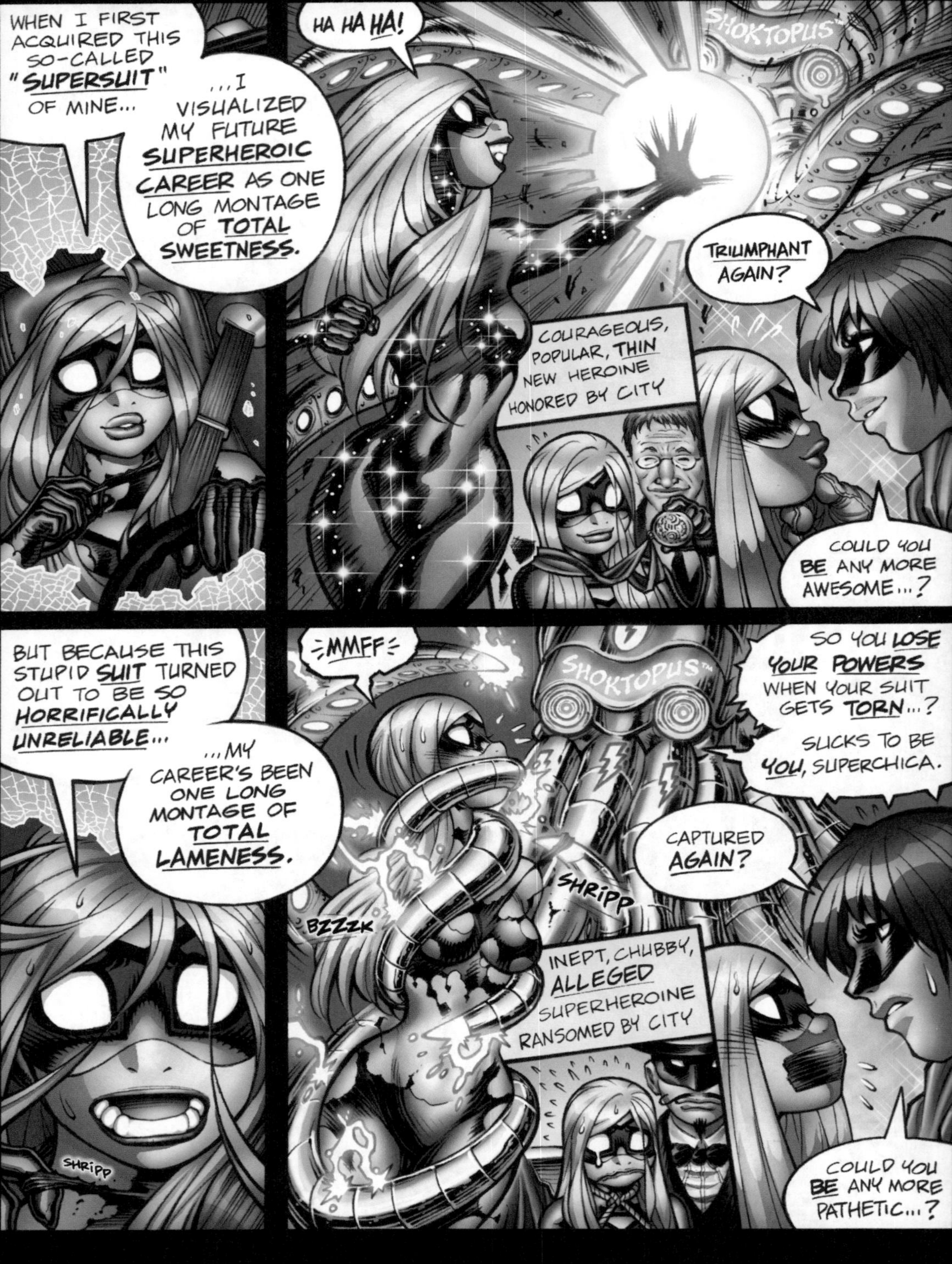

WHEN I FIRST ACQUIRED THIS SO-CALLED "SUPERSUIT" OF MINE...
...I VISUALIZED MY FUTURE SUPERHEROIC CAREER AS ONE LONG MONTAGE OF TOTAL SWEETNESS.
HA HA HA!
SHOKTOPUS™
TRIUMPHANT AGAIN?
COURAGEOUS, POPULAR, THIN NEW HEROINE HONORED BY CITY
COULD YOU BE ANY MORE AWESOME...?
BUT BECAUSE THIS STUPID SUIT TURNED OUT TO BE SO HORRIFICALLY UNRELIABLE...
...MY CAREER'S BEEN ONE LONG MONTAGE OF TOTAL LAMENESS.
SHRIPP
MMFF
SHOKTOPUS™
SO YOU LOSE YOUR POWERS WHEN YOUR SUIT GETS TORN...?
SUCKS TO BE YOU, SUPERCHICA.
CAPTURED AGAIN?
SHRIPP
BZZZK
INEPT, CHUBBY, ALLEGED SUPERHEROINE RANSOMED BY CITY
COULD YOU BE ANY MORE PATHETIC...?

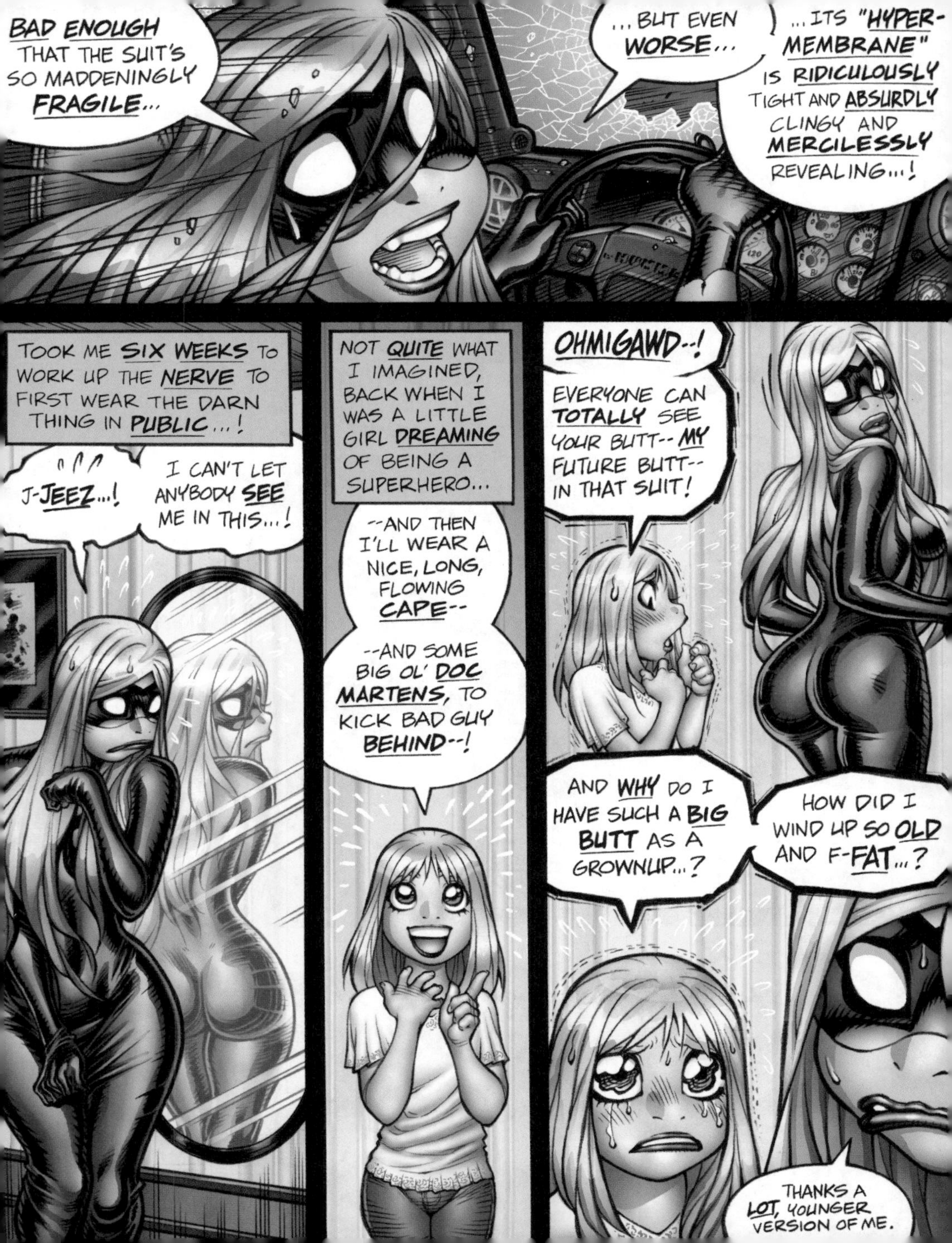
BAD ENOUGH THAT THE SUIT'S SO MADDENINGLY FRAGILE...
...BUT EVEN WORSE...
...ITS "HYPER-MEMBRANE" IS RIDICULOUSLY TIGHT AND ABSURDLY CLINGY AND MERCILESSLY REVEALING...!
TOOK ME SIX WEEKS TO WORK UP THE NERVE TO FIRST WEAR THE DARN THING IN PUBLIC...!
J-JEEZ...!
I CAN'T LET ANYBODY SEE ME IN THIS...!
NOT QUITE WHAT I IMAGINED, BACK WHEN I WAS A LITTLE GIRL DREAMING OF BEING A SUPERHERO...
--AND THEN I'LL WEAR A NICE, LONG, FLOWING CAPE--
--AND SOME BIG OL' DOC MARTENS, TO KICK BAD GUY BEHIND--!
OHMIGAWD--!
EVERYONE CAN TOTALLY SEE YOUR BUTT-- MY FUTURE BUTT-- IN THAT SUIT!
AND WHY DO I HAVE SUCH A BIG BUTT AS A GROWNUP...?
HOW DID I WIND UP SO OLD AND F-FAT...?
THANKS A LOT, YOUNGER VERSION OF ME.

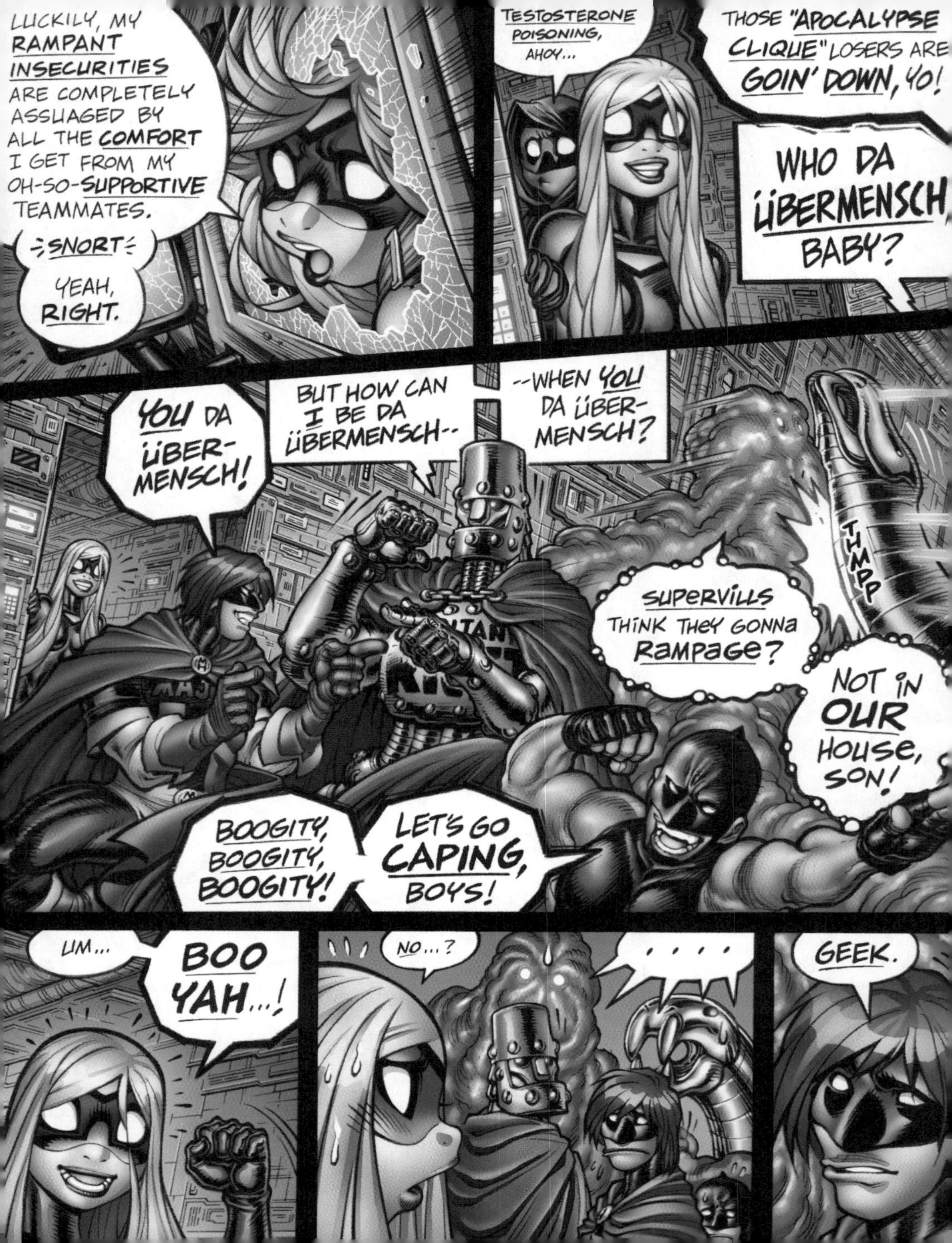

LUCKILY, MY RAMPANT INSECURITIES ARE COMPLETELY ASSUAGED BY ALL THE COMFORT I GET FROM MY OH-SO-SUPPORTIVE TEAMMATES.
SNORT
YEAH, RIGHT.
TESTOSTERONE POISONING, AHOY...
THOSE "APOCALYPSE CLIQUE" LOSERS ARE GOIN' DOWN, YO!
WHO DA ÜBERMENSCH BABY?
YOU DA ÜBER-MENSCH!
BUT HOW CAN I BE DA ÜBERMENSCH--
--WHEN YOU DA ÜBER-MENSCH?
THMPP
SUPERVILLS THINK THEY GONNA RAMPAGE?
NOT IN OUR HOUSE, SON!
BOOGITY, BOOGITY, BOOGITY!
LET'S GO CAPING, BOYS!
UM...
BOO YAH...!
NO...?
. . . .
GEEK.

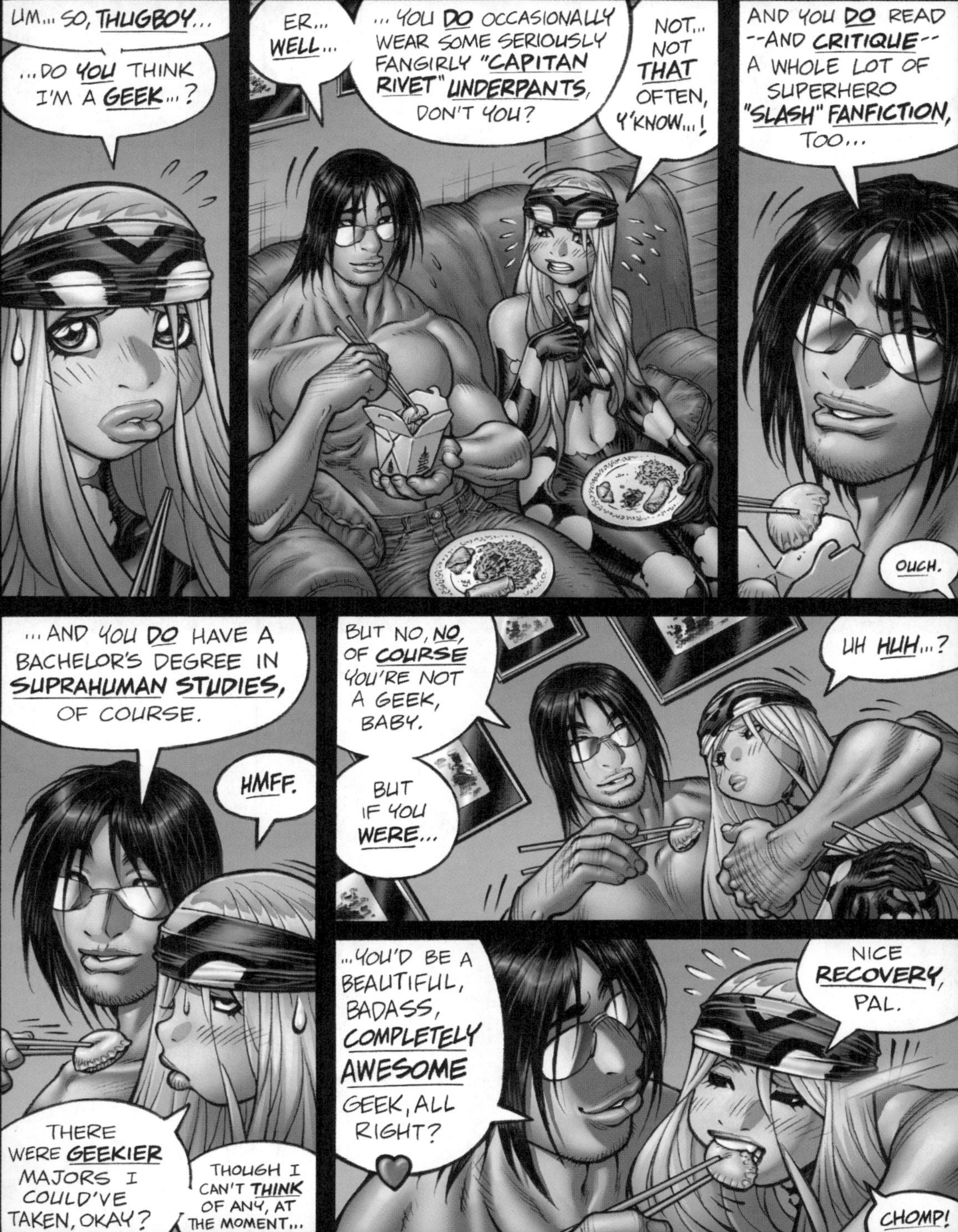
UM... SO, THUGBOY...
...DO YOU THINK I'M A GEEK...?
ER... WELL...
...YOU DO OCCASIONALLY WEAR SOME SERIOUSLY FANGIRLY "CAPITAN RIVET" UNDERPANTS, DON'T YOU?
NOT... NOT THAT OFTEN, Y'KNOW...!
AND YOU DO READ --AND CRITIQUE-- A WHOLE LOT OF SUPERHERO "SLASH" FANFICTION, TOO...
OUCH.
...AND YOU DO HAVE A BACHELOR'S DEGREE IN SUPRAHUMAN STUDIES, OF COURSE.
HMFF.
THERE WERE GEEKIER MAJORS I COULD'VE TAKEN, OKAY?
THOUGH I CAN'T THINK OF ANY, AT THE MOMENT...
BUT NO, NO, OF COURSE YOU'RE NOT A GEEK, BABY.
UH HUH...?
BUT IF YOU WERE...
...YOU'D BE A BEAUTIFUL, BADASS, COMPLETELY AWESOME GEEK, ALL RIGHT?
NICE RECOVERY, PAL.
CHOMP!

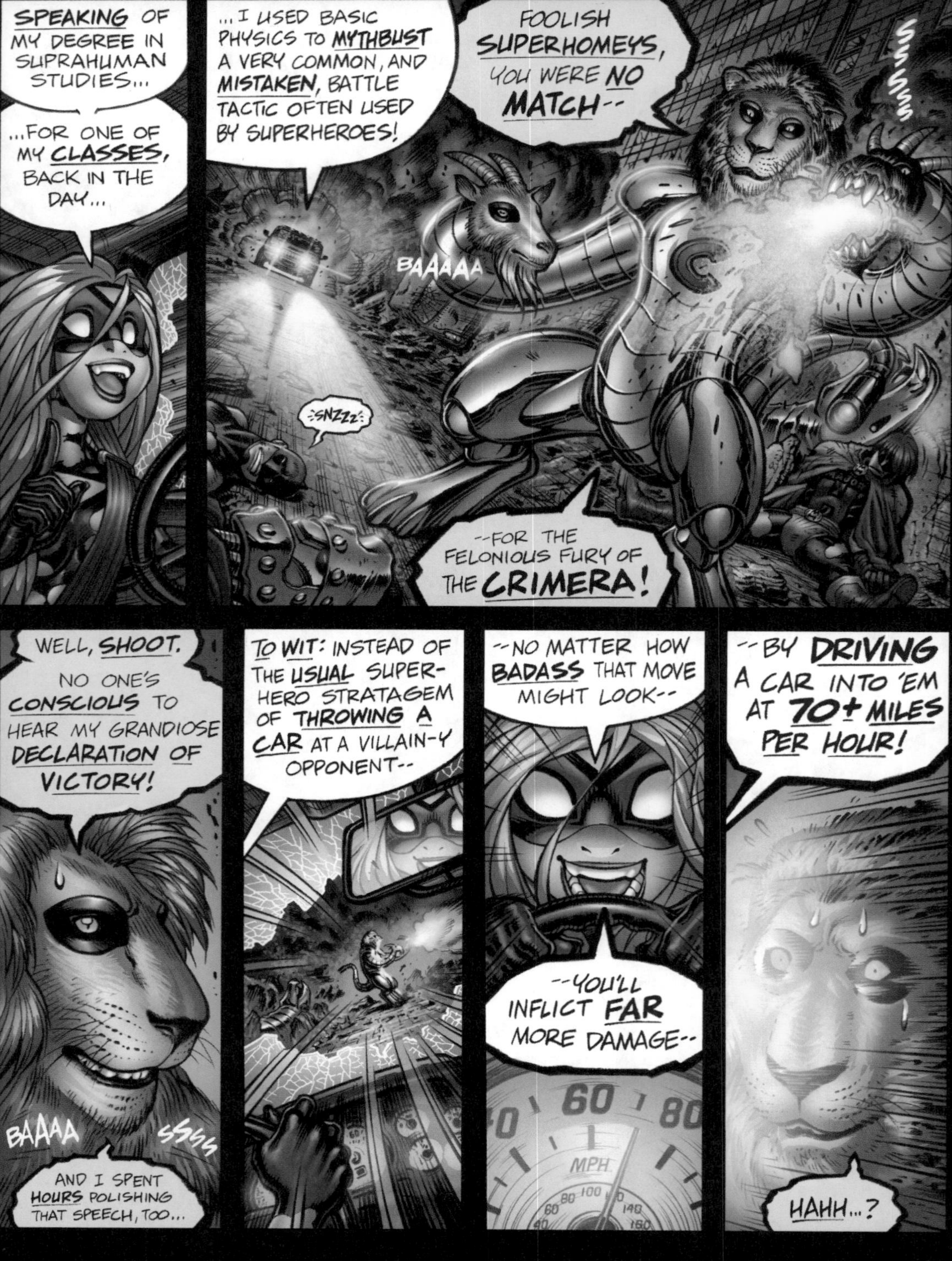
SPEAKING OF MY DEGREE IN SUPRAHUMAN STUDIES...
...FOR ONE OF MY CLASSES, BACK IN THE DAY...
...I USED BASIC PHYSICS TO MYTHBUST A VERY COMMON, AND MISTAKEN, BATTLE TACTIC OFTEN USED BY SUPERHEROES!
FOOLISH SUPERHOMEYS, YOU WERE NO MATCH--
SSSSS
BAAAAA
SNZZZ
--FOR THE FELONIOUS FURY OF THE CRIMERA!
WELL, SHOOT.
NO ONE'S CONSCIOUS TO HEAR MY GRANDIOSE DECLARATION OF VICTORY!
BAAAA
SSSS
AND I SPENT HOURS POLISHING THAT SPEECH, TOO...
TO WIT: INSTEAD OF THE USUAL SUPER-HERO STRATAGEM OF THROWING A CAR AT A VILLAIN-Y OPPONENT--
--NO MATTER HOW BADASS THAT MOVE MIGHT LOOK--
--YOU'LL INFLICT FAR MORE DAMAGE--
MPH
--BY DRIVING A CAR INTO 'EM AT 70+ MILES PER HOUR!
HAHH...?

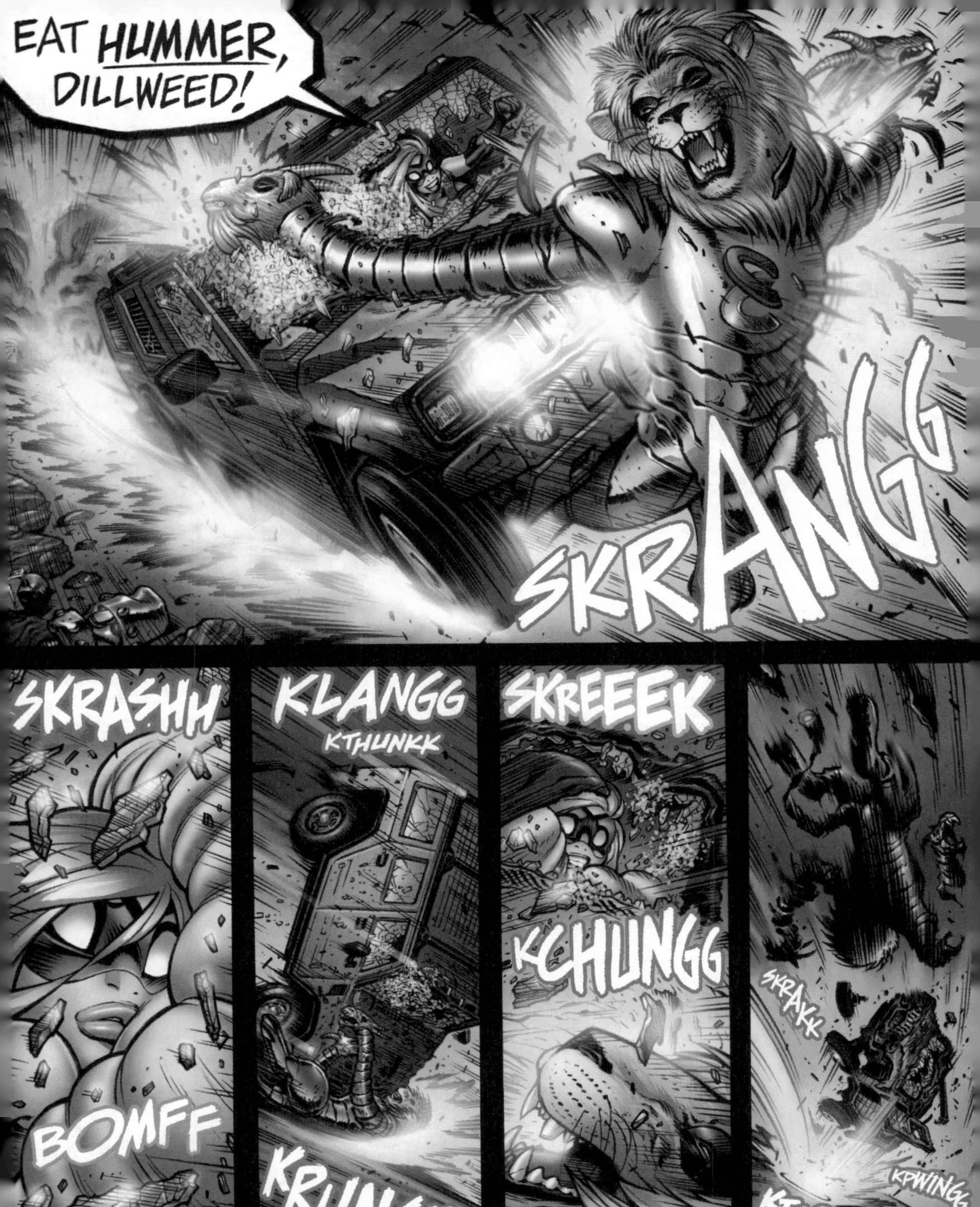
EAT HUMMER, DILLWEED!
SKRANGG
SKRASHH
BOMFF
KLANGG
KTHUNKK
KRUNCHH
SKREEEK
KCHUNGG
SKRAKK
KPWINGG
KTHOOM

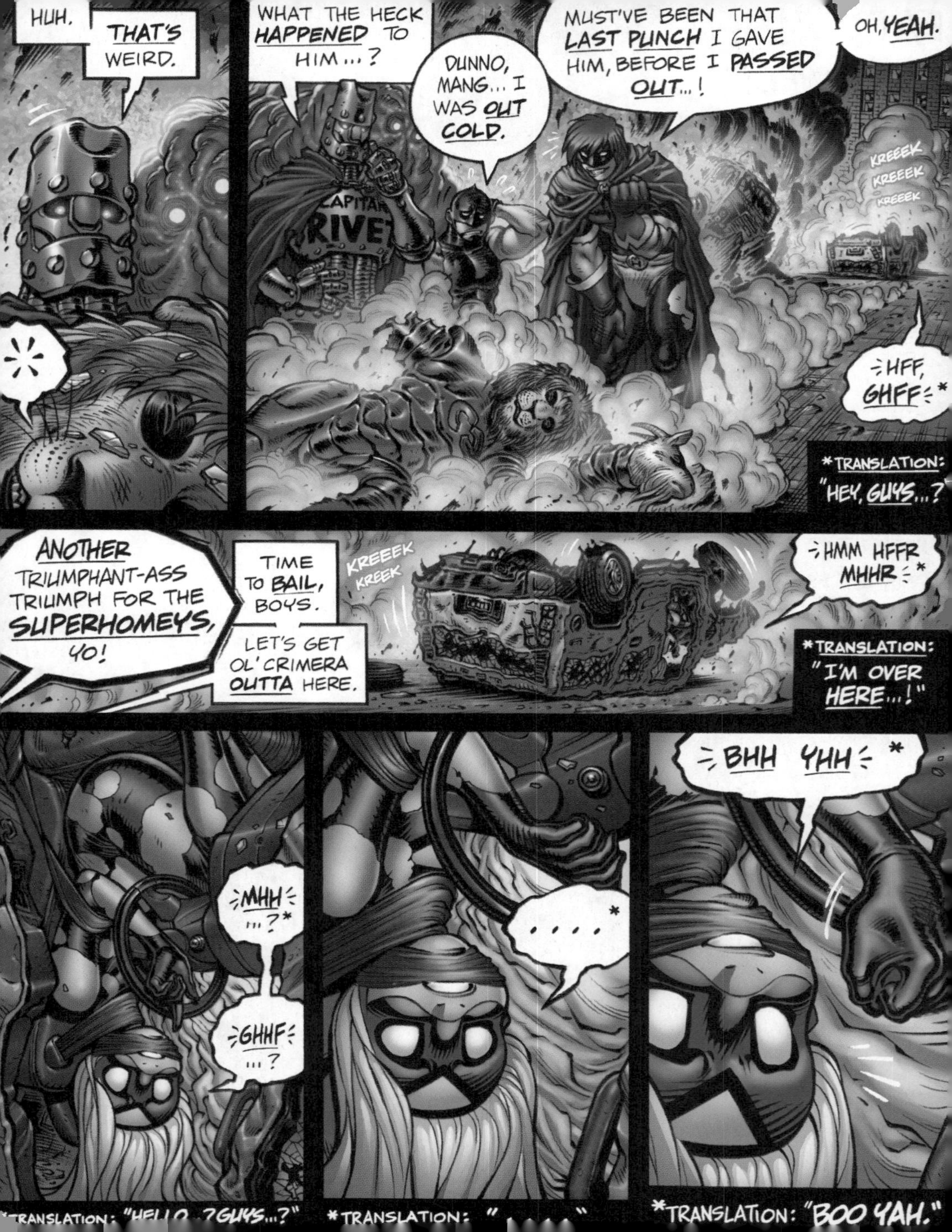
HUH.
THAT'S WEIRD.
WHAT THE HECK HAPPENED TO HIM...?
DUNNO, MANG... I WAS OUT COLD.
MUST'VE BEEN THAT LAST PUNCH I GAVE HIM, BEFORE I PASSED OUT...!
OH, YEAH.
KREEEK KREEEK KREEEK
HFF, GHFF *
*TRANSLATION: "HEY, GUYS...?
ANOTHER TRIUMPHANT-ASS TRIUMPH FOR THE SUPERHOMEYS, YO!
TIME TO BAIL, BOYS.
LET'S GET OL' CRIMERA OUTTA HERE.
KREEEK KREEK
HMM HFFR MHHR *
*TRANSLATION: "I'M OVER HERE...!"
MHH ...?*
GHHF ...?
*TRANSLATION: "HELLO...?GUYS...?"
....*
*TRANSLATION: "....."
BHH YHH *
*TRANSLATION: "BOO YAH."

Empowered™

General Hospitality

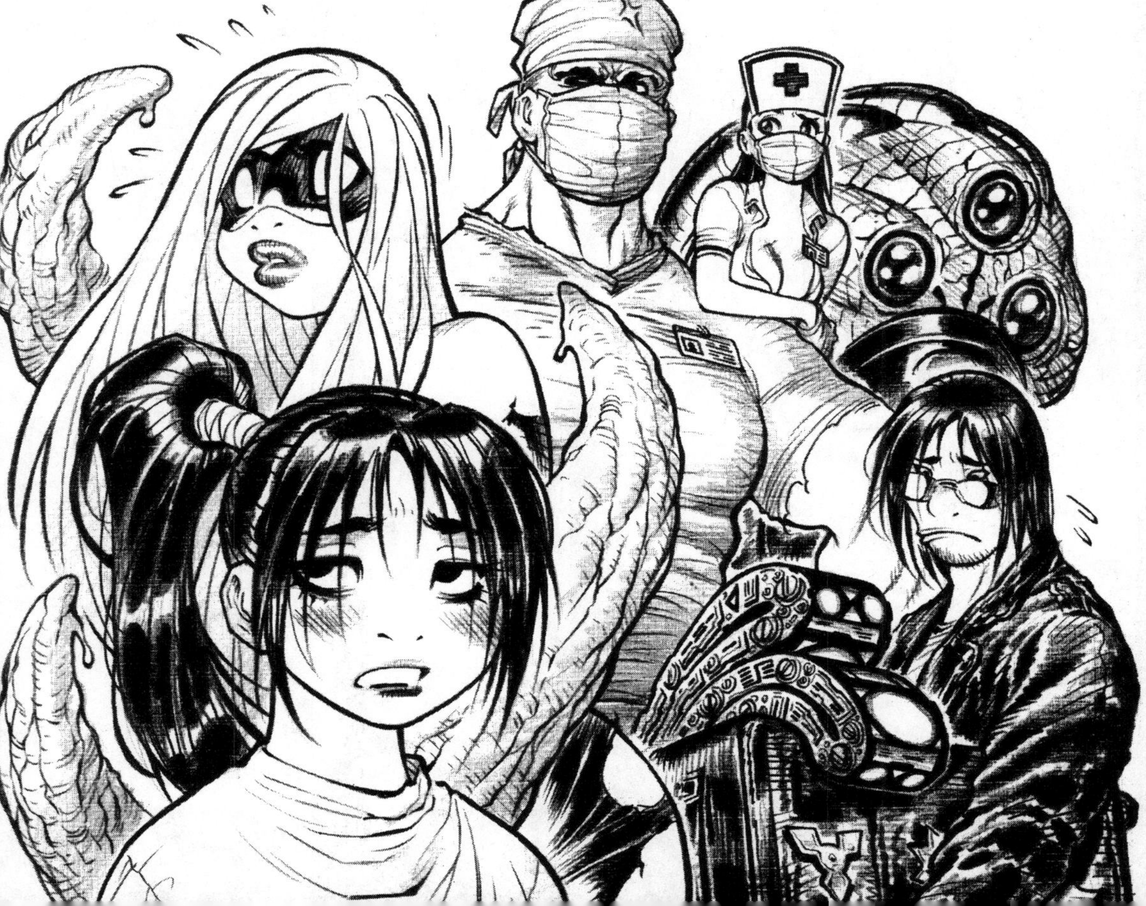

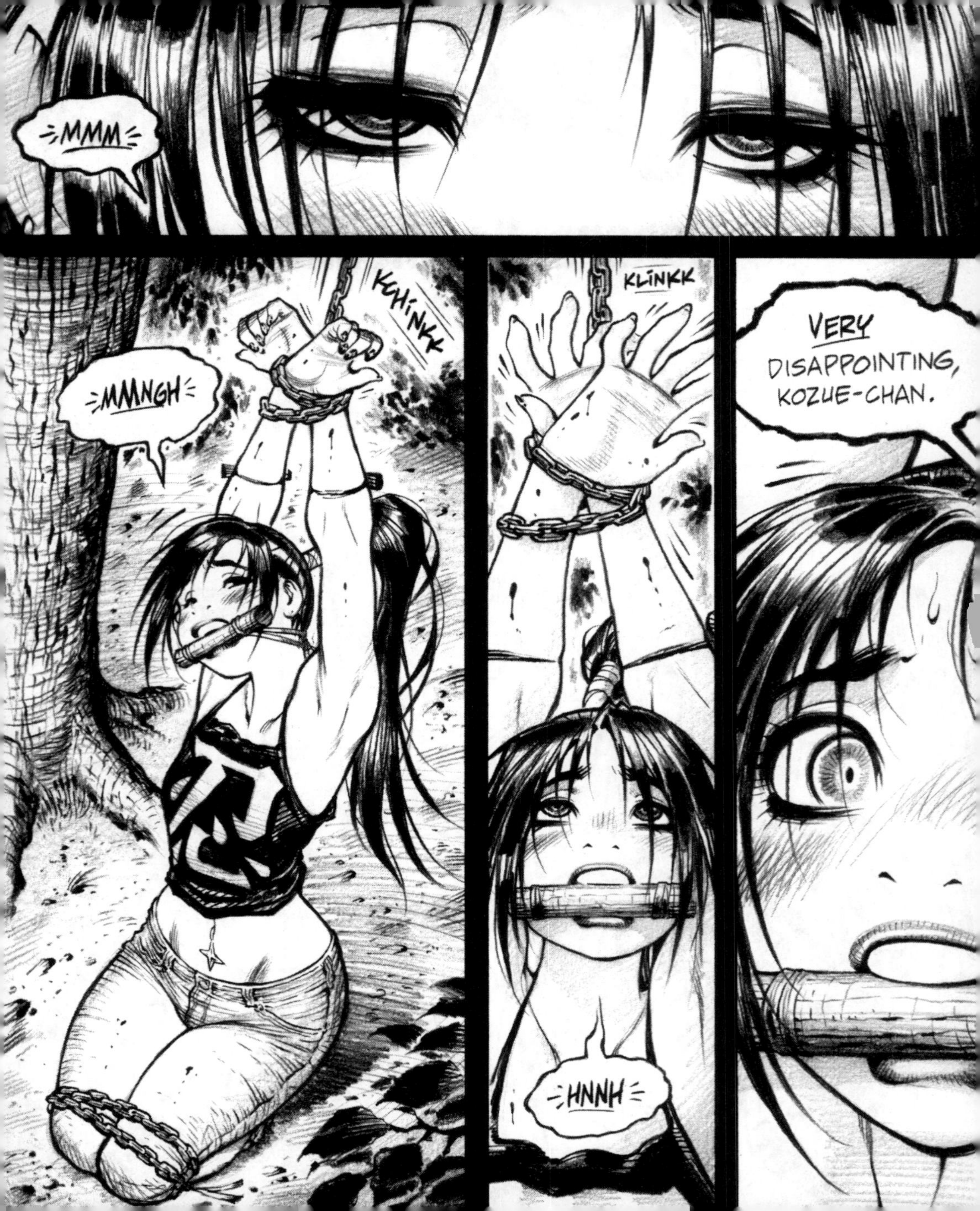
MMM
MMNGH
KCHINKK
KLINKK
HNNH
VERY DISAPPOINTING, KOZUE-CHAN.

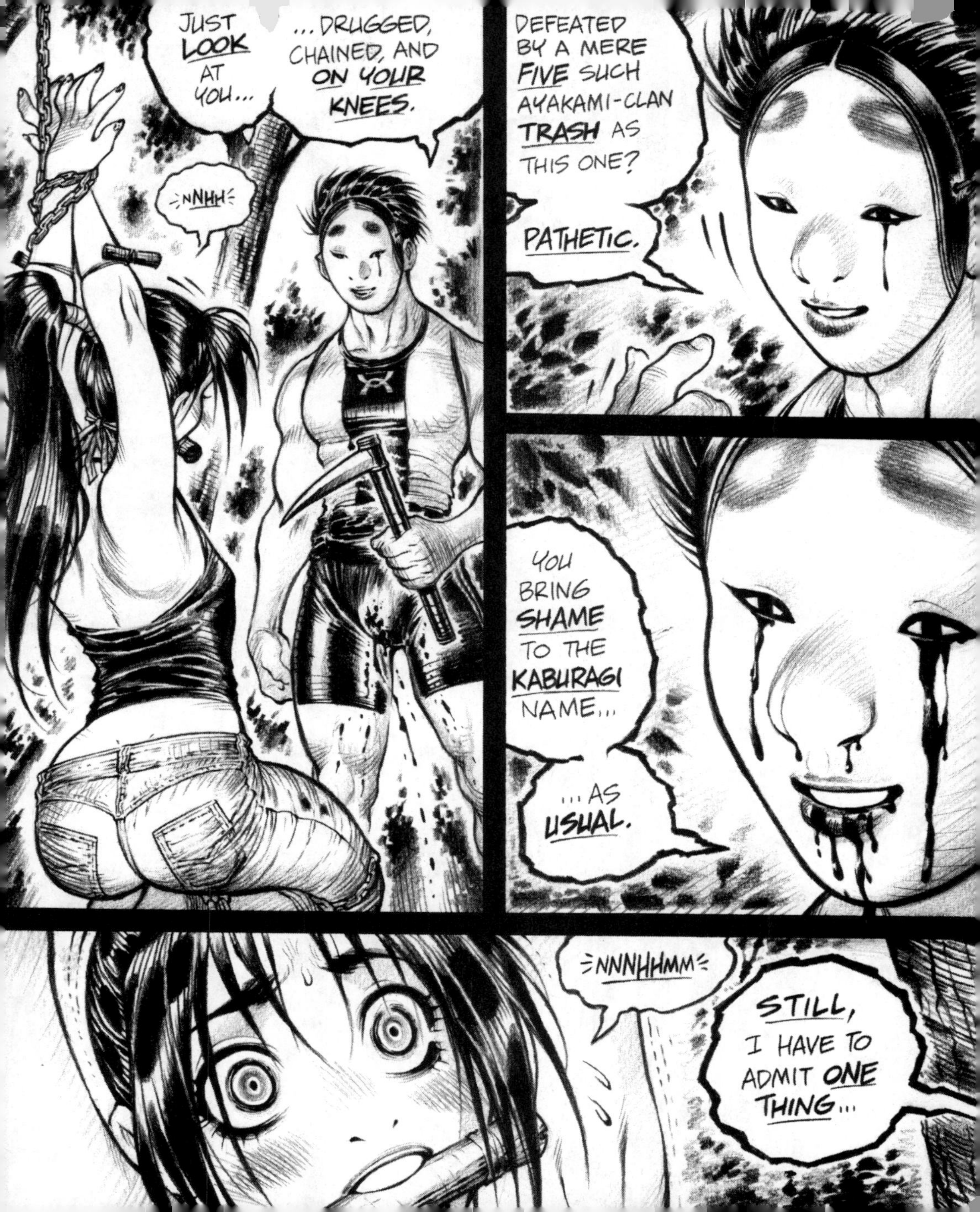
JUST LOOK AT YOU...
...DRUGGED, CHAINED, AND ON YOUR KNEES.
NNHH
DEFEATED BY A MERE FIVE SUCH AYAKAMI-CLAN TRASH AS THIS ONE?
PATHETIC.
YOU BRING SHAME TO THE KABURAGI NAME...
...AS USUAL.
NNNHHMM
STILL, I HAVE TO ADMIT ONE THING...

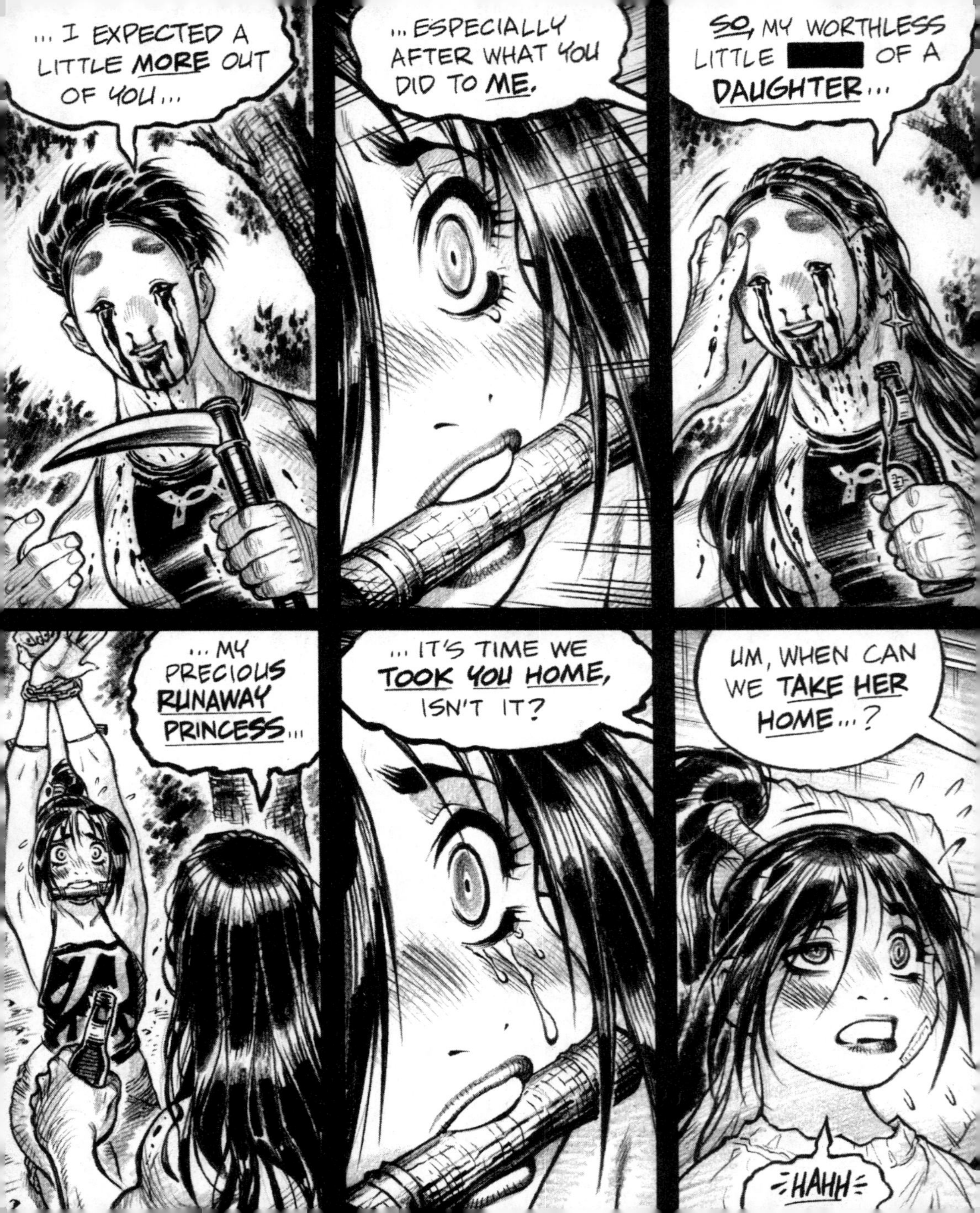
... I EXPECTED A LITTLE MORE OUT OF YOU...
... ESPECIALLY AFTER WHAT YOU DID TO ME.
SO, MY WORTHLESS LITTLE [redacted] OF A DAUGHTER...
... MY PRECIOUS RUNAWAY PRINCESS...
... IT'S TIME WE TOOK YOU HOME, ISN'T IT?
UM, WHEN CAN WE TAKE HER HOME...?
HAHH

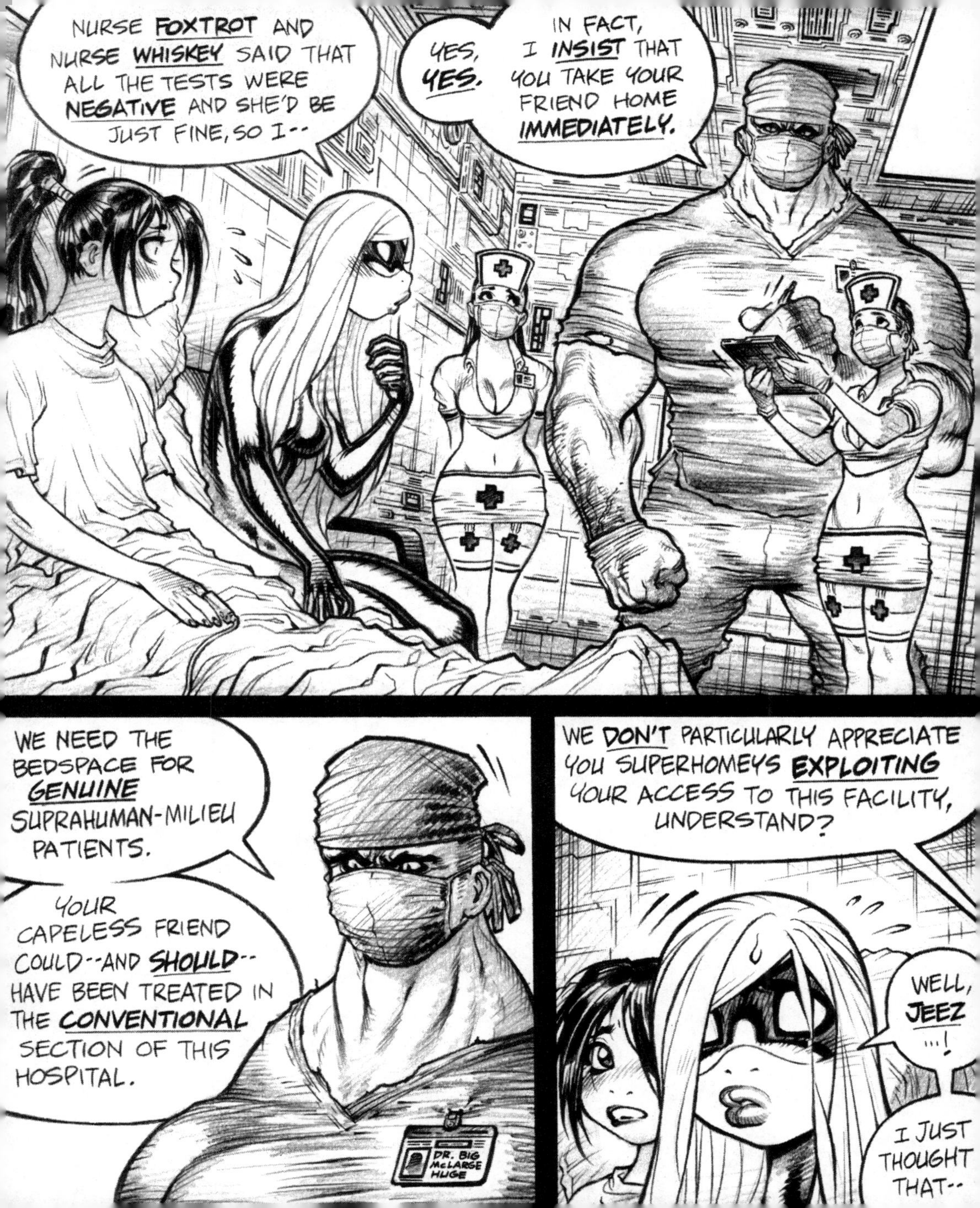
NURSE FOXTROT AND NURSE WHISKEY SAID THAT ALL THE TESTS WERE NEGATIVE AND SHE'D BE JUST FINE, SO I--
YES, YES.
IN FACT, I INSIST THAT YOU TAKE YOUR FRIEND HOME IMMEDIATELY.
WE NEED THE BEDSPACE FOR GENUINE SUPRAHUMAN-MILIEU PATIENTS.
YOUR CAPELESS FRIEND COULD--AND SHOULD--HAVE BEEN TREATED IN THE CONVENTIONAL SECTION OF THIS HOSPITAL.
DR. BIG McLARGE HUGE
WE DON'T PARTICULARLY APPRECIATE YOU SUPERHOMEYS EXPLOITING YOUR ACCESS TO THIS FACILITY, UNDERSTAND?
WELL, JEEZ ...!
I JUST THOUGHT THAT--

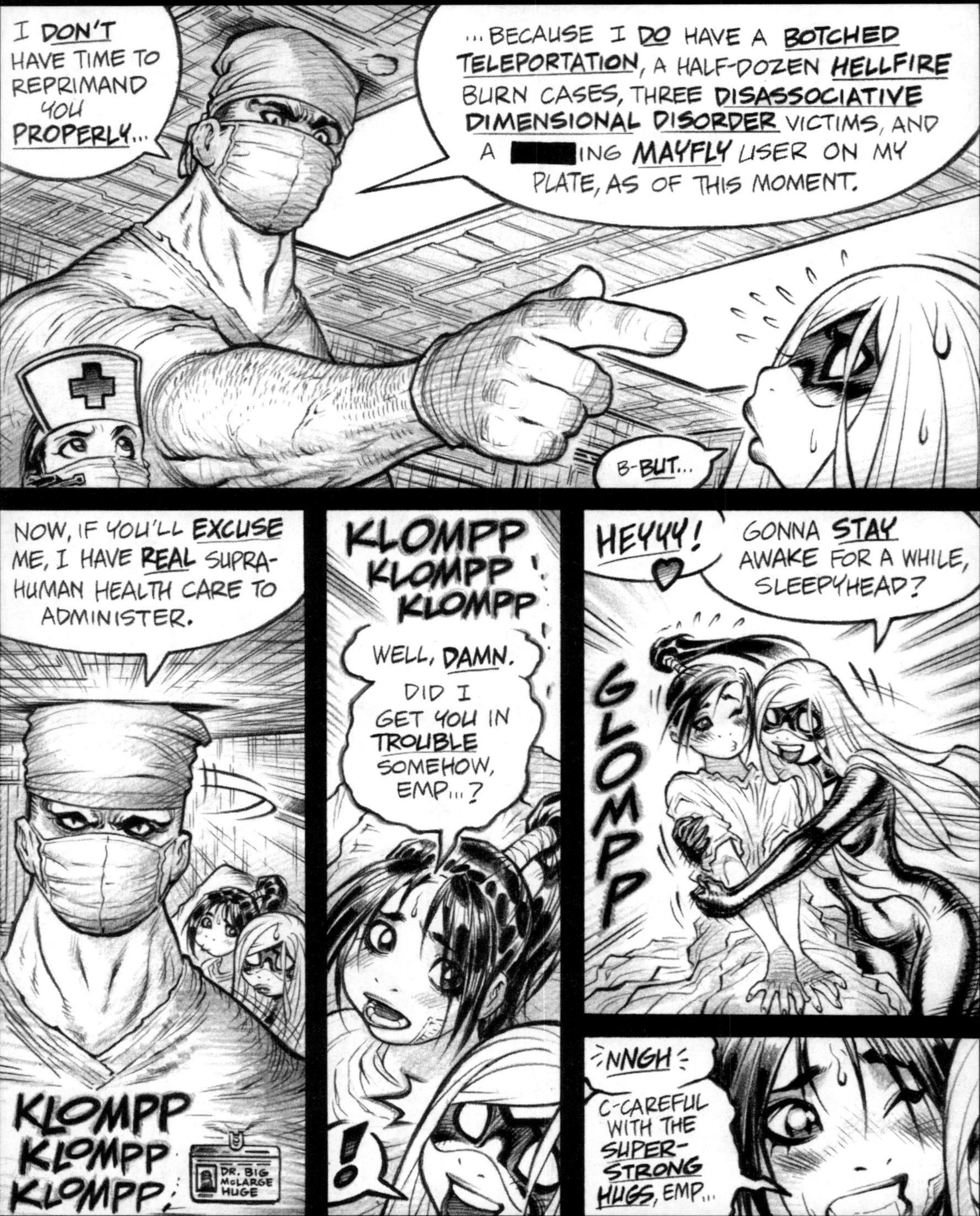
I DON'T HAVE TIME TO REPRIMAND YOU PROPERLY...
...BECAUSE I DO HAVE A BOTCHED TELEPORTATION, A HALF-DOZEN HELLFIRE BURN CASES, THREE DISASSOCIATIVE DIMENSIONAL DISORDER VICTIMS, AND A [redacted]ING MAYFLY USER ON MY PLATE, AS OF THIS MOMENT.
B-BUT...
NOW, IF YOU'LL EXCUSE ME, I HAVE REAL SUPRA-HUMAN HEALTH CARE TO ADMINISTER.
KLOMPP KLOMPP KLOMPP
DR. BIG McLARGE HUGE
KLOMPP KLOMPP KLOMPP
WELL, DAMN.
DID I GET YOU IN TROUBLE SOMEHOW, EMP...?
!
HEYYY!
GONNA STAY AWAKE FOR A WHILE, SLEEPYHEAD?
GLOMPP
NNGH
C-CAREFUL WITH THE SUPER-STRONG HUGS, EMP...

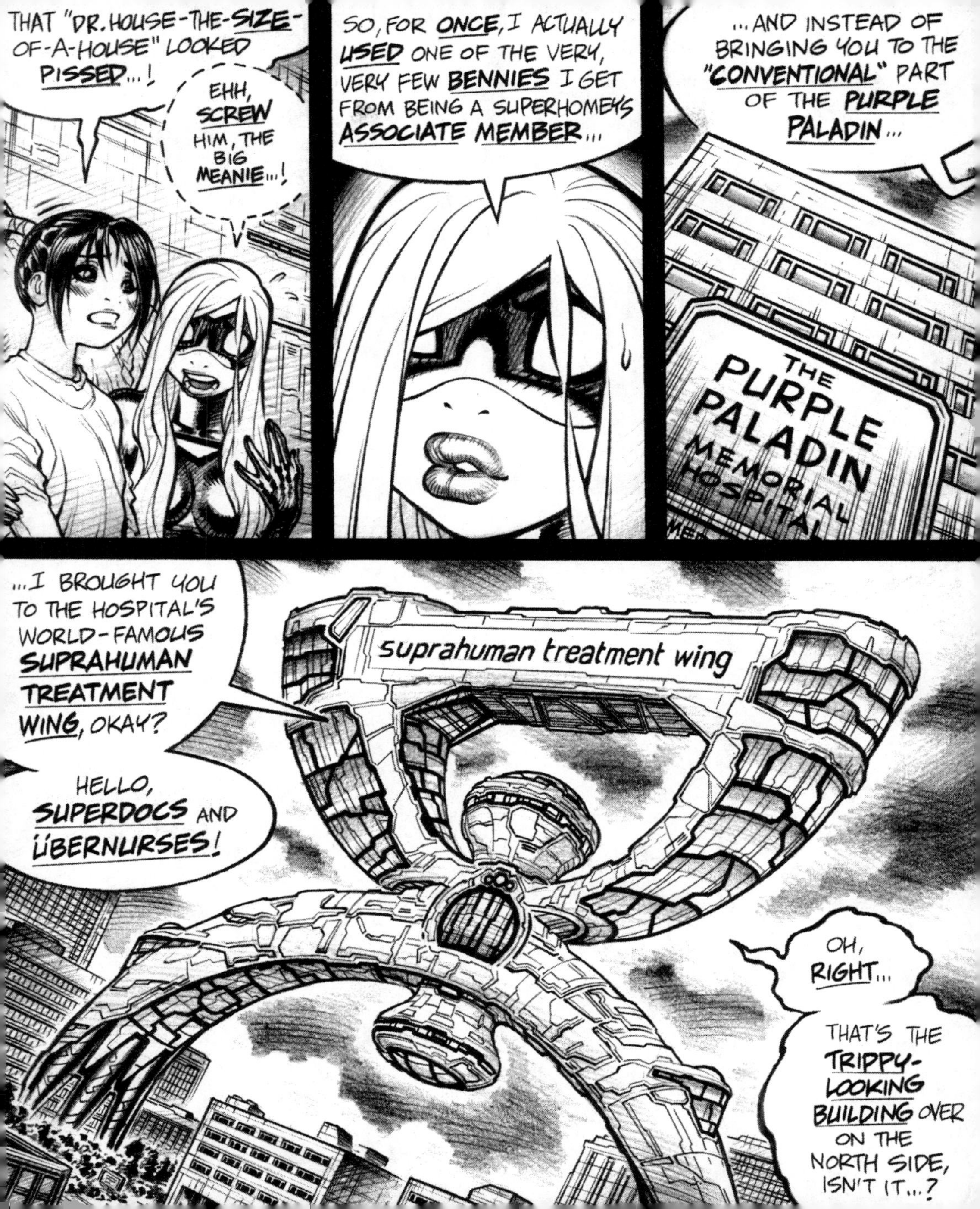
THAT "DR. HOUSE-THE-SIZE-OF-A-HOUSE" LOOKED PISSED...!
EHH, SCREW HIM, THE BIG MEANIE...!
SO, FOR ONCE, I ACTUALLY USED ONE OF THE VERY, VERY FEW BENNIES I GET FROM BEING A SUPERHOMEYS ASSOCIATE MEMBER...
...AND INSTEAD OF BRINGING YOU TO THE "CONVENTIONAL" PART OF THE PURPLE PALADIN...
THE PURPLE PALADIN MEMORIAL HOSPITAL
...I BROUGHT YOU TO THE HOSPITAL'S WORLD-FAMOUS SUPRAHUMAN TREATMENT WING, OKAY?
suprahuman treatment wing
HELLO, SUPERDOCS AND ÜBERNURSES!
OH, RIGHT...
THAT'S THE TRIPPY-LOOKING BUILDING OVER ON THE NORTH SIDE, ISN'T IT...?

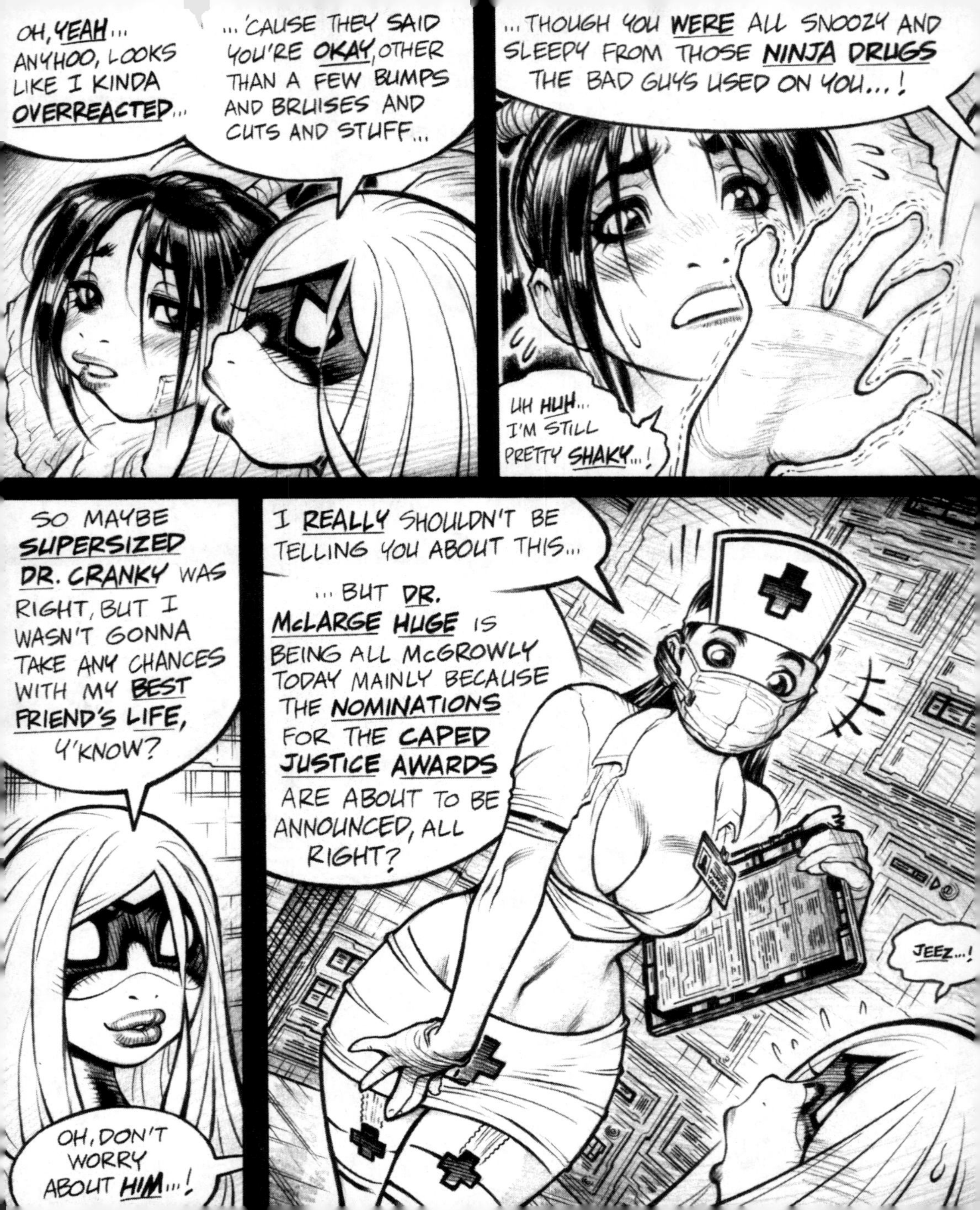
OH, YEAH... ANYHOO, LOOKS LIKE I KINDA OVERREACTED...
...'CAUSE THEY SAID YOU'RE OKAY, OTHER THAN A FEW BUMPS AND BRUISES AND CUTS AND STUFF...
...THOUGH YOU WERE ALL SNOOZY AND SLEEPY FROM THOSE NINJA DRUGS THE BAD GUYS USED ON YOU...!
UH HUH... I'M STILL PRETTY SHAKY...!
SO MAYBE SUPERSIZED DR. CRANKY WAS RIGHT, BUT I WASN'T GONNA TAKE ANY CHANCES WITH MY BEST FRIEND'S LIFE, Y'KNOW?
OH, DON'T WORRY ABOUT HIM...!
I REALLY SHOULDN'T BE TELLING YOU ABOUT THIS...
...BUT DR. McLARGE HUGE IS BEING ALL McGROWLY TODAY MAINLY BECAUSE THE NOMINATIONS FOR THE CAPED JUSTICE AWARDS ARE ABOUT TO BE ANNOUNCED, ALL RIGHT?
JEEZ...!

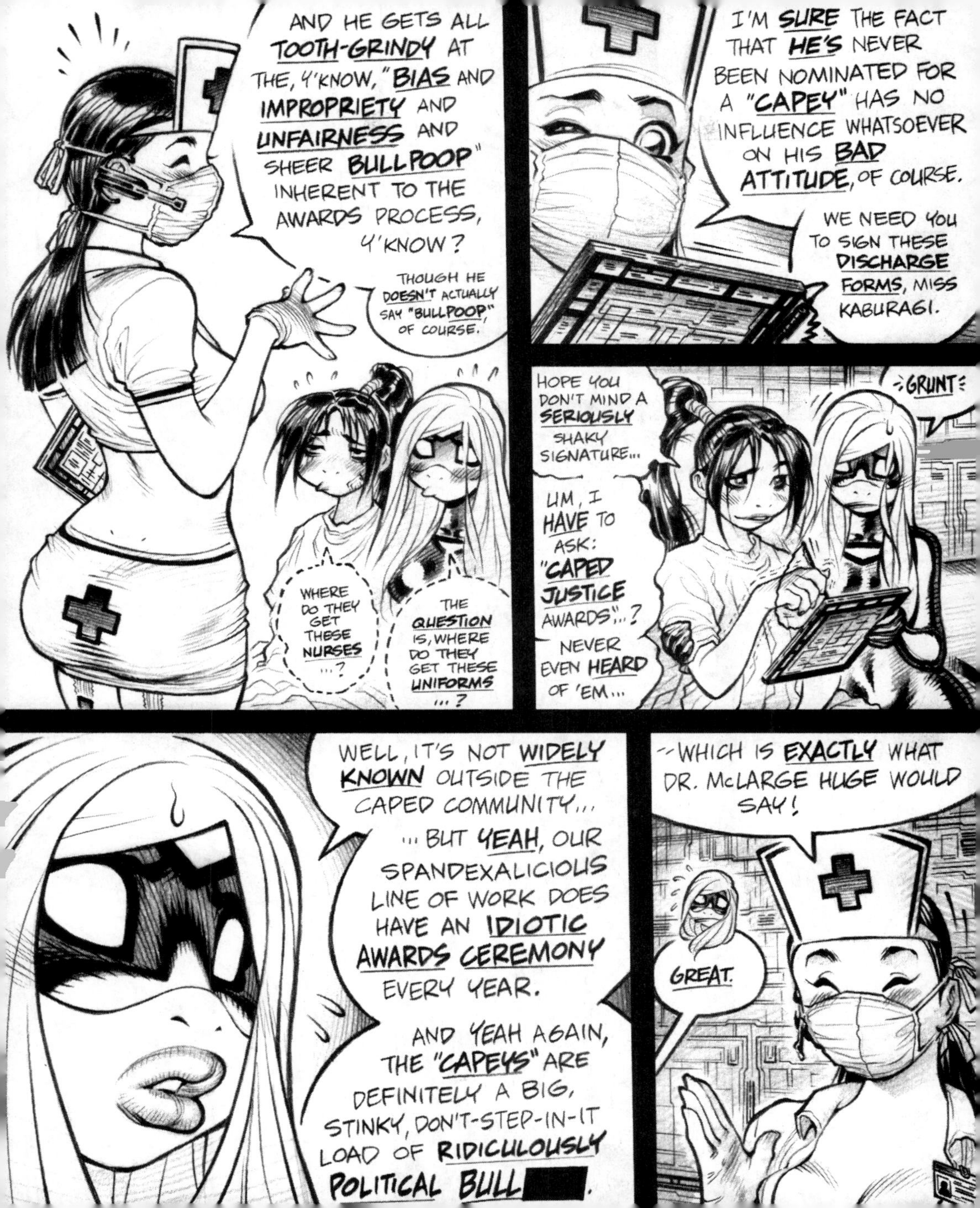
AND HE GETS ALL TOOTH-GRINDY AT THE, Y'KNOW, "BIAS AND IMPROPRIETY AND UNFAIRNESS AND SHEER BULLPOOP" INHERENT TO THE AWARDS PROCESS, Y'KNOW?
THOUGH HE DOESN'T ACTUALLY SAY "BULLPOOP," OF COURSE.
WHERE DO THEY GET THESE NURSES ...?
THE QUESTION IS, WHERE DO THEY GET THESE UNIFORMS ...?
I'M SURE THE FACT THAT HE'S NEVER BEEN NOMINATED FOR A "CAPEY" HAS NO INFLUENCE WHATSOEVER ON HIS BAD ATTITUDE, OF COURSE.
WE NEED YOU TO SIGN THESE DISCHARGE FORMS, MISS KABURAGI.
HOPE YOU DON'T MIND A SERIOUSLY SHAKY SIGNATURE...
UM, I HAVE TO ASK: "CAPED JUSTICE AWARDS"...? NEVER EVEN HEARD OF 'EM...
GRUNT
WELL, IT'S NOT WIDELY KNOWN OUTSIDE THE CAPED COMMUNITY...
... BUT YEAH, OUR SPANDEXALICIOUS LINE OF WORK DOES HAVE AN IDIOTIC AWARDS CEREMONY EVERY YEAR.
AND YEAH AGAIN, THE "CAPEYS" ARE DEFINITELY A BIG, STINKY, DON'T-STEP-IN-IT LOAD OF RIDICULOUSLY POLITICAL BULL[redacted].
-- WHICH IS EXACTLY WHAT DR. McLARGE HUGE WOULD SAY!
GREAT.

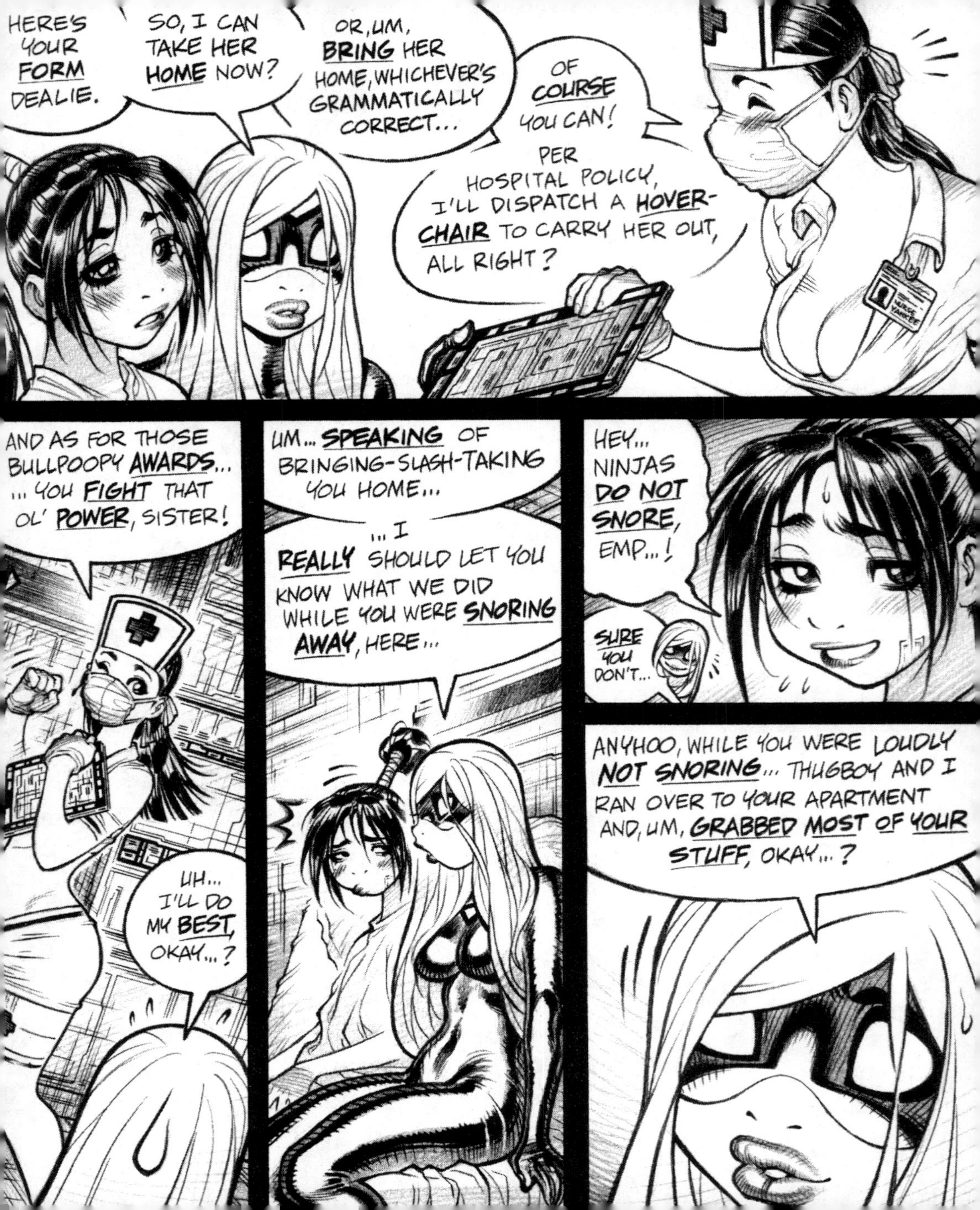
HERE'S YOUR FORM DEALIE.
SO, I CAN TAKE HER HOME NOW?
OR, UM, BRING HER HOME, WHICHEVER'S GRAMMATICALLY CORRECT...
OF COURSE YOU CAN!
PER HOSPITAL POLICY, I'LL DISPATCH A HOVER-CHAIR TO CARRY HER OUT, ALL RIGHT?
AND AS FOR THOSE BULLPOOPY AWARDS... ...YOU FIGHT THAT OL' POWER, SISTER!
UH... I'LL DO MY BEST, OKAY...?
UM... SPEAKING OF BRINGING-SLASH-TAKING YOU HOME...
...I REALLY SHOULD LET YOU KNOW WHAT WE DID WHILE YOU WERE SNORING AWAY, HERE...
HEY... NINJAS DO NOT SNORE, EMP...!
SURE YOU DON'T...
ANYHOO, WHILE YOU WERE LOUDLY NOT SNORING... THUGBOY AND I RAN OVER TO YOUR APARTMENT AND, UM, GRABBED MOST OF YOUR STUFF, OKAY...?

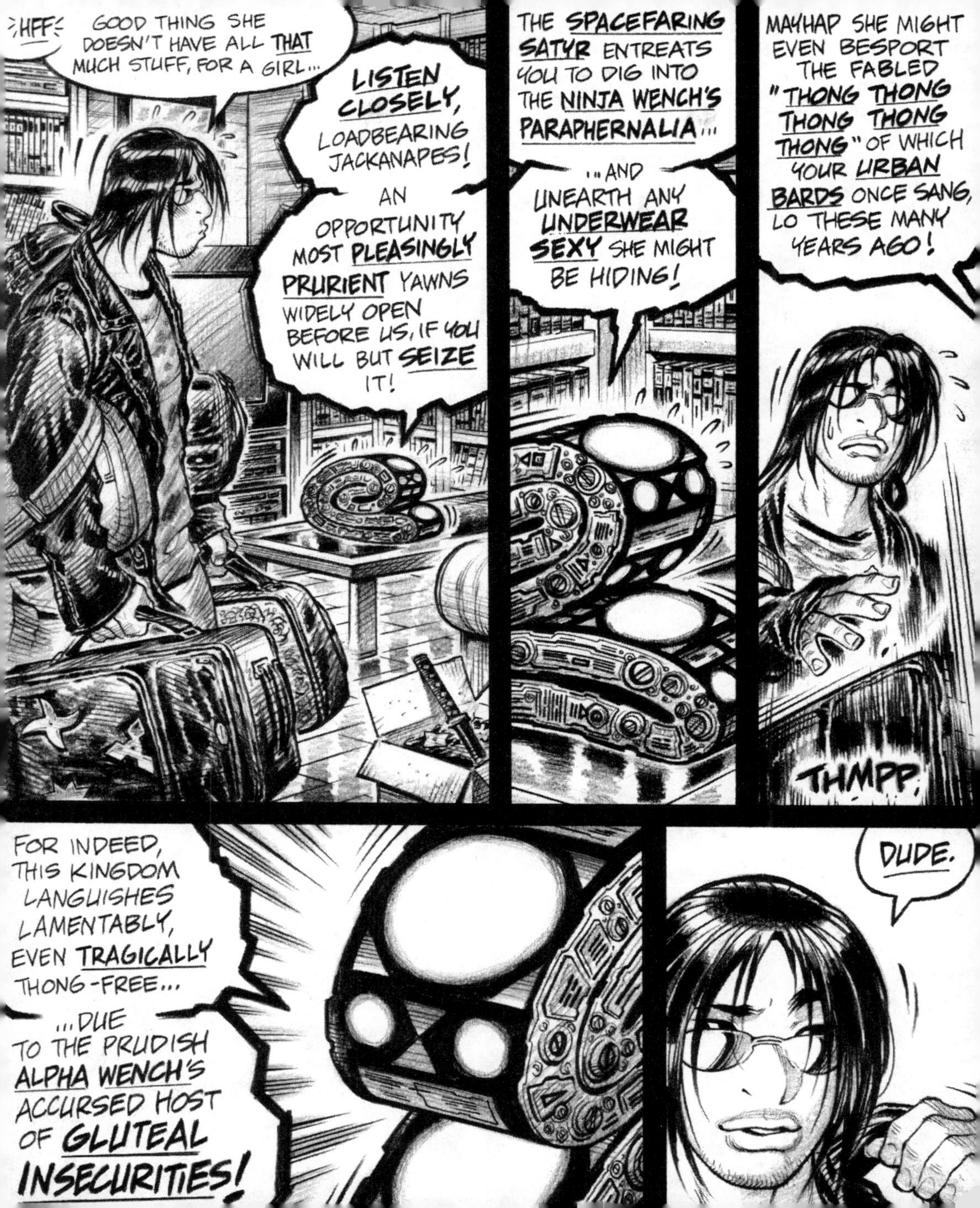
HFF
GOOD THING SHE DOESN'T HAVE ALL THAT MUCH STUFF, FOR A GIRL...
LISTEN CLOSELY, LOADBEARING JACKANAPES!
AN OPPORTUNITY MOST PLEASINGLY PRURIENT YAWNS WIDELY OPEN BEFORE US, IF YOU WILL BUT SEIZE IT!
THE SPACEFARING SATYR ENTREATS YOU TO DIG INTO THE NINJA WENCH'S PARAPHERNALIA...
...AND UNEARTH ANY UNDERWEAR SEXY SHE MIGHT BE HIDING!
MAYHAP SHE MIGHT EVEN BESPORT THE FABLED "THONG THONG THONG THONG THONG" OF WHICH YOUR URBAN BARDS ONCE SANG, LO THESE MANY YEARS AGO!
THMPP
FOR INDEED, THIS KINGDOM LANGUISHES LAMENTABLY, EVEN TRAGICALLY THONG-FREE...
...DUE TO THE PRUDISH ALPHA WENCH'S ACCURSED HOST OF GLUTEAL INSECURITIES!
DUDE.

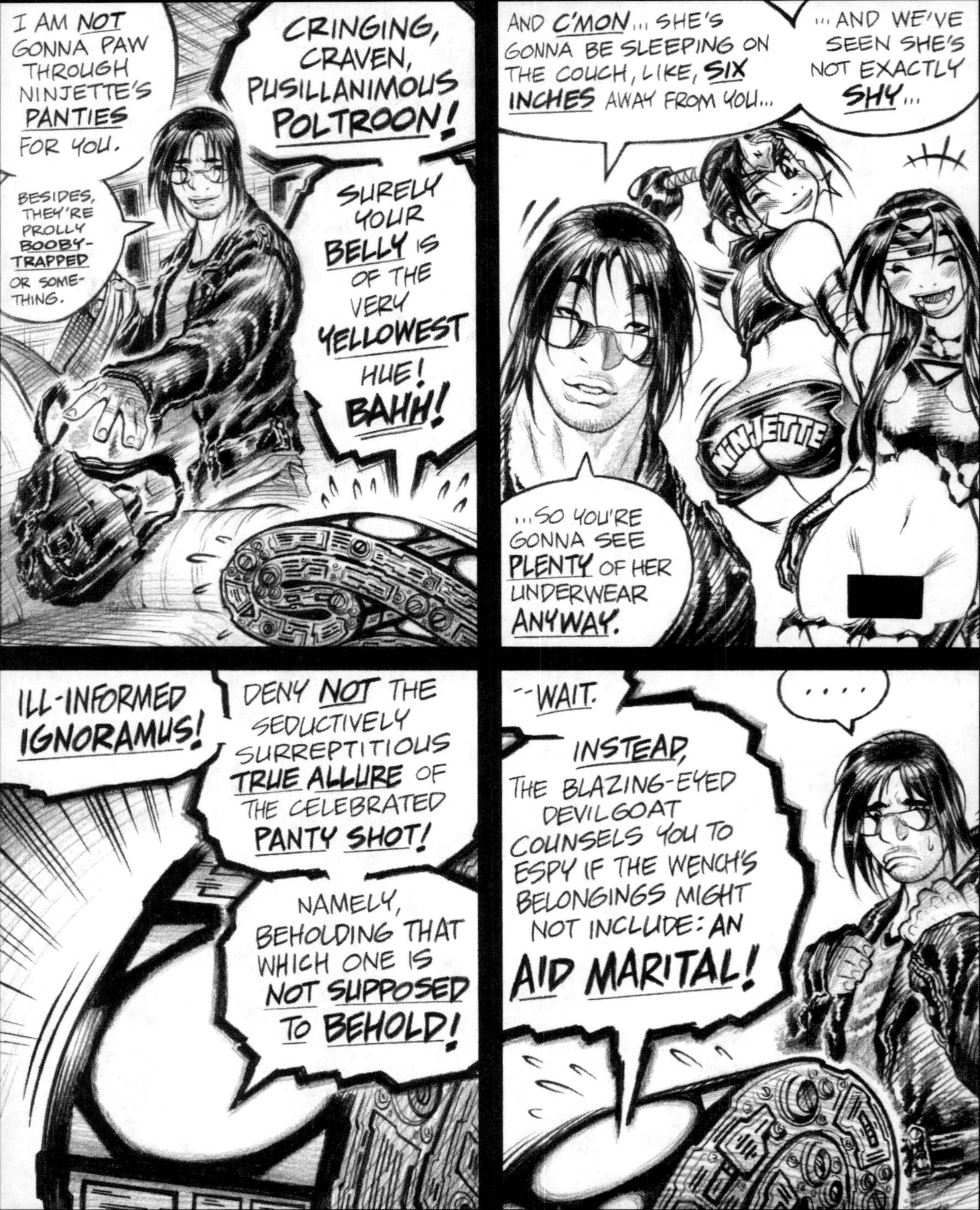
I AM NOT GONNA PAW THROUGH NINJETTE'S PANTIES FOR YOU.
CRINGING, CRAVEN, PUSILLANIMOUS POLTROON!
BESIDES, THEY'RE PROLLY BOOBY-TRAPPED OR SOME-THING.
SURELY YOUR BELLY IS OF THE VERY YELLOWEST HUE! BAHH!
AND C'MON... SHE'S GONNA BE SLEEPING ON THE COUCH, LIKE, SIX INCHES AWAY FROM YOU...
...AND WE'VE SEEN SHE'S NOT EXACTLY SHY...
NINJETTE
...SO YOU'RE GONNA SEE PLENTY OF HER UNDERWEAR ANYWAY.
ILL-INFORMED IGNORAMUS!
DENY NOT THE SEDUCTIVELY SURREPTITIOUS TRUE ALLURE OF THE CELEBRATED PANTY SHOT!
NAMELY, BEHOLDING THAT WHICH ONE IS NOT SUPPOSED TO BEHOLD!
--WAIT.
....
INSTEAD, THE BLAZING-EYED DEVILGOAT COUNSELS YOU TO ESPY IF THE WENCH'S BELONGINGS MIGHT NOT INCLUDE: AN AID MARITAL!

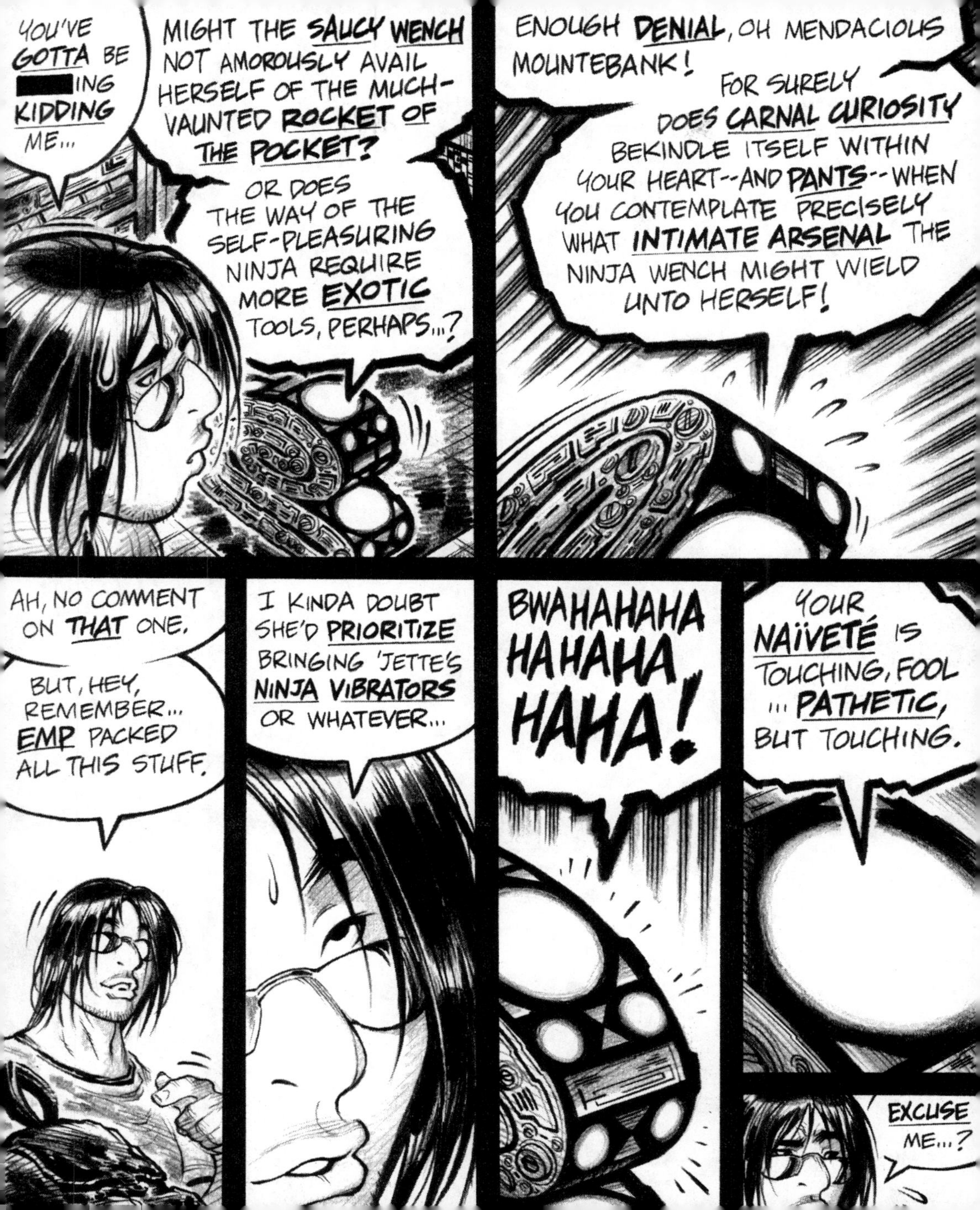
YOU'VE GOTTA BE [redacted]ING KIDDING ME...
MIGHT THE SAUCY WENCH NOT AMOROUSLY AVAIL HERSELF OF THE MUCH-VAUNTED ROCKET OF THE POCKET?
OR DOES THE WAY OF THE SELF-PLEASURING NINJA REQUIRE MORE EXOTIC TOOLS, PERHAPS...?
ENOUGH DENIAL, OH MENDACIOUS MOUNTEBANK!
FOR SURELY DOES CARNAL CURIOSITY BEKINDLE ITSELF WITHIN YOUR HEART--AND PANTS--WHEN YOU CONTEMPLATE PRECISELY WHAT INTIMATE ARSENAL THE NINJA WENCH MIGHT WIELD UNTO HERSELF!
AH, NO COMMENT ON THAT ONE.
BUT, HEY, REMEMBER... EMP PACKED ALL THIS STUFF.
I KINDA DOUBT SHE'D PRIORITIZE BRINGING 'JETTE'S NINJA VIBRATORS OR WHATEVER...
BWAHAHAHA HAHAHA HAHA!
YOUR NAÏVETÉ IS TOUCHING, FOOL ... PATHETIC, BUT TOUCHING.
EXCUSE ME...?

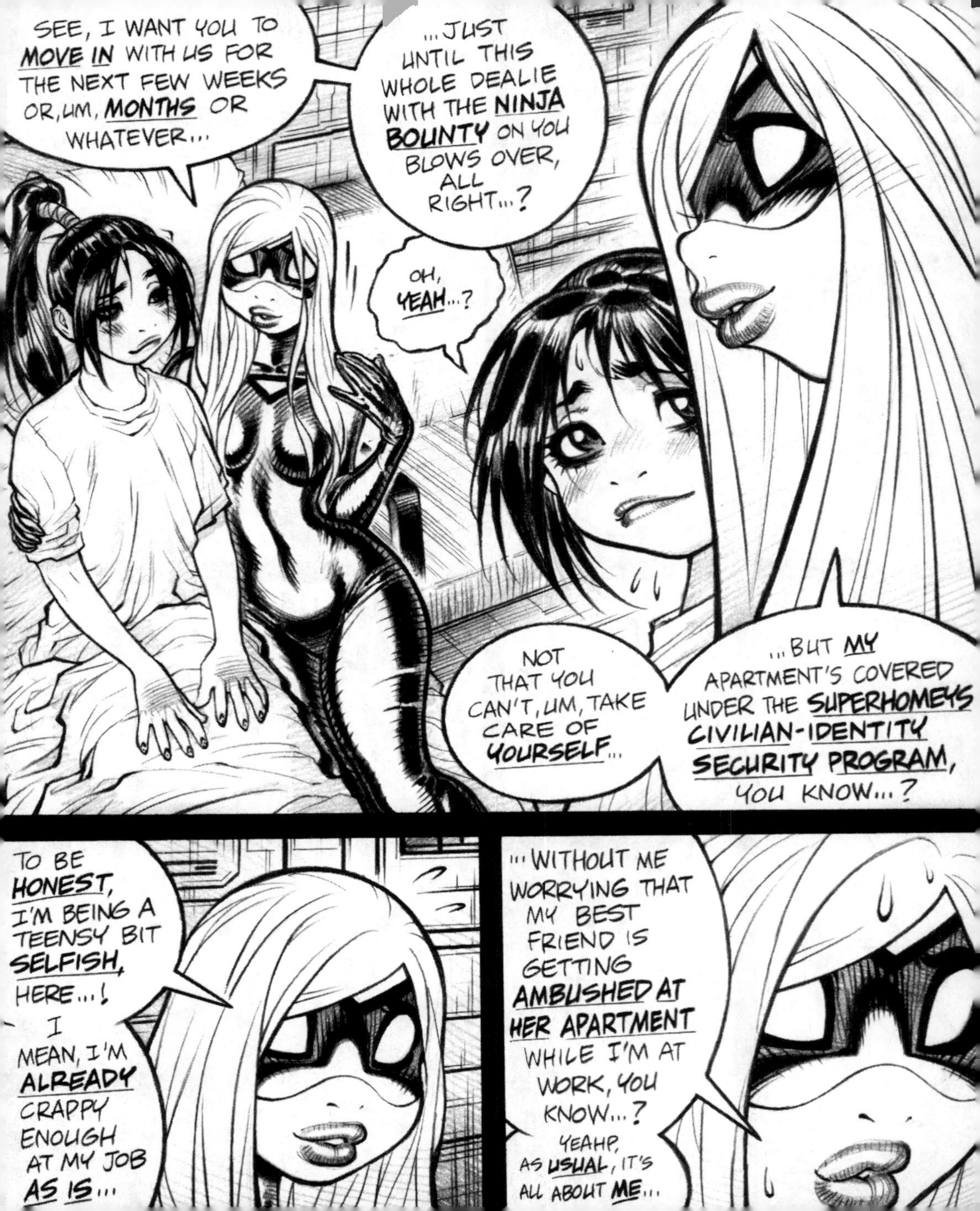

SEE, I WANT YOU TO **MOVE IN** WITH US FOR THE NEXT FEW WEEKS OR, UM, **MONTHS** OR WHATEVER...
...JUST UNTIL THIS WHOLE DEALIE WITH THE **NINJA BOUNTY** ON YOU BLOWS OVER, ALL RIGHT...?
OH, **YEAH**...?
NOT THAT YOU CAN'T, UM, TAKE CARE OF **YOURSELF**...
...BUT **MY** APARTMENT'S COVERED UNDER THE **SUPERHOMEYS CIVILIAN-IDENTITY SECURITY PROGRAM**, YOU KNOW...?
TO BE **HONEST**, I'M BEING A TEENSY BIT **SELFISH**, HERE...!
I MEAN, I'M **ALREADY** CRAPPY ENOUGH AT MY JOB **AS IS**...
...WITHOUT ME WORRYING THAT MY BEST FRIEND IS GETTING **AMBUSHED AT HER APARTMENT** WHILE I'M AT WORK, YOU KNOW...?
YEAHP, AS **USUAL**, IT'S ALL ABOUT **ME**...

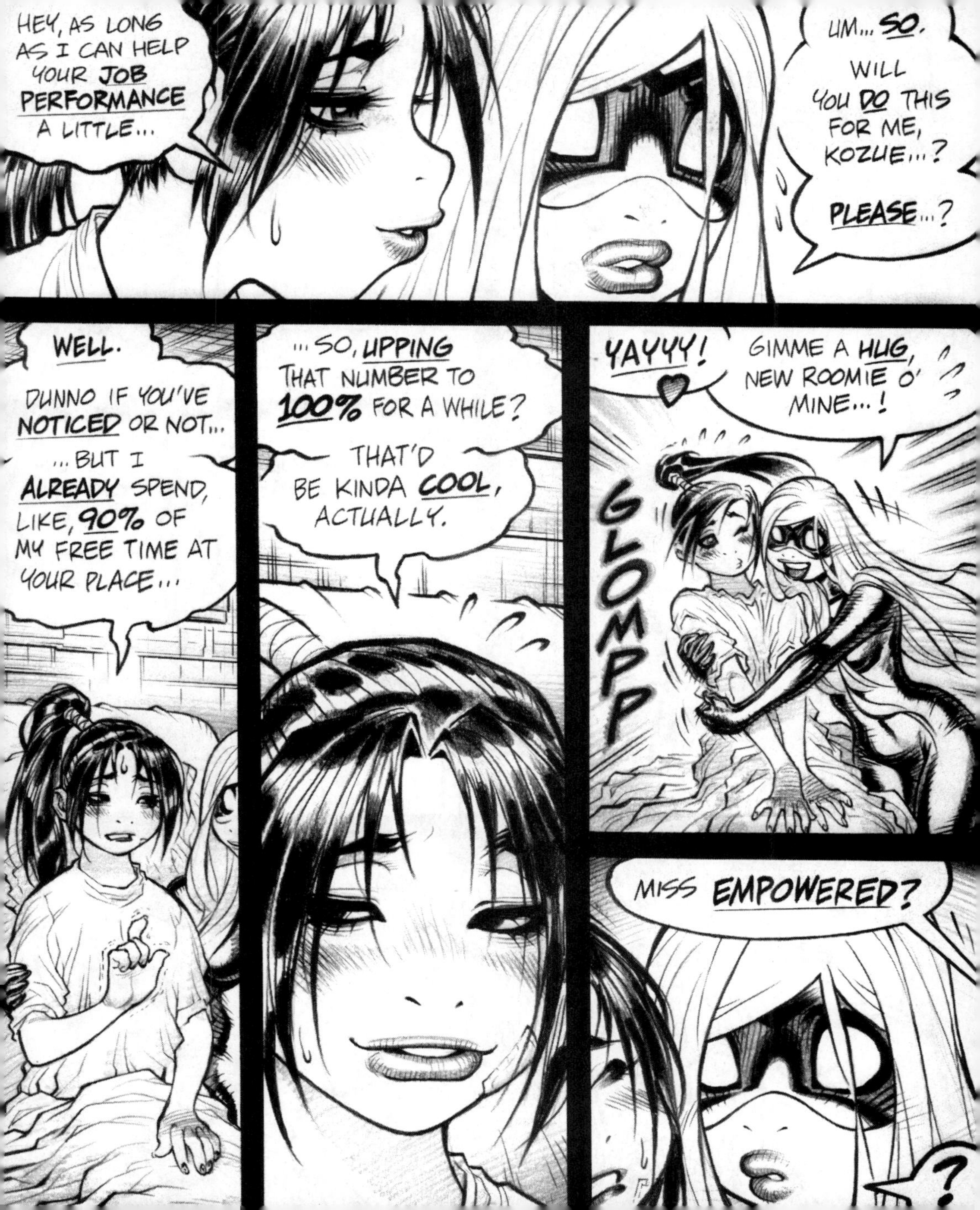
HEY, AS LONG AS I CAN HELP YOUR JOB PERFORMANCE A LITTLE...
UM... SO. WILL YOU DO THIS FOR ME, KOZUE...? PLEASE...?
WELL.
DUNNO IF YOU'VE NOTICED OR NOT...
...BUT I ALREADY SPEND, LIKE, 90% OF MY FREE TIME AT YOUR PLACE...
...SO, UPPING THAT NUMBER TO 100% FOR A WHILE?
THAT'D BE KINDA COOL, ACTUALLY.
YAYYY!
GIMME A HUG, NEW ROOMIE O' MINE...!
GLOMPP
MISS EMPOWERED?
?

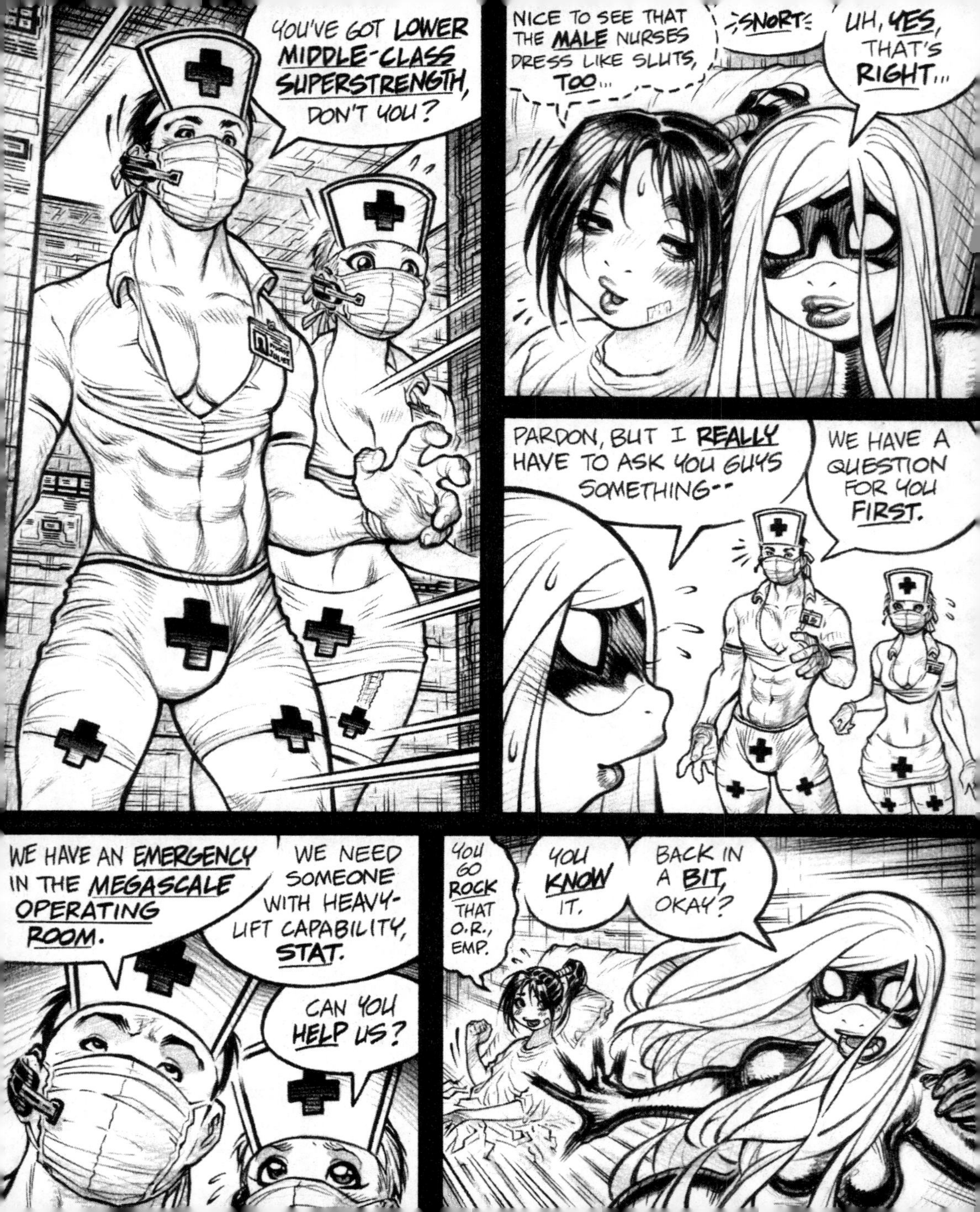
YOU'VE GOT LOWER MIDDLE-CLASS SUPERSTRENGTH, DON'T YOU?
NICE TO SEE THAT THE MALE NURSES DRESS LIKE SLUTS, TOO...
SNORT
UH, YES, THAT'S RIGHT...
PARDON, BUT I REALLY HAVE TO ASK YOU GUYS SOMETHING--
WE HAVE A QUESTION FOR YOU FIRST.
WE HAVE AN EMERGENCY IN THE MEGASCALE OPERATING ROOM.
WE NEED SOMEONE WITH HEAVY-LIFT CAPABILITY, STAT.
CAN YOU HELP US?
YOU GO ROCK THAT O.R., EMP.
YOU KNOW IT.
BACK IN A BIT, OKAY?

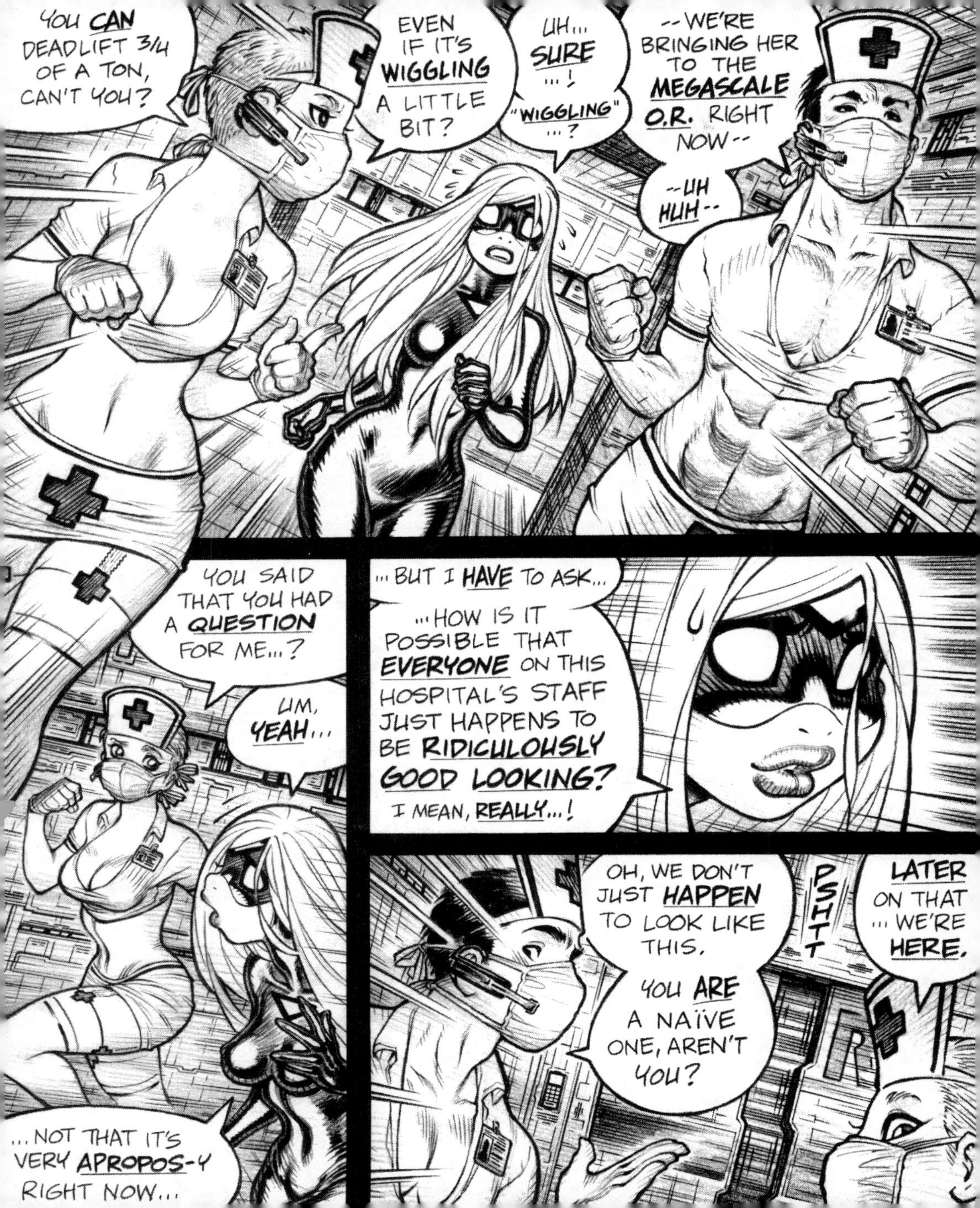
YOU CAN DEADLIFT 3/4 OF A TON, CAN'T YOU?
EVEN IF IT'S WIGGLING A LITTLE BIT?
UH... SURE ...!
"WIGGLING" ...?
--WE'RE BRINGING HER TO THE MEGASCALE O.R. RIGHT NOW--
--UH HUH--
YOU SAID THAT YOU HAD A QUESTION FOR ME...?
UM, YEAH...
...NOT THAT IT'S VERY APROPOS-Y RIGHT NOW...
...BUT I HAVE TO ASK...
...HOW IS IT POSSIBLE THAT EVERYONE ON THIS HOSPITAL'S STAFF JUST HAPPENS TO BE RIDICULOUSLY GOOD LOOKING?
I MEAN, REALLY...!
OH, WE DON'T JUST HAPPEN TO LOOK LIKE THIS.
YOU ARE A NAÏVE ONE, AREN'T YOU?
PSHTT
LATER ON THAT ...WE'RE HERE.

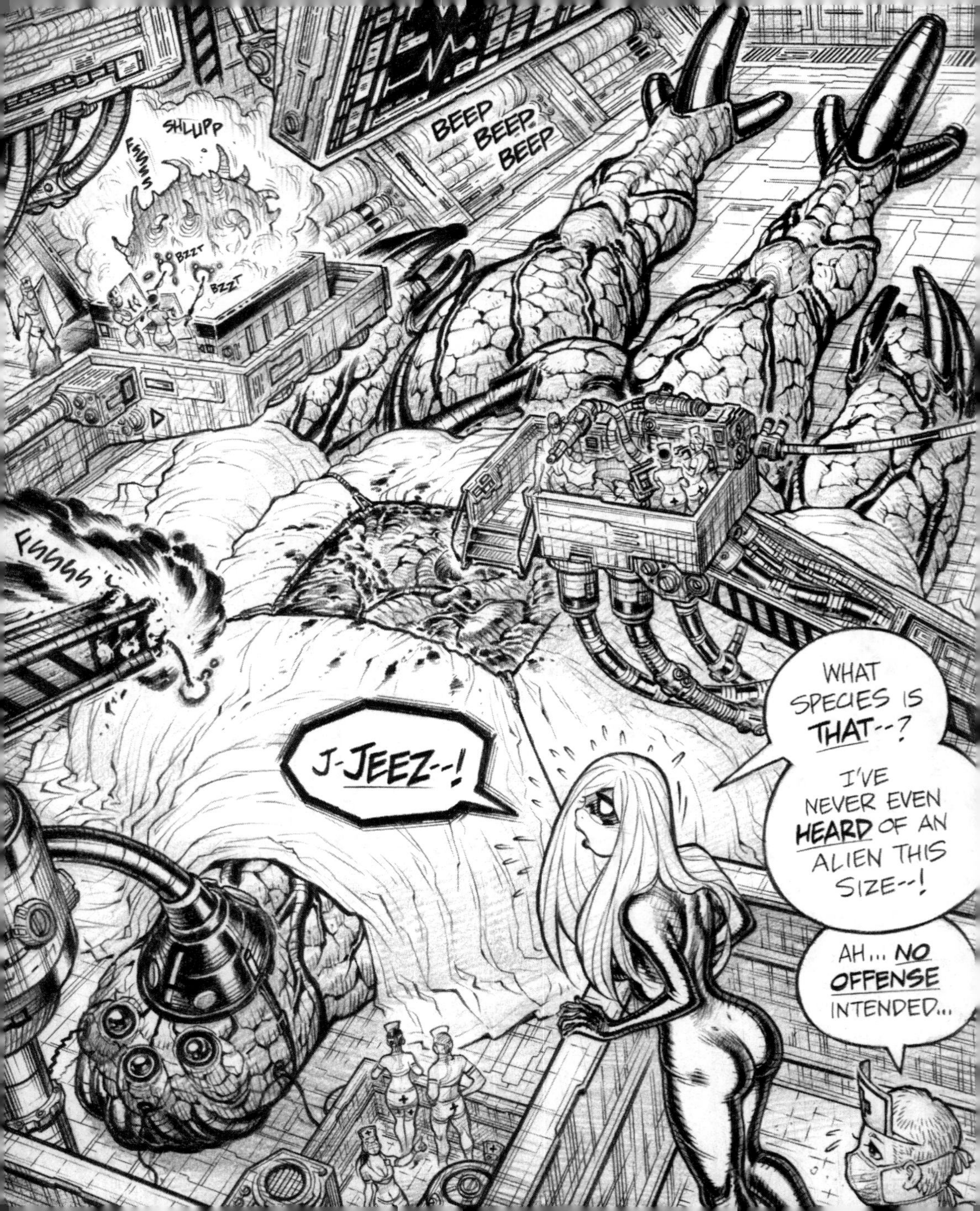
SHLUPP
FSSSSS
BZZT
BZZT
BEEP BEEP BEEP
FSSSSS
J-JEEZ--!
WHAT SPECIES IS THAT--?
I'VE NEVER EVEN HEARD OF AN ALIEN THIS SIZE--!
AH... NO OFFENSE INTENDED...

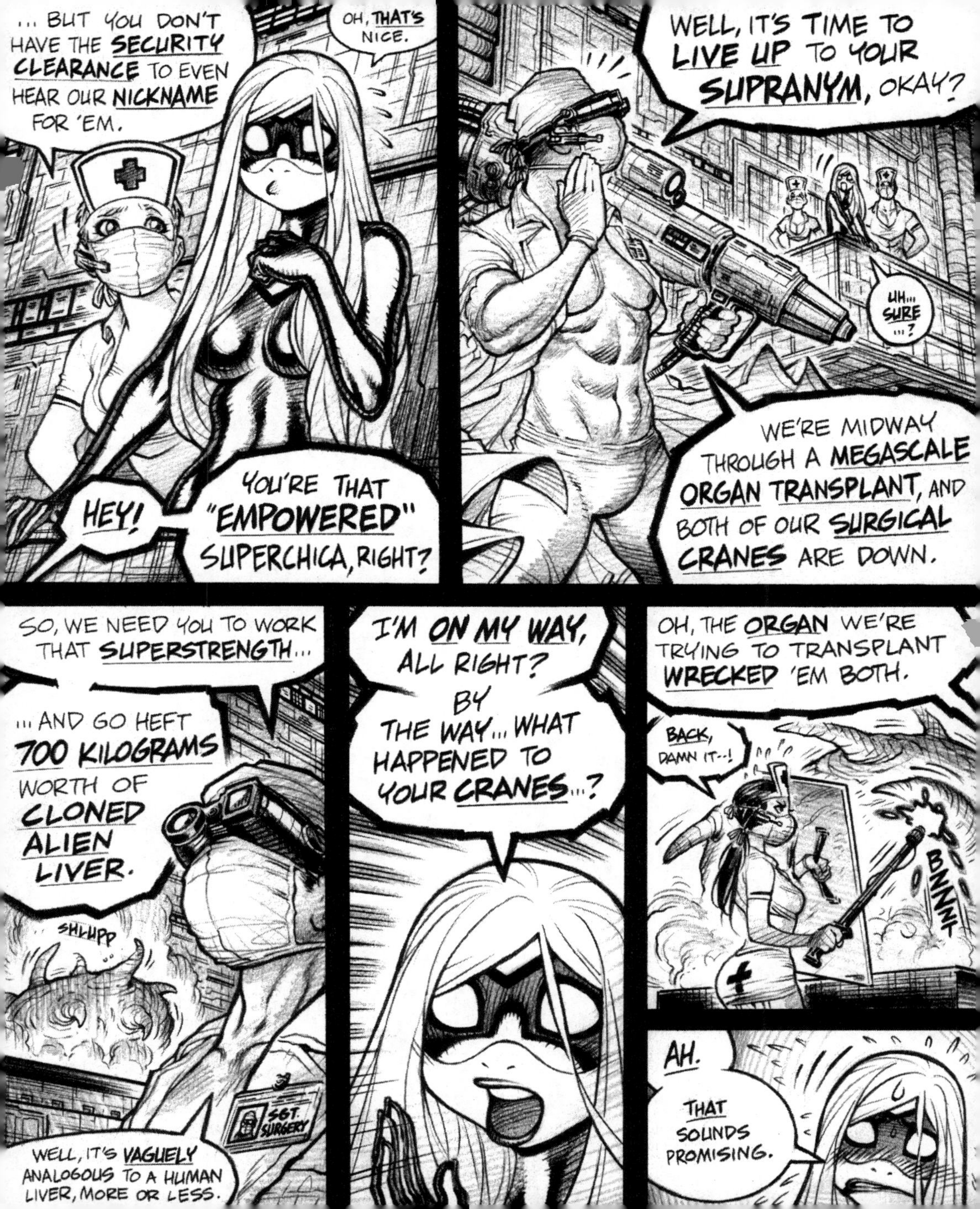
... BUT YOU DON'T HAVE THE SECURITY CLEARANCE TO EVEN HEAR OUR NICKNAME FOR 'EM.
OH, THAT'S NICE.
HEY!
YOU'RE THAT "EMPOWERED" SUPERCHICA, RIGHT?
WELL, IT'S TIME TO LIVE UP TO YOUR SUPRANYM, OKAY?
UH... SURE ...?
WE'RE MIDWAY THROUGH A MEGASCALE ORGAN TRANSPLANT, AND BOTH OF OUR SURGICAL CRANES ARE DOWN.
SO, WE NEED YOU TO WORK THAT SUPERSTRENGTH...
... AND GO HEFT 700 KILOGRAMS WORTH OF CLONED ALIEN LIVER.
SHLUPP
SGT. SURGERY
WELL, IT'S VAGUELY ANALOGOUS TO A HUMAN LIVER, MORE OR LESS.
I'M ON MY WAY, ALL RIGHT?
BY THE WAY... WHAT HAPPENED TO YOUR CRANES...?
OH, THE ORGAN WE'RE TRYING TO TRANSPLANT WRECKED 'EM BOTH.
BACK, DAMN IT--!
BZZZT
AH.
THAT SOUNDS PROMISING.

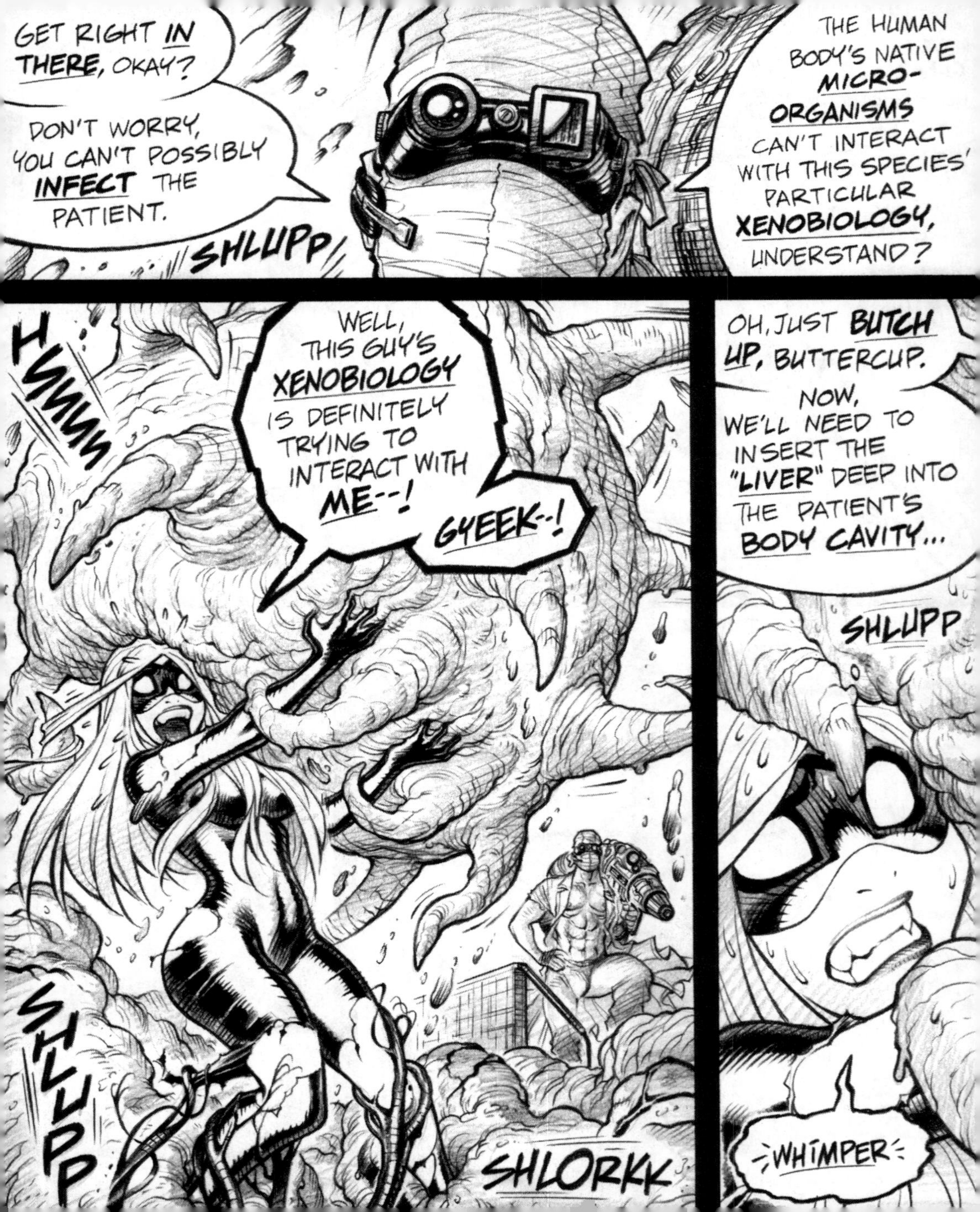

GET RIGHT IN THERE, OKAY?
DON'T WORRY, YOU CAN'T POSSIBLY INFECT THE PATIENT.
SHLUPP
THE HUMAN BODY'S NATIVE MICRO-ORGANISMS CAN'T INTERACT WITH THIS SPECIES' PARTICULAR XENOBIOLOGY, UNDERSTAND?
HMMMM
WELL, THIS GUY'S XENOBIOLOGY IS DEFINITELY TRYING TO INTERACT WITH ME--!
GYEEK--!
SHLUPP
SHLORKK
OH, JUST BUTCH UP, BUTTERCUP.
NOW, WE'LL NEED TO INSERT THE "LIVER" DEEP INTO THE PATIENT'S BODY CAVITY...
SHLUPP
WHIMPER

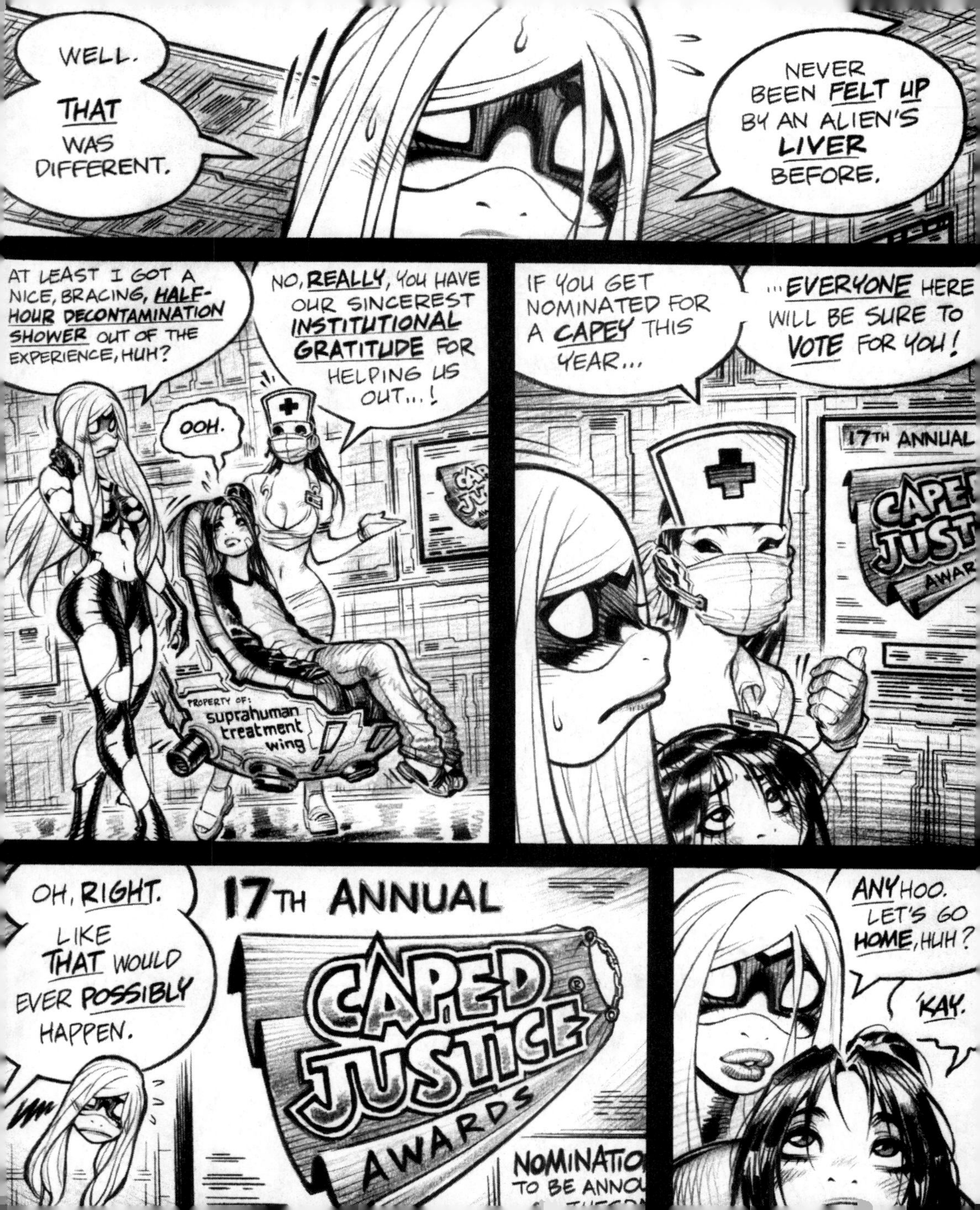
WELL.
THAT WAS DIFFERENT.
NEVER BEEN FELT UP BY AN ALIEN'S LIVER BEFORE.
AT LEAST I GOT A NICE, BRACING, HALF-HOUR DECONTAMINATION SHOWER OUT OF THE EXPERIENCE, HUH?
NO, REALLY, YOU HAVE OUR SINCEREST INSTITUTIONAL GRATITUDE FOR HELPING US OUT...!
OOH.
PROPERTY OF: suprahuman treatment wing
IF YOU GET NOMINATED FOR A CAPEY THIS YEAR...
...EVERYONE HERE WILL BE SURE TO VOTE FOR YOU!
17TH ANNUAL
OH, RIGHT.
LIKE THAT WOULD EVER POSSIBLY HAPPEN.
17TH ANNUAL
CAPED JUSTICE AWARDS
NOMINATIO
TO BE ANNOU
ANYHOO. LET'S GO HOME, HUH?
'KAY.

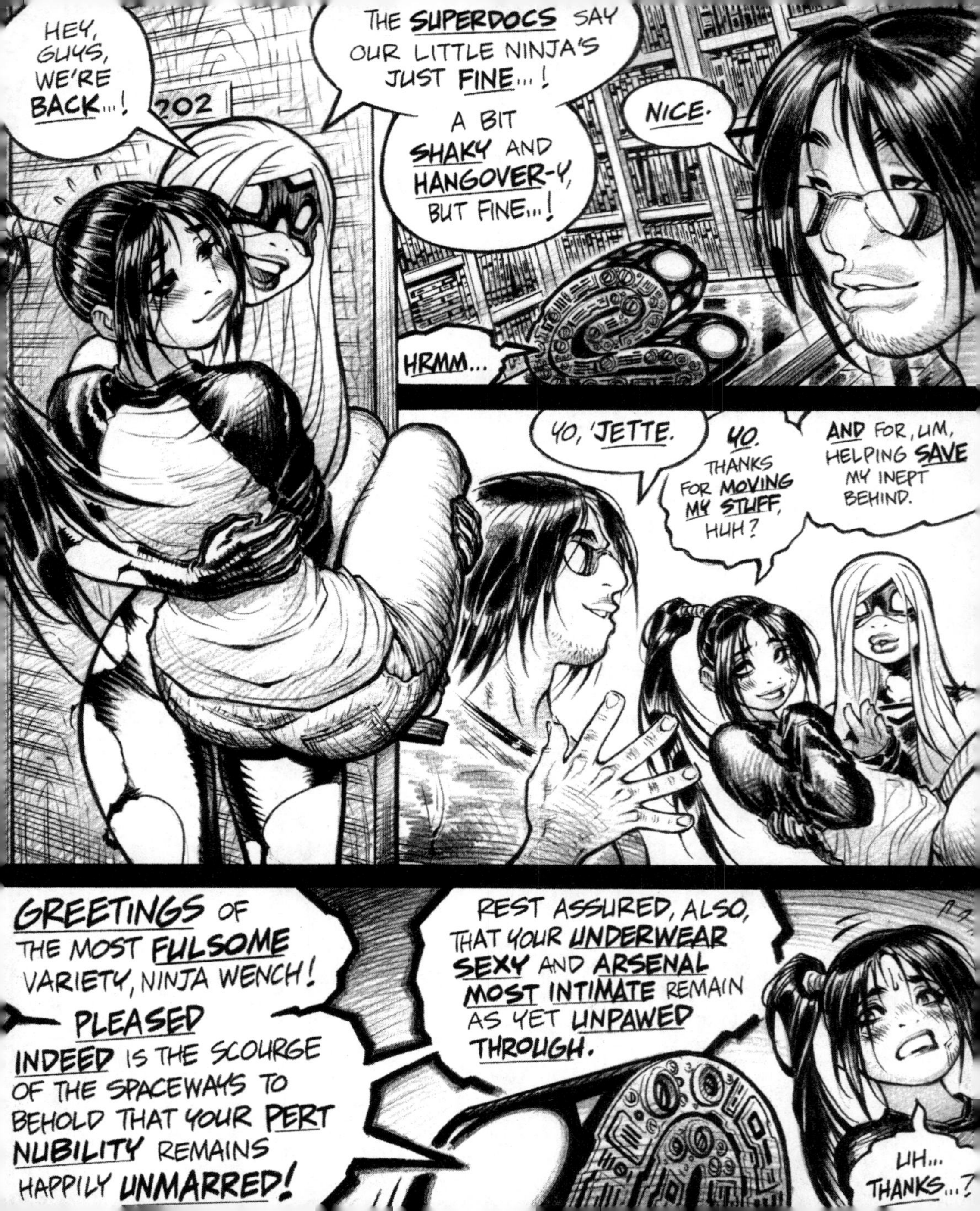
HEY, GUYS, WE'RE BACK...!
202
THE SUPERDOCS SAY OUR LITTLE NINJA'S JUST FINE...!
A BIT SHAKY AND HANGOVER-Y, BUT FINE...!
NICE.
HRMM...
YO, 'JETTE.
YO. THANKS FOR MOVING MY STUFF, HUH?
AND FOR, UM, HELPING SAVE MY INEPT BEHIND.
GREETINGS OF THE MOST FULSOME VARIETY, NINJA WENCH!
— PLEASED INDEED IS THE SCOURGE OF THE SPACEWAYS TO BEHOLD THAT YOUR PERT NUBILITY REMAINS HAPPILY UNMARRED!
REST ASSURED, ALSO, THAT YOUR UNDERWEAR SEXY AND ARSENAL MOST INTIMATE REMAIN AS YET UNPAWED THROUGH.
UH... THANKS...?

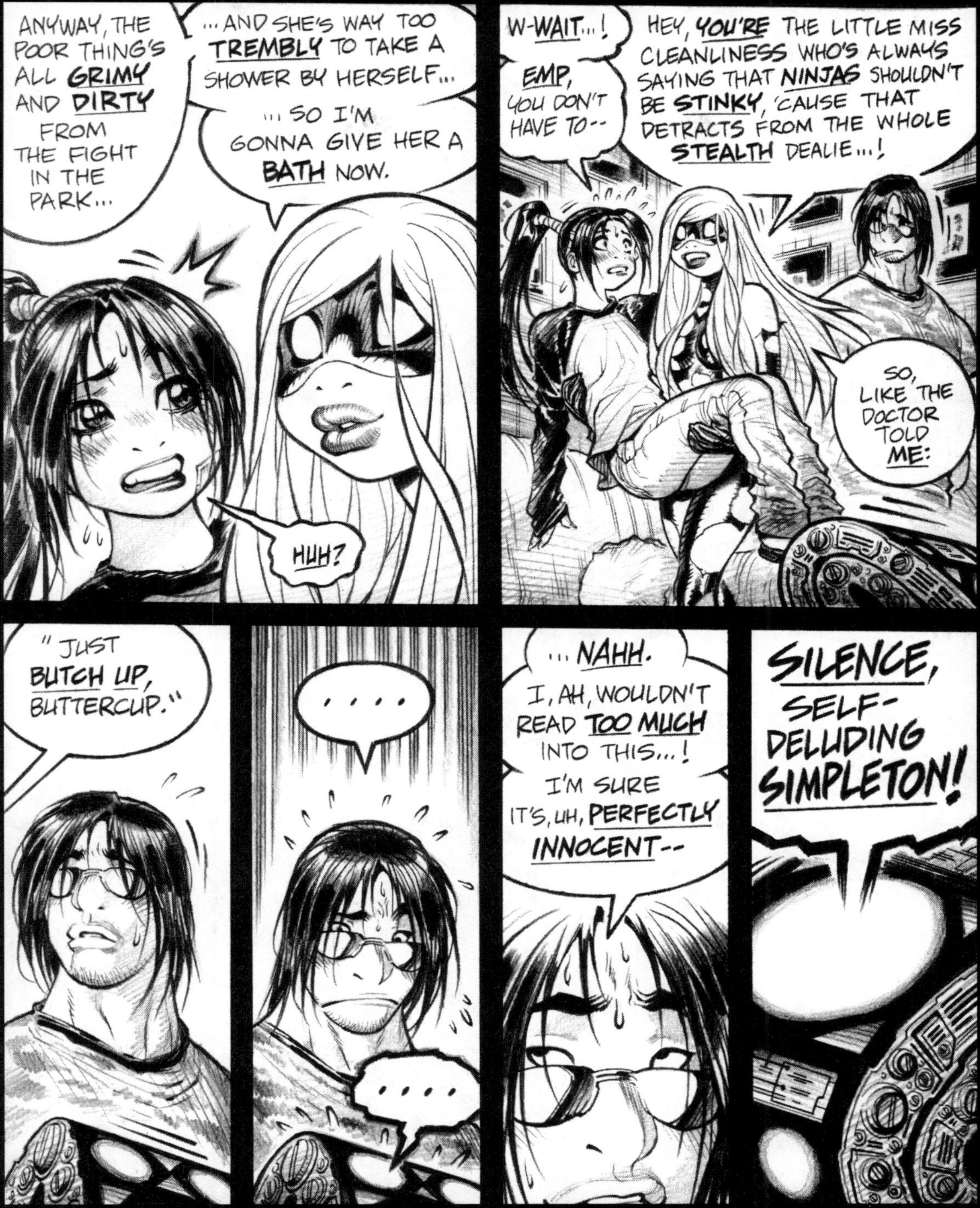
ANYWAY, THE POOR THING'S ALL GRIMY AND DIRTY FROM THE FIGHT IN THE PARK...
...AND SHE'S WAY TOO TREMBLY TO TAKE A SHOWER BY HERSELF...
...SO I'M GONNA GIVE HER A BATH NOW.
HUH?
W-WAIT...!
EMP, YOU DON'T HAVE TO--
HEY, YOU'RE THE LITTLE MISS CLEANLINESS WHO'S ALWAYS SAYING THAT NINJAS SHOULDN'T BE STINKY, 'CAUSE THAT DETRACTS FROM THE WHOLE STEALTH DEALIE...!
SO, LIKE THE DOCTOR TOLD ME:
"JUST BUTCH UP, BUTTERCUP."
....
....
...NAHH.
I, AH, WOULDN'T READ TOO MUCH INTO THIS...!
I'M SURE IT'S, UH, PERFECTLY INNOCENT--
SILENCE, SELF-DELUDING SIMPLETON!

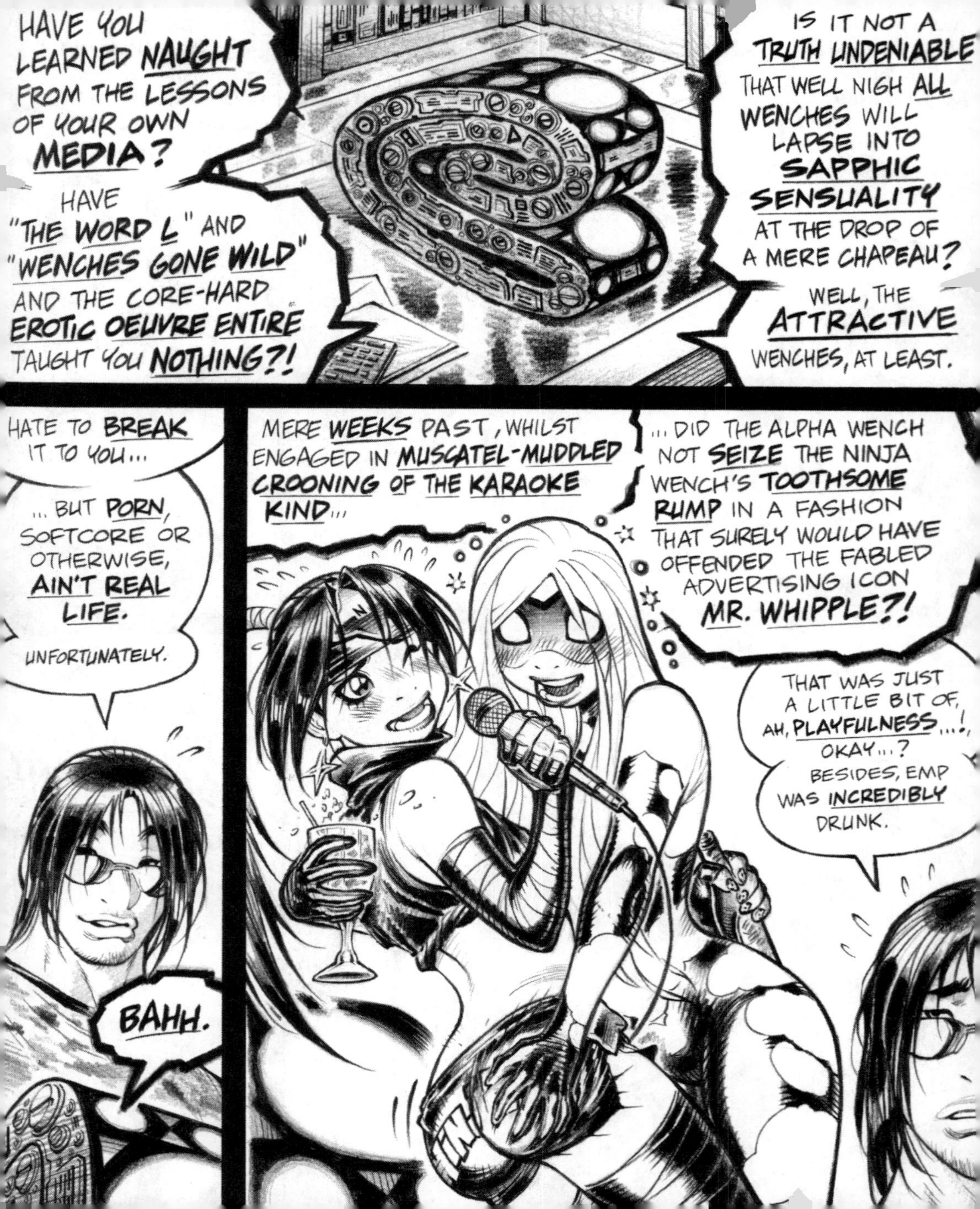
HAVE YOU LEARNED NAUGHT FROM THE LESSONS OF YOUR OWN MEDIA?
HAVE "THE WORD L" AND "WENCHES GONE WILD" AND THE CORE-HARD EROTIC OEUVRE ENTIRE TAUGHT YOU NOTHING?!
IS IT NOT A TRUTH UNDENIABLE THAT WELL NIGH ALL WENCHES WILL LAPSE INTO SAPPHIC SENSUALITY AT THE DROP OF A MERE CHAPEAU?
WELL, THE ATTRACTIVE WENCHES, AT LEAST.
HATE TO BREAK IT TO YOU...
...BUT PORN, SOFTCORE OR OTHERWISE, AIN'T REAL LIFE.
UNFORTUNATELY.
BAHH.
MERE WEEKS PAST, WHILST ENGAGED IN MUSCATEL-MUDDLED CROONING OF THE KARAOKE KIND...
...DID THE ALPHA WENCH NOT SEIZE THE NINJA WENCH'S TOOTHSOME RUMP IN A FASHION THAT SURELY WOULD HAVE OFFENDED THE FABLED ADVERTISING ICON MR. WHIPPLE?!
THAT WAS JUST A LITTLE BIT OF, AH, PLAYFULNESS...!, OKAY...?
BESIDES, EMP WAS INCREDIBLY DRUNK.

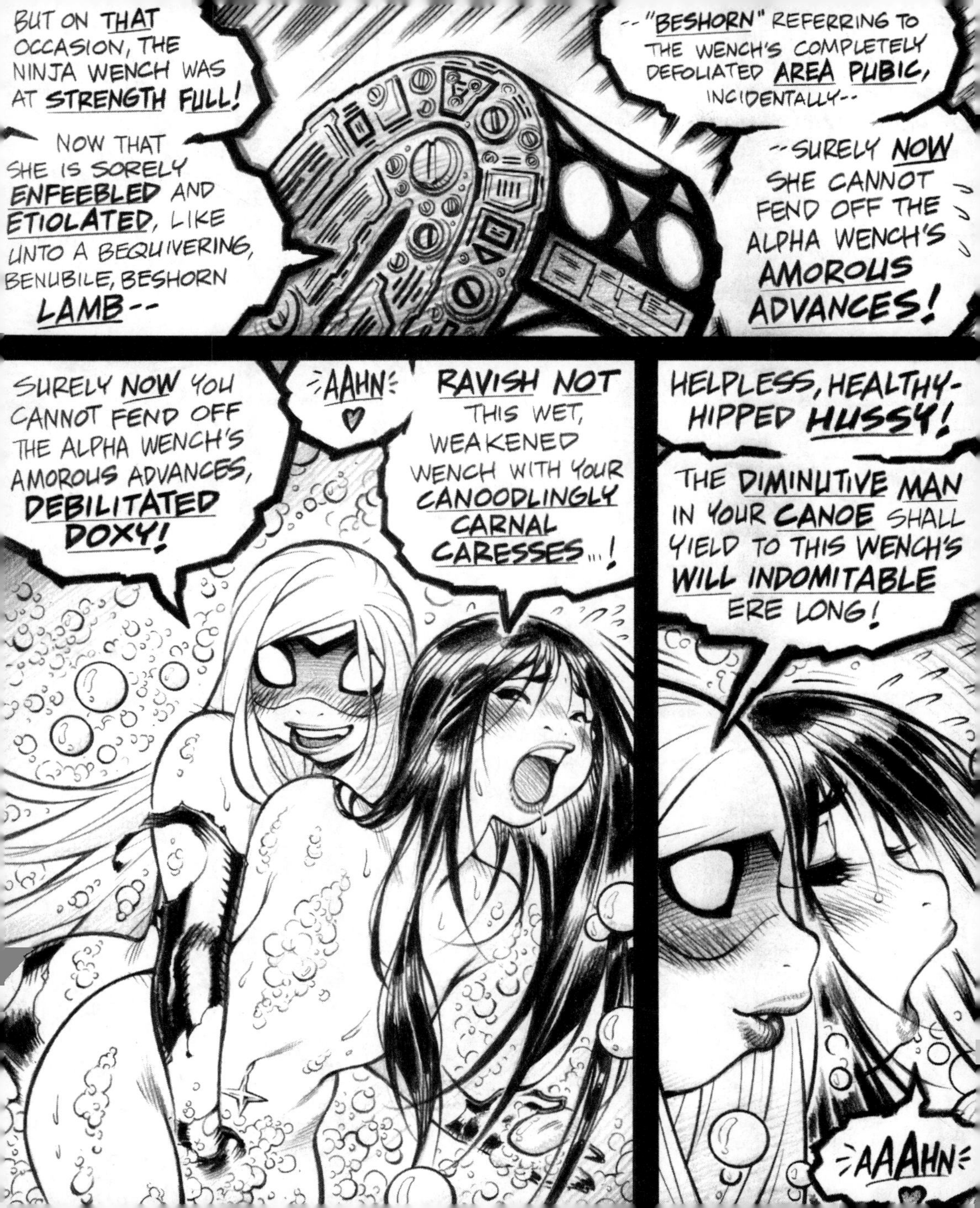
BUT ON THAT OCCASION, THE NINJA WENCH WAS AT STRENGTH FULL!
NOW THAT SHE IS SORELY ENFEEBLED AND ETIOLATED, LIKE UNTO A BEQUIVERING, BENUBILE, BESHORN LAMB--
--"BESHORN" REFERRING TO THE WENCH'S COMPLETELY DEFOLIATED AREA PUBIC, INCIDENTALLY--
--SURELY NOW SHE CANNOT FEND OFF THE ALPHA WENCH'S AMOROUS ADVANCES!
SURELY NOW YOU CANNOT FEND OFF THE ALPHA WENCH'S AMOROUS ADVANCES, DEBILITATED DOXY!
AAHN
RAVISH NOT THIS WET, WEAKENED WENCH WITH YOUR CANOODLINGLY CARNAL CARESSES...!
HELPLESS, HEALTHY-HIPPED HUSSY!
THE DIMINUTIVE MAN IN YOUR CANOE SHALL YIELD TO THIS WENCH'S WILL INDOMITABLE ERE LONG!
AAAHN

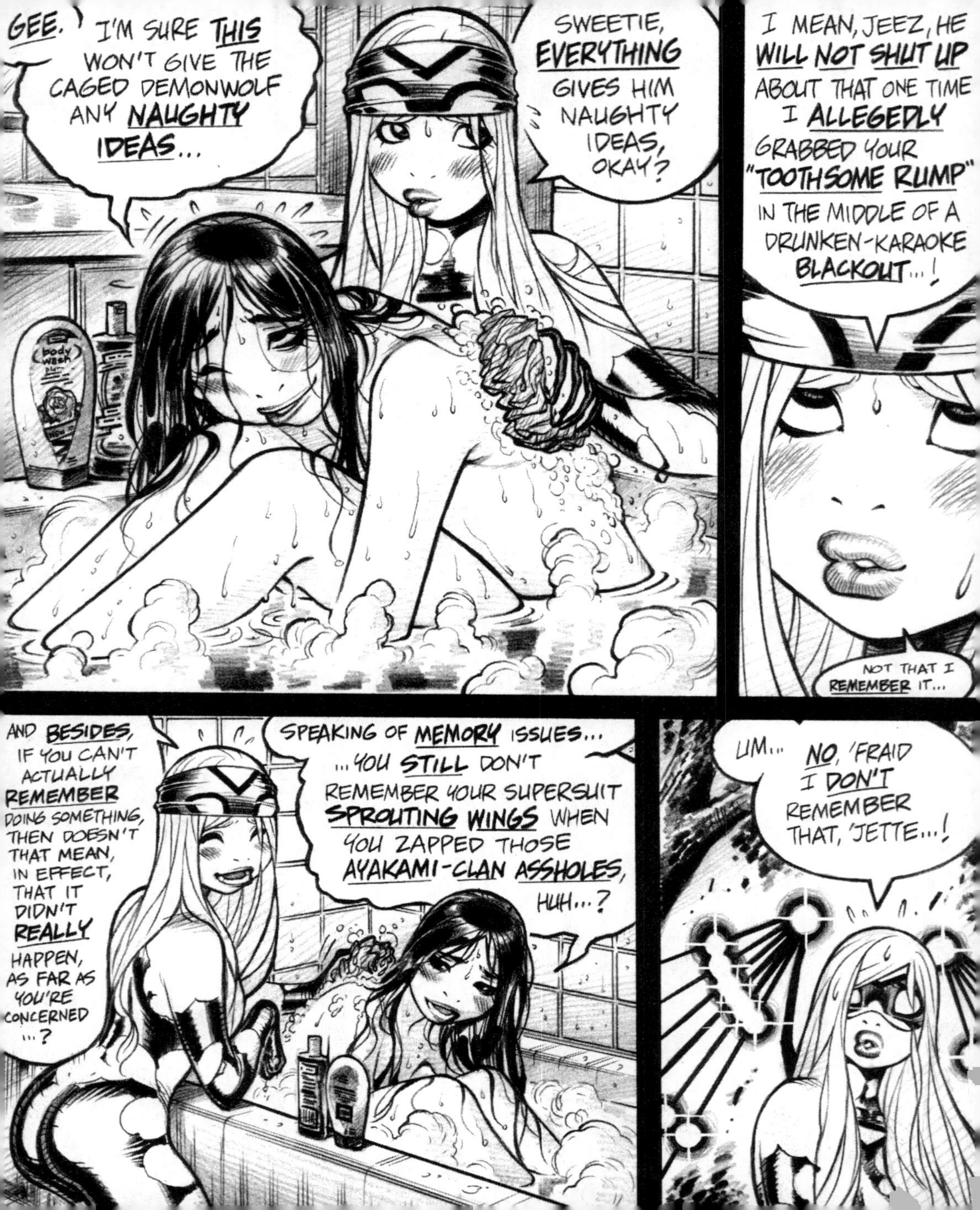
GEE.
I'M SURE THIS WON'T GIVE THE CAGED DEMONWOLF ANY NAUGHTY IDEAS...
SWEETIE, EVERYTHING GIVES HIM NAUGHTY IDEAS, OKAY?
I MEAN, JEEZ, HE WILL NOT SHUT UP ABOUT THAT ONE TIME I ALLEGEDLY GRABBED YOUR "TOOTHSOME RUMP" IN THE MIDDLE OF A DRUNKEN-KARAOKE BLACKOUT...!
NOT THAT I REMEMBER IT...
AND BESIDES, IF YOU CAN'T ACTUALLY REMEMBER DOING SOMETHING, THEN DOESN'T THAT MEAN, IN EFFECT, THAT IT DIDN'T REALLY HAPPEN, AS FAR AS YOU'RE CONCERNED ...?
SPEAKING OF MEMORY ISSUES...
...YOU STILL DON'T REMEMBER YOUR SUPERSUIT SPROUTING WINGS WHEN YOU ZAPPED THOSE AYAKAMI-CLAN ASSHOLES, HUH...?
UM... NO, 'FRAID I DON'T REMEMBER THAT, 'JETTE...!

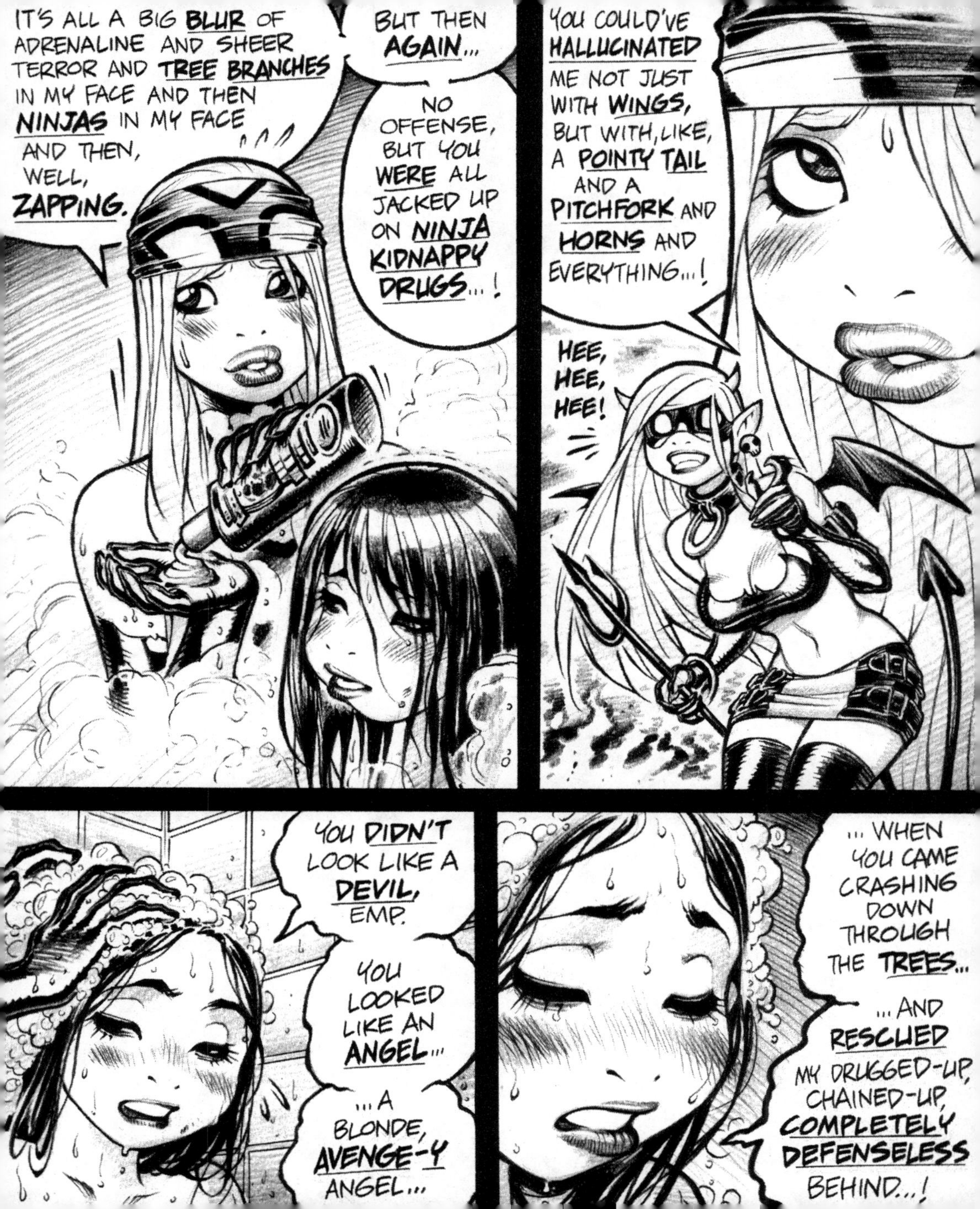
IT'S ALL A BIG BLUR OF ADRENALINE AND SHEER TERROR AND TREE BRANCHES IN MY FACE AND THEN NINJAS IN MY FACE AND THEN, WELL, ZAPPING.
BUT THEN AGAIN...
NO OFFENSE, BUT YOU WERE ALL JACKED UP ON NINJA KIDNAPPY DRUGS...!
YOU COULD'VE HALLUCINATED ME NOT JUST WITH WINGS, BUT WITH, LIKE, A POINTY TAIL AND A PITCHFORK AND HORNS AND EVERYTHING...!
HEE, HEE, HEE!
YOU DIDN'T LOOK LIKE A DEVIL, EMP.
YOU LOOKED LIKE AN ANGEL...
...A BLONDE, AVENGE-Y ANGEL...
...WHEN YOU CAME CRASHING DOWN THROUGH THE TREES...
...AND RESCUED MY DRUGGED-UP, CHAINED-UP, COMPLETELY DEFENSELESS BEHIND...!

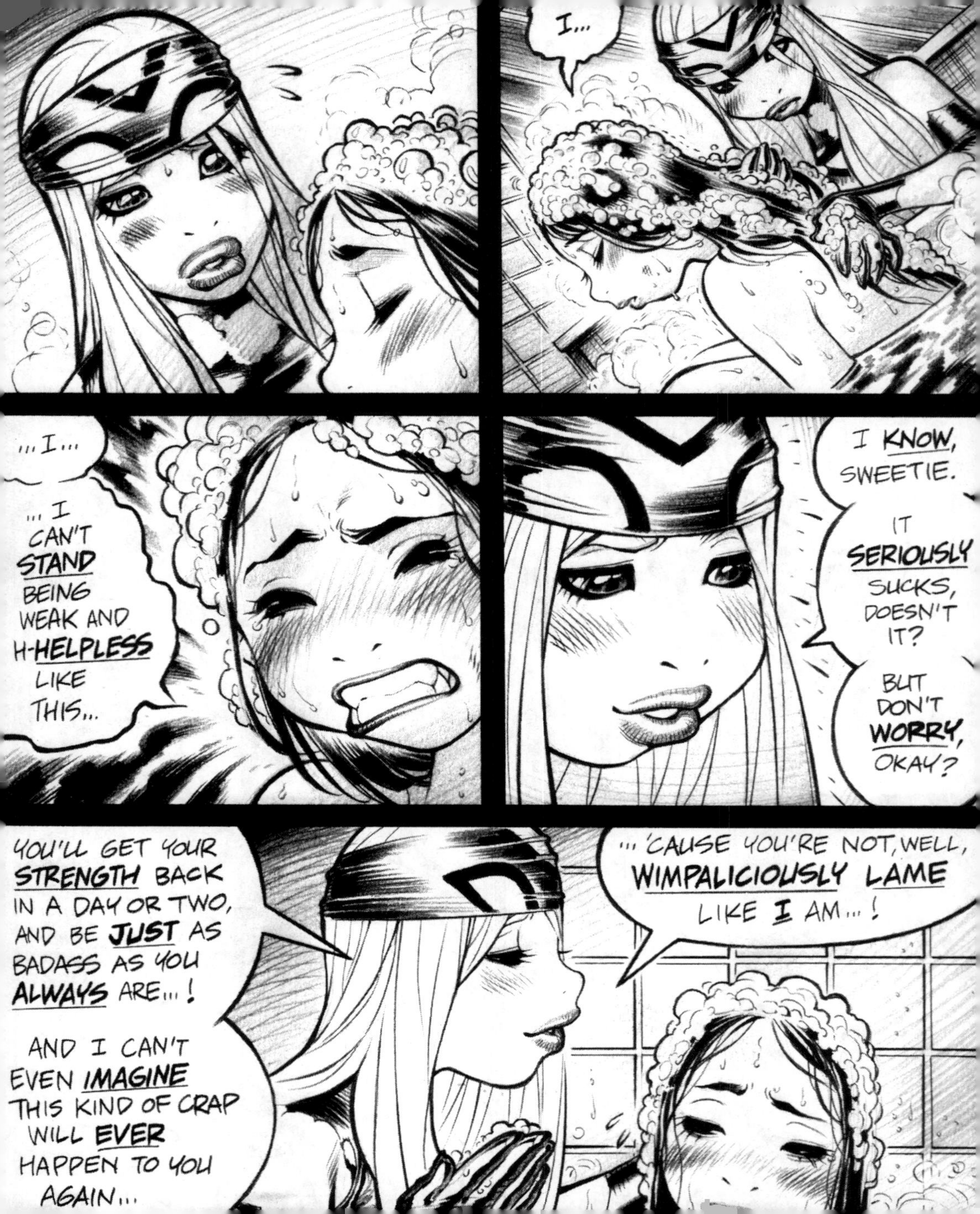
I...
...I...
...I CAN'T STAND BEING WEAK AND H-HELPLESS LIKE THIS...
I KNOW, SWEETIE.
IT SERIOUSLY SUCKS, DOESN'T IT?
BUT DON'T WORRY, OKAY?
YOU'LL GET YOUR STRENGTH BACK IN A DAY OR TWO, AND BE JUST AS BADASS AS YOU ALWAYS ARE...!
AND I CAN'T EVEN IMAGINE THIS KIND OF CRAP WILL EVER HAPPEN TO YOU AGAIN...
...'CAUSE YOU'RE NOT, WELL, WIMPALICIOUSLY LAME LIKE I AM...!

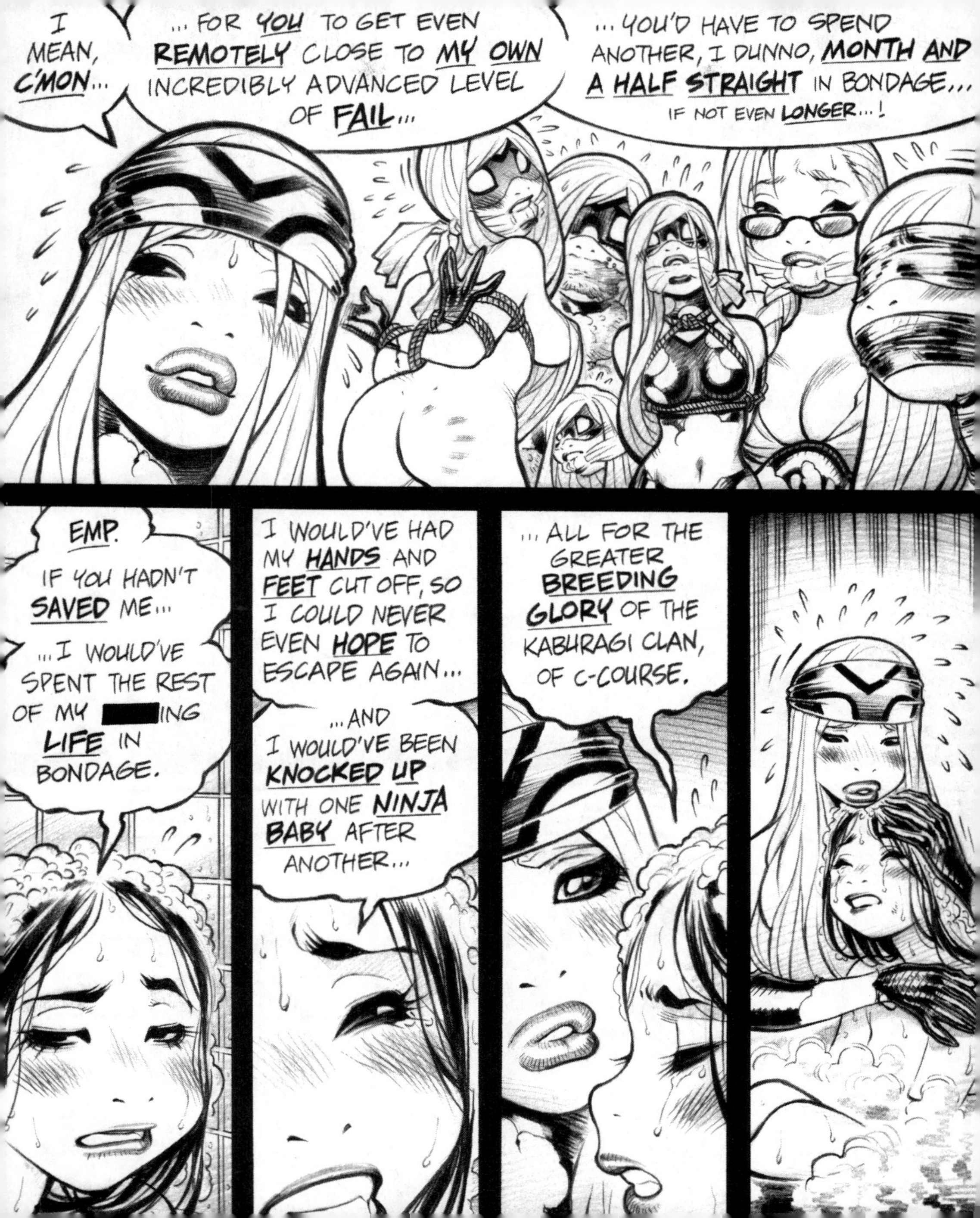
I MEAN, C'MON...
... FOR YOU TO GET EVEN REMOTELY CLOSE TO MY OWN INCREDIBLY ADVANCED LEVEL OF FAIL...
... YOU'D HAVE TO SPEND ANOTHER, I DUNNO, MONTH AND A HALF STRAIGHT IN BONDAGE... IF NOT EVEN LONGER...!
EMP.
IF YOU HADN'T SAVED ME...
...I WOULD'VE SPENT THE REST OF MY [redacted]ING LIFE IN BONDAGE.
I WOULD'VE HAD MY HANDS AND FEET CUT OFF, SO I COULD NEVER EVEN HOPE TO ESCAPE AGAIN...
...AND I WOULD'VE BEEN KNOCKED UP WITH ONE NINJA BABY AFTER ANOTHER...
...ALL FOR THE GREATER BREEDING GLORY OF THE KABURAGI CLAN, OF C-COURSE.

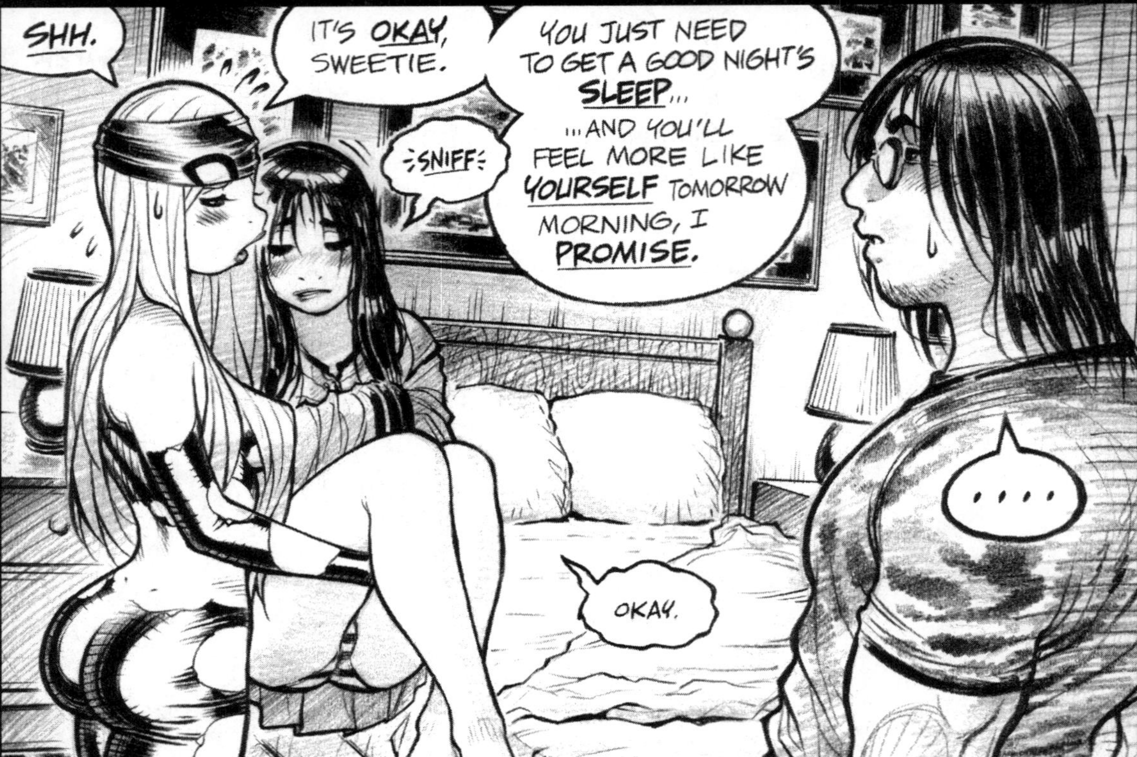
SHH.
IT'S OKAY, SWEETIE.
YOU JUST NEED TO GET A GOOD NIGHT'S SLEEP...
...AND YOU'LL FEEL MORE LIKE YOURSELF TOMORROW MORNING, I PROMISE.
SNIFF
....
OKAY.
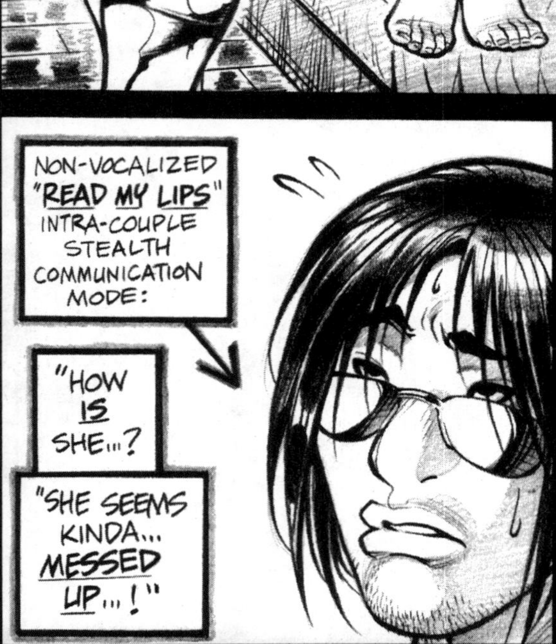
NON-VOCALIZED "READ MY LIPS" INTRA-COUPLE STEALTH COMMUNICATION MODE:
"HOW IS SHE...?
"SHE SEEMS KINDA... MESSED UP...!"
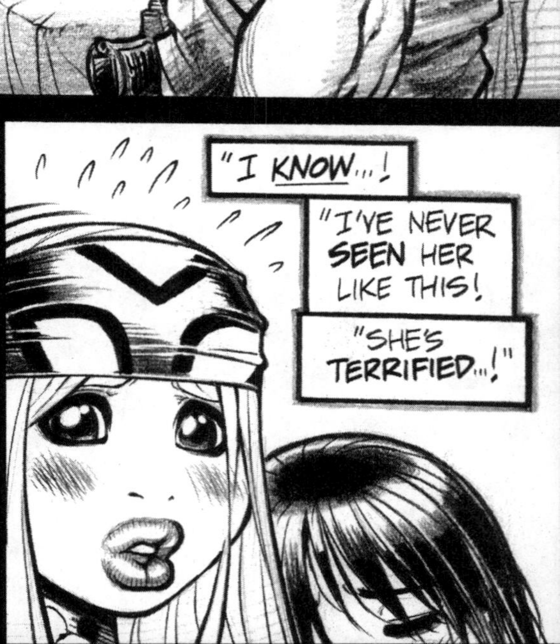
"I KNOW...!
"I'VE NEVER SEEN HER LIKE THIS!
"SHE'S TERRIFIED...!"

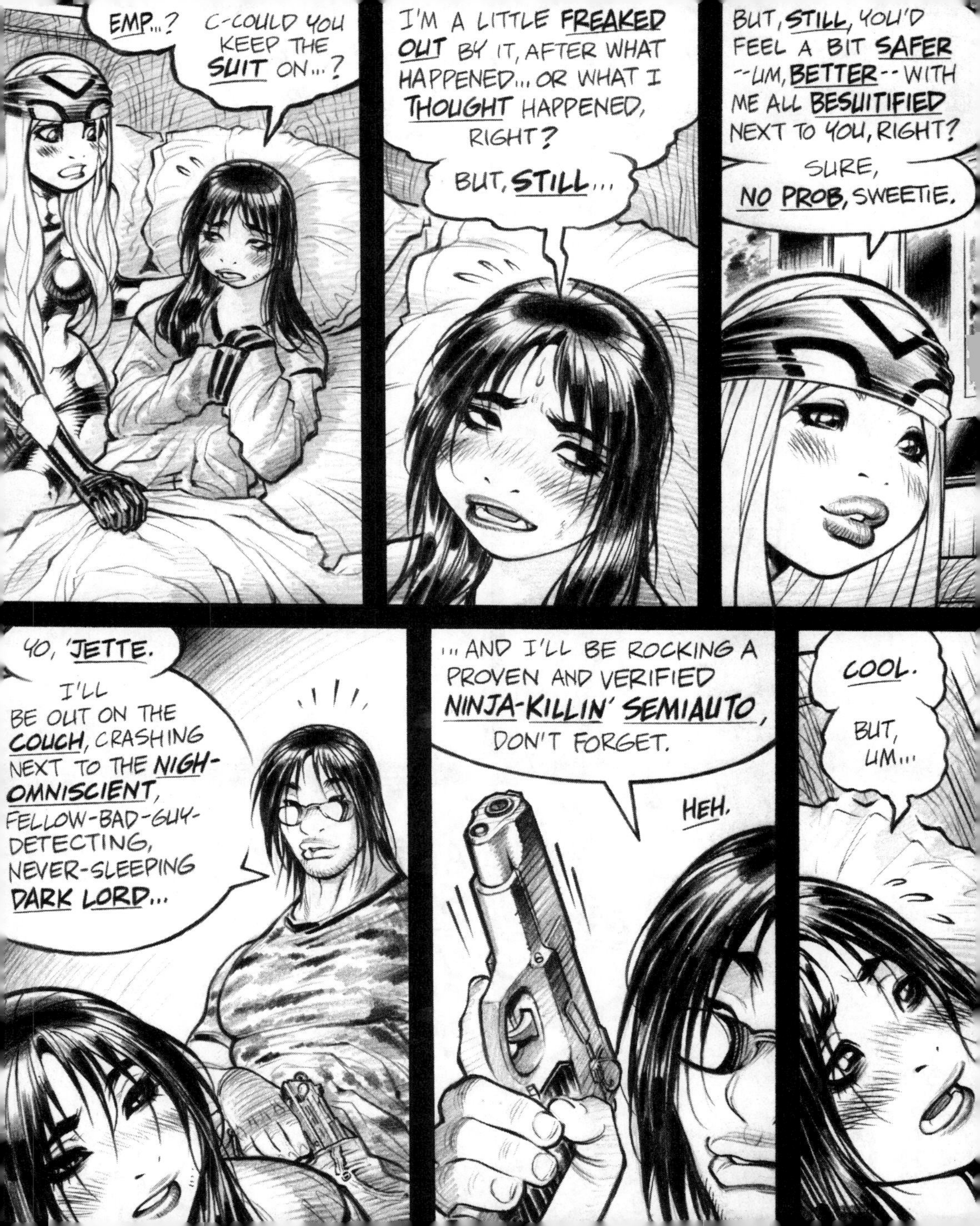
EMP...?
C-COULD YOU KEEP THE SUIT ON...?
I'M A LITTLE FREAKED OUT BY IT, AFTER WHAT HAPPENED... OR WHAT I THOUGHT HAPPENED, RIGHT?
BUT, STILL...
BUT, STILL, YOU'D FEEL A BIT SAFER --UM, BETTER-- WITH ME ALL BESUITIFIED NEXT TO YOU, RIGHT?
SURE, NO PROB, SWEETIE.
YO, 'JETTE.
I'LL BE OUT ON THE COUCH, CRASHING NEXT TO THE NIGH-OMNISCIENT, FELLOW-BAD-GUY-DETECTING, NEVER-SLEEPING DARK LORD...
...AND I'LL BE ROCKING A PROVEN AND VERIFIED NINJA-KILLIN' SEMIAUTO, DON'T FORGET.
HEH.
COOL.
BUT, UM...

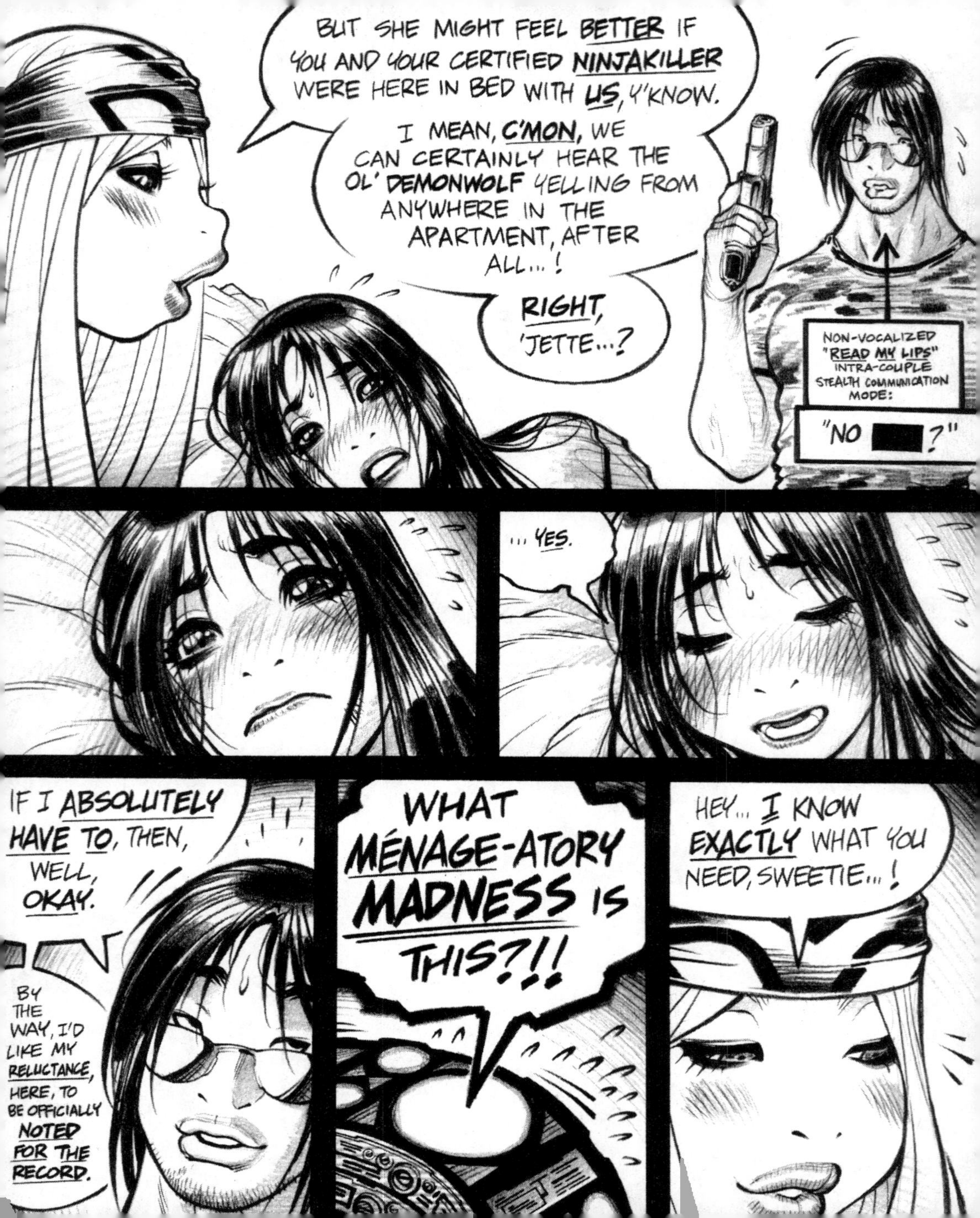
BUT SHE MIGHT FEEL BETTER IF YOU AND YOUR CERTIFIED NINJAKILLER WERE HERE IN BED WITH US, Y'KNOW.
I MEAN, C'MON, WE CAN CERTAINLY HEAR THE OL' DEMONWOLF YELLING FROM ANYWHERE IN THE APARTMENT, AFTER ALL...!
RIGHT, 'JETTE...?
NON-VOCALIZED "READ MY LIPS" INTRA-COUPLE STEALTH COMMUNICATION MODE:
"NO [redacted]?"
...YES.
IF I ABSOLUTELY HAVE TO, THEN, WELL, OKAY.
BY THE WAY, I'D LIKE MY RELUCTANCE, HERE, TO BE OFFICIALLY NOTED FOR THE RECORD.
WHAT MÉNAGE-ATORY MADNESS IS THIS?!!
HEY... I KNOW EXACTLY WHAT YOU NEED, SWEETIE...!

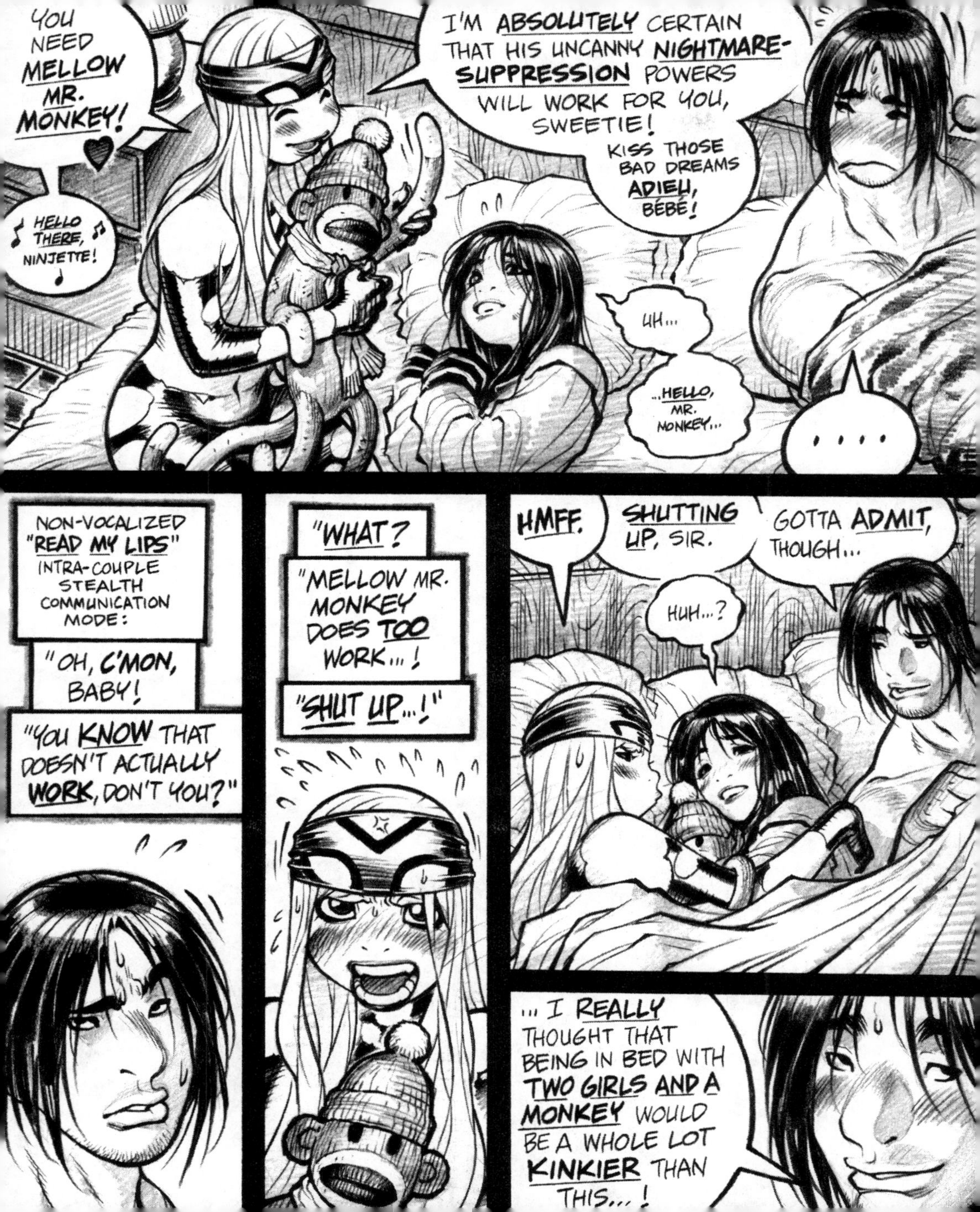
YOU NEED MELLOW MR. MONKEY! ♥
♪ HELLO THERE, NINJETTE! ♪
I'M ABSOLUTELY CERTAIN THAT HIS UNCANNY NIGHTMARE-SUPPRESSION POWERS WILL WORK FOR YOU, SWEETIE!
KISS THOSE BAD DREAMS ADIEU, BÉBÉ!
UH...
...HELLO, MR. MONKEY...
....
NON-VOCALIZED "READ MY LIPS" INTRA-COUPLE STEALTH COMMUNICATION MODE:
"OH, C'MON, BABY!
"YOU KNOW THAT DOESN'T ACTUALLY WORK, DON'T YOU?"
"WHAT?
"MELLOW MR. MONKEY DOES TOO WORK...!
"SHUT UP...!"
HMFF.
SHUTTING UP, SIR.
GOTTA ADMIT, THOUGH...
HUH...?
... I REALLY THOUGHT THAT BEING IN BED WITH TWO GIRLS AND A MONKEY WOULD BE A WHOLE LOT KINKIER THAN THIS... !

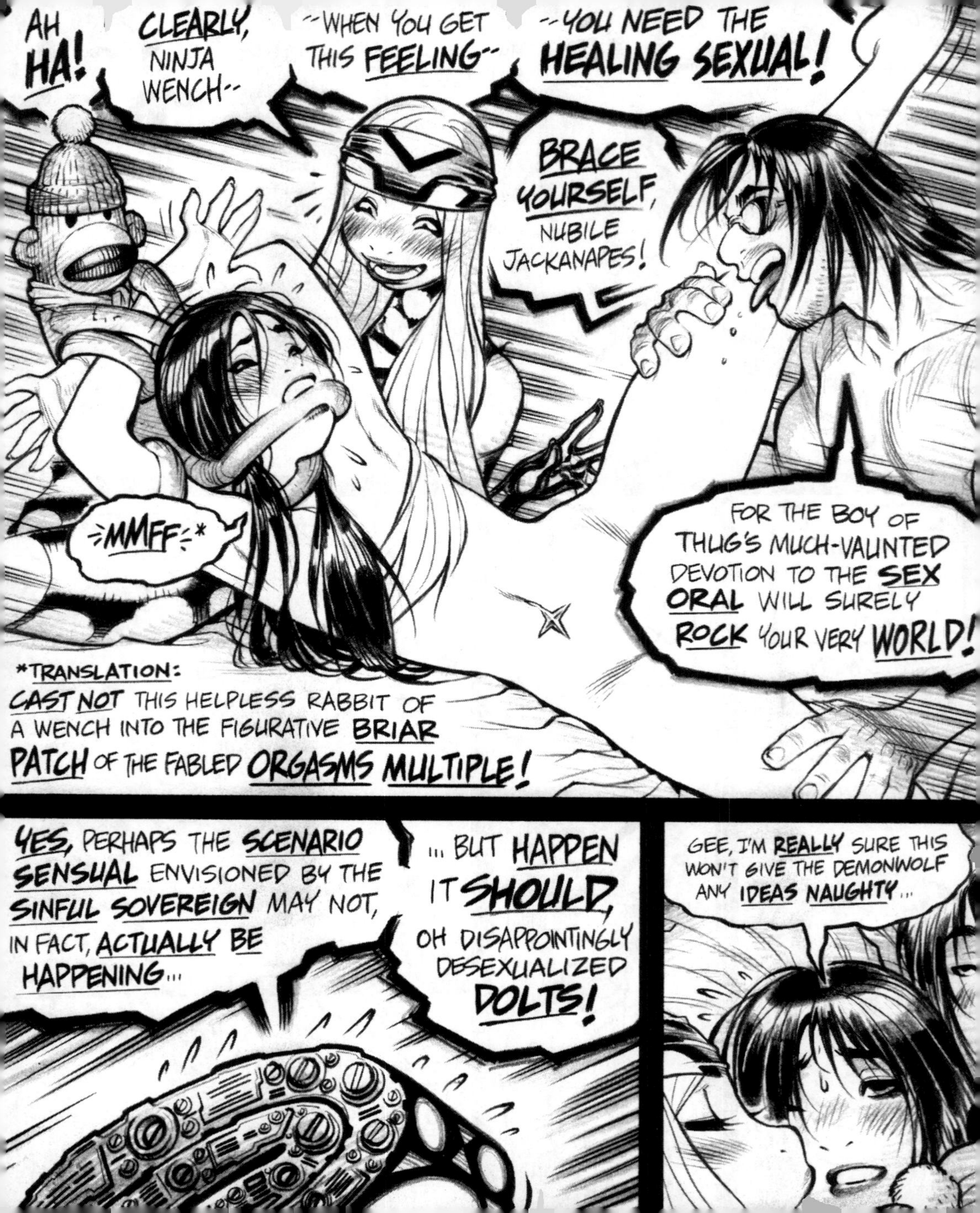
AH HA!
CLEARLY, NINJA WENCH--
--WHEN YOU GET THIS FEELING--
--YOU NEED THE HEALING SEXUAL!
BRACE YOURSELF, NUBILE JACKANAPES!
MMFF*
FOR THE BOY OF THUG'S MUCH-VAUNTED DEVOTION TO THE SEX ORAL WILL SURELY ROCK YOUR VERY WORLD!
*TRANSLATION: CAST NOT THIS HELPLESS RABBIT OF A WENCH INTO THE FIGURATIVE BRIAR PATCH OF THE FABLED ORGASMS MULTIPLE!
YES, PERHAPS THE SCENARIO SENSUAL ENVISIONED BY THE SINFUL SOVEREIGN MAY NOT, IN FACT, ACTUALLY BE HAPPENING...
...BUT HAPPEN IT SHOULD, OH DISAPPOINTINGLY DESEXUALIZED DOLTS!
GEE, I'M REALLY SURE THIS WON'T GIVE THE DEMONWOLF ANY IDEAS NAUGHTY...

eMpowered ™

Elephants, Cups, and Canoes

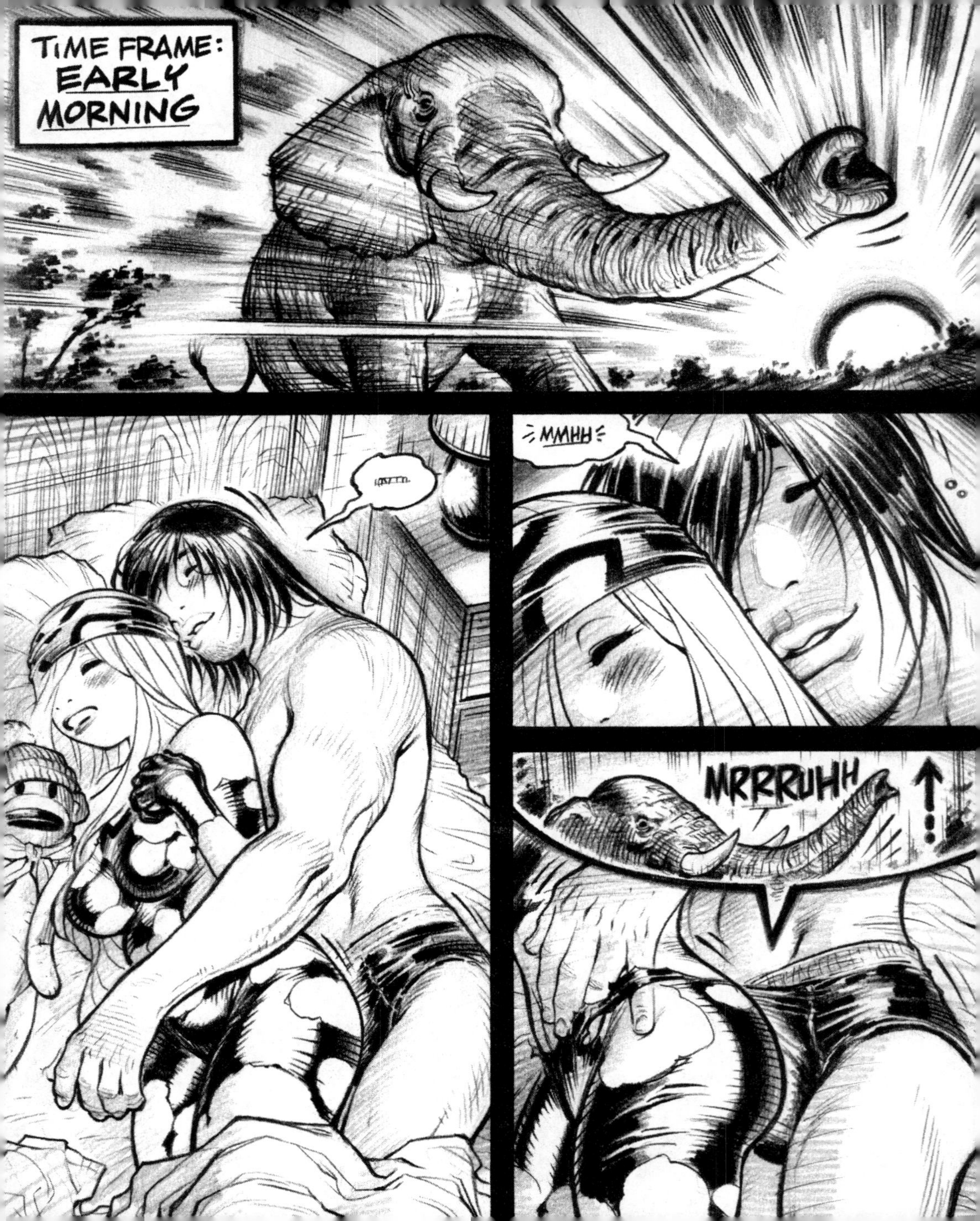
TIME FRAME:
EARLY
MORNING
MMHH
MRRRUHH

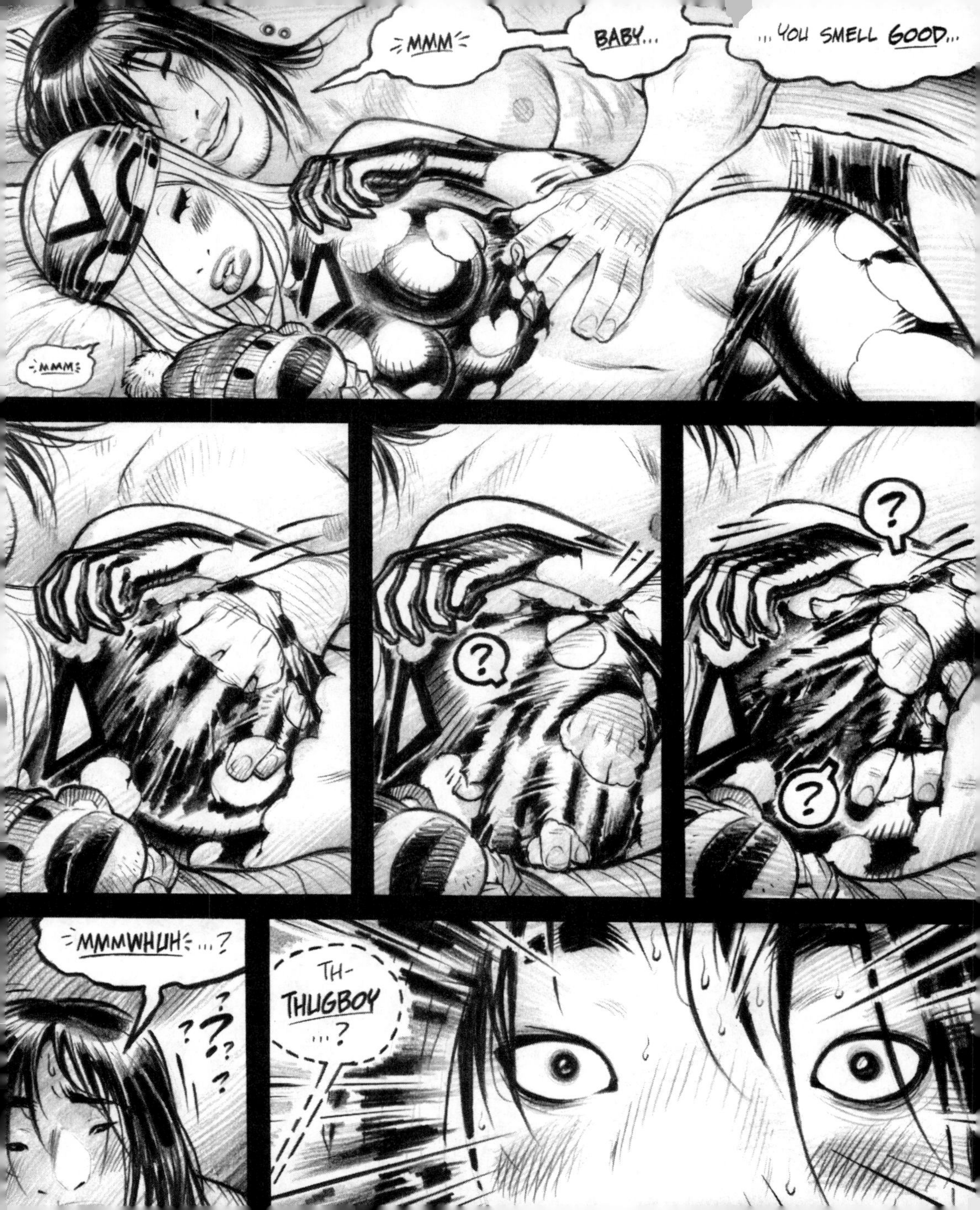
MMM
BABY...
...YOU SMELL GOOD...
MMM
?
?
?
MMMWHUH...?
? ? ? ?
TH-
THUGBOY
...?

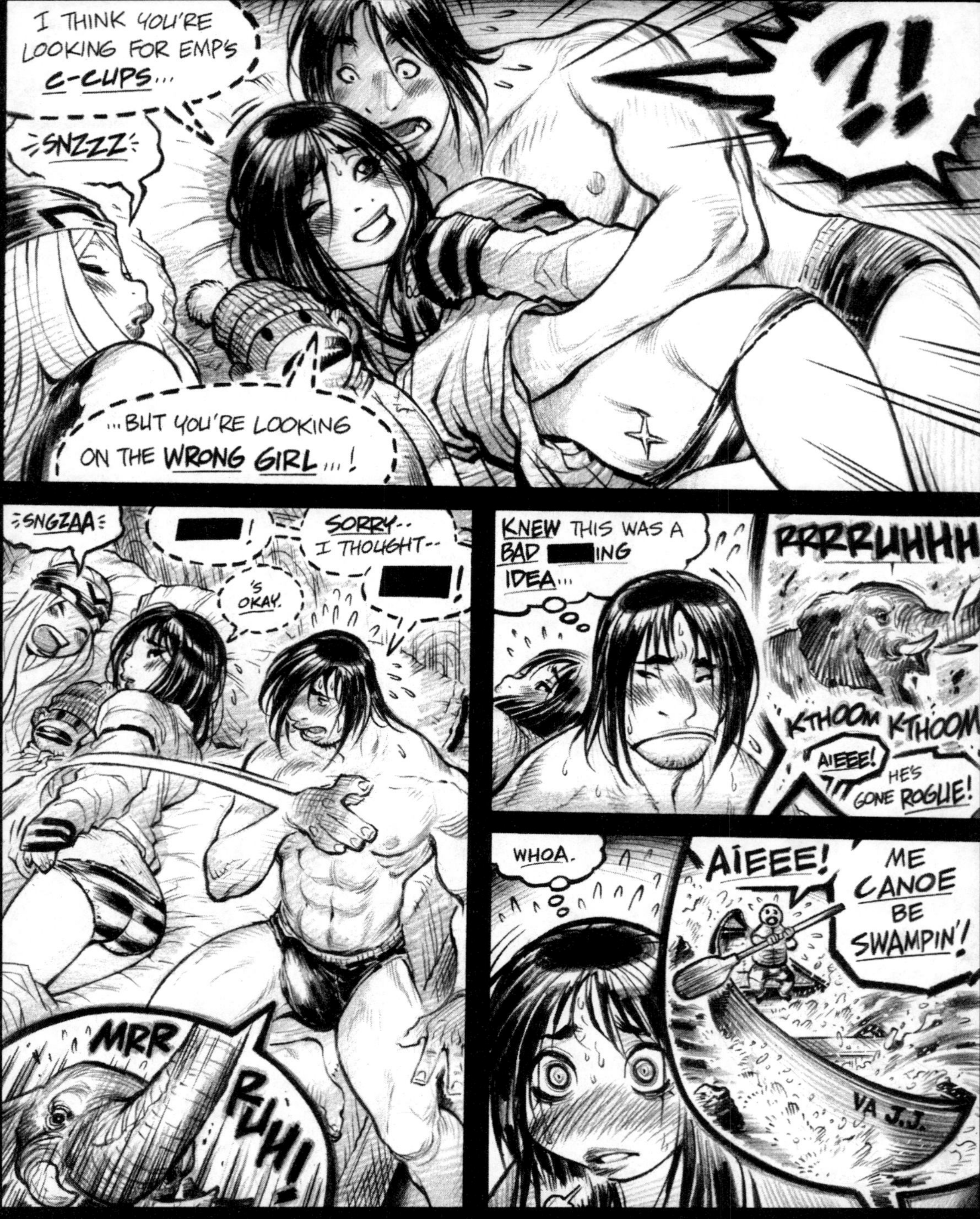
I THINK YOU'RE LOOKING FOR EMP'S C-CUPS...
SNZZZ
?!
...BUT YOU'RE LOOKING ON THE WRONG GIRL...!
SNGZAA
[redacted]!
SORRY.. I THOUGHT--
'S OKAY.
[redacted]!
MRR RUH!
KNEW THIS WAS A BAD [redacted]ING IDEA...
RRRRUHHH
KTHOOM KTHOOM
AIEEE!
HE'S GONE ROGUE!
WHOA.
AIEEE!
ME CANOE BE SWAMPIN'!
VA J.J.

Empowered™

Of Maids and Wet Blankets

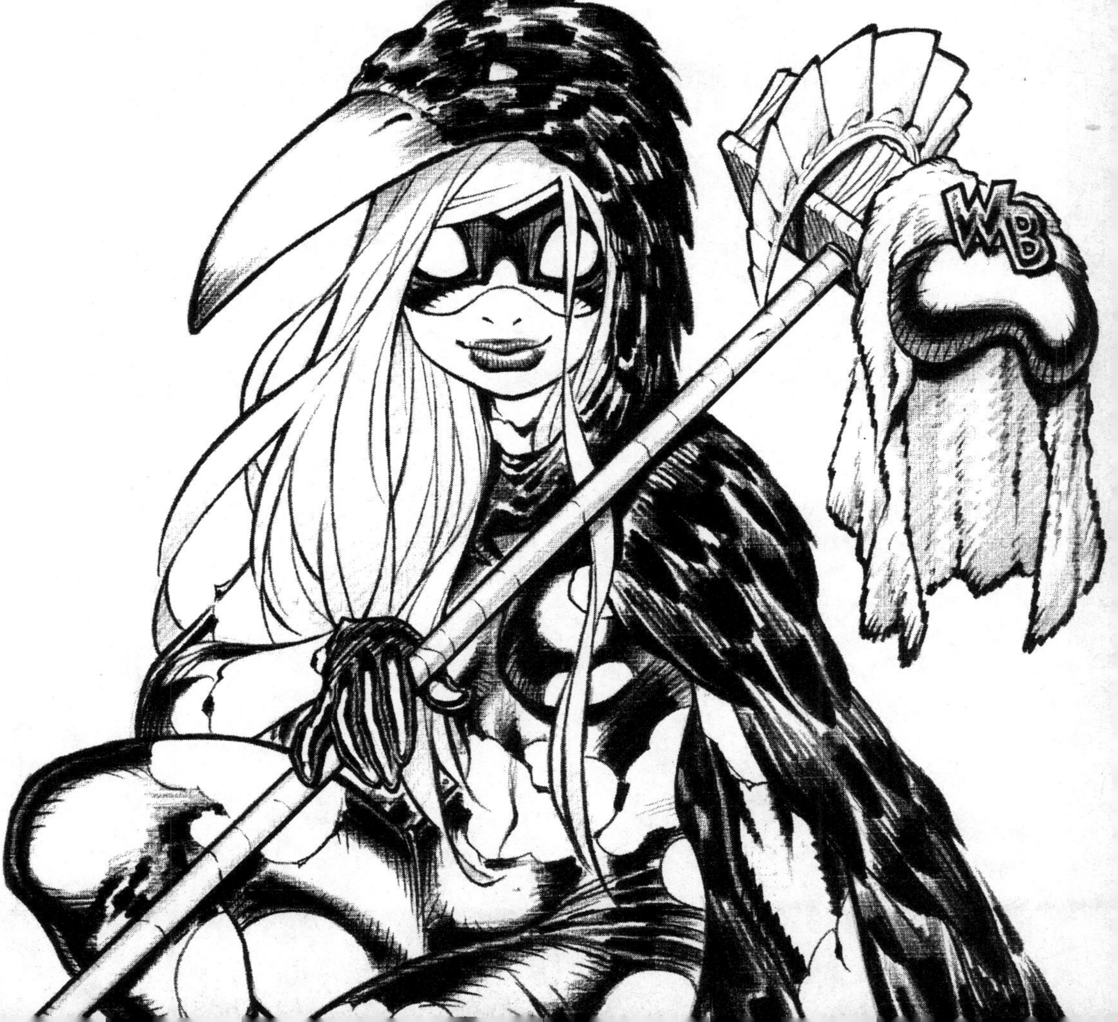
WB

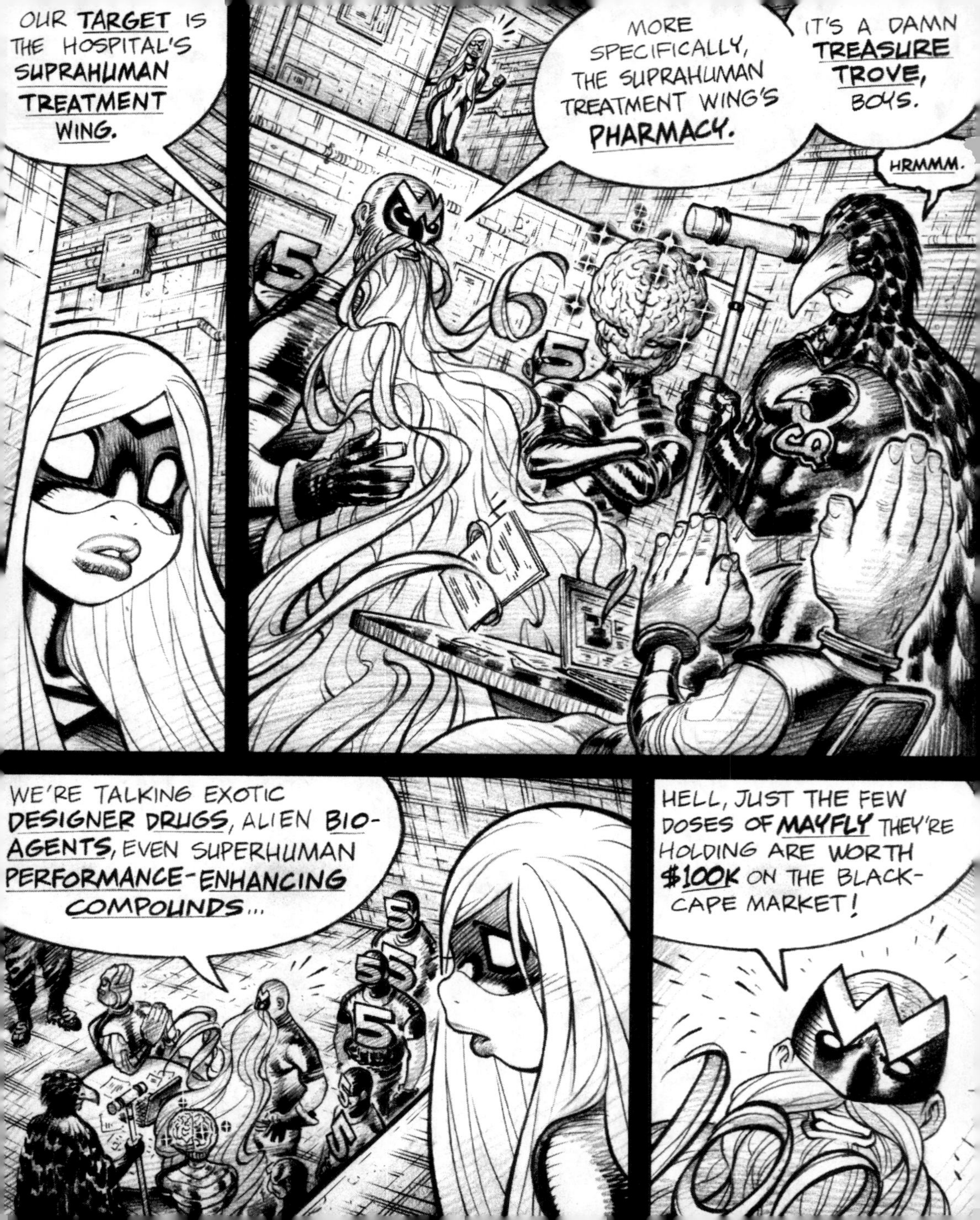
OUR TARGET IS THE HOSPITAL'S SUPRAHUMAN TREATMENT WING.
MORE SPECIFICALLY, THE SUPRAHUMAN TREATMENT WING'S PHARMACY.
IT'S A DAMN TREASURE TROVE, BOYS.
HRMMM.
WE'RE TALKING EXOTIC DESIGNER DRUGS, ALIEN BIO-AGENTS, EVEN SUPERHUMAN PERFORMANCE-ENHANCING COMPOUNDS...
HELL, JUST THE FEW DOSES OF MAYFLY THEY'RE HOLDING ARE WORTH $100K ON THE BLACK-CAPE MARKET!

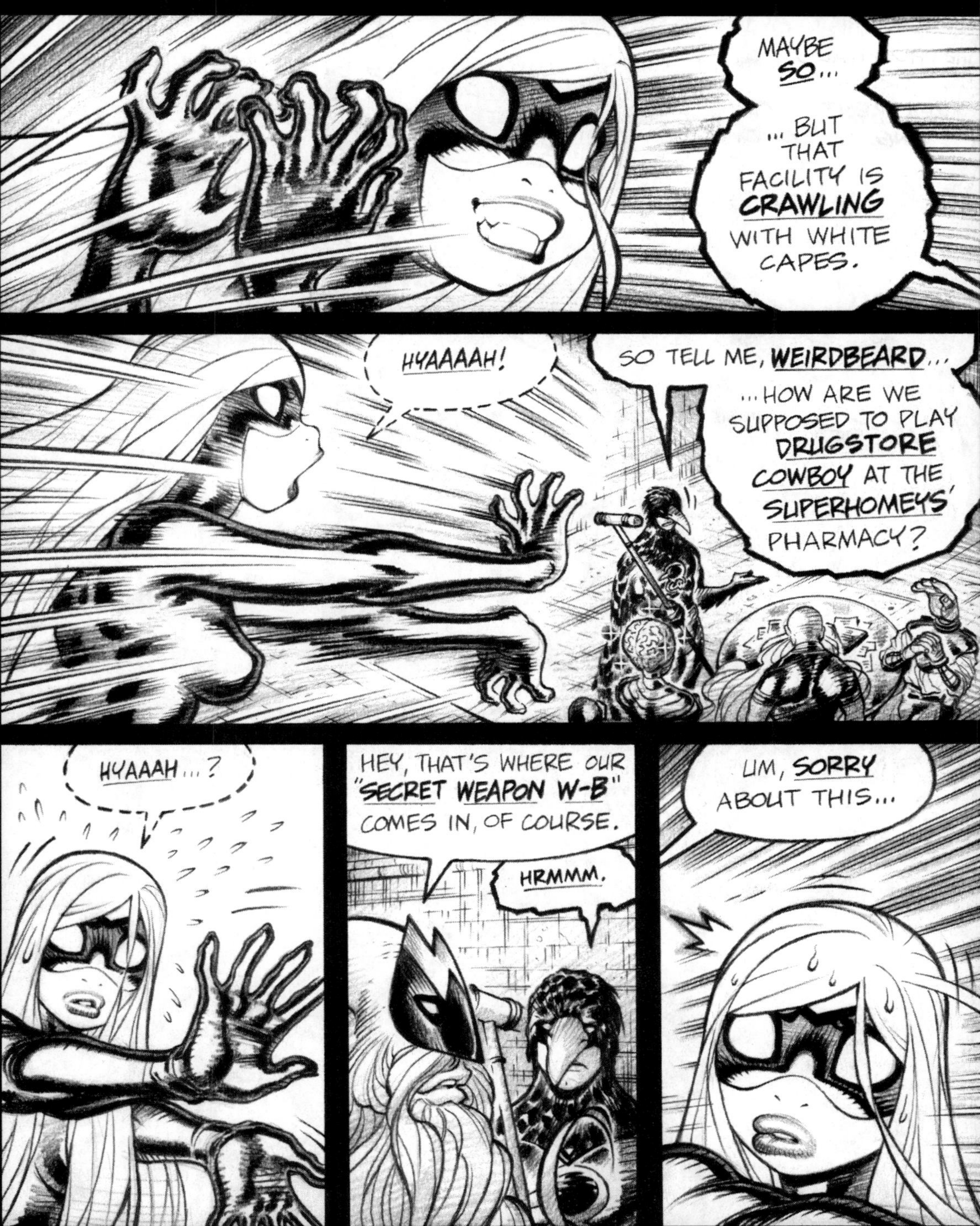
MAYBE SO...
... BUT THAT FACILITY IS CRAWLING WITH WHITE CAPES.
HYAAAAH!
SO TELL ME, WEIRDBEARD...
...HOW ARE WE SUPPOSED TO PLAY DRUGSTORE COWBOY AT THE SUPERHOMEYS' PHARMACY?
HYAAAH...?
HEY, THAT'S WHERE OUR "SECRET WEAPON W-B" COMES IN, OF COURSE.
HRMMM.
UM, SORRY ABOUT THIS...

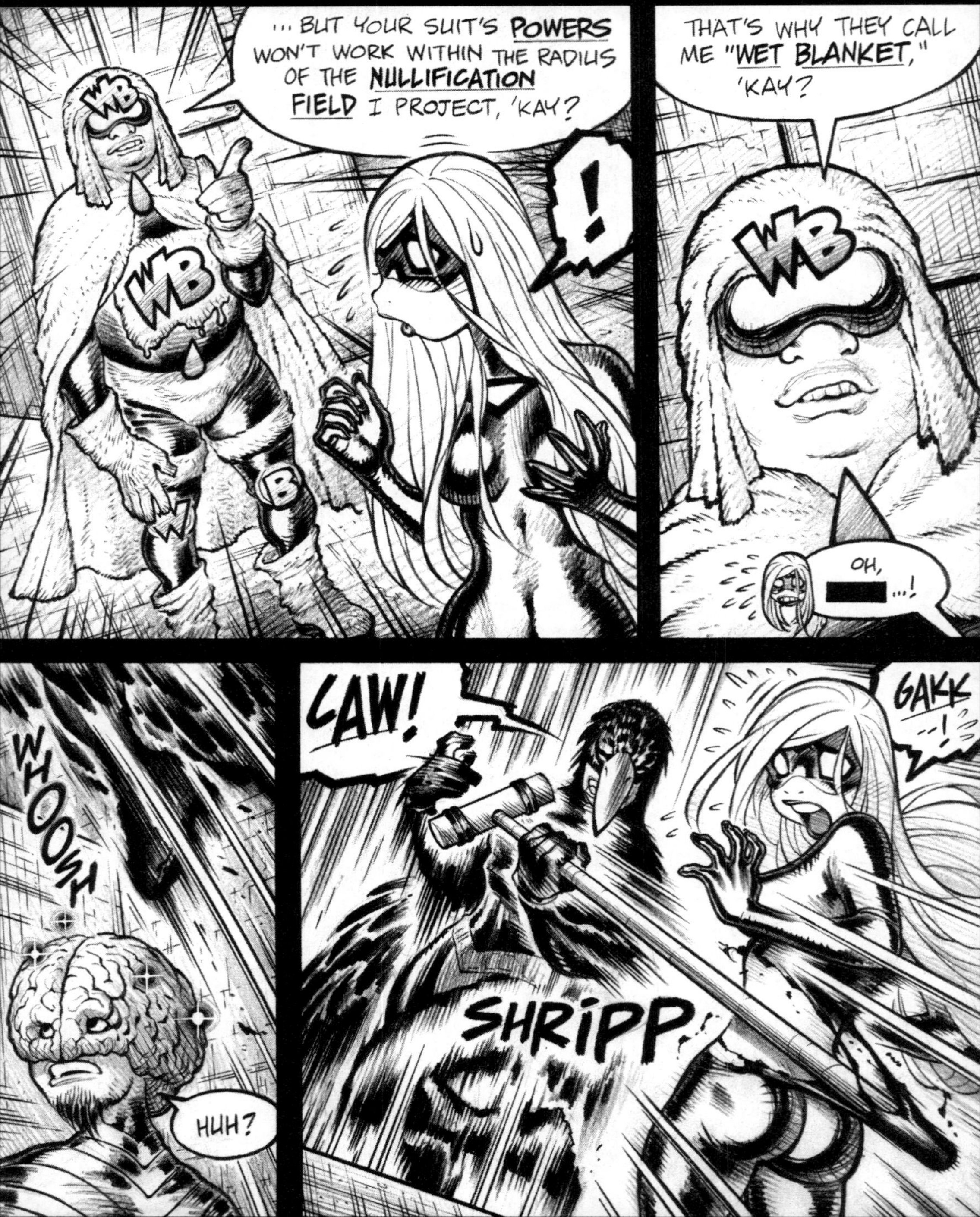
...BUT YOUR SUIT'S POWERS WON'T WORK WITHIN THE RADIUS OF THE NULLIFICATION FIELD I PROJECT, 'KAY?
!
THAT'S WHY THEY CALL ME "WET BLANKET," 'KAY?
OH, [redacted]...!
WHOOSH
HUH?
CAW!
GAKK--!
SHRIPP

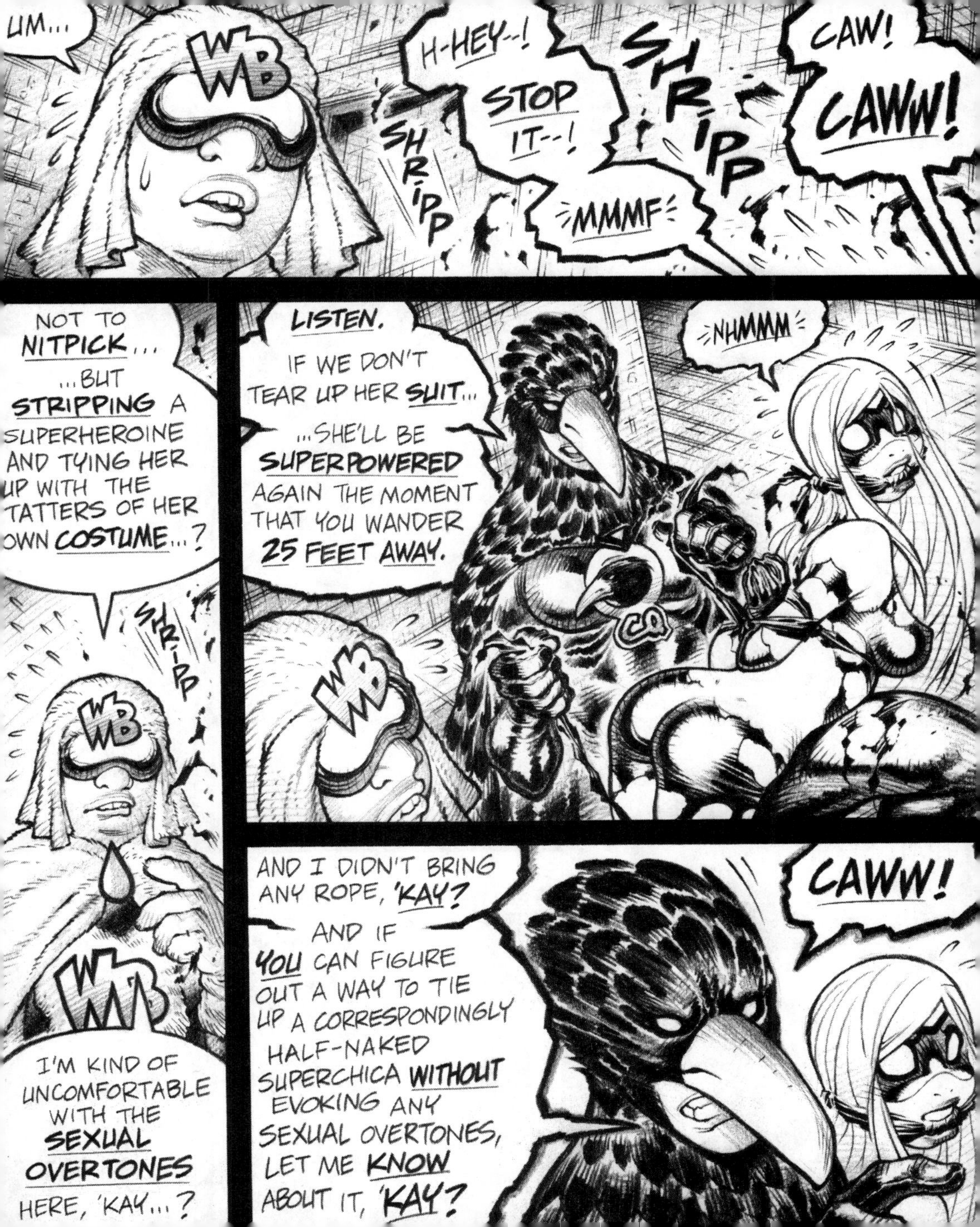
UM...
SHRIPP
H-HEY--! STOP IT--!
MMMF
SHRIPP
CAW! CAWW!
NOT TO NITPICK... ...BUT STRIPPING A SUPERHEROINE AND TYING HER UP WITH THE TATTERS OF HER OWN COSTUME...?
SHRIPP
I'M KIND OF UNCOMFORTABLE WITH THE SEXUAL OVERTONES HERE, 'KAY...?
LISTEN. IF WE DON'T TEAR UP HER SUIT... ...SHE'LL BE SUPERPOWERED AGAIN THE MOMENT THAT YOU WANDER 25 FEET AWAY.
NHMMM
AND I DIDN'T BRING ANY ROPE, 'KAY? AND IF YOU CAN FIGURE OUT A WAY TO TIE UP A CORRESPONDINGLY HALF-NAKED SUPERCHICA WITHOUT EVOKING ANY SEXUAL OVERTONES, LET ME KNOW ABOUT IT, 'KAY?
CAWW!

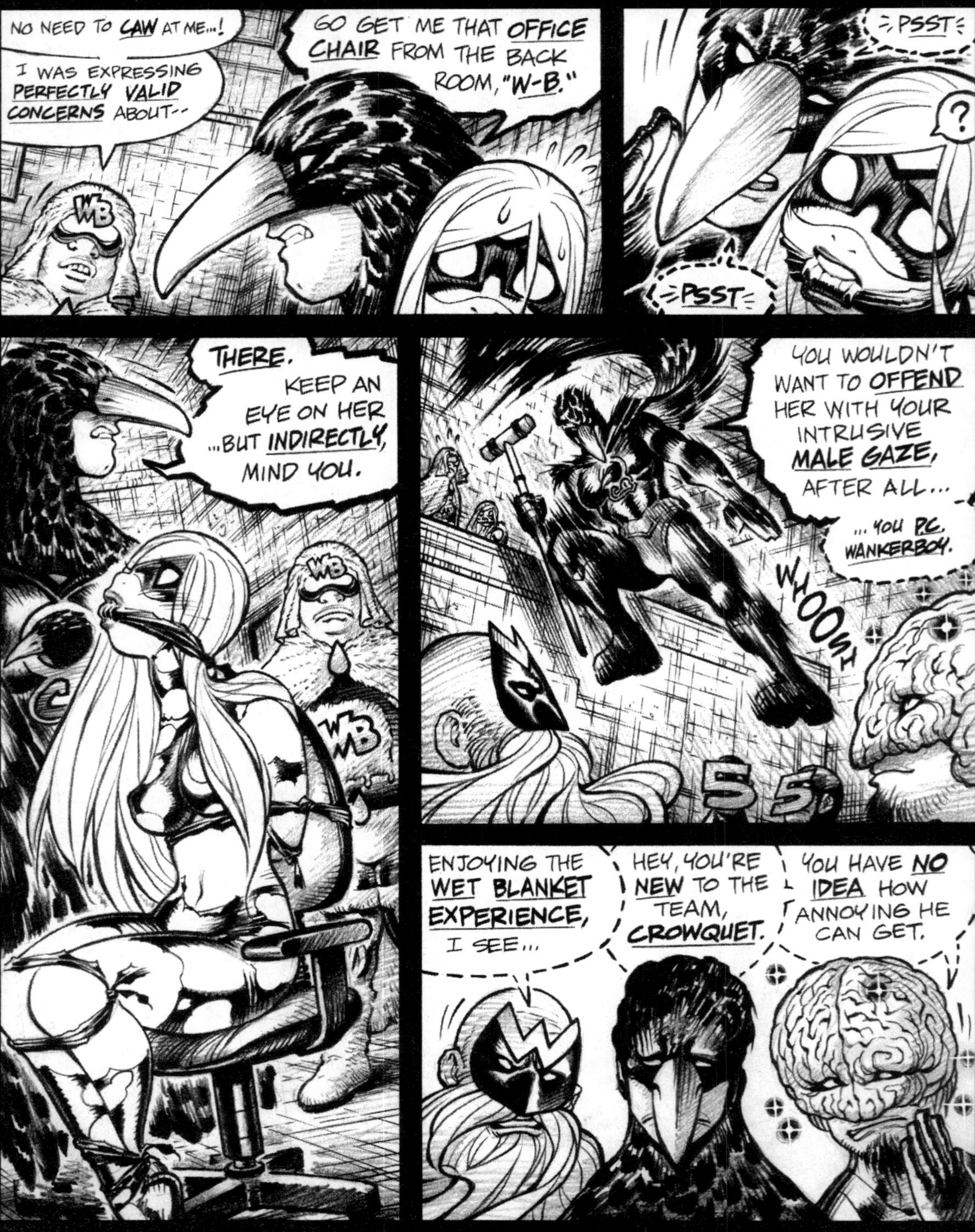

NO NEED TO CAW AT ME...!
I WAS EXPRESSING PERFECTLY VALID CONCERNS ABOUT--
GO GET ME THAT OFFICE CHAIR FROM THE BACK ROOM, "W-B."
PSST
?
PSST
THERE. KEEP AN EYE ON HER ...BUT INDIRECTLY, MIND YOU.
YOU WOULDN'T WANT TO OFFEND HER WITH YOUR INTRUSIVE MALE GAZE, AFTER ALL...
...YOU P.C. WANKERBOY.
WHOOSH
ENJOYING THE WET BLANKET EXPERIENCE, I SEE...
HEY, YOU'RE NEW TO THE TEAM, CROWQUET.
YOU HAVE NO IDEA HOW ANNOYING HE CAN GET.

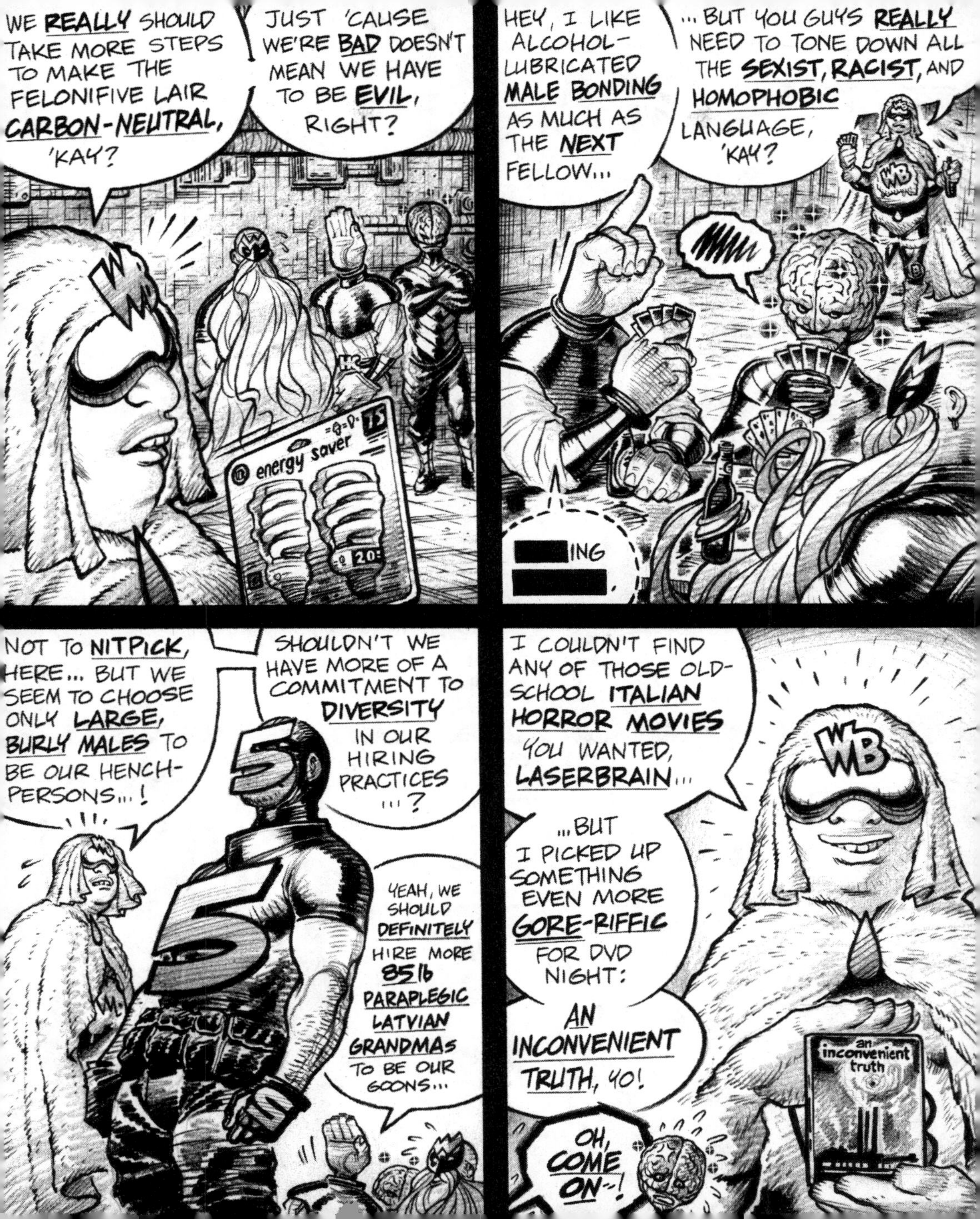
WE REALLY SHOULD TAKE MORE STEPS TO MAKE THE FELONIFIVE LAIR CARBON-NEUTRAL, 'KAY?
JUST 'CAUSE WE'RE BAD DOESN'T MEAN WE HAVE TO BE EVIL, RIGHT?
energy saver
HEY, I LIKE ALCOHOL-LUBRICATED MALE BONDING AS MUCH AS THE NEXT FELLOW...
...BUT YOU GUYS REALLY NEED TO TONE DOWN ALL THE SEXIST, RACIST, AND HOMOPHOBIC LANGUAGE, 'KAY?
[redacted]ING [redacted]
NOT TO NITPICK, HERE... BUT WE SEEM TO CHOOSE ONLY LARGE, BURLY MALES TO BE OUR HENCH-PERSONS...!
SHOULDN'T WE HAVE MORE OF A COMMITMENT TO DIVERSITY IN OUR HIRING PRACTICES...?
YEAH, WE SHOULD DEFINITELY HIRE MORE 85lb PARAPLEGIC LATVIAN GRANDMAs TO BE OUR GOONS...
I COULDN'T FIND ANY OF THOSE OLD-SCHOOL ITALIAN HORROR MOVIES YOU WANTED, LASERBRAIN...
...BUT I PICKED UP SOMETHING EVEN MORE GORE-RIFFIC FOR DVD NIGHT:
AN INCONVENIENT TRUTH, YO!
an inconvenient truth
OH, COME ON--!

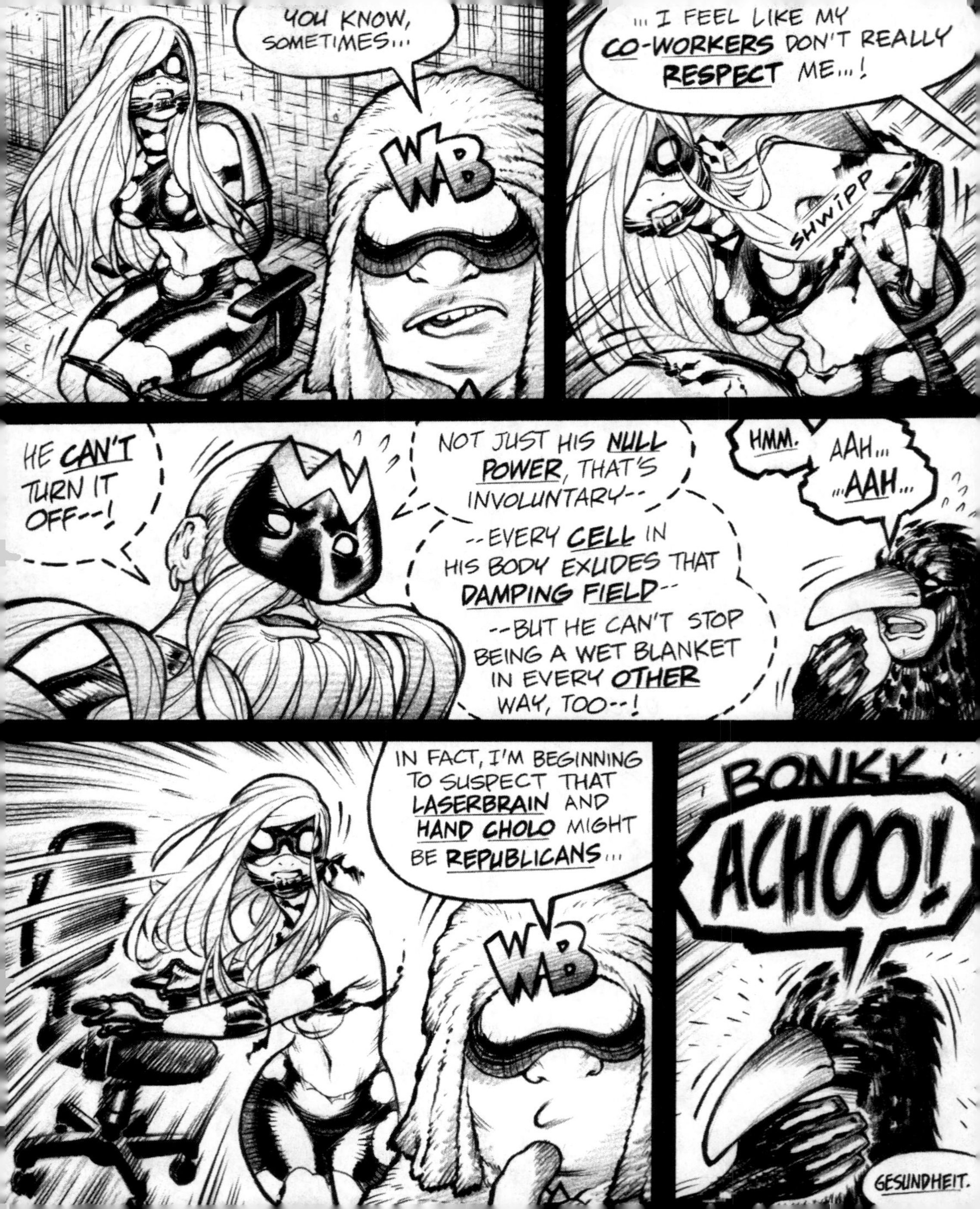
YOU KNOW, SOMETIMES...
WB
...I FEEL LIKE MY CO-WORKERS DON'T REALLY RESPECT ME...!
SHWIPP
HE CAN'T TURN IT OFF--!
NOT JUST HIS NULL POWER, THAT'S INVOLUNTARY--
--EVERY CELL IN HIS BODY EXUDES THAT DAMPING FIELD--
--BUT HE CAN'T STOP BEING A WET BLANKET IN EVERY OTHER WAY, TOO--!
HMM.
AAH... ...AAH...
IN FACT, I'M BEGINNING TO SUSPECT THAT LASERBRAIN AND HAND CHOLO MIGHT BE REPUBLICANS...
WB
BONKK
ACHOO!
GESUNDHEIT.

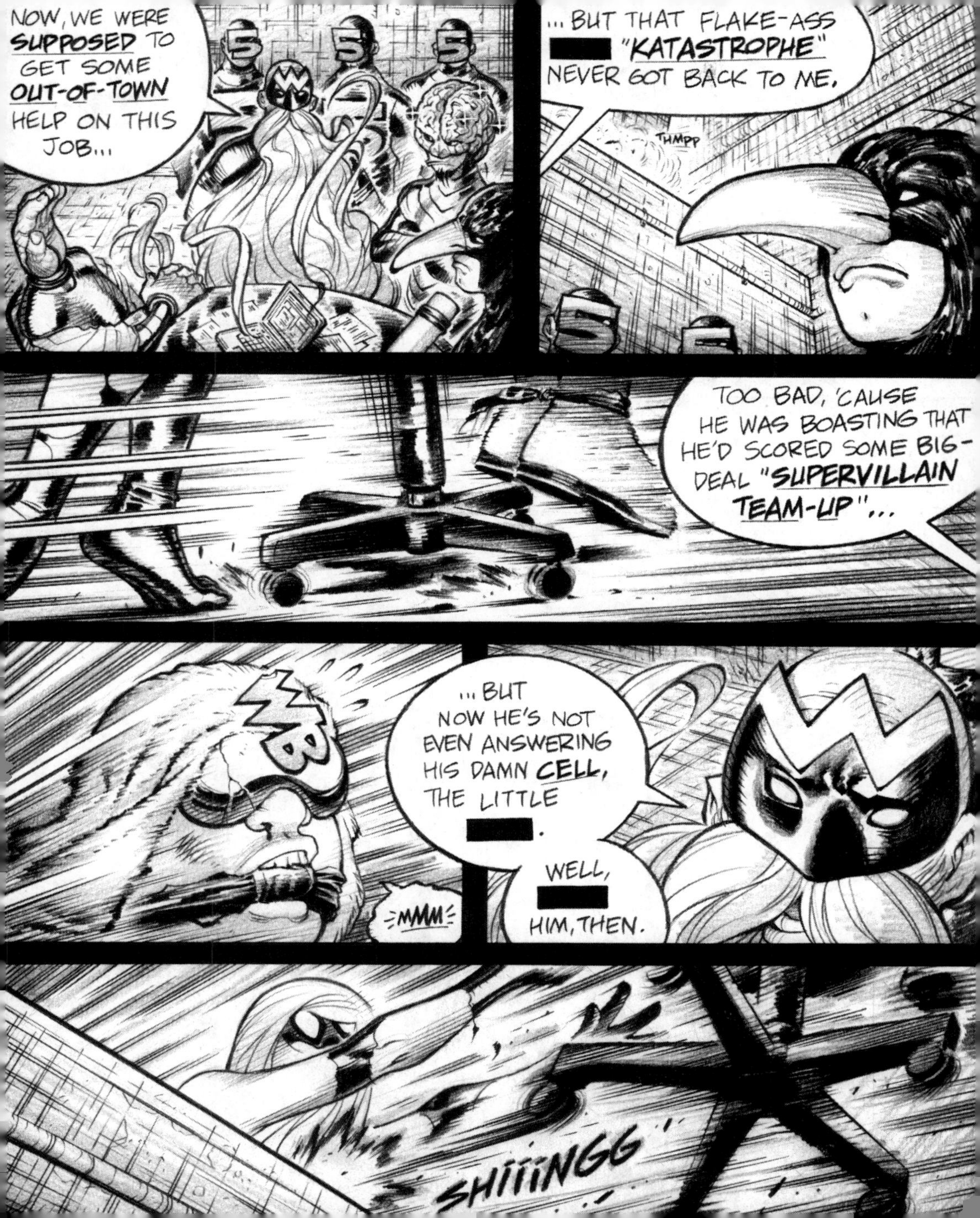
NOW, WE WERE SUPPOSED TO GET SOME OUT-OF-TOWN HELP ON THIS JOB...
...BUT THAT FLAKE-ASS [redacted] "KATASTROPHE" NEVER GOT BACK TO ME.
THMPP
TOO BAD, 'CAUSE HE WAS BOASTING THAT HE'D SCORED SOME BIG-DEAL "SUPERVILLAIN TEAM-UP"...
MMM
...BUT NOW HE'S NOT EVEN ANSWERING HIS DAMN CELL, THE LITTLE [redacted].
WELL, [redacted] HIM, THEN.
SHIIIINGG

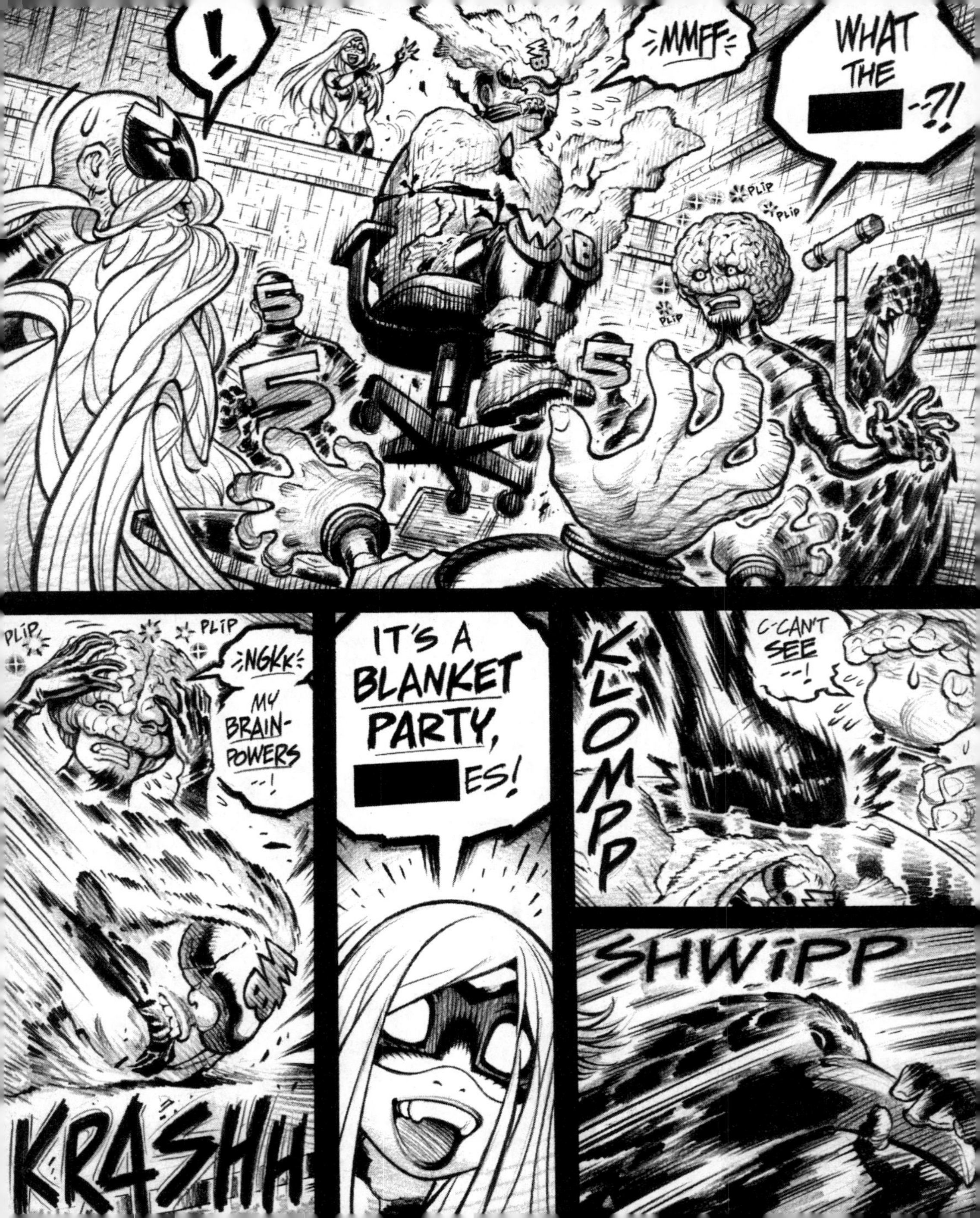
!
MMFF
WHAT THE [redacted]--?!
PLIP
PLIP
PLIP
PLIP
PLIP
NGKK
MY BRAIN-POWERS--!
KRASHH
IT'S A BLANKET PARTY, [redacted]ES!
KLOMPP
C-CAN'T SEE--!
SHWIPP

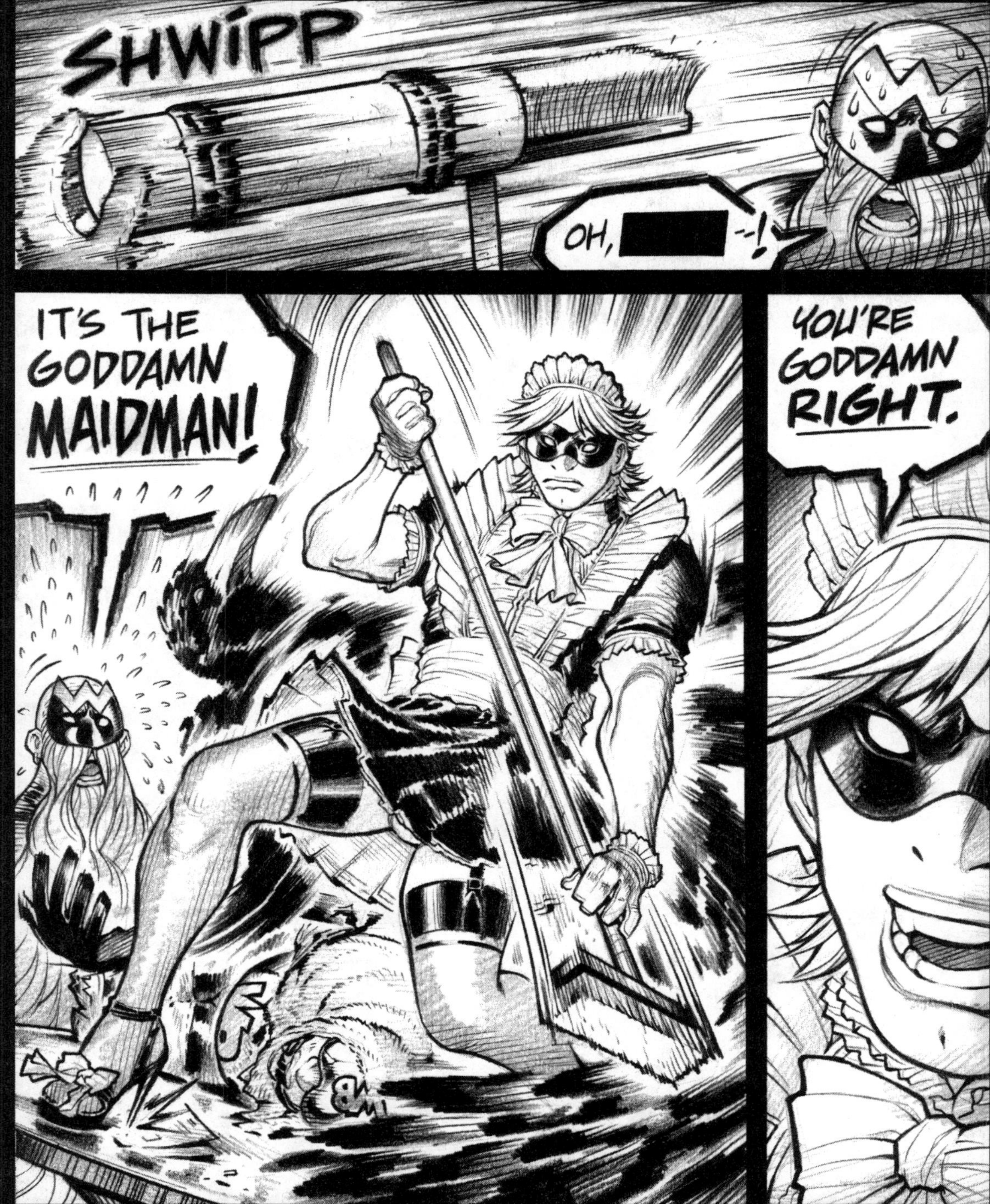
SHWIPP
OH, [redacted]--!
IT'S THE GODDAMN MAIDMAN!
YOU'RE GODDAMN RIGHT.

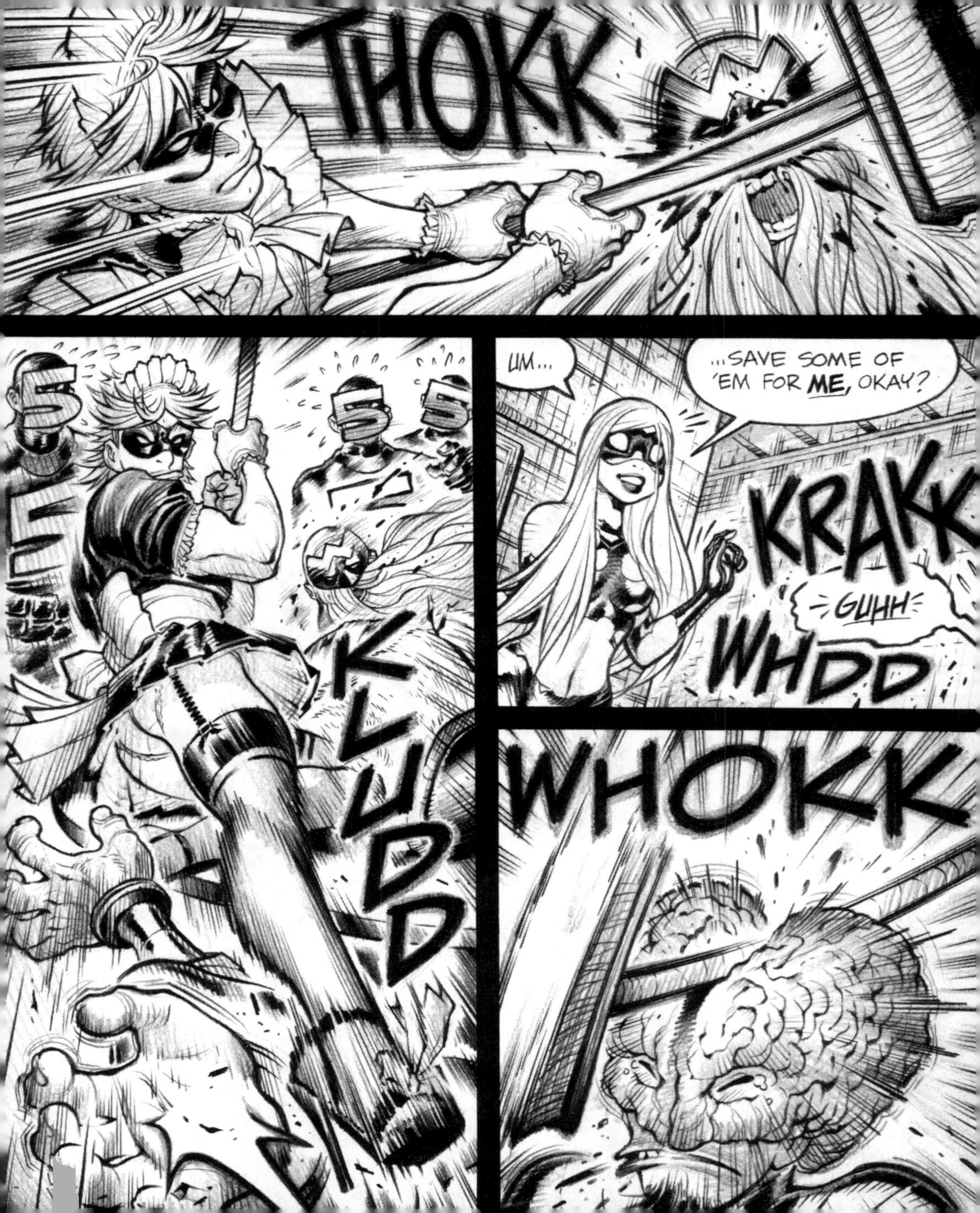
THOKK
KLUDD
UM...
...SAVE SOME OF 'EM FOR ME, OKAY?
KRAKK
GUHH
WHDD
WHOKK

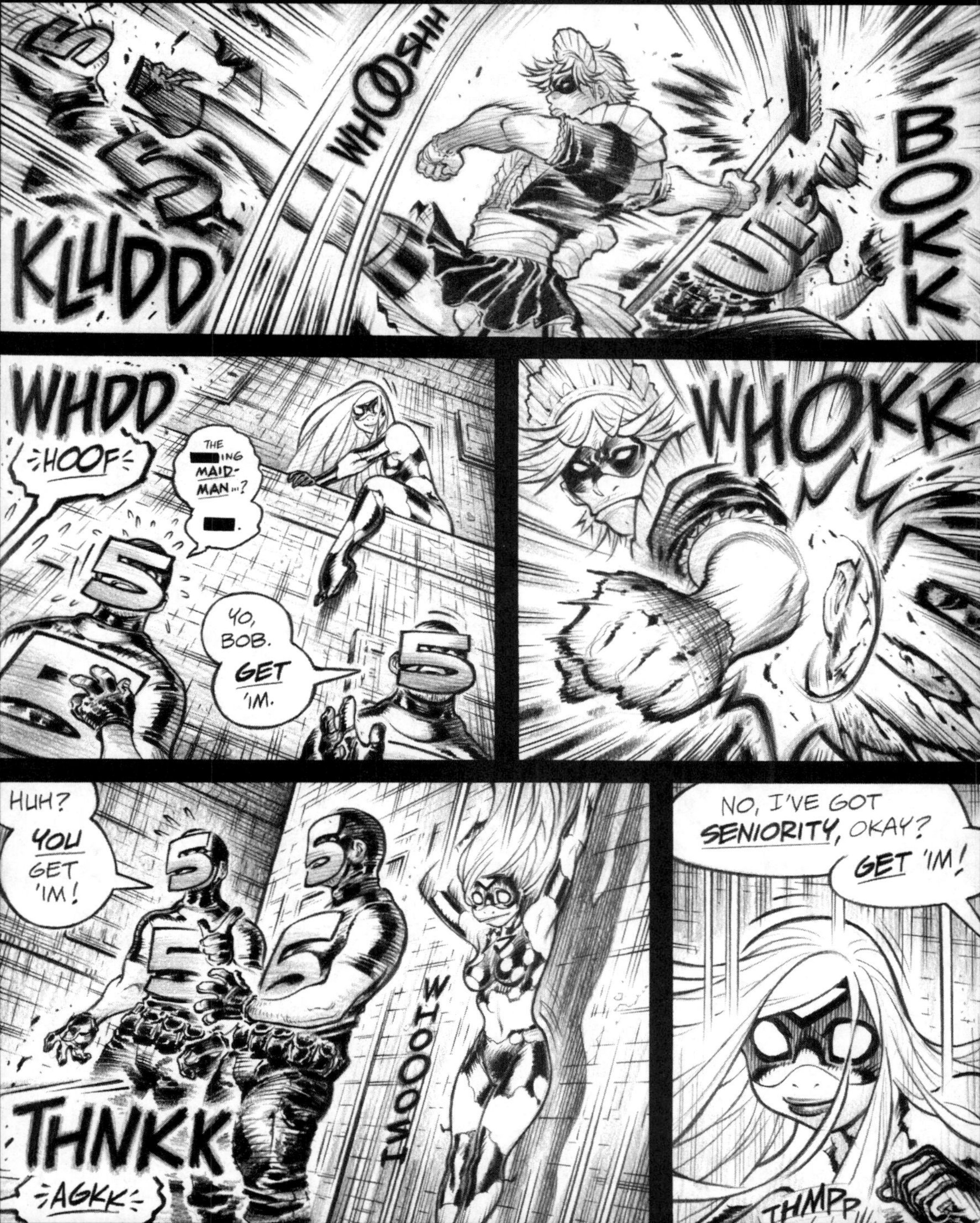
KLUDD
WHOOSH
BOKK
WHDD
HOOF
THE [redacted]ING MAID-MAN...? [redacted].
YO, BOB. GET 'IM.
WHOKK
HUH? YOU GET 'IM!
WHOOOSH
THNKK
AGKK
NO, I'VE GOT SENIORITY, OKAY? GET 'IM!
THMPP

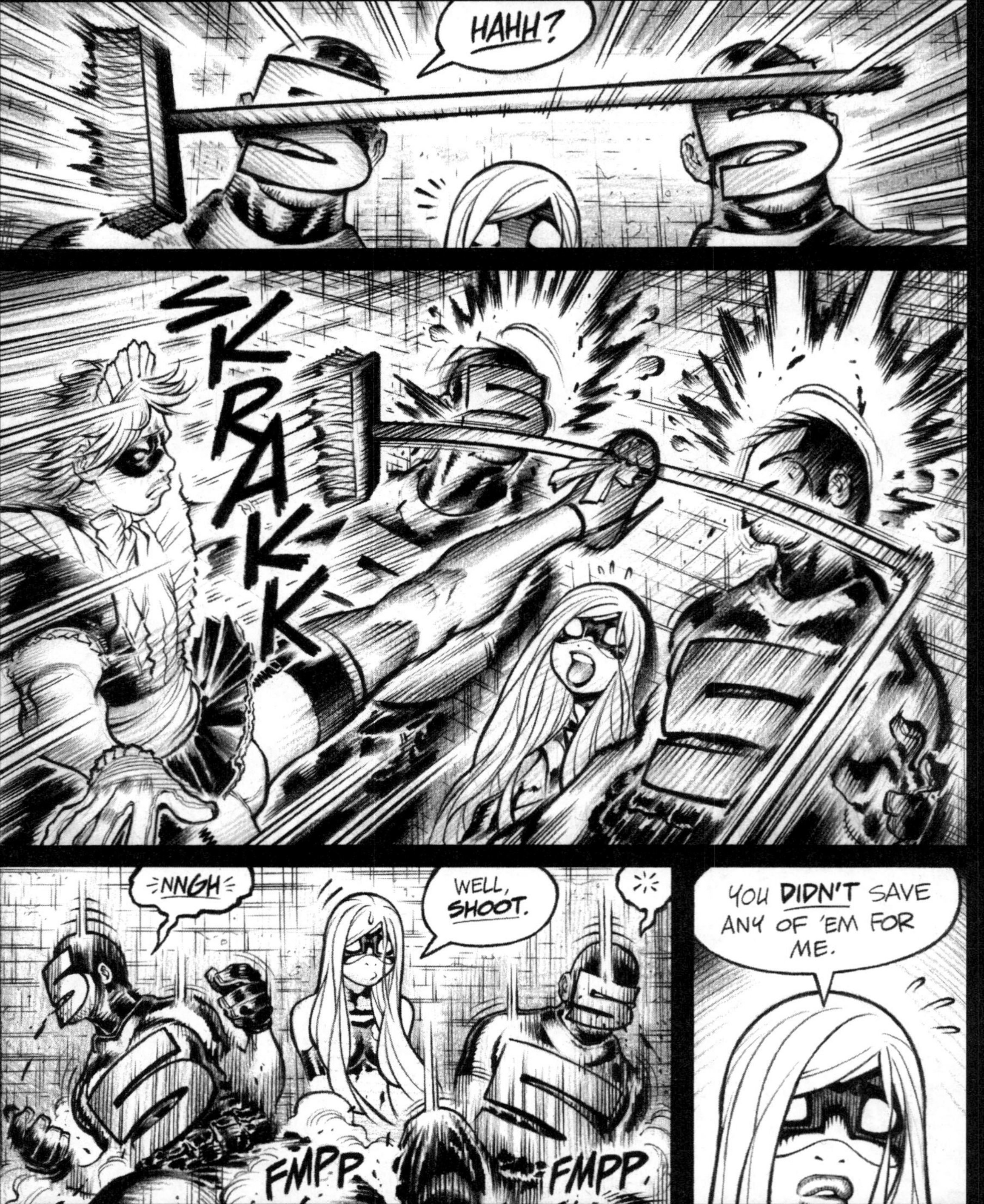
HAHH?
SKRAKKK
NNGH
WELL, SHOOT.
YOU DIDN'T SAVE ANY OF 'EM FOR ME.
FMPP
FMPP

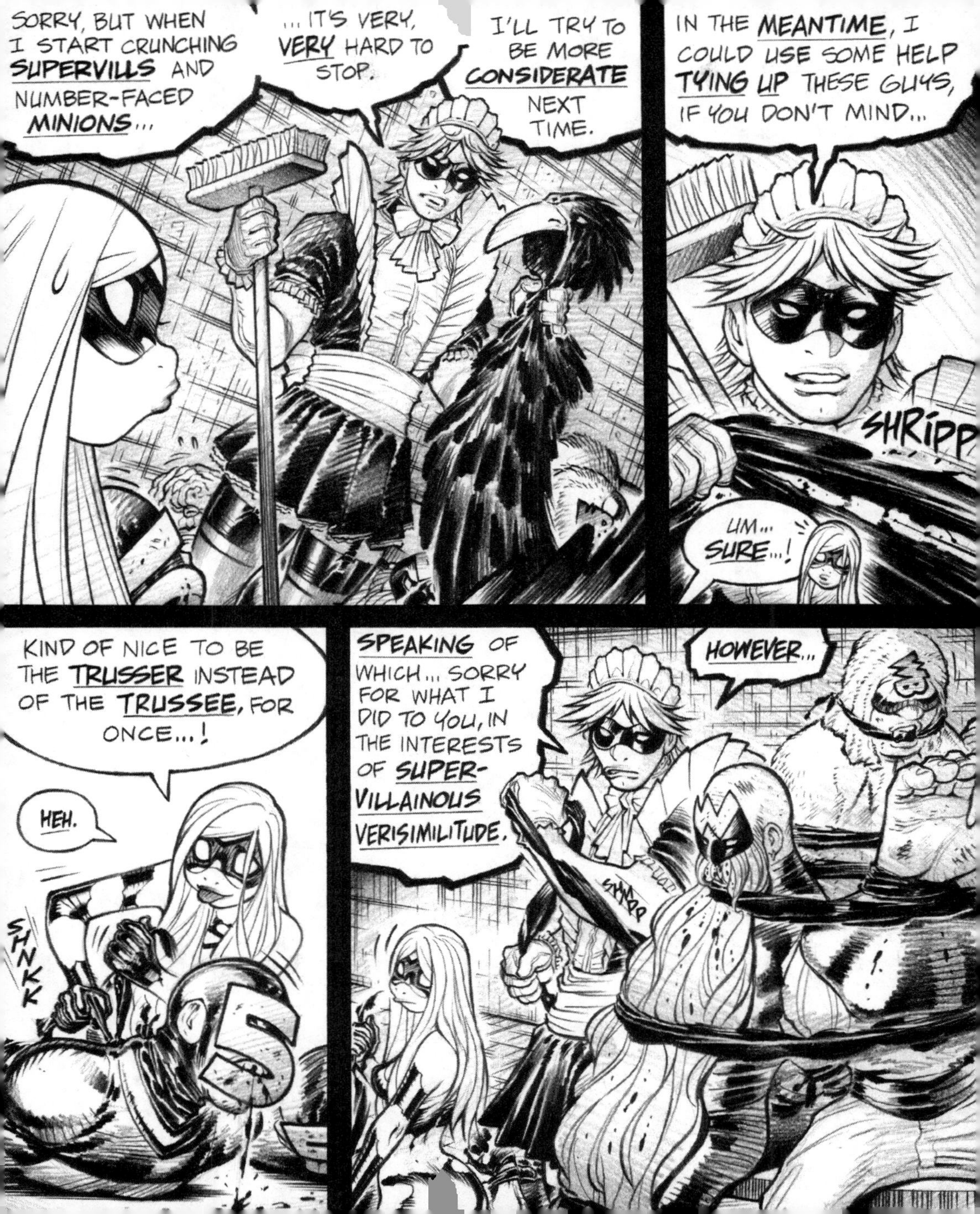

SORRY, BUT WHEN I START CRUNCHING SUPERVILLS AND NUMBER-FACED MINIONS...
...IT'S VERY, VERY HARD TO STOP.
I'LL TRY TO BE MORE CONSIDERATE NEXT TIME.
IN THE MEANTIME, I COULD USE SOME HELP TYING UP THESE GUYS, IF YOU DON'T MIND...
SHRIPP
UM... SURE...!
KIND OF NICE TO BE THE TRUSSER INSTEAD OF THE TRUSSEE, FOR ONCE...!
HEH.
SHNKK
SPEAKING OF WHICH... SORRY FOR WHAT I DID TO YOU, IN THE INTERESTS OF SUPER-VILLAINOUS VERISIMILITUDE.
HOWEVER...

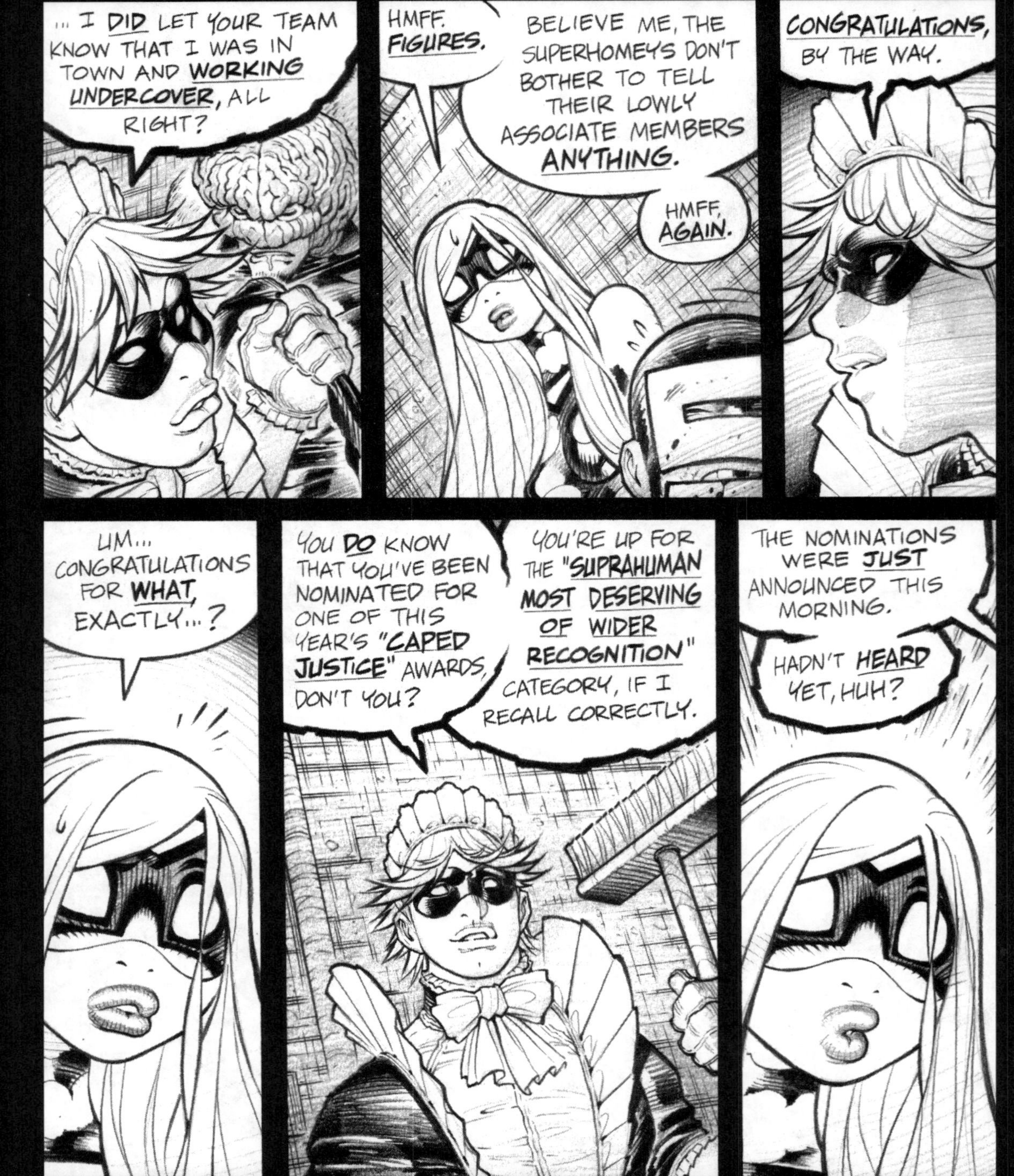
... I DID LET YOUR TEAM KNOW THAT I WAS IN TOWN AND WORKING UNDERCOVER, ALL RIGHT?
HMFF. FIGURES.
BELIEVE ME, THE SUPERHOMEYS DON'T BOTHER TO TELL THEIR LOWLY ASSOCIATE MEMBERS ANYTHING.
HMFF, AGAIN.
CONGRATULATIONS, BY THE WAY.
UM... CONGRATULATIONS FOR WHAT, EXACTLY...?
YOU DO KNOW THAT YOU'VE BEEN NOMINATED FOR ONE OF THIS YEAR'S "CAPED JUSTICE" AWARDS, DON'T YOU?
YOU'RE UP FOR THE "SUPRAHUMAN MOST DESERVING OF WIDER RECOGNITION" CATEGORY, IF I RECALL CORRECTLY.
THE NOMINATIONS WERE JUST ANNOUNCED THIS MORNING.
HADN'T HEARD YET, HUH?

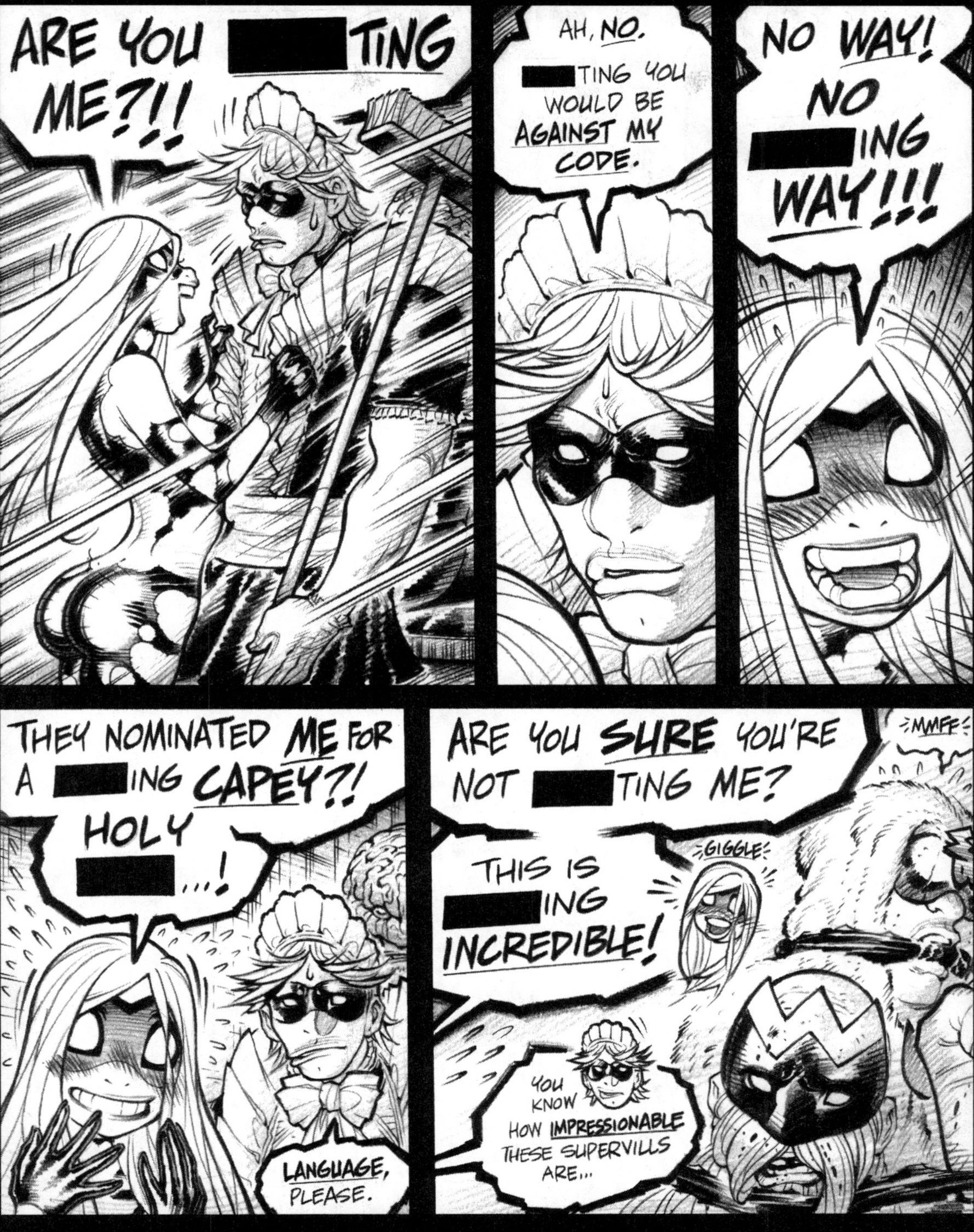
ARE YOU [redacted]TING ME?!!
AH, NO.
[redacted]TING YOU WOULD BE AGAINST MY CODE.
NO WAY! NO [redacted]ING WAY!!!
THEY NOMINATED ME FOR A [redacted]ING CAPEY?!
HOLY [redacted]...!
LANGUAGE, PLEASE.
ARE YOU SURE YOU'RE NOT [redacted]TING ME?
MMFF
GIGGLE
THIS IS [redacted]ING INCREDIBLE!
YOU KNOW HOW IMPRESSIONABLE THESE SUPERVILLS ARE...

Empowered™

My Definition of Team-Up

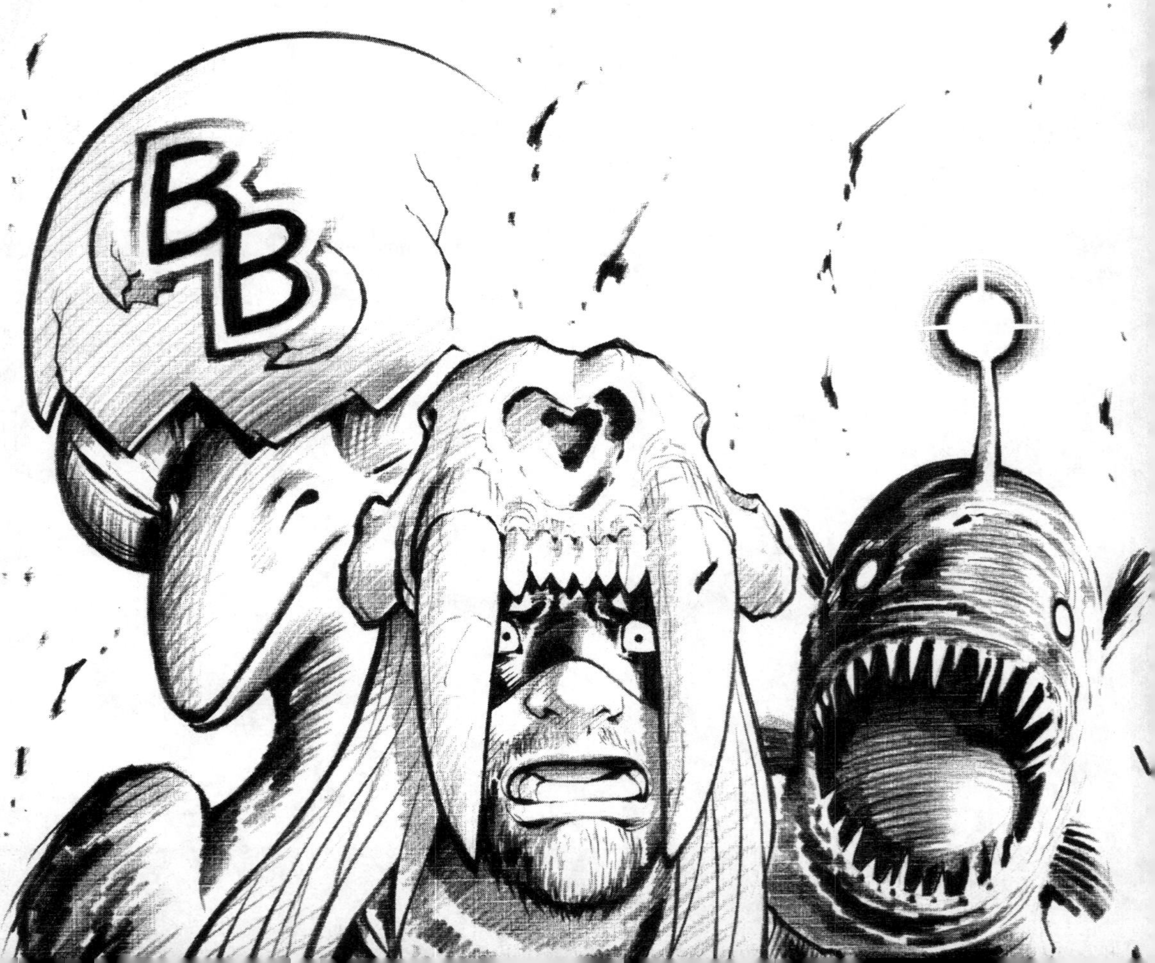
BB

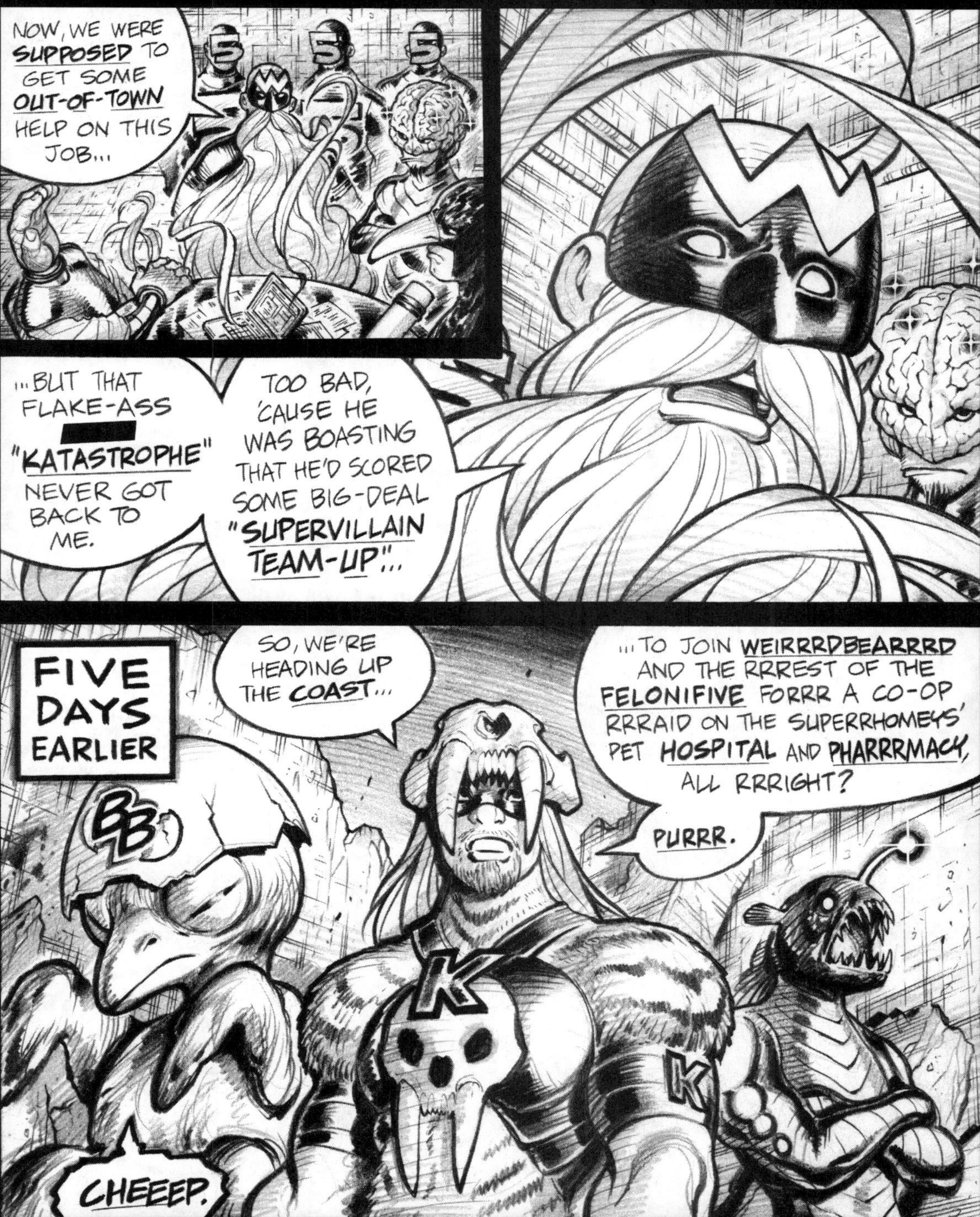
NOW, WE WERE SUPPOSED TO GET SOME OUT-OF-TOWN HELP ON THIS JOB...
...BUT THAT FLAKE-ASS [redacted] "KATASTROPHE" NEVER GOT BACK TO ME.
TOO BAD, 'CAUSE HE WAS BOASTING THAT HE'D SCORED SOME BIG-DEAL "SUPERVILLAIN TEAM-UP"...
FIVE DAYS EARLIER
SO, WE'RE HEADING UP THE COAST...
...TO JOIN WEIRRRDBEARRRD AND THE RRREST OF THE FELONIFIVE FORRR A CO-OP RRRAID ON THE SUPERRHOMEYS' PET HOSPITAL AND PHARRRMACY, ALL RRRIGHT?
BB
PURRR.
CHEEEP.

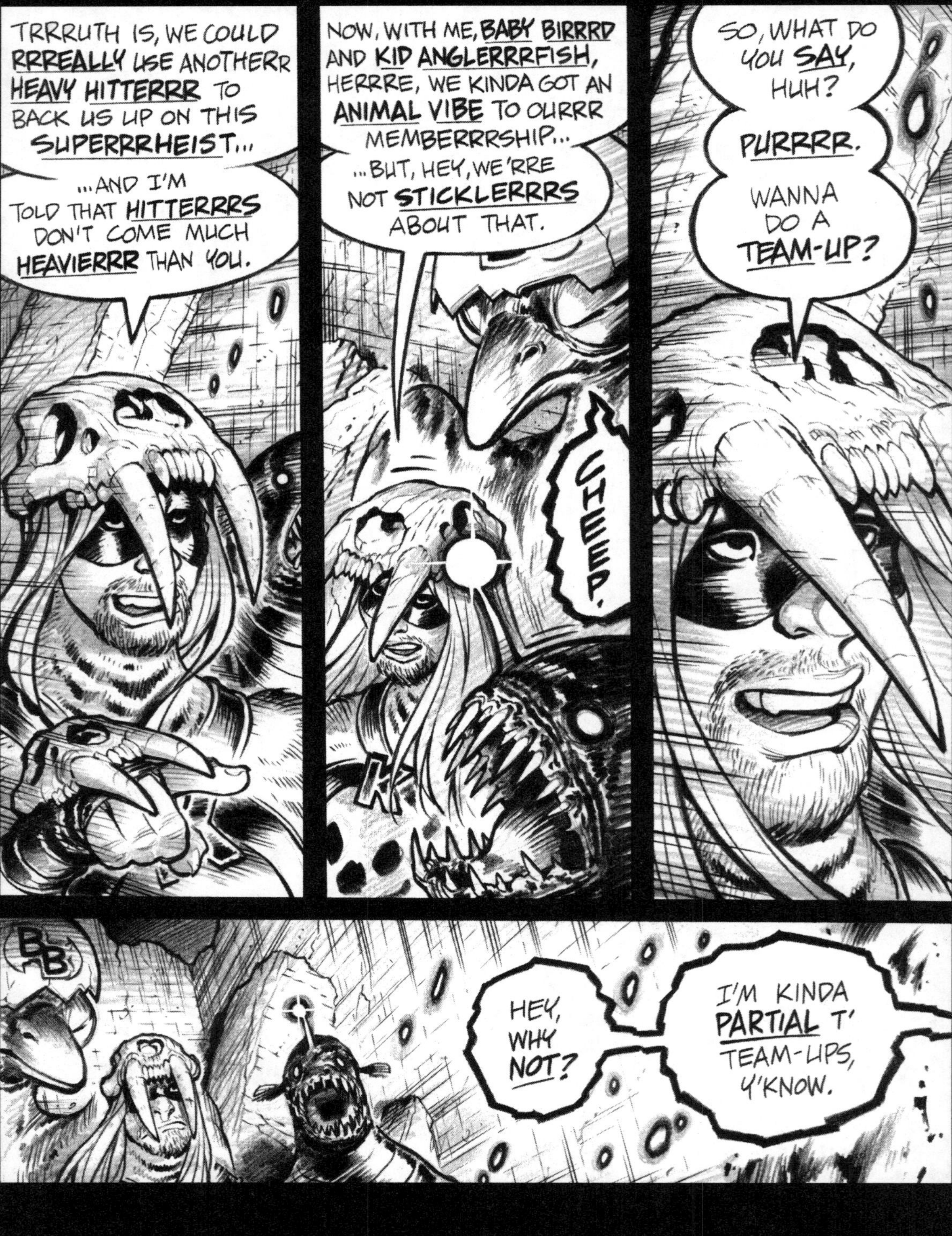
TRRRUTH IS, WE COULD RRREALLY USE ANOTHERR HEAVY HITTERRR TO BACK US UP ON THIS SUPERRRHEIST...
...AND I'M TOLD THAT HITTERRRS DON'T COME MUCH HEAVIERRR THAN YOU.
NOW, WITH ME, BABY BIRRRD AND KID ANGLERRRFISH, HERRRE, WE KINDA GOT AN ANIMAL VIBE TO OURRR MEMBERRRSHIP...
...BUT, HEY, WE'RRE NOT STICKLERRRS ABOUT THAT.
CHEEP.
SO, WHAT DO YOU SAY, HUH?
PURRRR.
WANNA DO A TEAM-UP?
HEY, WHY NOT?
I'M KINDA PARTIAL T' TEAM-UPS, Y'KNOW.

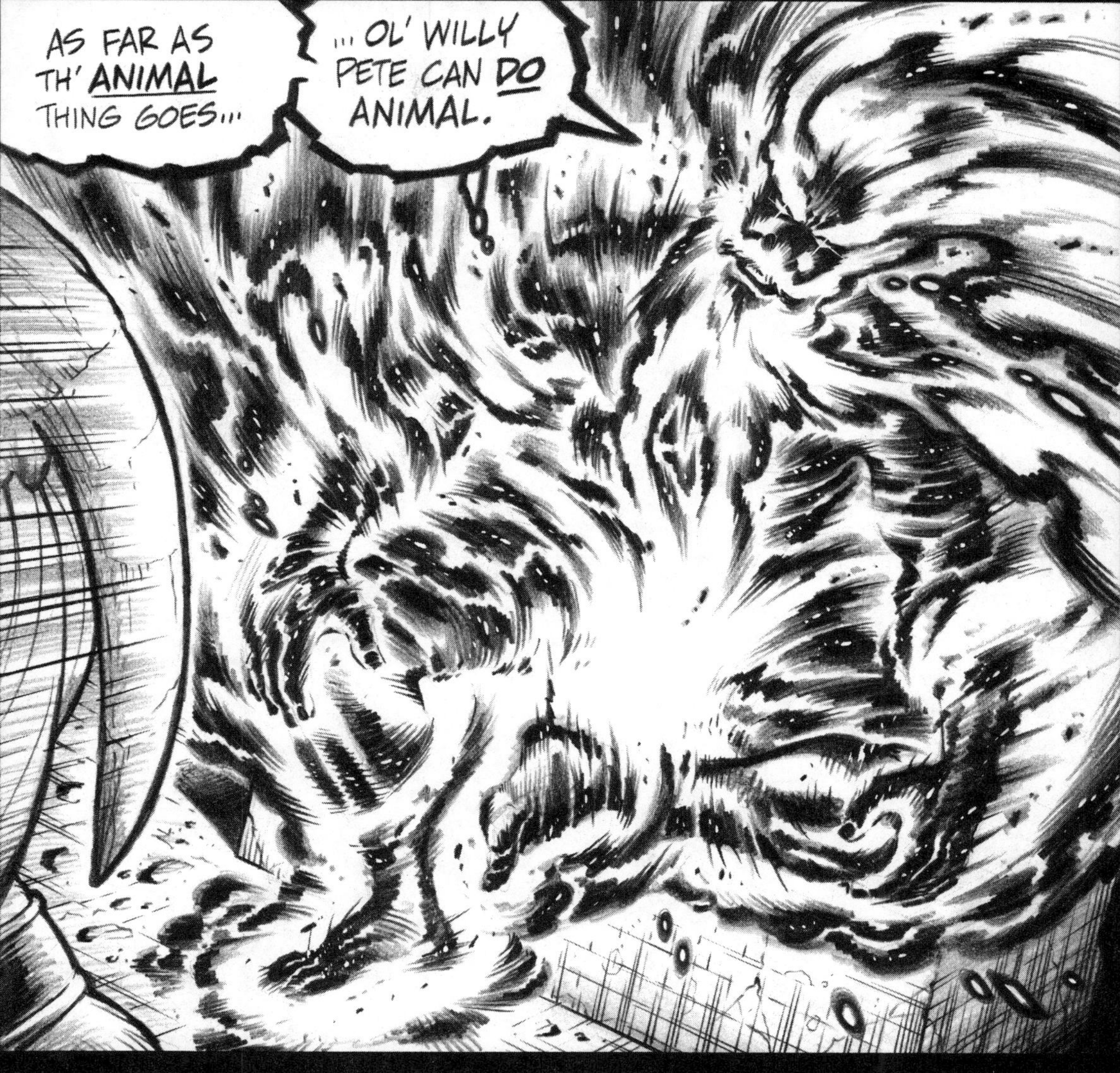
AS FAR AS TH' ANIMAL THING GOES...
...OL' WILLY PETE CAN DO ANIMAL.
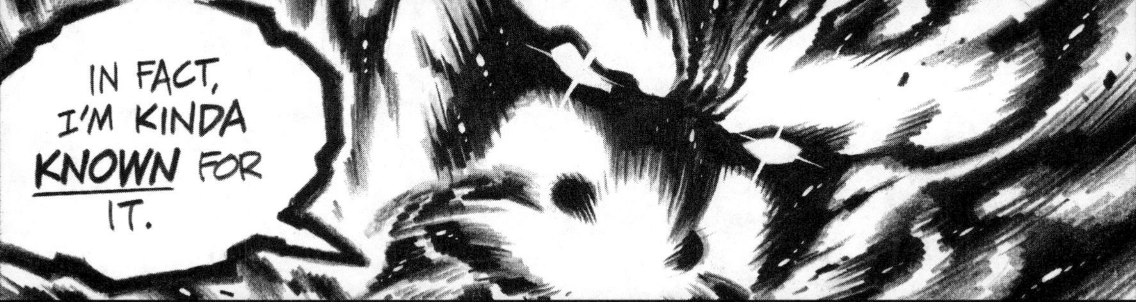
IN FACT, I'M KINDA KNOWN FOR IT.

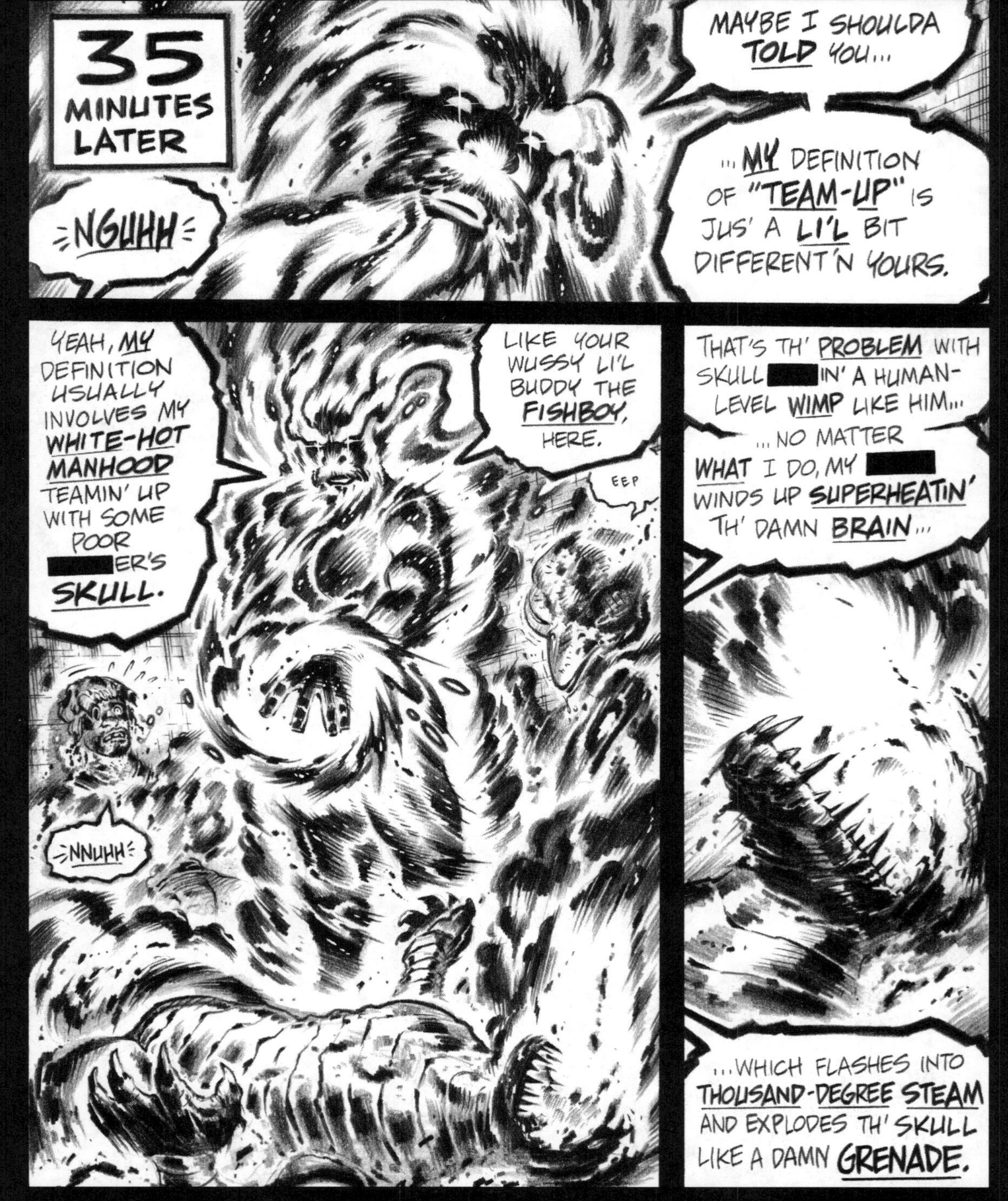
35 MINUTES LATER
NGUHH
MAYBE I SHOULDA TOLD YOU...
...MY DEFINITION OF "TEAM-UP" IS JUS' A LI'L BIT DIFFERENT'N YOURS.
YEAH, MY DEFINITION USUALLY INVOLVES MY WHITE-HOT MANHOOD TEAMIN' UP WITH SOME POOR [redacted]ER'S SKULL.
LIKE YOUR WUSSY LI'L BUDDY THE FISHBOY, HERE.
EEP
NNUHH
THAT'S TH' PROBLEM WITH SKULL[redacted]IN' A HUMAN-LEVEL WIMP LIKE HIM...
...NO MATTER WHAT I DO, MY [redacted] WINDS UP SUPERHEATIN' TH' DAMN BRAIN...
...WHICH FLASHES INTO THOUSAND-DEGREE STEAM AND EXPLODES TH' SKULL LIKE A DAMN GRENADE.

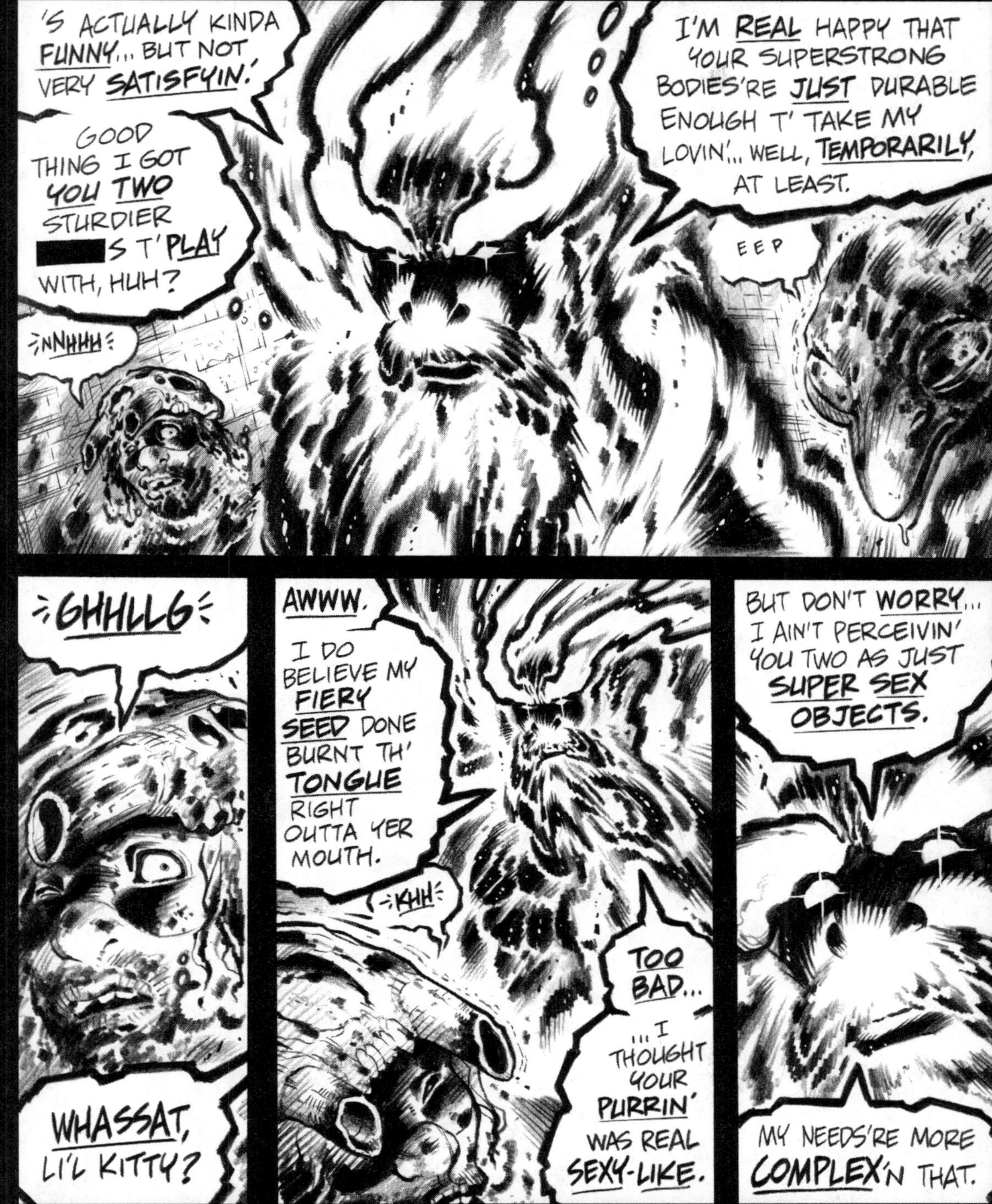
'S ACTUALLY KINDA FUNNY... BUT NOT VERY SATISFYIN'.
I'M REAL HAPPY THAT YOUR SUPERSTRONG BODIES'RE JUST DURABLE ENOUGH T' TAKE MY LOVIN'... WELL, TEMPORARILY, AT LEAST.
GOOD THING I GOT YOU TWO STURDIER [redacted]S T' PLAY WITH, HUH?
EEP
NNHHH
GHHLLG
WHASSAT, LI'L KITTY?
AWWW.
I DO BELIEVE MY FIERY SEED DONE BURNT TH' TONGUE RIGHT OUTTA YER MOUTH.
KHH
TOO BAD...
...I THOUGHT YOUR PURRIN' WAS REAL SEXY-LIKE.
BUT DON'T WORRY... I AIN'T PERCEIVIN' YOU TWO AS JUST SUPER SEX OBJECTS.
MY NEEDS'RE MORE COMPLEX'N THAT.

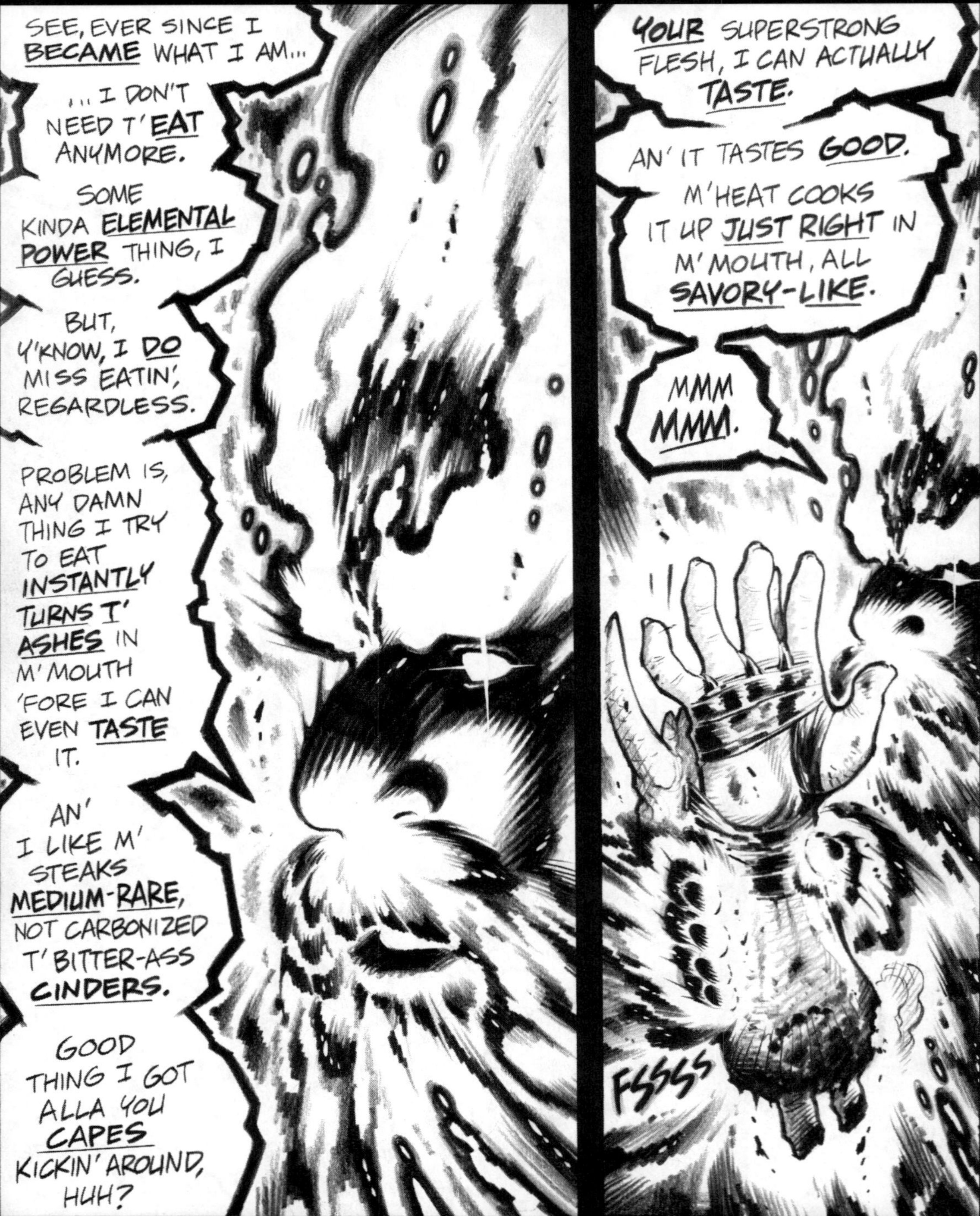
SEE, EVER SINCE I BECAME WHAT I AM...
...I DON'T NEED T' EAT ANYMORE.
SOME KINDA ELEMENTAL POWER THING, I GUESS.
BUT, Y'KNOW, I DO MISS EATIN', REGARDLESS.
PROBLEM IS, ANY DAMN THING I TRY TO EAT INSTANTLY TURNS T' ASHES IN M' MOUTH 'FORE I CAN EVEN TASTE IT.
AN' I LIKE M' STEAKS MEDIUM-RARE, NOT CARBONIZED T' BITTER-ASS CINDERS.
GOOD THING I GOT ALLA YOU CAPES KICKIN' AROUND, HUH?
YOUR SUPERSTRONG FLESH, I CAN ACTUALLY TASTE.
AN' IT TASTES GOOD.
M'HEAT COOKS IT UP JUST RIGHT IN M' MOUTH, ALL SAVORY-LIKE.
MMM MMM.
FSSSS

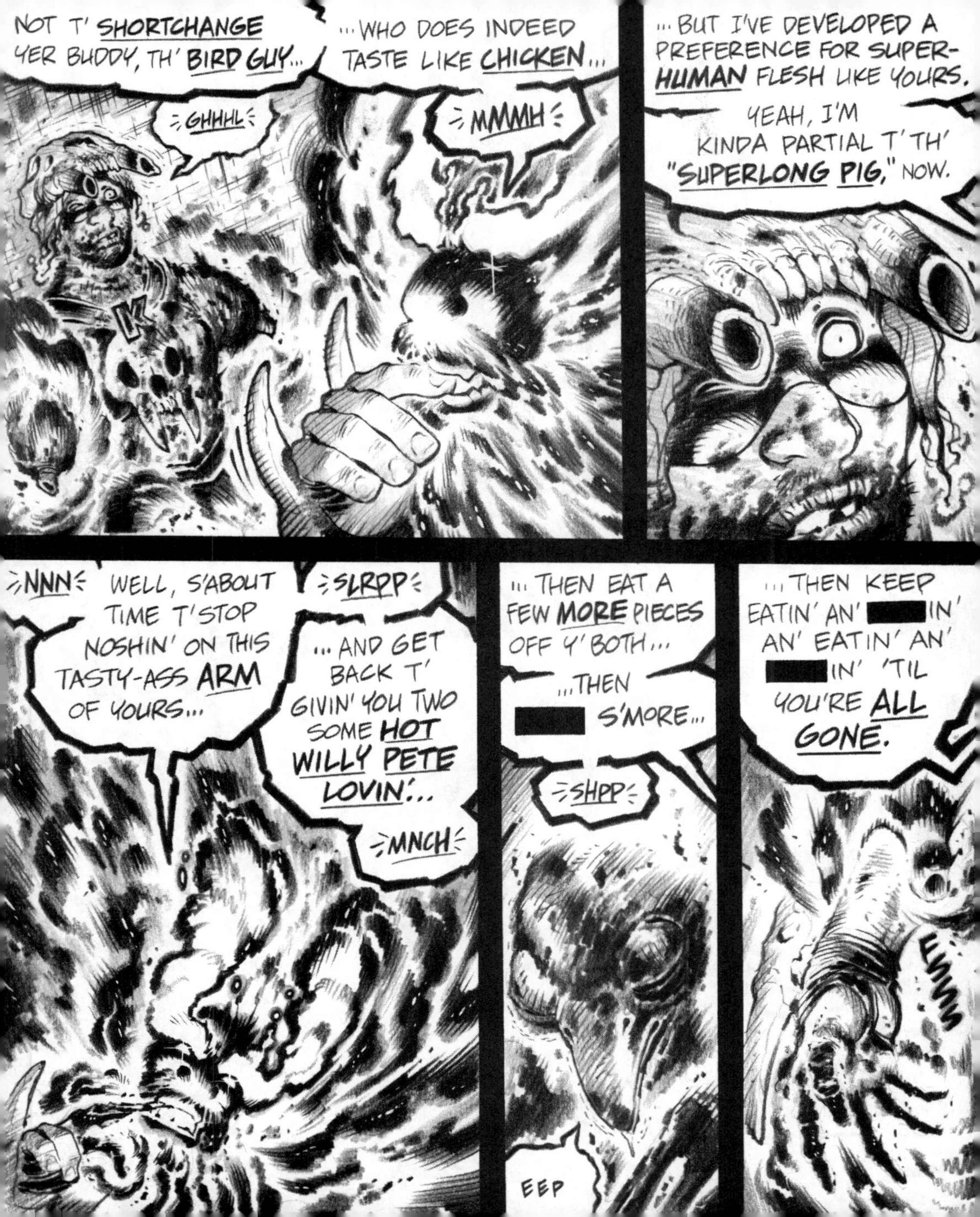
NOT T' SHORTCHANGE YER BUDDY, TH' BIRD GUY...
...WHO DOES INDEED TASTE LIKE CHICKEN...
GHHHL
MMMH
...BUT I'VE DEVELOPED A PREFERENCE FOR SUPER-HUMAN FLESH LIKE YOURS.
YEAH, I'M KINDA PARTIAL T' TH' "SUPERLONG PIG," NOW.
NNN
WELL, S'ABOUT TIME T'STOP NOSHIN' ON THIS TASTY-ASS ARM OF YOURS...
SLRPP
...AND GET BACK T' GIVIN' YOU TWO SOME HOT WILLY PETE LOVIN'...
MNCH
...THEN EAT A FEW MORE PIECES OFF Y' BOTH...
...THEN [redacted] S'MORE...
SHPP
EEP
...THEN KEEP EATIN' AN' [redacted]IN' AN' EATIN' AN' [redacted]IN' 'TIL YOU'RE ALL GONE.
EMMM

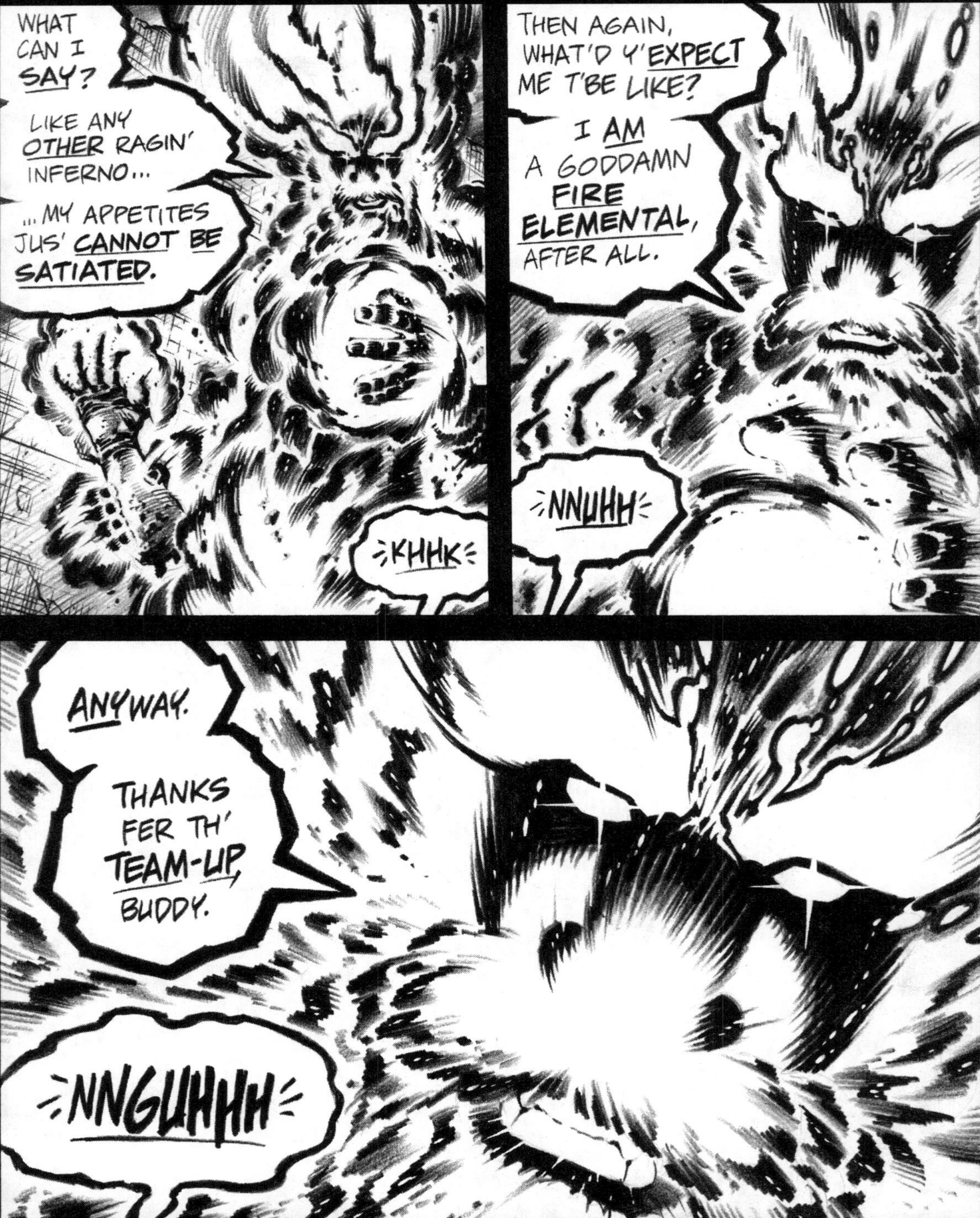
WHAT CAN I SAY?
LIKE ANY OTHER RAGIN' INFERNO...
...MY APPETITES JUS' CANNOT BE SATIATED.
KHHK
THEN AGAIN, WHAT'D Y'EXPECT ME T'BE LIKE?
I AM A GODDAMN FIRE ELEMENTAL, AFTER ALL.
NNUHH
ANYWAY.
THANKS FER TH' TEAM-UP, BUDDY.
NNGUHHH

Empowered™

Bemused, Bekittened, and Bepantied

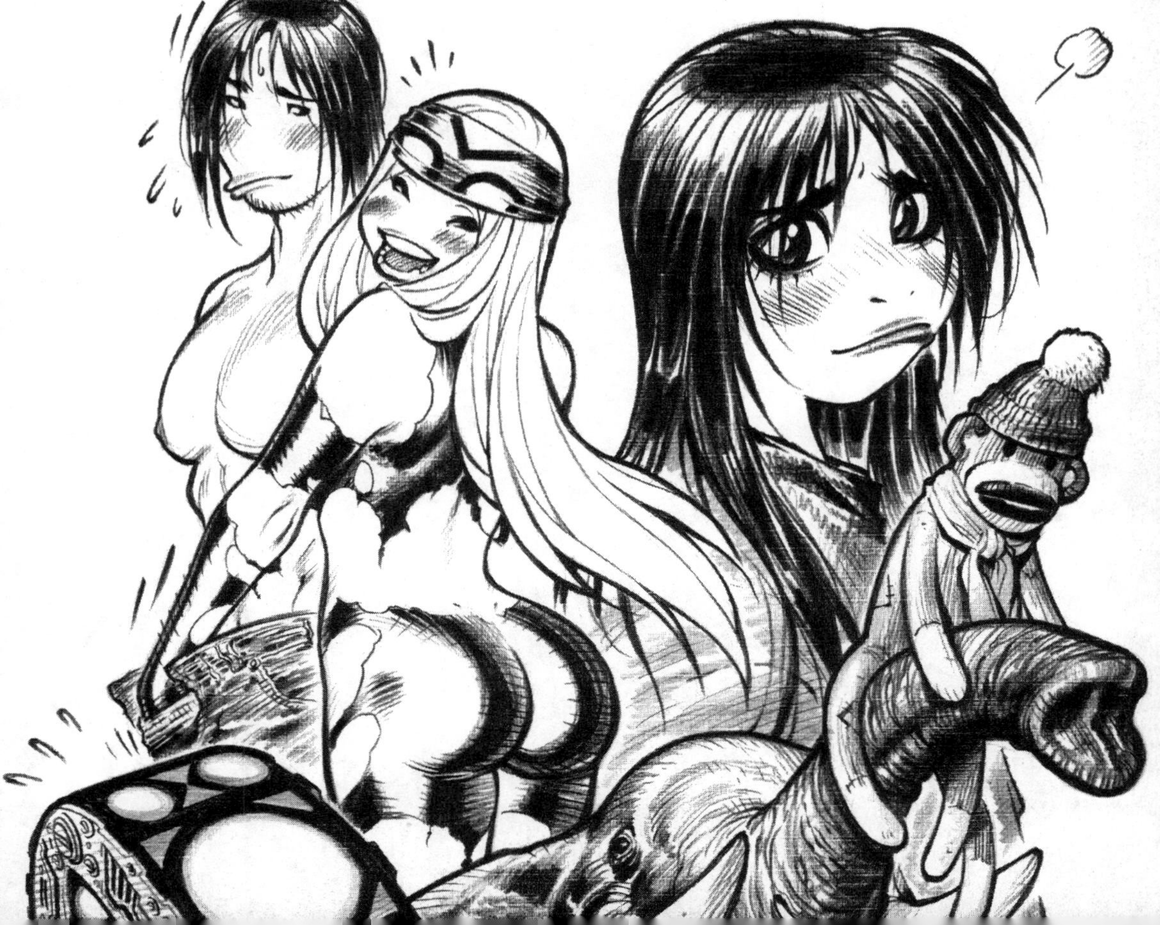

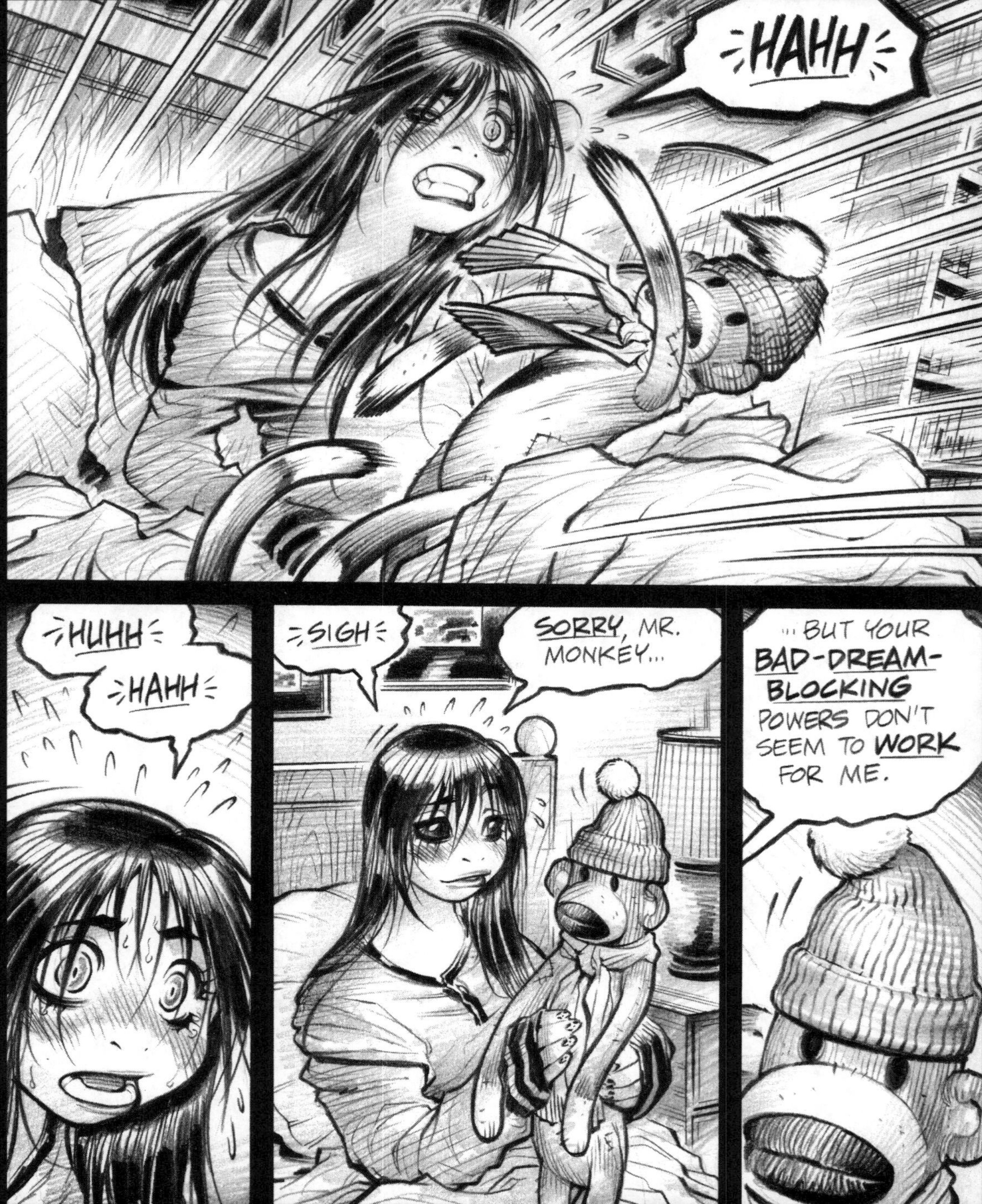
HAHH
HUHH
HAHH
SIGH
SORRY, MR. MONKEY...
...BUT YOUR BAD-DREAM-BLOCKING POWERS DON'T SEEM TO WORK FOR ME.

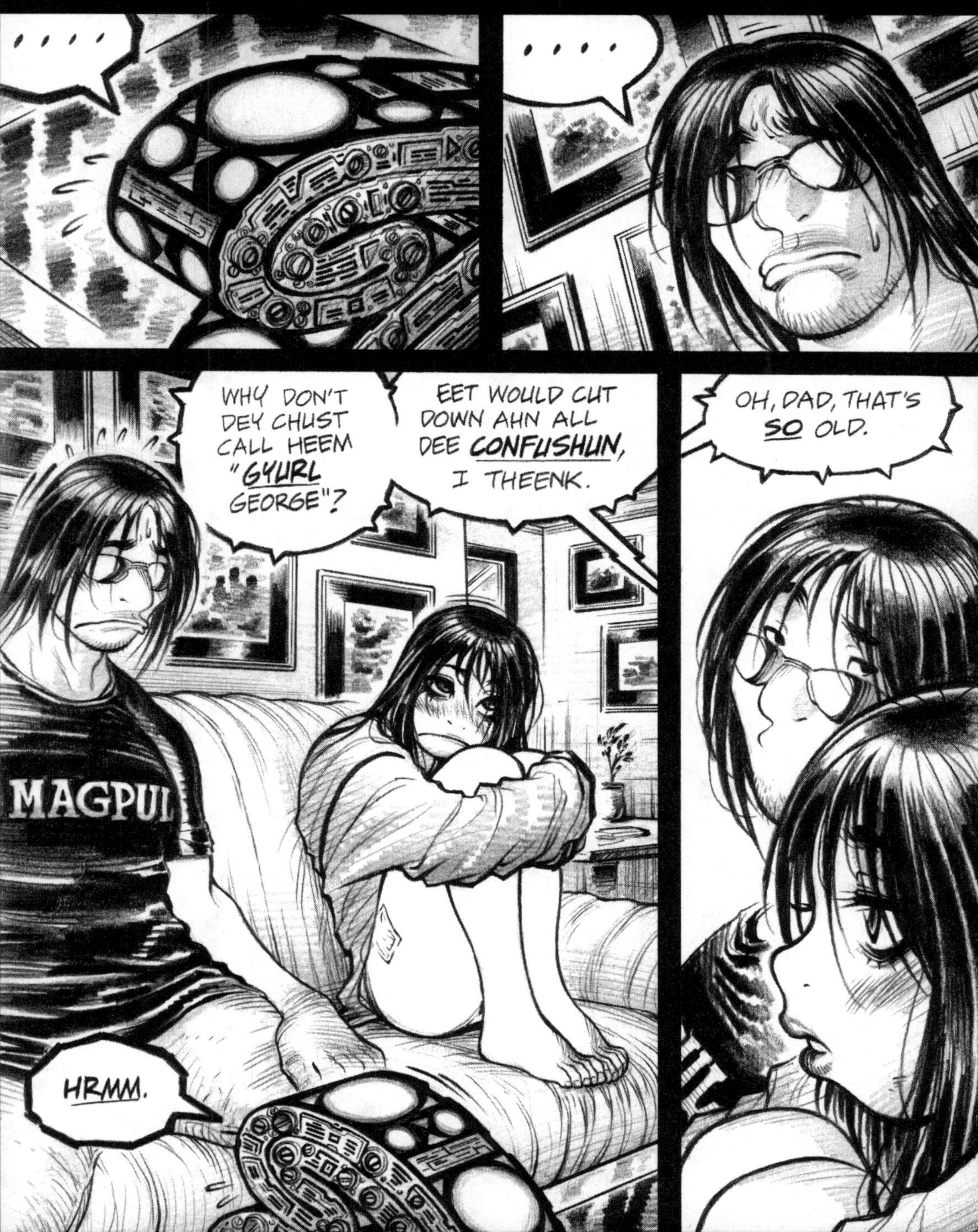
. . . .
. . . .
WHY DON'T DEY CHUST CALL HEEM "GYURL GEORGE"?
EET WOULD CUT DOWN AHN ALL DEE CONFUSHUN, I THEENK.
MAGPUL
HRMM.
OH, DAD, THAT'S SO OLD.

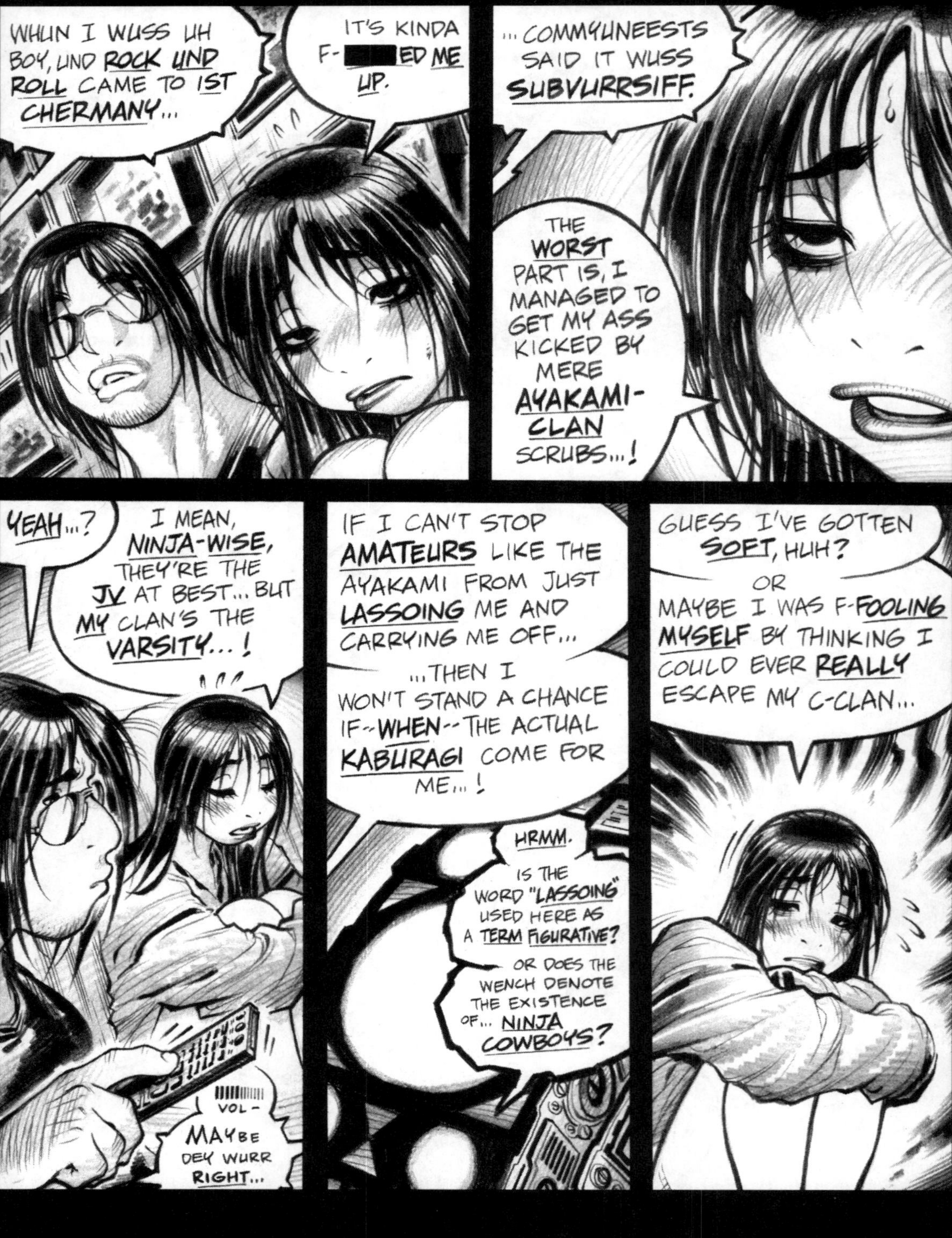
WHUN I WUSS UH BOY, UND ROCK UND ROLL CAME TO IST CHERMANY...
IT'S KINDA F-[redacted]ED ME UP.
...COMMYUNEESTS SAID IT WUSS SUBVURRSIFF.
THE WORST PART IS, I MANAGED TO GET MY ASS KICKED BY MERE AYAKAMI-CLAN SCRUBS...!
YEAH...?
I MEAN, NINJA-WISE, THEY'RE THE JV AT BEST... BUT MY CLAN'S THE VARSITY...!
VOL-
MAYBE DEY WURR RIGHT...
IF I CAN'T STOP AMATEURS LIKE THE AYAKAMI FROM JUST LASSOING ME AND CARRYING ME OFF...
...THEN I WON'T STAND A CHANCE IF--WHEN--THE ACTUAL KABURAGI COME FOR ME...!
HRMM.
IS THE WORD "LASSOING" USED HERE AS A TERM FIGURATIVE?
OR DOES THE WENCH DENOTE THE EXISTENCE OF... NINJA COWBOYS?
GUESS I'VE GOTTEN SOFT, HUH?
OR MAYBE I WAS F-FOOLING MYSELF BY THINKING I COULD EVER REALLY ESCAPE MY C-CLAN...

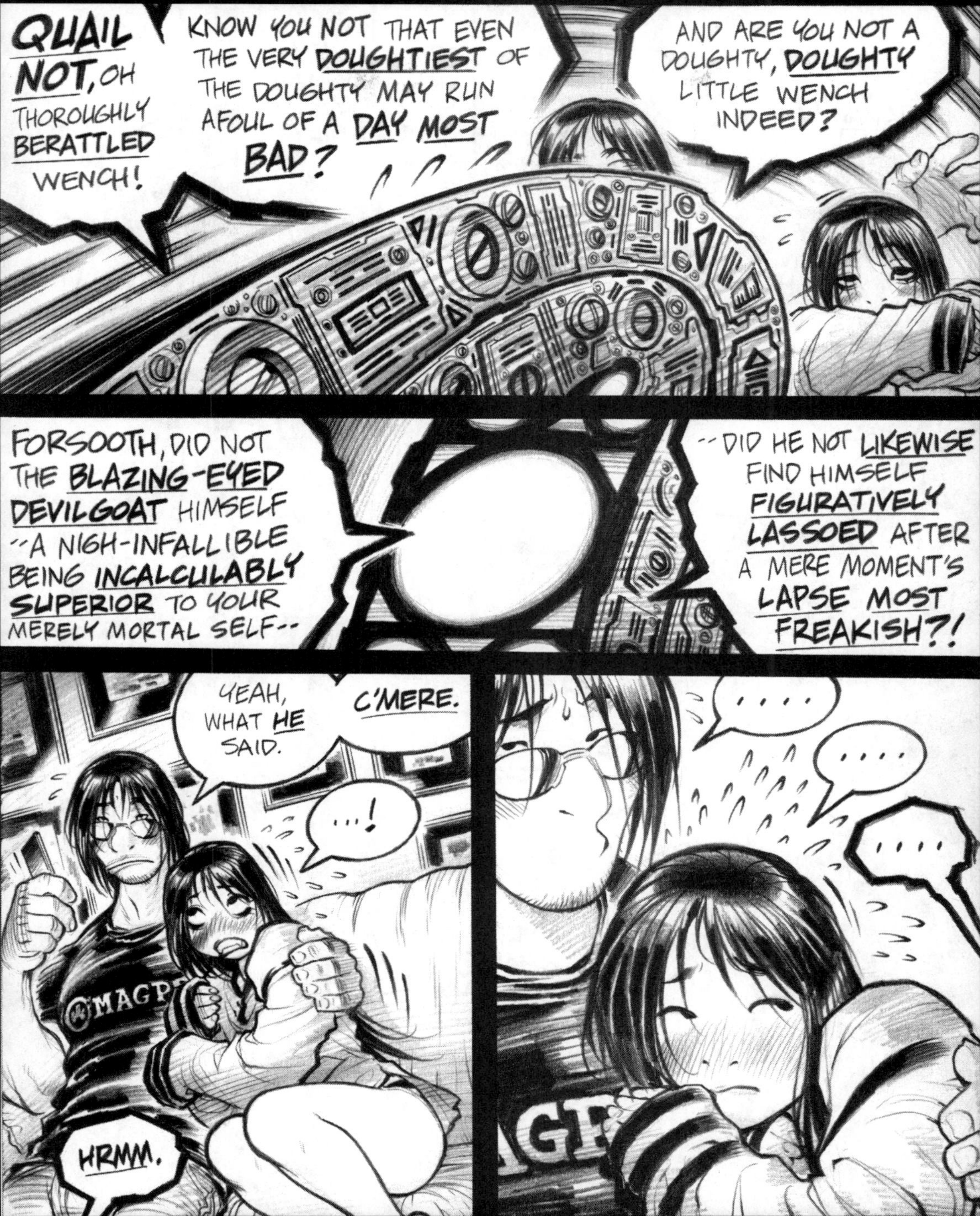
QUAIL NOT, OH THOROUGHLY BERATTLED WENCH!
KNOW YOU NOT THAT EVEN THE VERY DOUGHTIEST OF THE DOUGHTY MAY RUN AFOUL OF A DAY MOST BAD?
AND ARE YOU NOT A DOUGHTY, DOUGHTY LITTLE WENCH INDEED?
FORSOOTH, DID NOT THE BLAZING-EYED DEVILGOAT HIMSELF --A NIGH-INFALLIBLE BEING INCALCULABLY SUPERIOR TO YOUR MERELY MORTAL SELF--
--DID HE NOT LIKEWISE FIND HIMSELF FIGURATIVELY LASSOED AFTER A MERE MOMENT'S LAPSE MOST FREAKISH?!
YEAH, WHAT HE SAID.
C'MERE.
...!
HRMM.
....
....
....

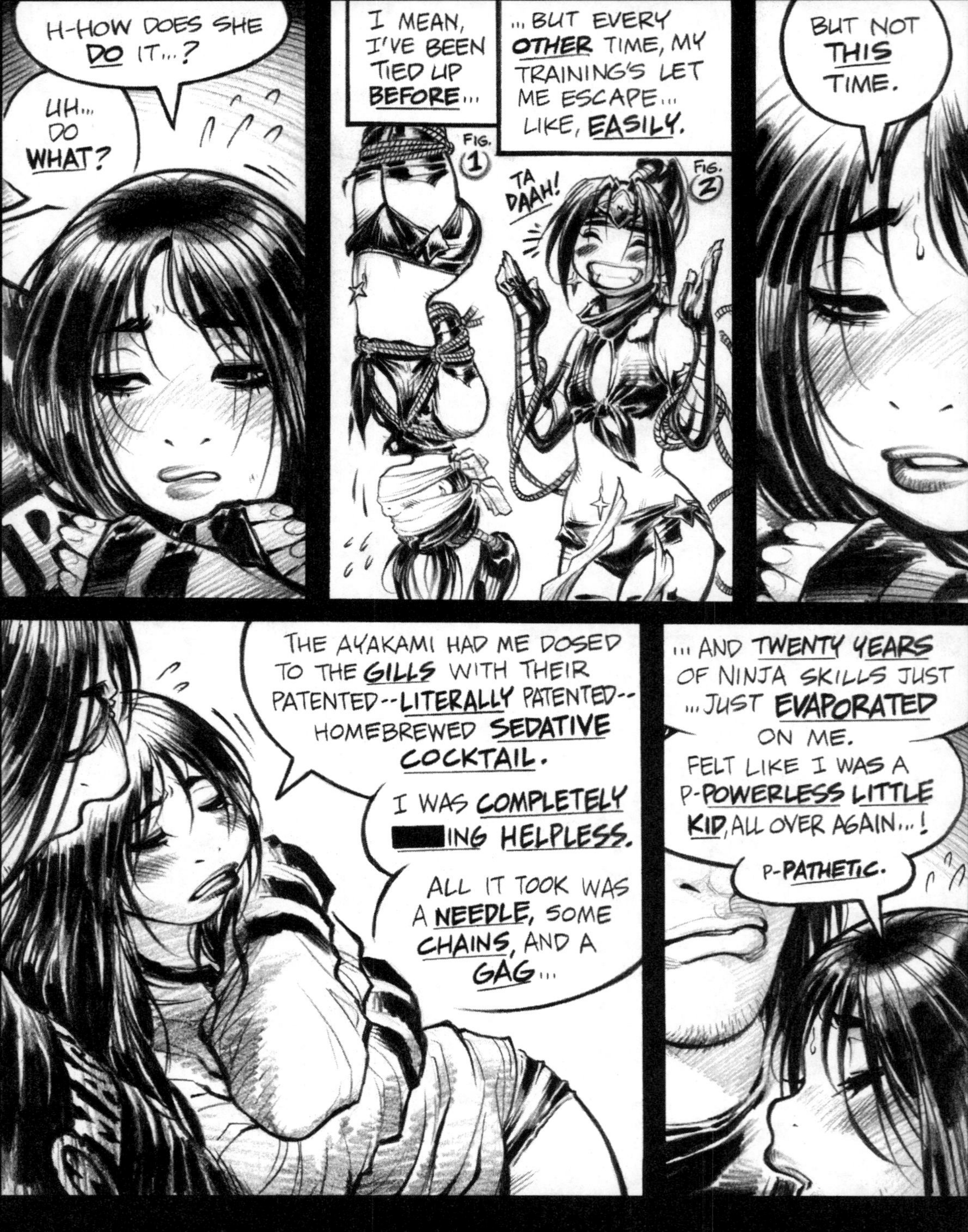

H-HOW DOES SHE DO IT...?
UH... DO WHAT?
I MEAN, I'VE BEEN TIED UP BEFORE...
...BUT EVERY OTHER TIME, MY TRAINING'S LET ME ESCAPE... LIKE, EASILY.
FIG. 1
TA DAAH!
FIG. 2
BUT NOT THIS TIME.
THE AYAKAMI HAD ME DOSED TO THE GILLS WITH THEIR PATENTED--LITERALLY PATENTED--HOMEBREWED SEDATIVE COCKTAIL.
I WAS COMPLETELY [redacted]ING HELPLESS.
ALL IT TOOK WAS A NEEDLE, SOME CHAINS, AND A GAG...
...AND TWENTY YEARS OF NINJA SKILLS JUST ...JUST EVAPORATED ON ME.
FELT LIKE I WAS A P-POWERLESS LITTLE KID, ALL OVER AGAIN...!
P-PATHETIC.

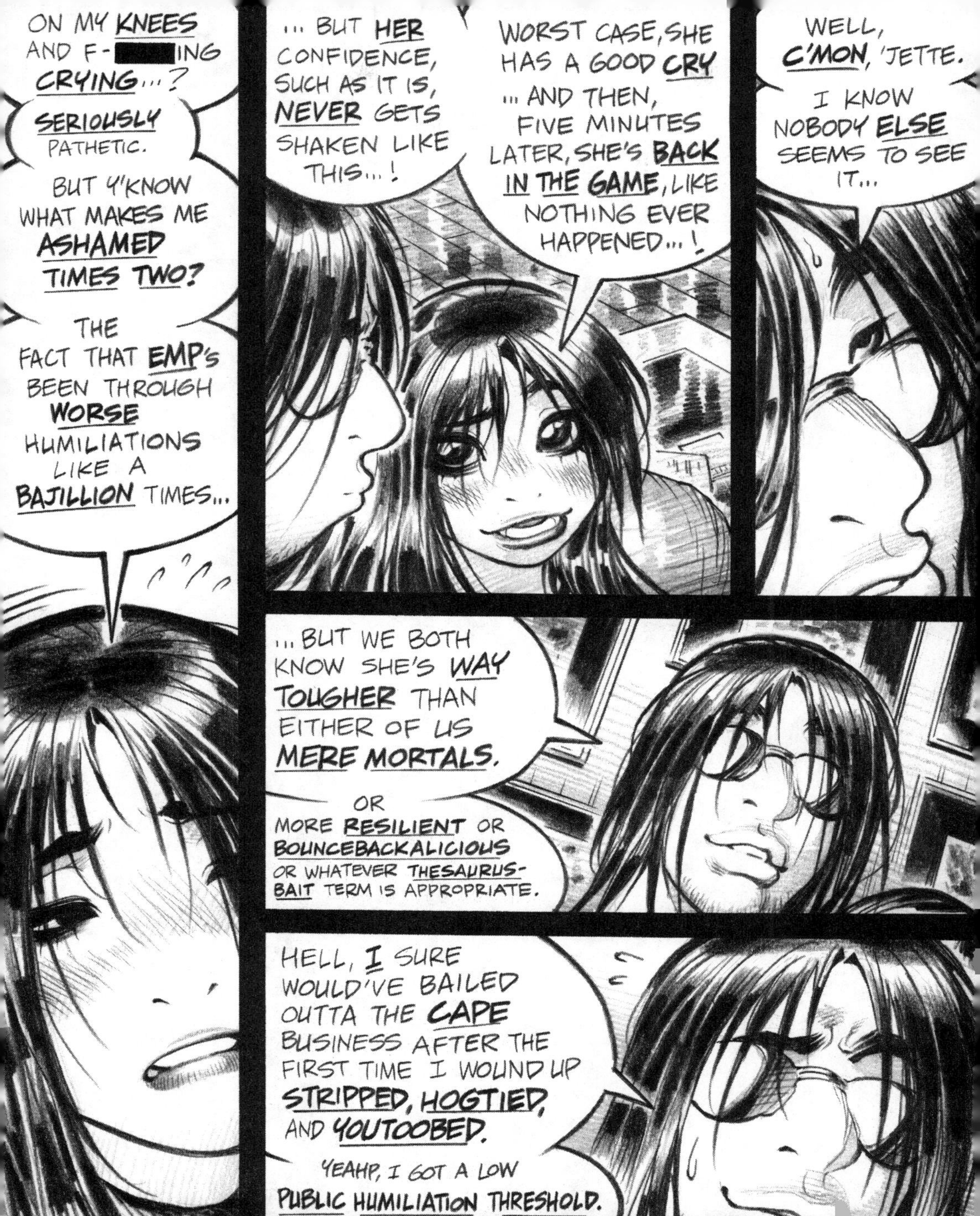
ON MY KNEES AND F-[redacted]ING CRYING...?
SERIOUSLY PATHETIC.
BUT Y'KNOW WHAT MAKES ME ASHAMED TIMES TWO?
THE FACT THAT EMP's BEEN THROUGH WORSE HUMILIATIONS LIKE A BAJILLION TIMES...
... BUT HER CONFIDENCE, SUCH AS IT IS, NEVER GETS SHAKEN LIKE THIS...!
WORST CASE, SHE HAS A GOOD CRY
... AND THEN, FIVE MINUTES LATER, SHE'S BACK IN THE GAME, LIKE NOTHING EVER HAPPENED...!
WELL, C'MON, 'JETTE.
I KNOW NOBODY ELSE SEEMS TO SEE IT...
... BUT WE BOTH KNOW SHE'S WAY TOUGHER THAN EITHER OF US MERE MORTALS.
OR MORE RESILIENT OR BOUNCEBACKALICIOUS OR WHATEVER THESAURUS-BAIT TERM IS APPROPRIATE.
HELL, I SURE WOULD'VE BAILED OUTTA THE CAPE BUSINESS AFTER THE FIRST TIME I WOUND UP STRIPPED, HOGTIED, AND YOUTOOBED.
YEAHP, I GOT A LOW PUBLIC HUMILIATION THRESHOLD.

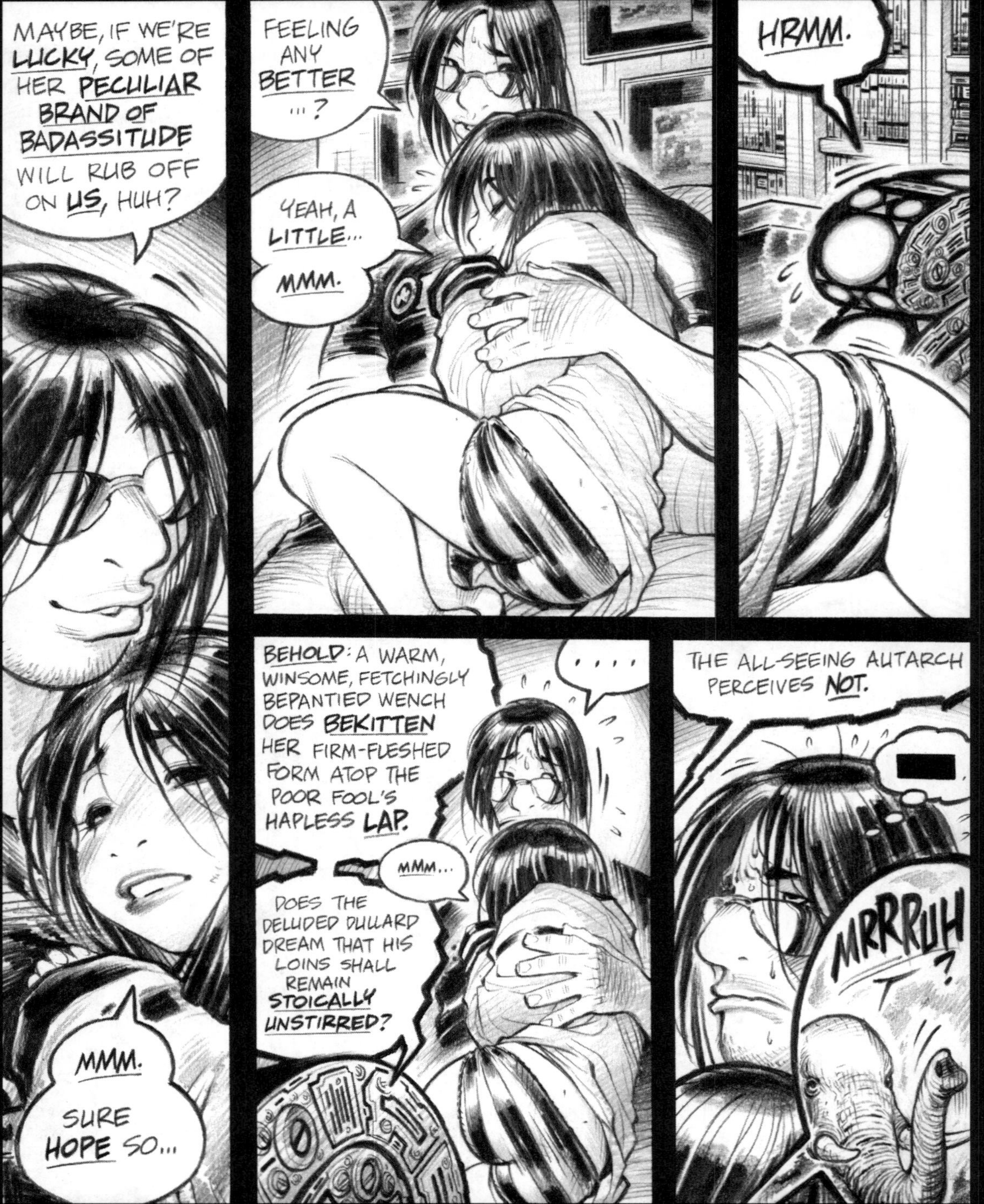
MAYBE, IF WE'RE LUCKY, SOME OF HER PECULIAR BRAND OF BADASSITUDE WILL RUB OFF ON US, HUH?
MMM.
SURE HOPE SO...
FEELING ANY BETTER ...?
YEAH, A LITTLE...
MMM.
HRMM.
BEHOLD: A WARM, WINSOME, FETCHINGLY BEPANTIED WENCH DOES BEKITTEN HER FIRM-FLESHED FORM ATOP THE POOR FOOL'S HAPLESS LAP.
....
MMM...
DOES THE DELUDED DULLARD DREAM THAT HIS LOINS SHALL REMAIN STOICALLY UNSTIRRED?
THE ALL-SEEING AUTARCH PERCEIVES NOT.
[redacted]
MRRRUH?

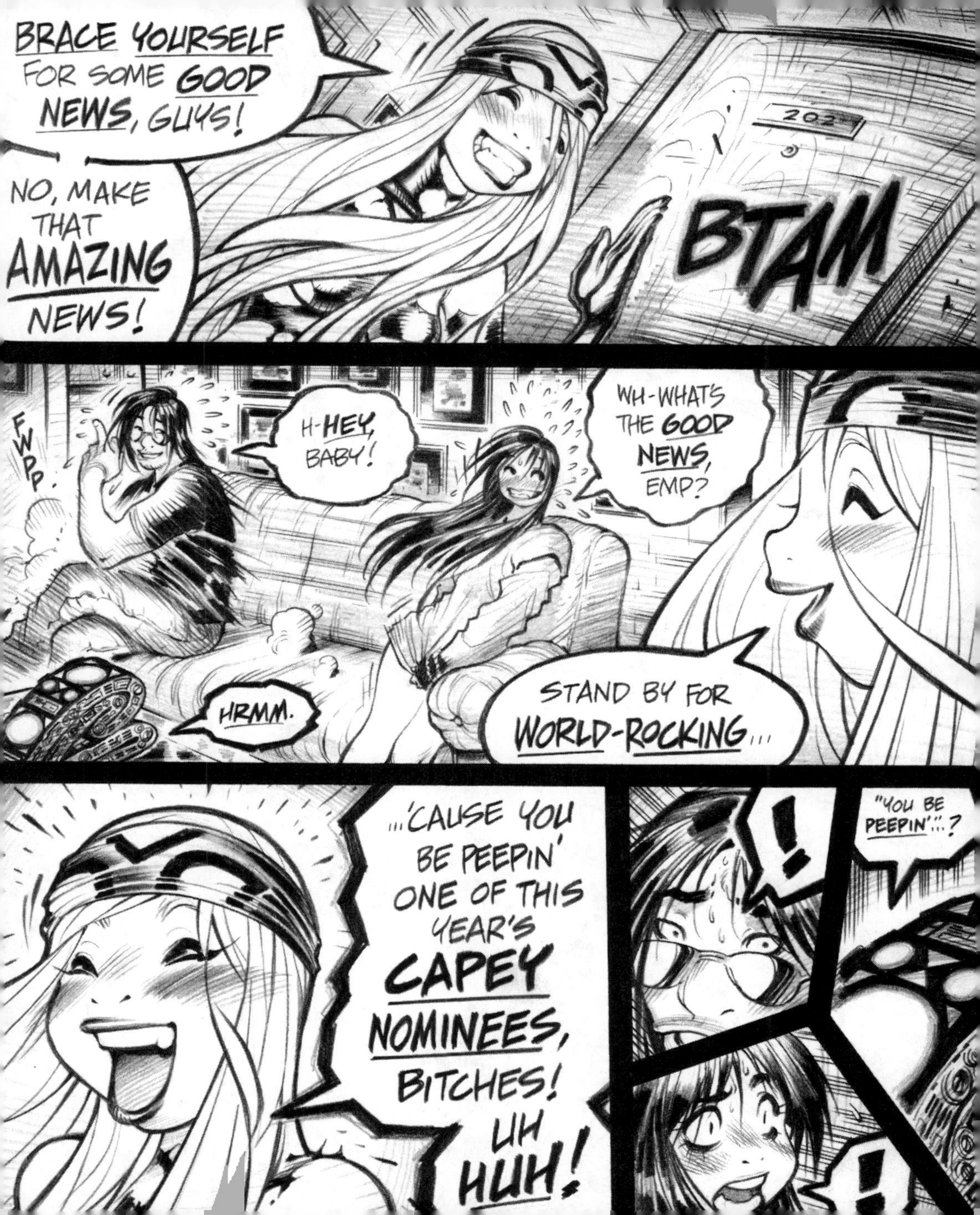
BRACE YOURSELF FOR SOME GOOD NEWS, GUYS!
NO, MAKE THAT AMAZING NEWS!
202
BTAM
FWPP
H-HEY, BABY!
WH-WHAT'S THE GOOD NEWS, EMP?
HRMM.
STAND BY FOR WORLD-ROCKING...
...'CAUSE YOU BE PEEPIN' ONE OF THIS YEAR'S CAPEY NOMINEES, BITCHES!
UH HUH!
!
"YOU BE PEEPIN'"...?
!

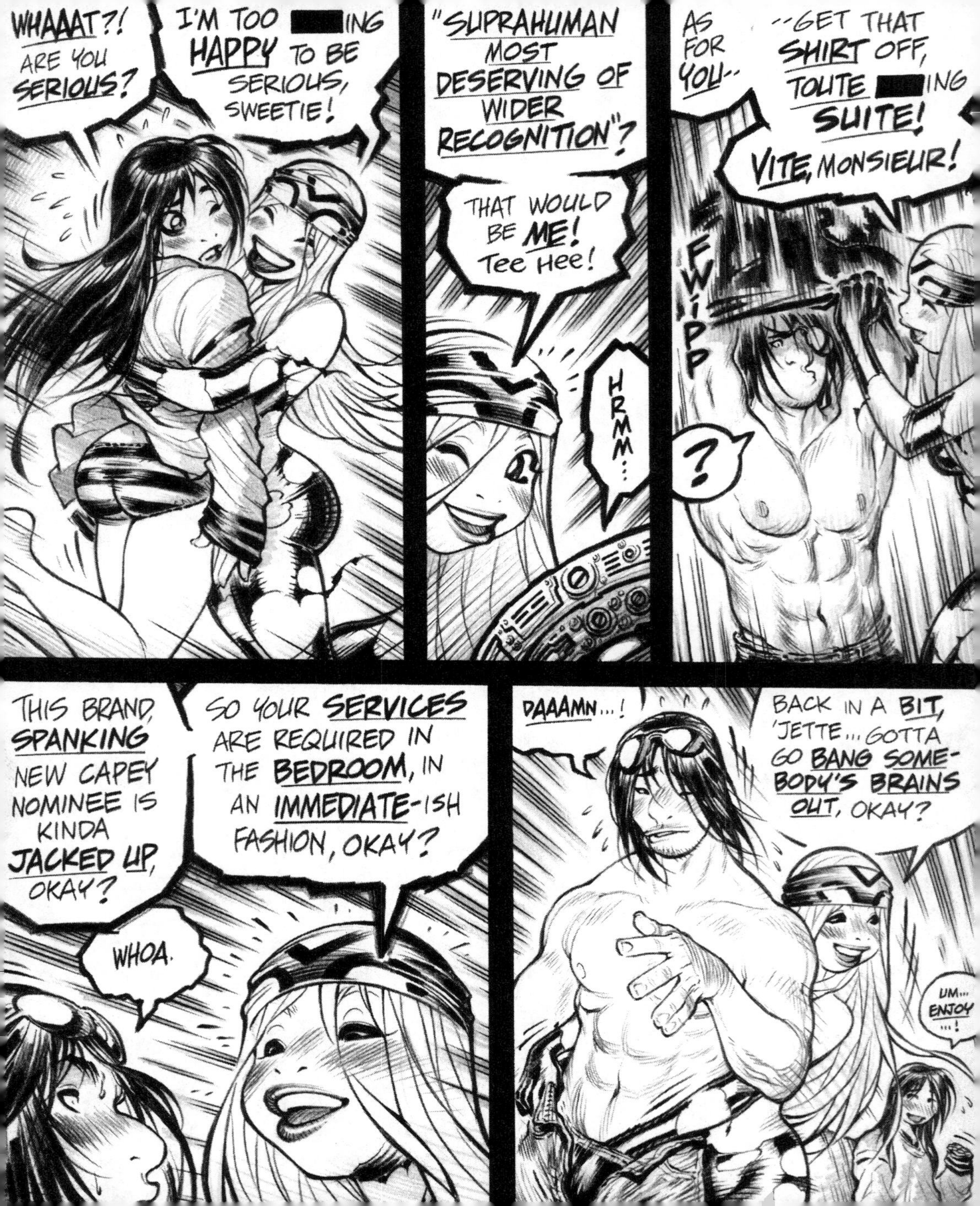

WHAAAT?! ARE YOU SERIOUS?
I'M TOO [redacted]ING HAPPY TO BE SERIOUS, SWEETIE!
"SUPRAHUMAN MOST DESERVING OF WIDER RECOGNITION"?
THAT WOULD BE ME! Tee Hee!
HRMM...
AS FOR YOU...
--GET THAT SHIRT OFF, TOUTE [redacted]ING SUITE! VITE, MONSIEUR!
FWIPP
?
THIS BRAND, SPANKING NEW CAPEY NOMINEE IS KINDA JACKED UP, OKAY?
SO YOUR SERVICES ARE REQUIRED IN THE BEDROOM, IN AN IMMEDIATE-ISH FASHION, OKAY?
WHOA.
DAAAMN...!
BACK IN A BIT, 'JETTE... GOTTA GO BANG SOMEBODY'S BRAINS OUT, OKAY?
UM... ENJOY...!

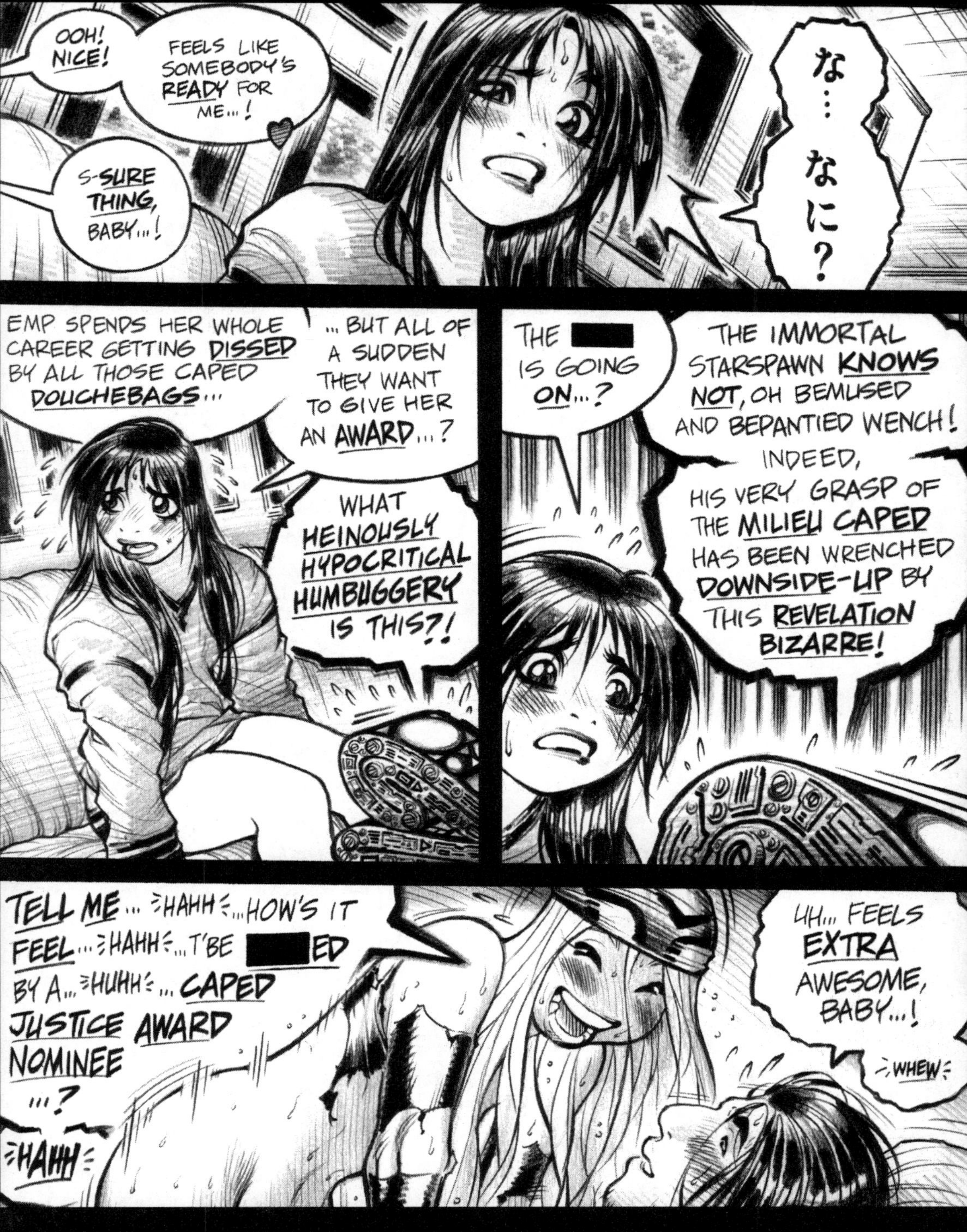
OOH! NICE!
FEELS LIKE SOMEBODY'S READY FOR ME...!
S-SURE THING, BABY...!
な…なに？
EMP SPENDS HER WHOLE CAREER GETTING DISSED BY ALL THOSE CAPED DOUCHEBAGS...
...BUT ALL OF A SUDDEN THEY WANT TO GIVE HER AN AWARD...?
WHAT HEINOUSLY HYPOCRITICAL HUMBUGGERY IS THIS?!
THE [redacted] IS GOING ON...?
THE IMMORTAL STARSPAWN KNOWS NOT, OH BEMUSED AND BEPANTIED WENCH!
INDEED, HIS VERY GRASP OF THE MILIEU CAPED HAS BEEN WRENCHED DOWNSIDE-UP BY THIS REVELATION BIZARRE!
TELL ME... HAHH ...HOW'S IT FEEL... HAHH ...T'BE [redacted]ED BY A... HUHH ... CAPED JUSTICE AWARD NOMINEE ...?
HAHH
UH... FEELS EXTRA AWESOME, BABY...!
WHEW

empowered™

The Downside of Hurricane Elissa

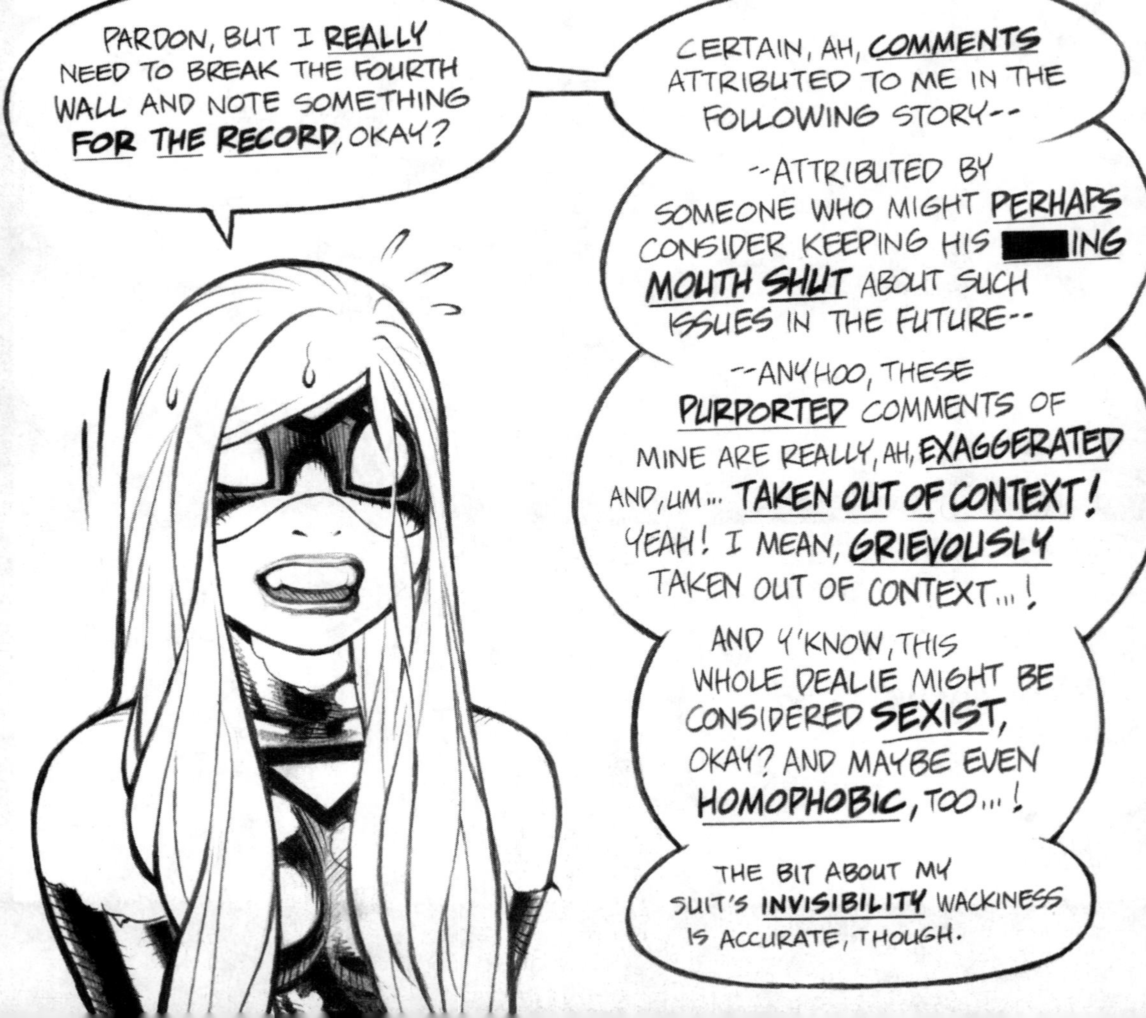
PARDON, BUT I REALLY NEED TO BREAK THE FOURTH WALL AND NOTE SOMETHING FOR THE RECORD, OKAY?
CERTAIN, AH, COMMENTS ATTRIBUTED TO ME IN THE FOLLOWING STORY--
--ATTRIBUTED BY SOMEONE WHO MIGHT PERHAPS CONSIDER KEEPING HIS [redacted]ING MOUTH SHUT ABOUT SUCH ISSUES IN THE FUTURE--
--ANYHOO, THESE PURPORTED COMMENTS OF MINE ARE REALLY, AH, EXAGGERATED AND, UM... TAKEN OUT OF CONTEXT! YEAH! I MEAN, GRIEVOUSLY TAKEN OUT OF CONTEXT...!
AND Y'KNOW, THIS WHOLE DEALIE MIGHT BE CONSIDERED SEXIST, OKAY? AND MAYBE EVEN HOMOPHOBIC, TOO...!
THE BIT ABOUT MY SUIT'S INVISIBILITY WACKINESS IS ACCURATE, THOUGH.

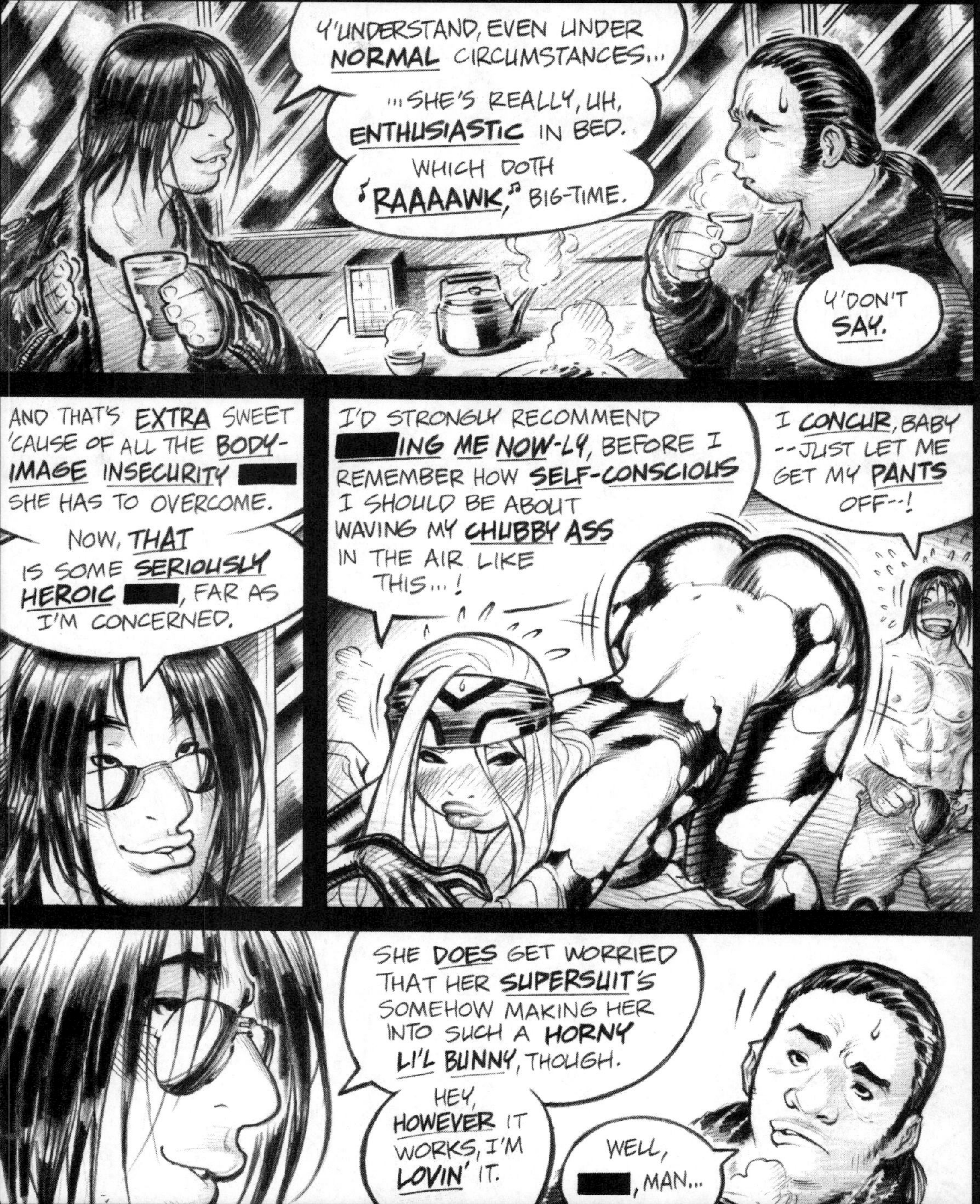
Y'UNDERSTAND, EVEN UNDER NORMAL CIRCUMSTANCES...
...SHE'S REALLY, UH, ENTHUSIASTIC IN BED.
WHICH DOTH ♪RAAAAWK,♪ BIG-TIME.
Y'DON'T SAY.
AND THAT'S EXTRA SWEET 'CAUSE OF ALL THE BODY-IMAGE INSECURITY [redacted] SHE HAS TO OVERCOME.
NOW, THAT IS SOME SERIOUSLY HEROIC [redacted], FAR AS I'M CONCERNED.
I'D STRONGLY RECOMMEND [redacted]ING ME NOW-LY, BEFORE I REMEMBER HOW SELF-CONSCIOUS I SHOULD BE ABOUT WAVING MY CHUBBY ASS IN THE AIR LIKE THIS...!
I CONCUR, BABY --JUST LET ME GET MY PANTS OFF--!
SHE DOES GET WORRIED THAT HER SUPERSUIT'S SOMEHOW MAKING HER INTO SUCH A HORNY LI'L BUNNY, THOUGH.
HEY, HOWEVER IT WORKS, I'M LOVIN' IT.
WELL, [redacted], MAN...

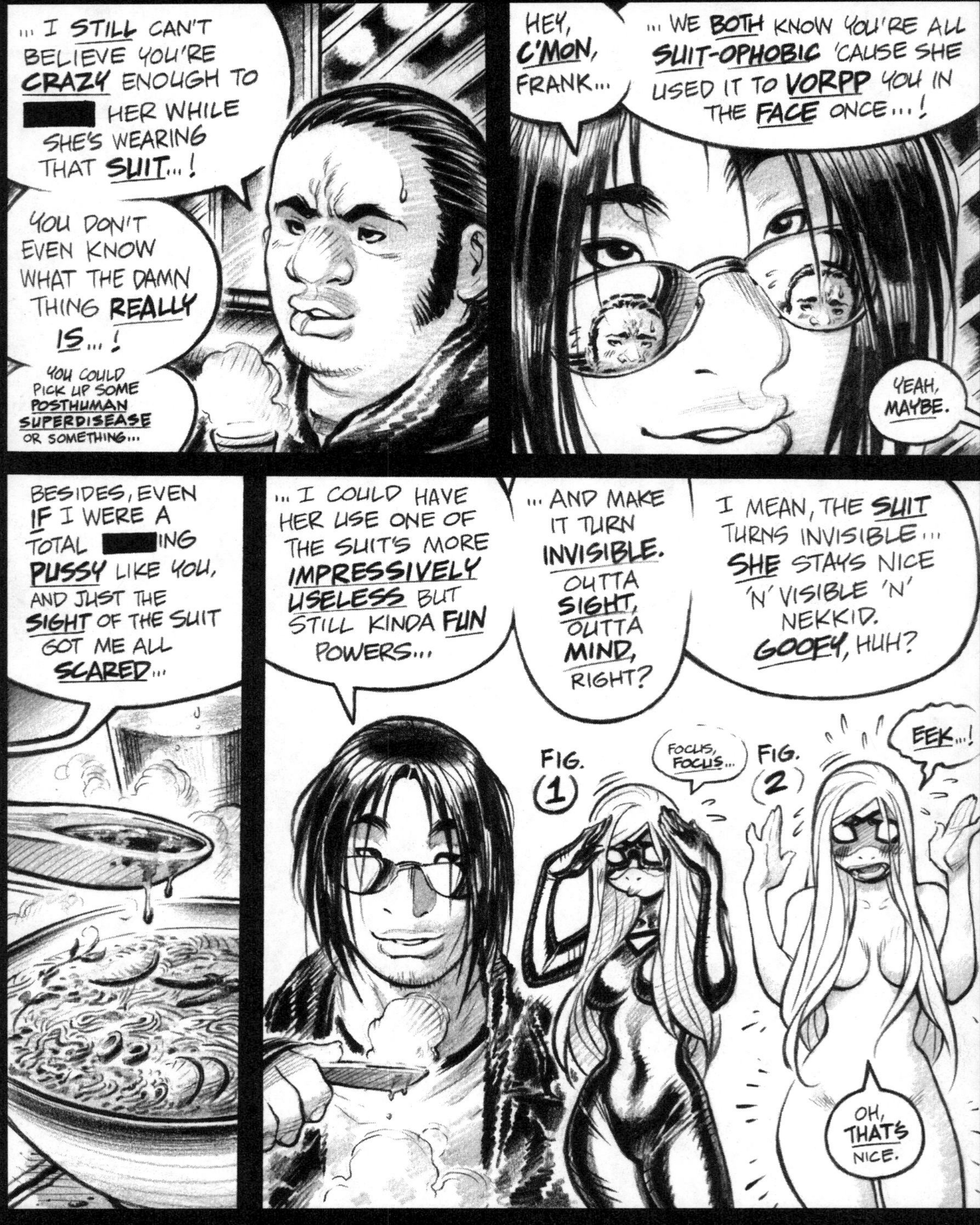
... I STILL CAN'T BELIEVE YOU'RE CRAZY ENOUGH TO [redacted] HER WHILE SHE'S WEARING THAT SUIT...!
YOU DON'T EVEN KNOW WHAT THE DAMN THING REALLY IS...!
YOU COULD PICK UP SOME POSTHUMAN SUPERDISEASE OR SOMETHING...
HEY, C'MON, FRANK...
... WE BOTH KNOW YOU'RE ALL SUIT-OPHOBIC 'CAUSE SHE USED IT TO VORPP YOU IN THE FACE ONCE...!
YEAH, MAYBE.
BESIDES, EVEN IF I WERE A TOTAL [redacted]ING PUSSY LIKE YOU, AND JUST THE SIGHT OF THE SUIT GOT ME ALL SCARED...
... I COULD HAVE HER USE ONE OF THE SUIT'S MORE IMPRESSIVELY USELESS BUT STILL KINDA FUN POWERS...
... AND MAKE IT TURN INVISIBLE. OUTTA SIGHT, OUTTA MIND, RIGHT?
I MEAN, THE SUIT TURNS INVISIBLE... SHE STAYS NICE 'N' VISIBLE 'N' NEKKID. GOOFY, HUH?
FIG. 1
FOCUS, FOCUS...
FIG. 2
EEK...!
OH, THAT'S NICE.

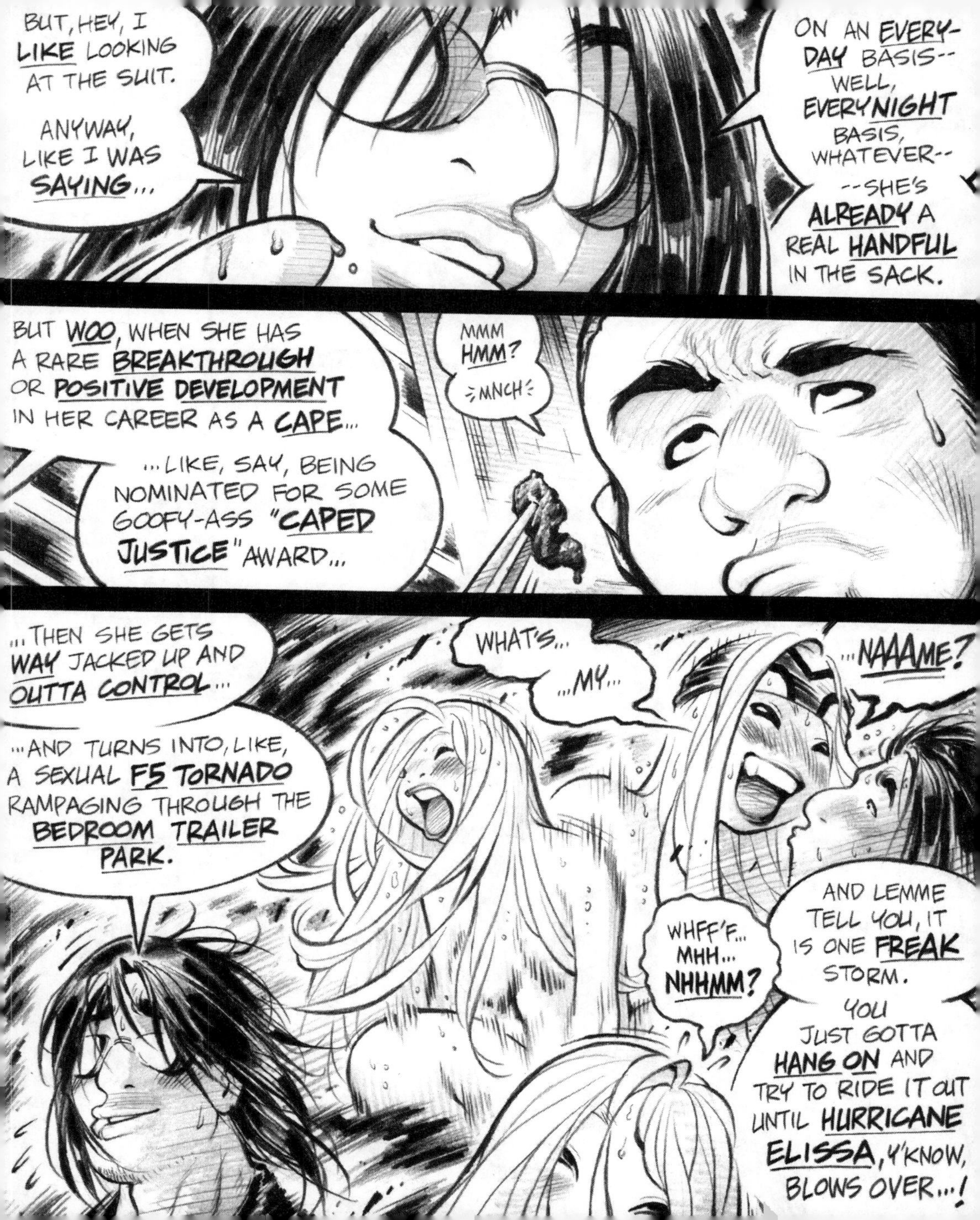
BUT, HEY, I LIKE LOOKING AT THE SUIT.
ANYWAY, LIKE I WAS SAYING...
ON AN EVERY-DAY BASIS-- WELL, EVERYNIGHT BASIS, WHATEVER--
--SHE'S ALREADY A REAL HANDFUL IN THE SACK.
BUT WOO, WHEN SHE HAS A RARE BREAKTHROUGH OR POSITIVE DEVELOPMENT IN HER CAREER AS A CAPE...
...LIKE, SAY, BEING NOMINATED FOR SOME GOOFY-ASS "CAPED JUSTICE" AWARD...
MMM HMM?
MNCH
...THEN SHE GETS WAY JACKED UP AND OUTTA CONTROL...
...AND TURNS INTO, LIKE, A SEXUAL F5 TORNADO RAMPAGING THROUGH THE BEDROOM TRAILER PARK.
WHAT'S...
...MY...
...NAAAME?
WHFF'F... MHH... NHHMM?
AND LEMME TELL YOU, IT IS ONE FREAK STORM.
YOU JUST GOTTA HANG ON AND TRY TO RIDE IT OUT UNTIL HURRICANE ELISSA, Y'KNOW, BLOWS OVER...!

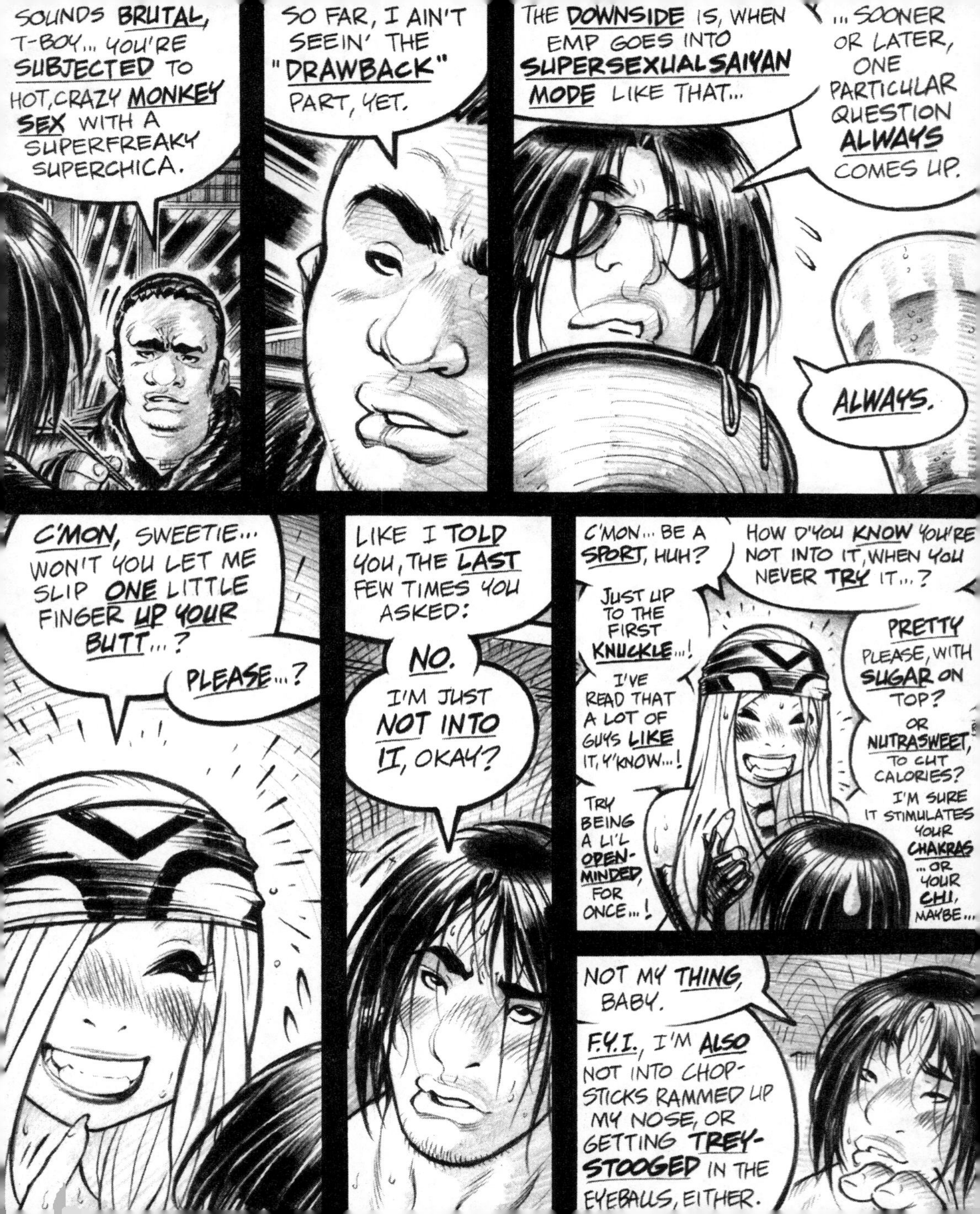
SOUNDS BRUTAL, T-BOY... YOU'RE SUBJECTED TO HOT, CRAZY MONKEY SEX WITH A SUPERFREAKY SUPERCHICA.
SO FAR, I AIN'T SEEIN' THE "DRAWBACK" PART, YET.
THE DOWNSIDE IS, WHEN EMP GOES INTO SUPERSEXUALSAIYAN MODE LIKE THAT...
...SOONER OR LATER, ONE PARTICULAR QUESTION ALWAYS COMES UP.
ALWAYS.
C'MON, SWEETIE... WON'T YOU LET ME SLIP ONE LITTLE FINGER UP YOUR BUTT...?
PLEASE...?
LIKE I TOLD YOU, THE LAST FEW TIMES YOU ASKED:
NO.
I'M JUST NOT INTO IT, OKAY?
C'MON... BE A SPORT, HUH?
JUST UP TO THE FIRST KNUCKLE...!
I'VE READ THAT A LOT OF GUYS LIKE IT, Y'KNOW...!
TRY BEING A LI'L OPEN-MINDED, FOR ONCE...!
HOW D'YOU KNOW YOU'RE NOT INTO IT, WHEN YOU NEVER TRY IT...?
PRETTY PLEASE, WITH SUGAR ON TOP?
OR NUTRASWEET, TO CUT CALORIES?
I'M SURE IT STIMULATES YOUR CHAKRAS ...OR YOUR CHI, MAYBE...
NOT MY THING, BABY.
F.Y.I., I'M ALSO NOT INTO CHOP-STICKS RAMMED UP MY NOSE, OR GETTING TREY-STOOGED IN THE EYEBALLS, EITHER.

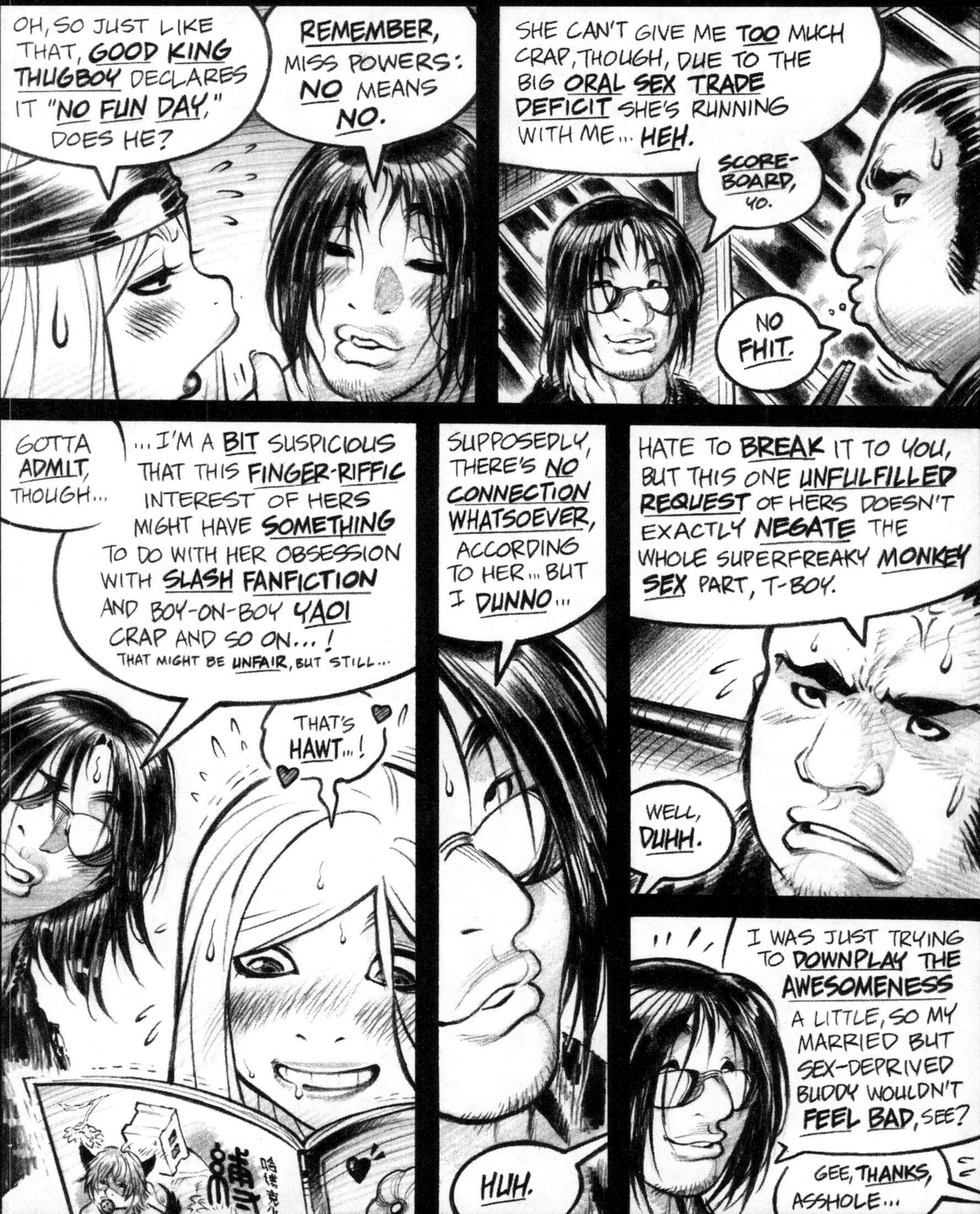
OH, SO JUST LIKE THAT, GOOD KING THUGBOY DECLARES IT "NO FUN DAY," DOES HE?
REMEMBER, MISS POWERS: NO MEANS NO.
SHE CAN'T GIVE ME TOO MUCH CRAP, THOUGH, DUE TO THE BIG ORAL SEX TRADE DEFICIT SHE'S RUNNING WITH ME... HEH.
SCORE-BOARD, YO.
NO FHIT.
GOTTA ADMIT, THOUGH...
...I'M A BIT SUSPICIOUS THAT THIS FINGER-RIFFIC INTEREST OF HERS MIGHT HAVE SOMETHING TO DO WITH HER OBSESSION WITH SLASH FANFICTION AND BOY-ON-BOY YAOI CRAP AND SO ON...! THAT MIGHT BE UNFAIR, BUT STILL...
THAT'S HAWT...!
SUPPOSEDLY, THERE'S NO CONNECTION WHATSOEVER, ACCORDING TO HER... BUT I DUNNO...
HUH.
HATE TO BREAK IT TO YOU, BUT THIS ONE UNFULFILLED REQUEST OF HERS DOESN'T EXACTLY NEGATE THE WHOLE SUPERFREAKY MONKEY SEX PART, T-BOY.
WELL, DUHH.
I WAS JUST TRYING TO DOWNPLAY THE AWESOMENESS A LITTLE, SO MY MARRIED BUT SEX-DEPRIVED BUDDY WOULDN'T FEEL BAD, SEE?
GEE, THANKS, ASSHOLE...

eMpoWered ™

Orbiting Spookums

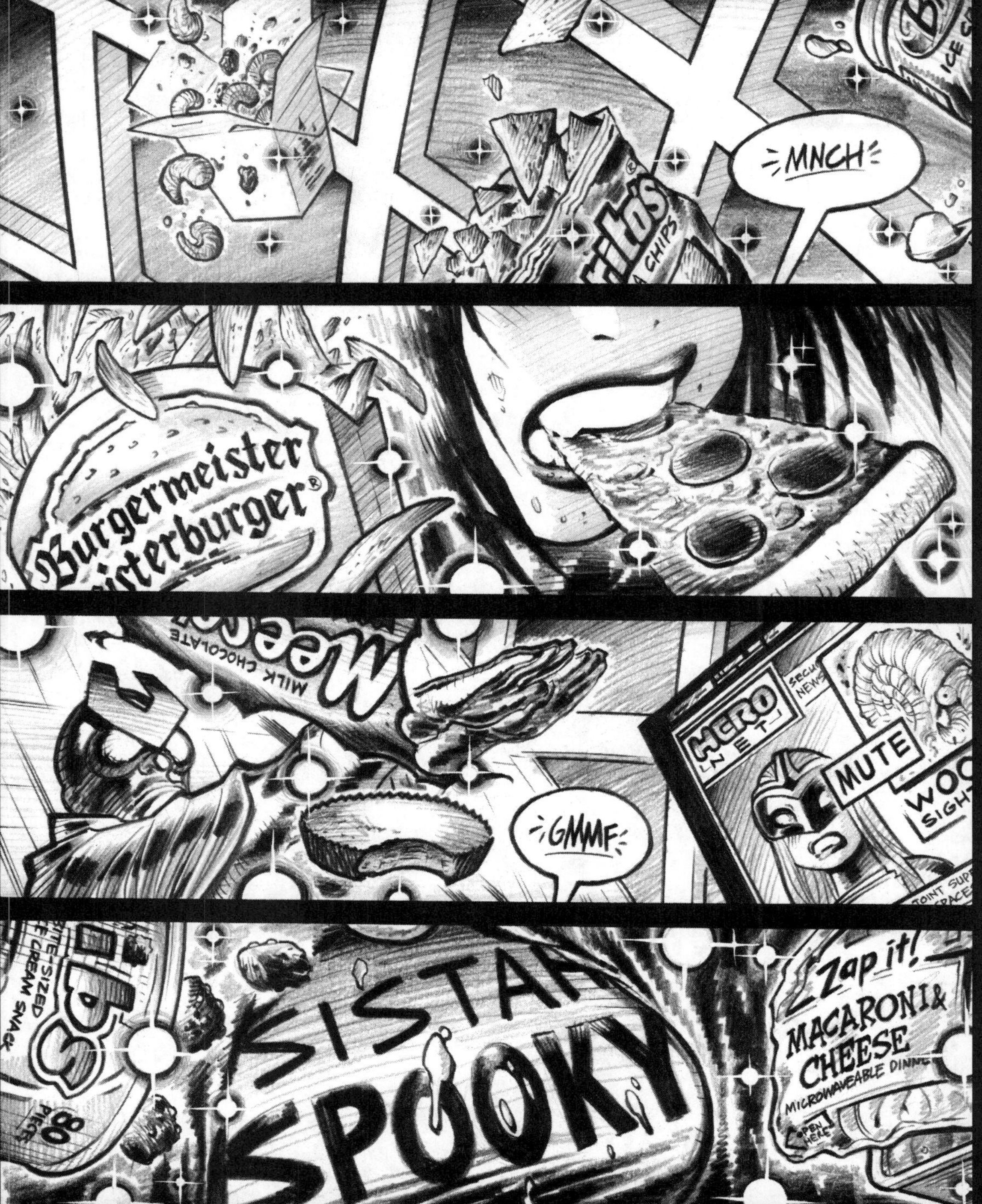

MNCH
CHIPS
Burgermeister
MILK CHOCOLATE
GMMF
MUTE
BITE-SIZED
CREAM SNACK
PIECE
SPOOKY
Zap it!
MACARONI & CHEESE
MICROWAVEABLE
OPEN HERE

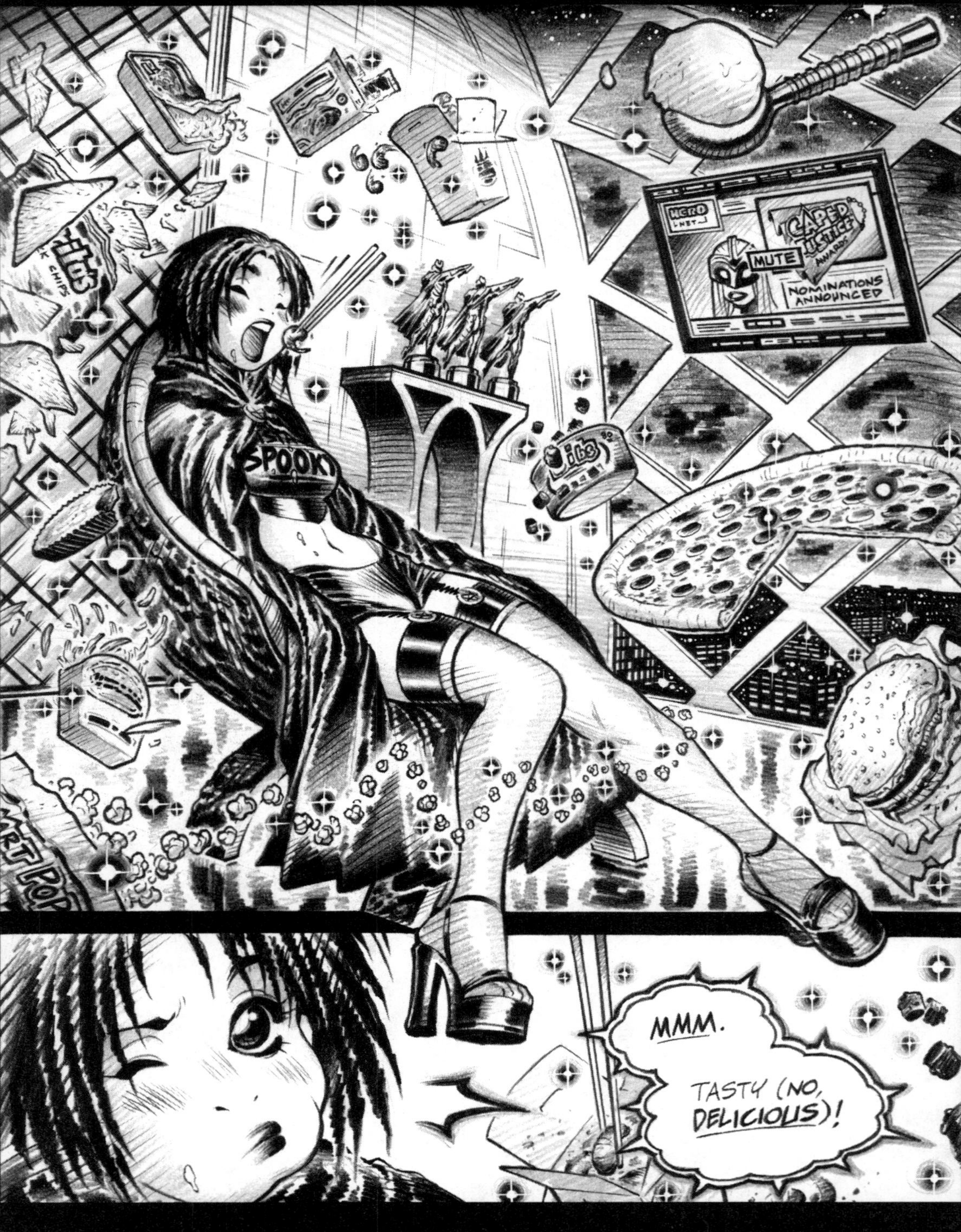
HERO NET
CAPED JUSTICE AWARDS
MUTE
NOMINATIONS ANNOUNCED
SPOOKY
MMM.
TASTY (NO, DELICIOUS)!

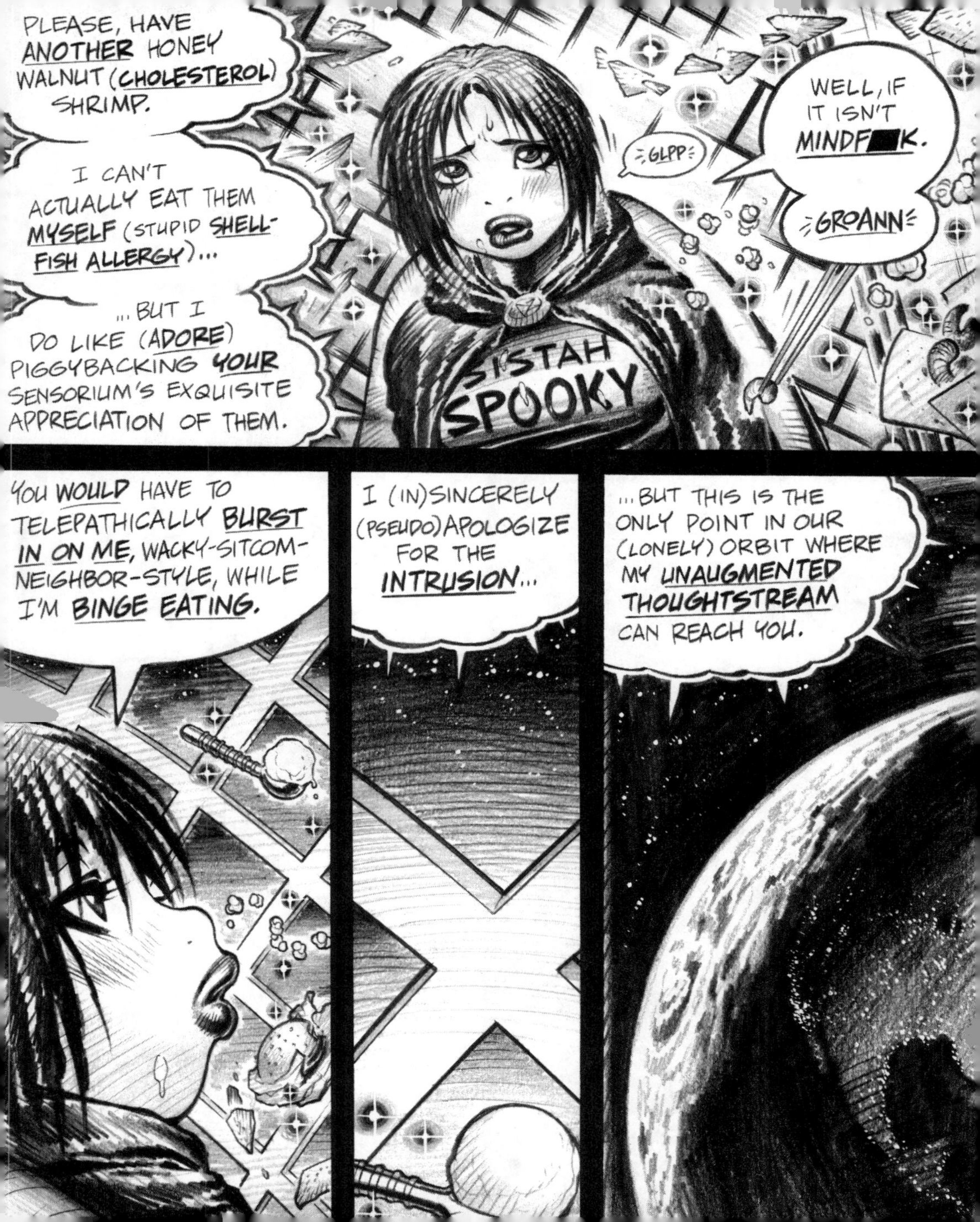
PLEASE, HAVE ANOTHER HONEY WALNUT (CHOLESTEROL) SHRIMP.
I CAN'T ACTUALLY EAT THEM MYSELF (STUPID SHELL-FISH ALLERGY)...
...BUT I DO LIKE (ADORE) PIGGYBACKING YOUR SENSORIUM'S EXQUISITE APPRECIATION OF THEM.
GLPP
SISTAH SPOOKY
WELL, IF IT ISN'T MINDF[redacted]K.
GROANN
YOU WOULD HAVE TO TELEPATHICALLY BURST IN ON ME, WACKY-SITCOM-NEIGHBOR-STYLE, WHILE I'M BINGE EATING.
I (IN)SINCERELY (PSEUDO)APOLOGIZE FOR THE INTRUSION...
...BUT THIS IS THE ONLY POINT IN OUR (LONELY) ORBIT WHERE MY UNAUGMENTED THOUGHTSTREAM CAN REACH YOU.

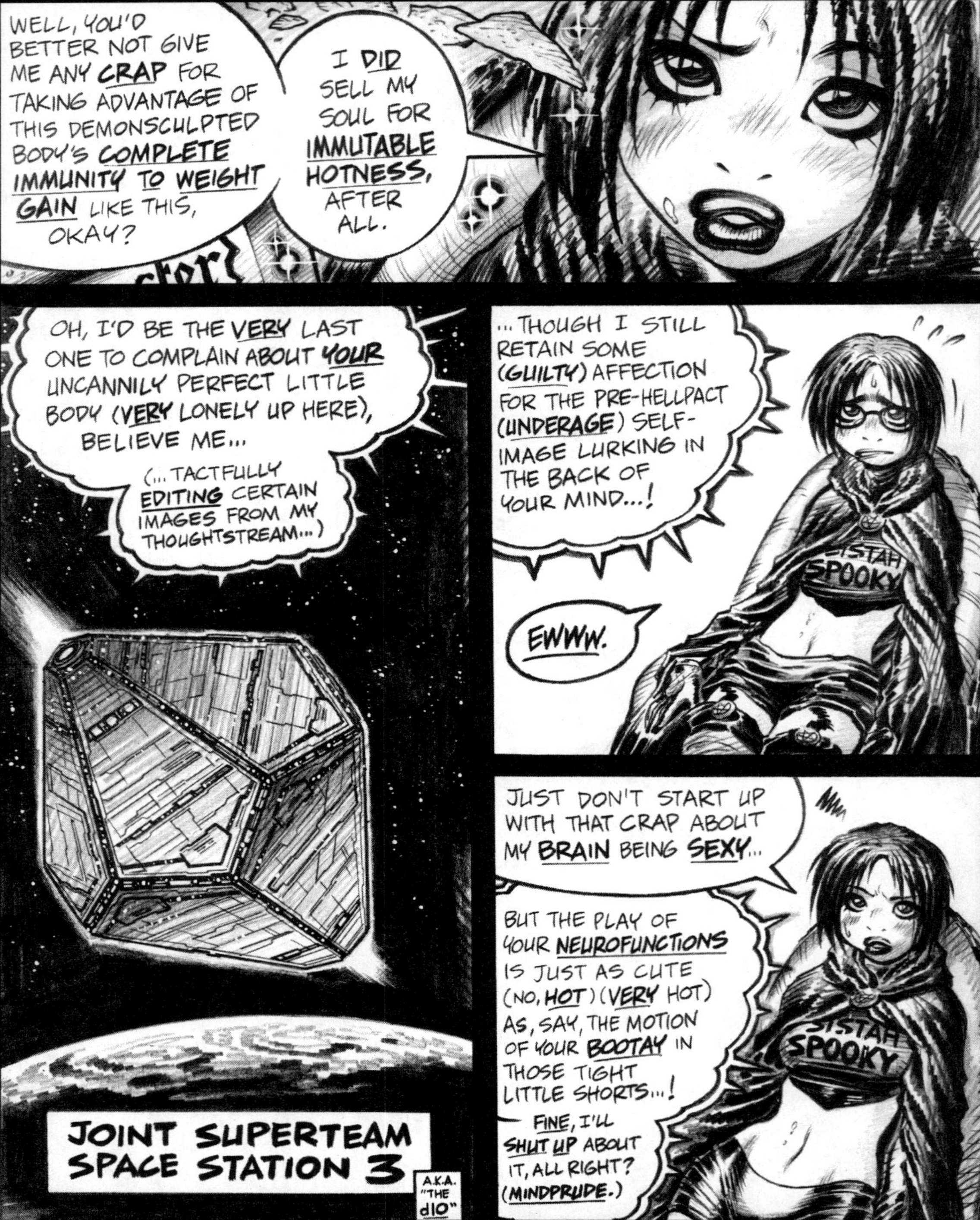

WELL, YOU'D BETTER NOT GIVE ME ANY CRAP FOR TAKING ADVANTAGE OF THIS DEMONSCULPTED BODY'S COMPLETE IMMUNITY TO WEIGHT GAIN LIKE THIS, OKAY?
I DID SELL MY SOUL FOR IMMUTABLE HOTNESS, AFTER ALL.
OH, I'D BE THE VERY LAST ONE TO COMPLAIN ABOUT YOUR UNCANNILY PERFECT LITTLE BODY (VERY LONELY UP HERE), BELIEVE ME...
(...TACTFULLY EDITING CERTAIN IMAGES FROM MY THOUGHTSTREAM...)
JOINT SUPERTEAM SPACE STATION 3
A.K.A. "THE d10"
...THOUGH I STILL RETAIN SOME (GUILTY) AFFECTION FOR THE PRE-HELLPACT (UNDERAGE) SELF-IMAGE LURKING IN THE BACK OF YOUR MIND...!
SISTAH SPOOKY
EWWW.
JUST DON'T START UP WITH THAT CRAP ABOUT MY BRAIN BEING SEXY...
BUT THE PLAY OF YOUR NEUROFUNCTIONS IS JUST AS CUTE (NO, HOT) (VERY HOT) AS, SAY, THE MOTION OF YOUR BOOTAY IN THOSE TIGHT LITTLE SHORTS...!
SISTAH SPOOKY
FINE, I'LL SHUT UP ABOUT IT, ALL RIGHT? (MINDPRUDE.)

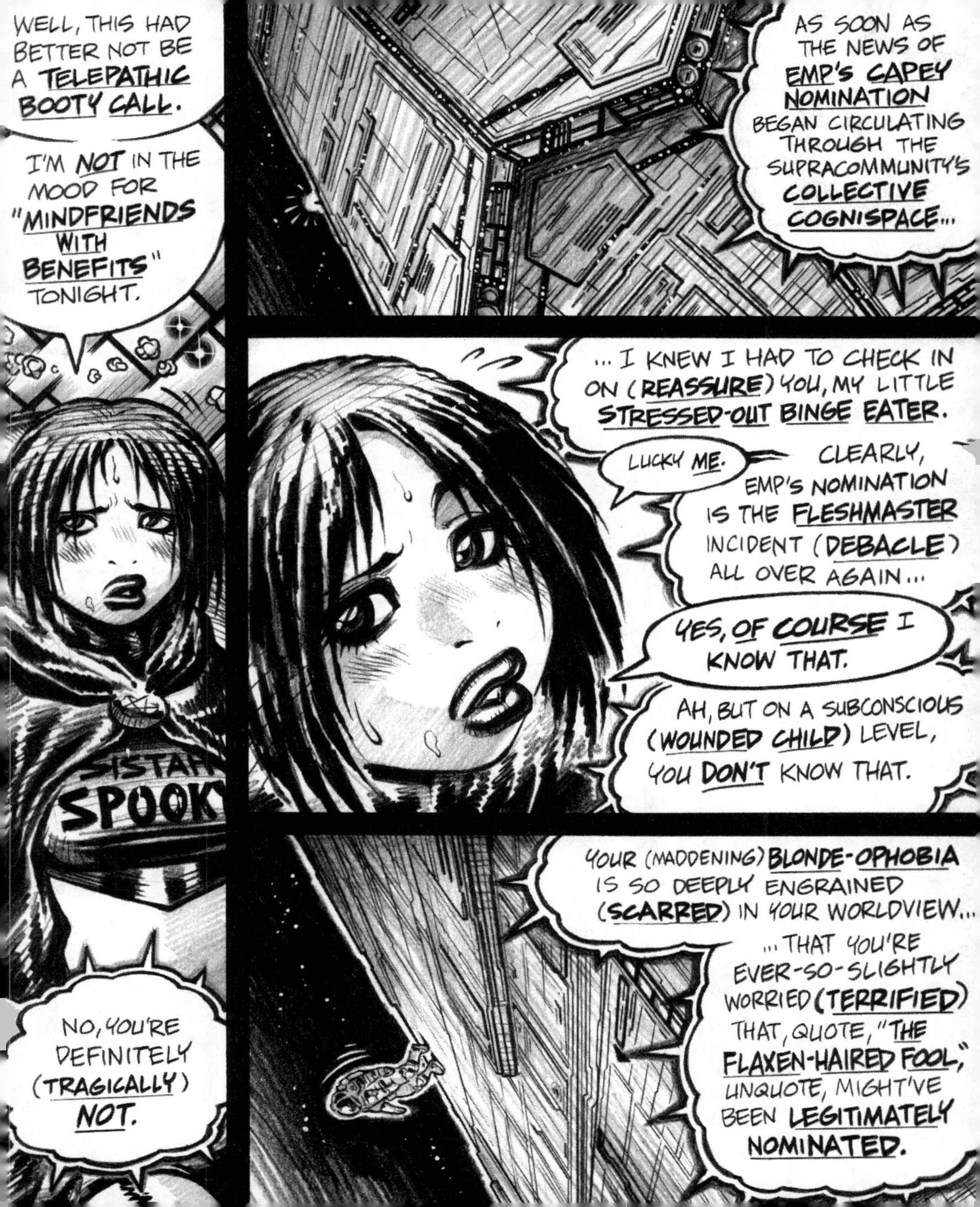
WELL, THIS HAD BETTER NOT BE A TELEPATHIC BOOTY CALL.
I'M NOT IN THE MOOD FOR "MINDFRIENDS WITH BENEFITS" TONIGHT.
AS SOON AS THE NEWS OF EMP'S CAPEY NOMINATION BEGAN CIRCULATING THROUGH THE SUPRACOMMUNITY'S COLLECTIVE COGNISPACE...
SISTAH SPOOKY
...I KNEW I HAD TO CHECK IN ON (REASSURE) YOU, MY LITTLE STRESSED-OUT BINGE EATER.
LUCKY ME.
CLEARLY, EMP'S NOMINATION IS THE FLESHMASTER INCIDENT (DEBACLE) ALL OVER AGAIN...
YES, OF COURSE I KNOW THAT.
AH, BUT ON A SUBCONSCIOUS (WOUNDED CHILD) LEVEL, YOU DON'T KNOW THAT.
NO, YOU'RE DEFINITELY (TRAGICALLY) NOT.
YOUR (MADDENING) BLONDE-OPHOBIA IS SO DEEPLY ENGRAINED (SCARRED) IN YOUR WORLDVIEW...
...THAT YOU'RE EVER-SO-SLIGHTLY WORRIED (TERRIFIED) THAT, QUOTE, "THE FLAXEN-HAIRED FOOL," UNQUOTE, MIGHT'VE BEEN LEGITIMATELY NOMINATED.

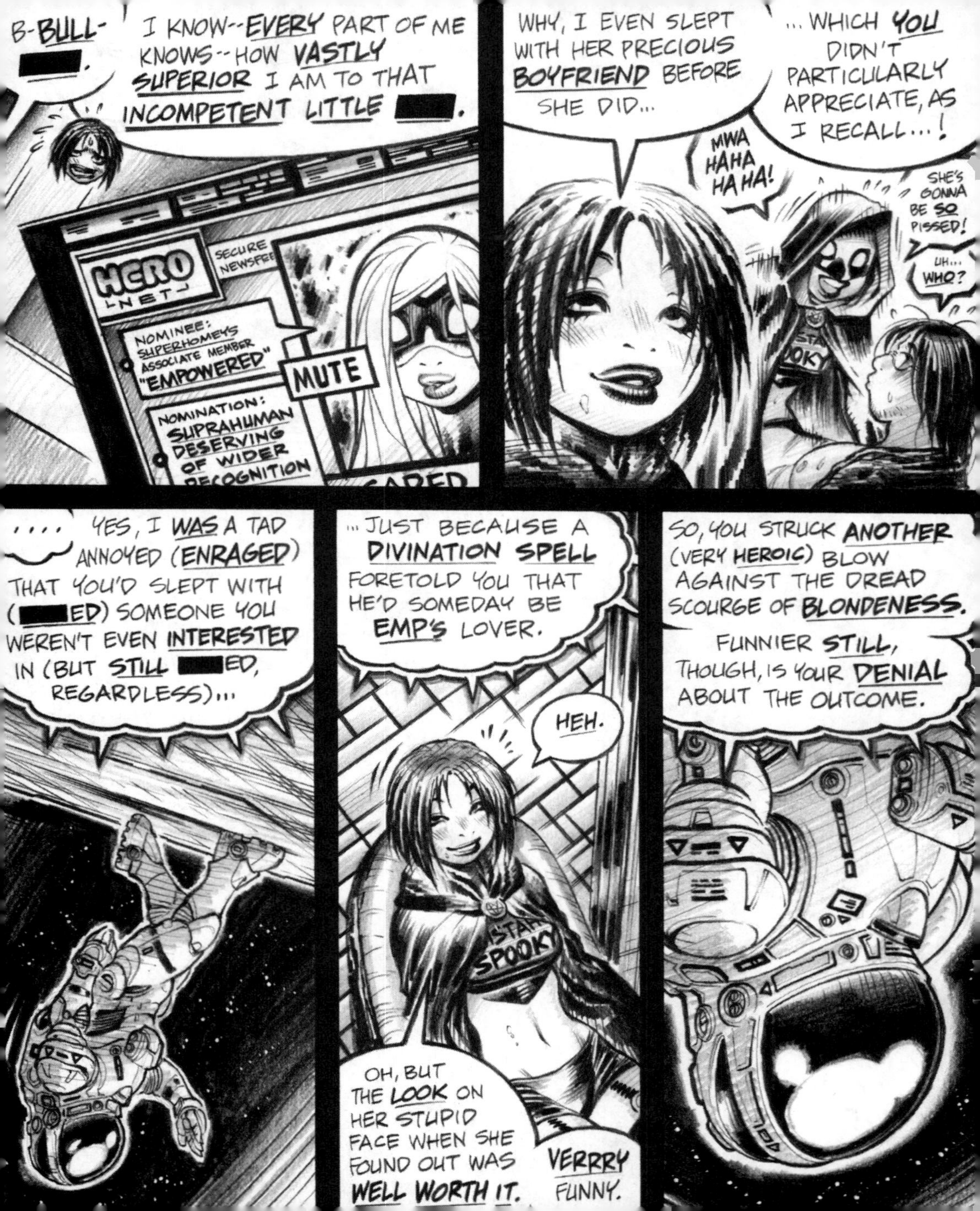

B-BULL-[redacted].
I KNOW--EVERY PART OF ME KNOWS--HOW VASTLY SUPERIOR I AM TO THAT INCOMPETENT LITTLE [redacted].
HERO NET
SECURE NEWSFEE
NOMINEE: SUPERHOMEYS ASSOCIATE MEMBER "EMPOWERED"
MUTE
NOMINATION: SUPRAHUMAN DESERVING OF WIDER RECOGNITION
WHY, I EVEN SLEPT WITH HER PRECIOUS BOYFRIEND BEFORE SHE DID...
...WHICH YOU DIDN'T PARTICULARLY APPRECIATE, AS I RECALL...!
MWA HAHA HAHA HA HA!
SHE'S GONNA BE SO PISSED!
UH... WHO?
....
YES, I WAS A TAD ANNOYED (ENRAGED) THAT YOU'D SLEPT WITH ([redacted]ED) SOMEONE YOU WEREN'T EVEN INTERESTED IN (BUT STILL [redacted]ED, REGARDLESS)...
...JUST BECAUSE A DIVINATION SPELL FORETOLD YOU THAT HE'D SOMEDAY BE EMP'S LOVER.
HEH.
SPOOKY
OH, BUT THE LOOK ON HER STUPID FACE WHEN SHE FOUND OUT WAS WELL WORTH IT.
VERRRY FUNNY.
SO, YOU STRUCK ANOTHER (VERY HEROIC) BLOW AGAINST THE DREAD SCOURGE OF BLONDENESS.
FUNNIER STILL, THOUGH, IS YOUR DENIAL ABOUT THE OUTCOME.

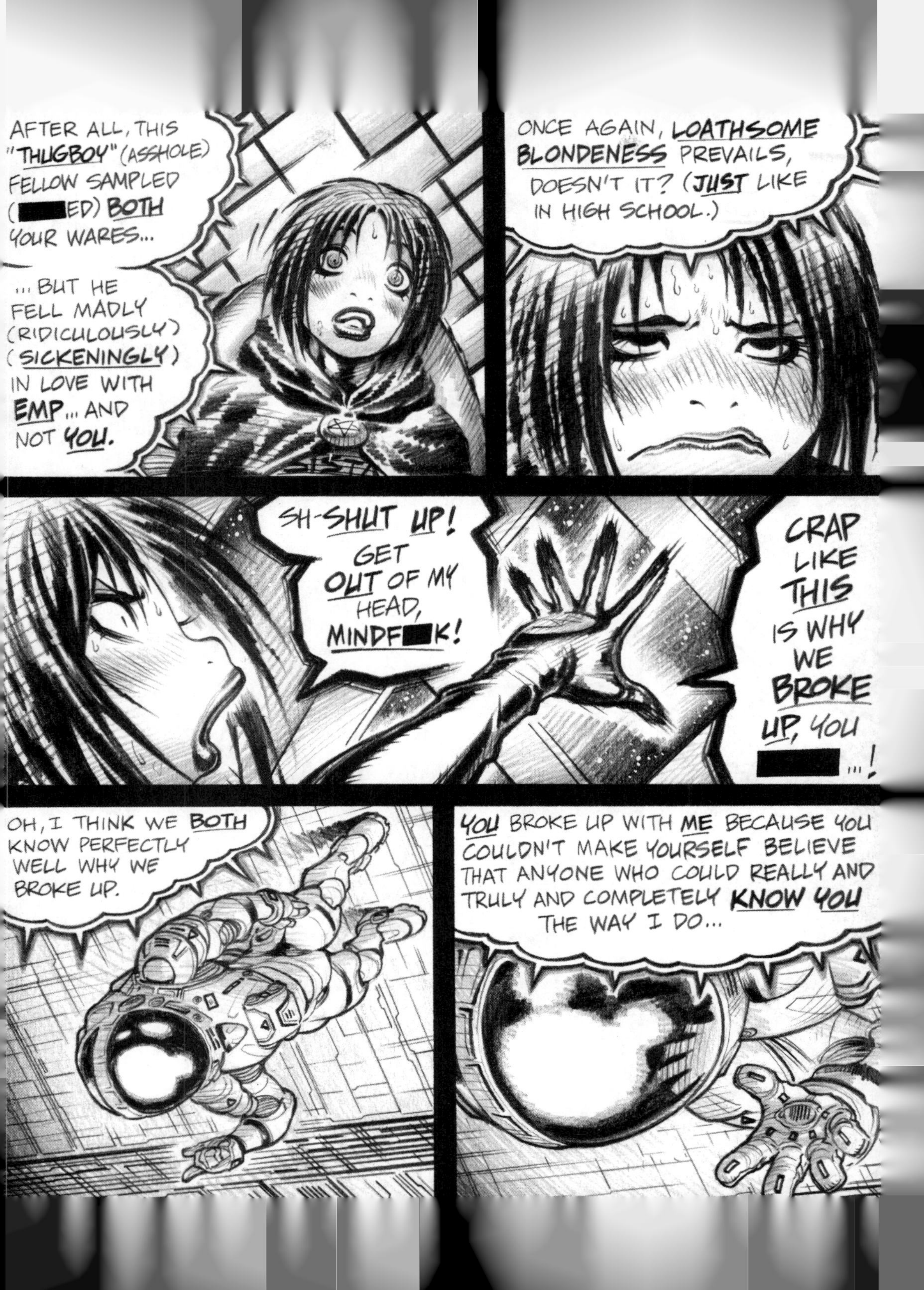
AFTER ALL, THIS "THUGBOY" (ASSHOLE) FELLOW SAMPLED ([redacted]ED) BOTH YOUR WARES...
... BUT HE FELL MADLY (RIDICULOUSLY) (SICKENINGLY) IN LOVE WITH EMP... AND NOT YOU.
ONCE AGAIN, LOATHSOME BLONDENESS PREVAILS, DOESN'T IT? (JUST LIKE IN HIGH SCHOOL.)
SH-SHUT UP! GET OUT OF MY HEAD, MINDF[redacted]K!
CRAP LIKE THIS IS WHY WE BROKE UP, YOU [redacted]...!
OH, I THINK WE BOTH KNOW PERFECTLY WELL WHY WE BROKE UP.
YOU BROKE UP WITH ME BECAUSE YOU COULDN'T MAKE YOURSELF BELIEVE THAT ANYONE WHO COULD REALLY AND TRULY AND COMPLETELY KNOW YOU THE WAY I DO...

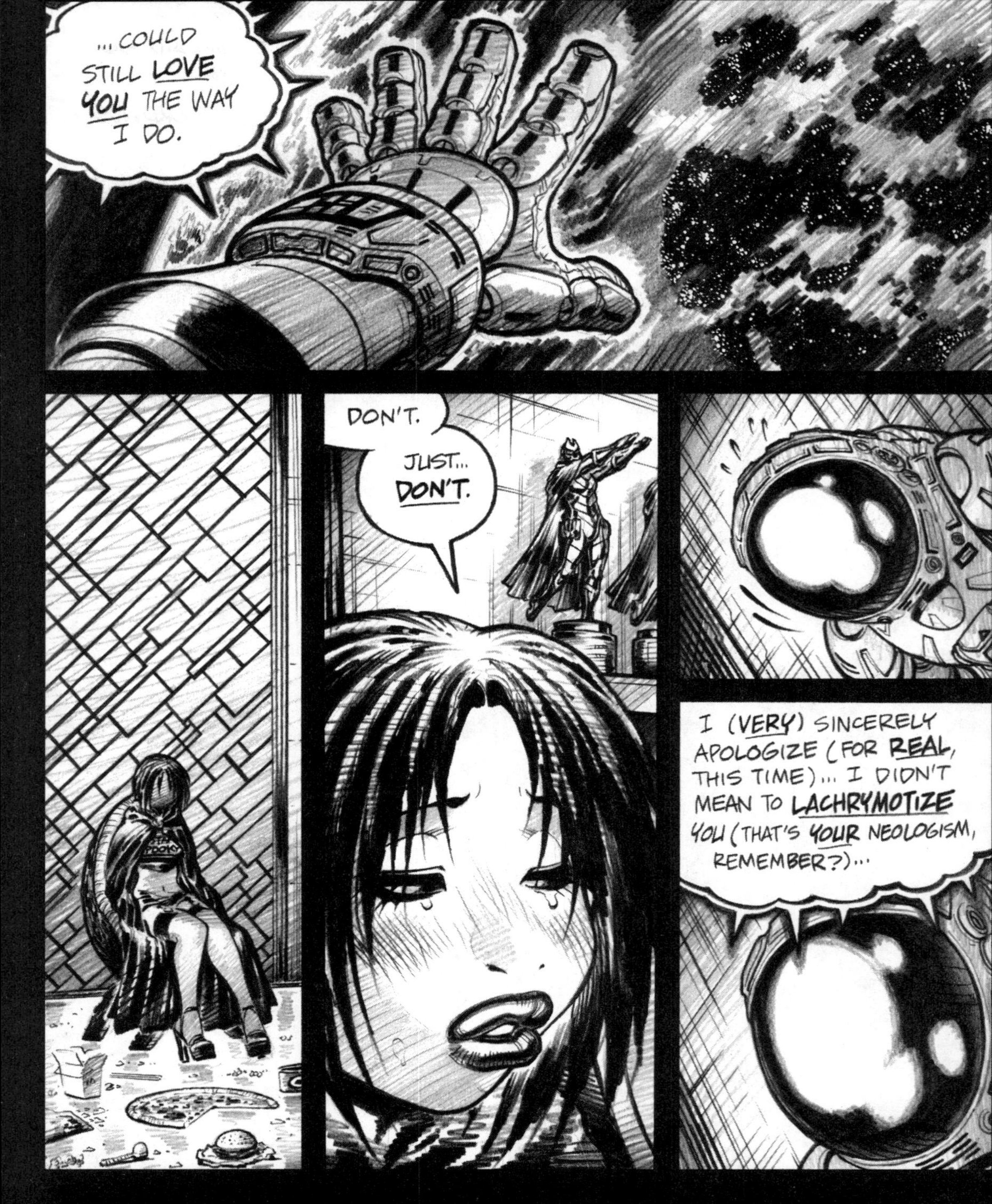
...COULD STILL LOVE YOU THE WAY I DO.
DON'T.
JUST... DON'T.
I (VERY) SINCERELY APOLOGIZE (FOR REAL, THIS TIME)... I DIDN'T MEAN TO LACHRYMOTIZE YOU (THAT'S YOUR NEOLOGISM, REMEMBER?)...

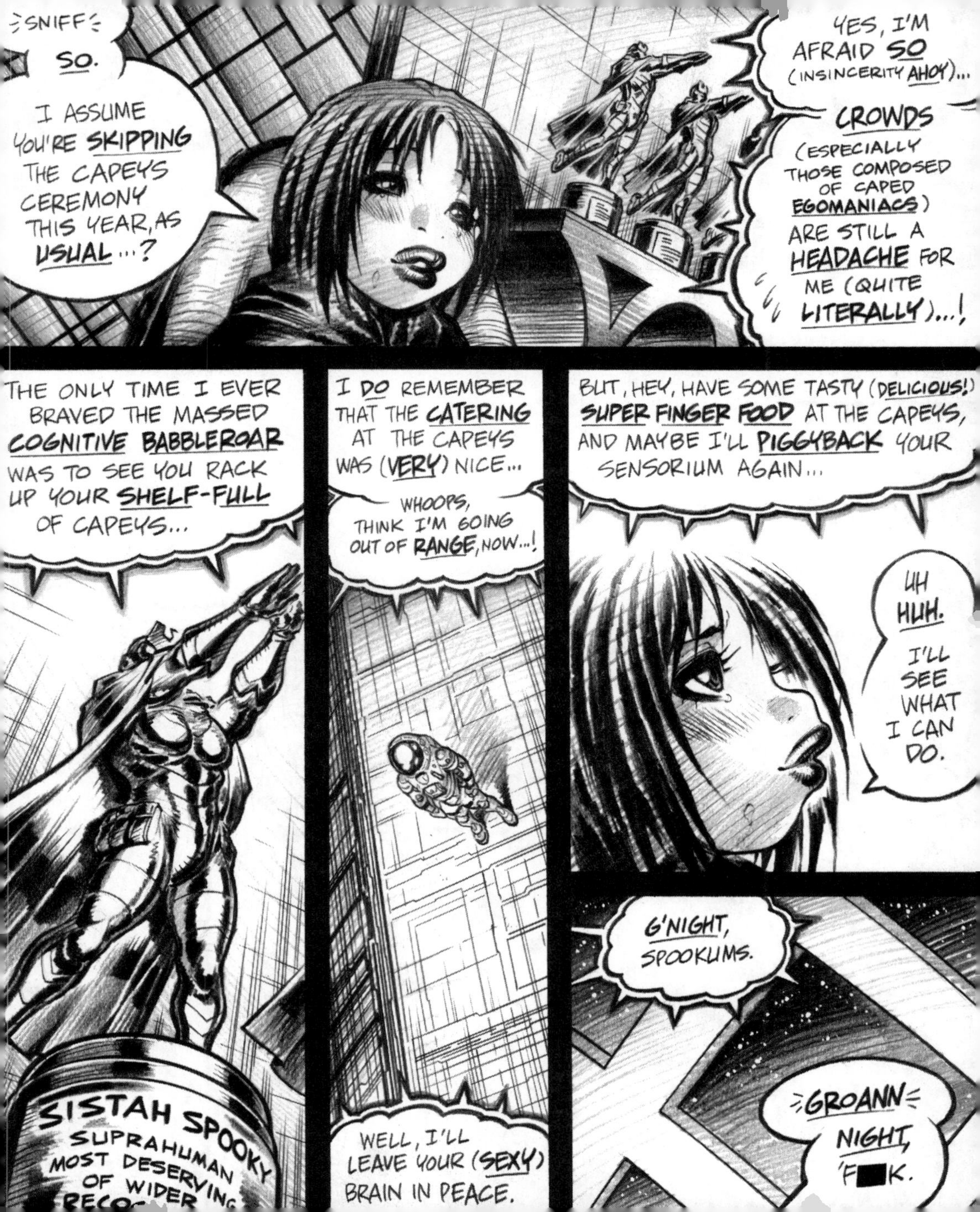

≡SNIFF≡ SO.
I ASSUME YOU'RE SKIPPING THE CAPEYS CEREMONY THIS YEAR, AS USUAL...?
YES, I'M AFRAID SO (INSINCERITY AHOY)...
CROWDS (ESPECIALLY THOSE COMPOSED OF CAPED EGOMANIACS) ARE STILL A HEADACHE FOR ME (QUITE LITERALLY)...!
THE ONLY TIME I EVER BRAVED THE MASSED COGNITIVE BABBLEROAR WAS TO SEE YOU RACK UP YOUR SHELF-FULL OF CAPEYS...
SISTAH SPOOKY
SUPRAHUMAN MOST DESERVING OF WIDER
I DO REMEMBER THAT THE CATERING AT THE CAPEYS WAS (VERY) NICE...
WHOOPS, THINK I'M GOING OUT OF RANGE, NOW...!
WELL, I'LL LEAVE YOUR (SEXY) BRAIN IN PEACE.
BUT, HEY, HAVE SOME TASTY (DELICIOUS!) SUPER FINGER FOOD AT THE CAPEYS, AND MAYBE I'LL PIGGYBACK YOUR SENSORIUM AGAIN...
UH HUH.
I'LL SEE WHAT I CAN DO.
G'NIGHT, SPOOKUMS.
≡GROANN≡
NIGHT, 'F[redacted]K.

eMpoWered

Of Wishes and Mayflies

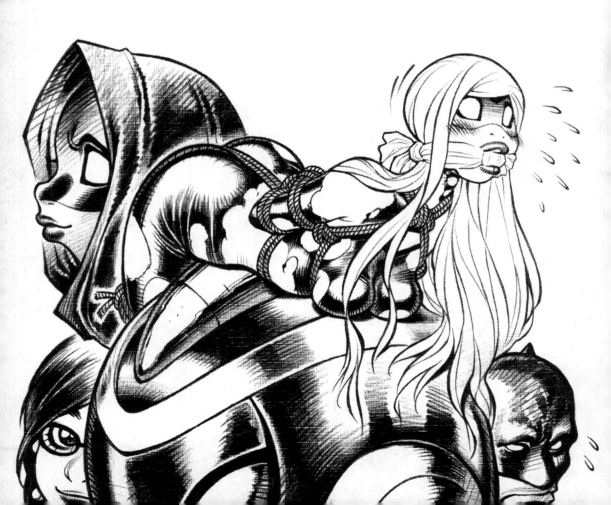

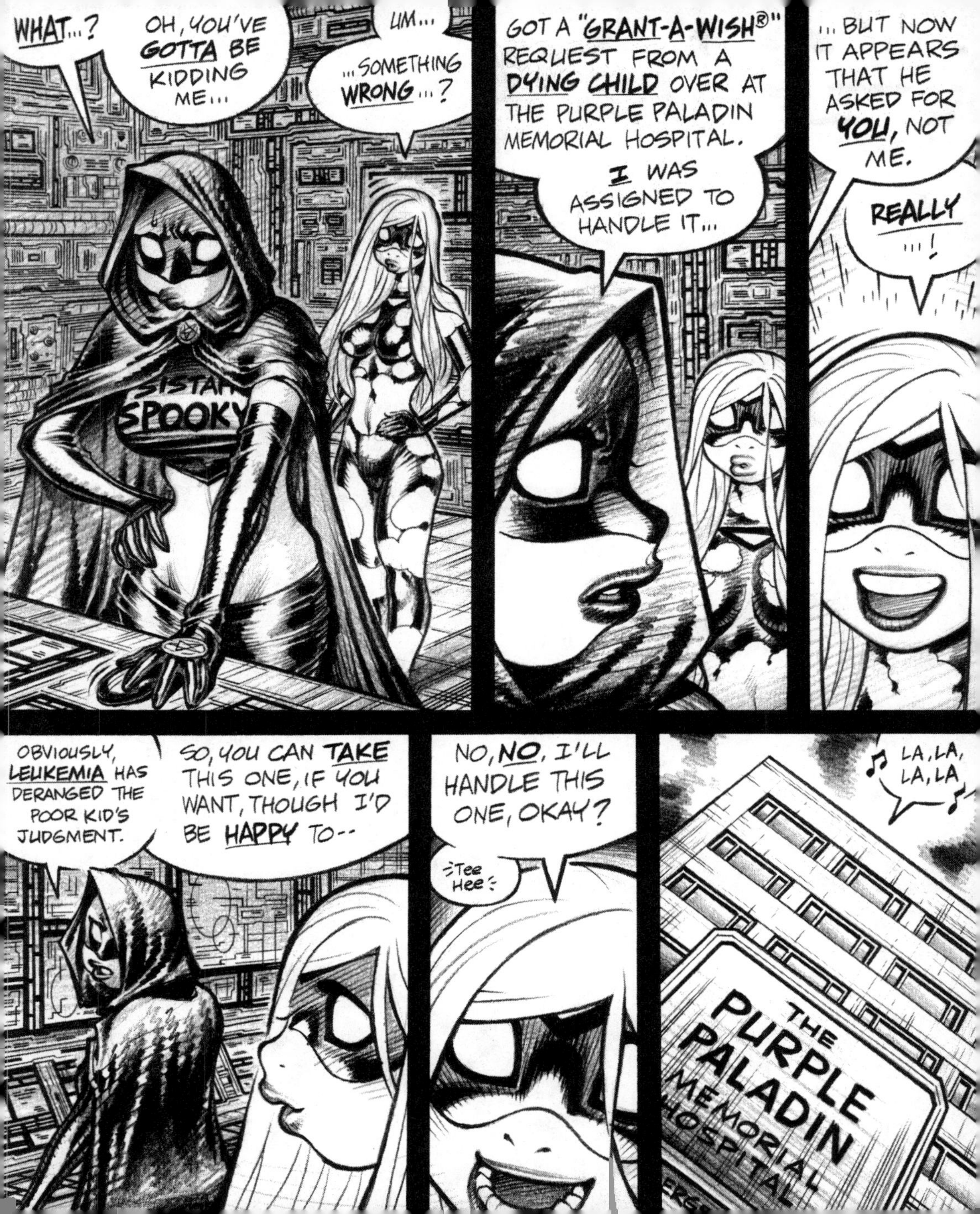
WHAT...?
OH, YOU'VE GOTTA BE KIDDING ME...
UM...
...SOMETHING WRONG...?
SISTAH SPOOKY
GOT A "GRANT-A-WISH®" REQUEST FROM A DYING CHILD OVER AT THE PURPLE PALADIN MEMORIAL HOSPITAL.
I WAS ASSIGNED TO HANDLE IT...
...BUT NOW IT APPEARS THAT HE ASKED FOR YOU, NOT ME.
REALLY...!
OBVIOUSLY, LEUKEMIA HAS DERANGED THE POOR KID'S JUDGMENT.
SO, YOU CAN TAKE THIS ONE, IF YOU WANT, THOUGH I'D BE HAPPY TO--
NO, NO, I'LL HANDLE THIS ONE, OKAY?
Tee Hee
LA, LA, LA, LA
THE PURPLE PALADIN MEMORIAL HOSPITAL

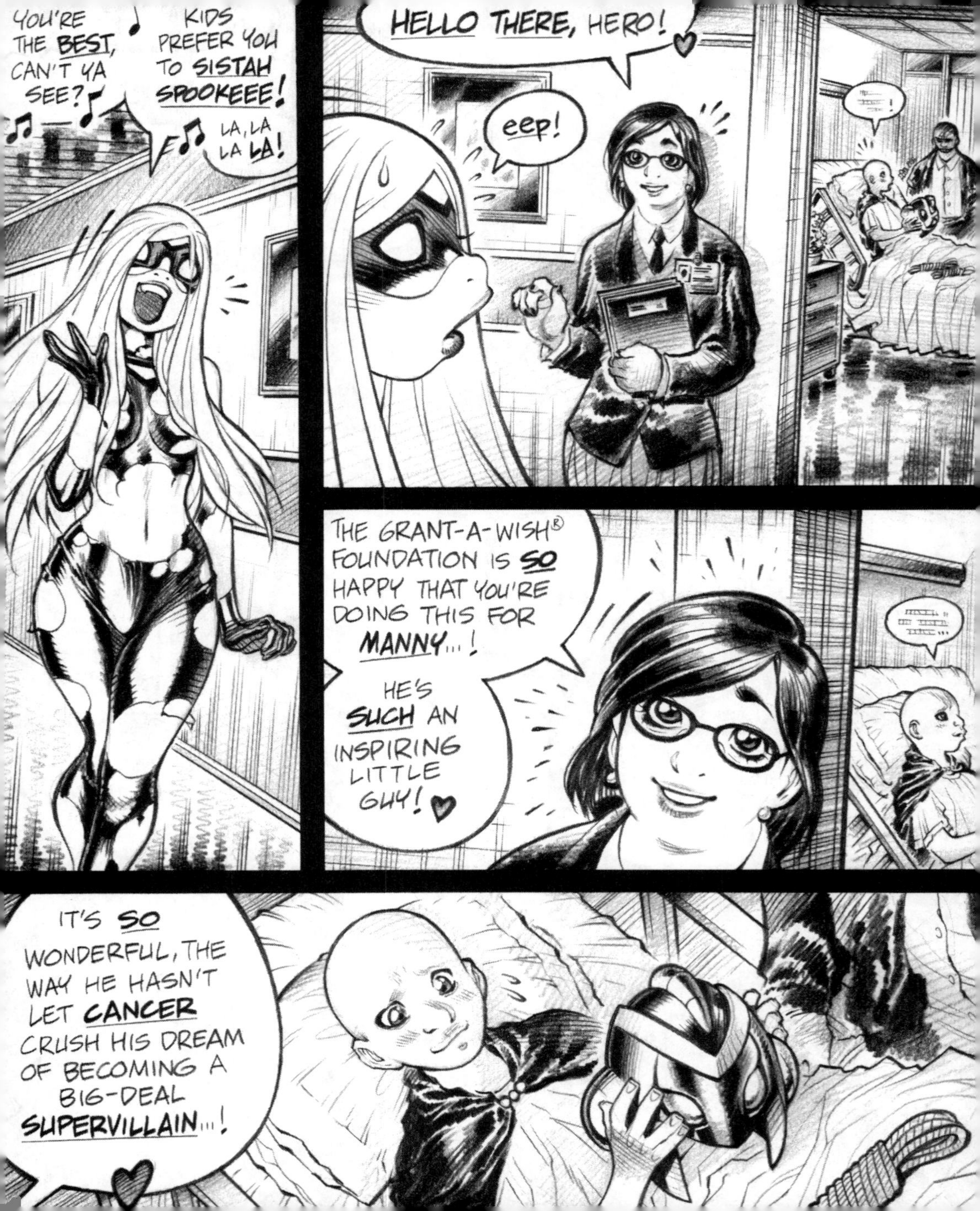
YOU'RE THE BEST, CAN'T YA SEE?
KIDS PREFER YOU TO SISTAH SPOOKEEE!
LA, LA LA LA!
HELLO THERE, HERO!
eep!
THE GRANT-A-WISH® FOUNDATION IS SO HAPPY THAT YOU'RE DOING THIS FOR MANNY...!
HE'S SUCH AN INSPIRING LITTLE GUY!
IT'S SO WONDERFUL, THE WAY HE HASN'T LET CANCER CRUSH HIS DREAM OF BECOMING A BIG-DEAL SUPERVILLAIN...!

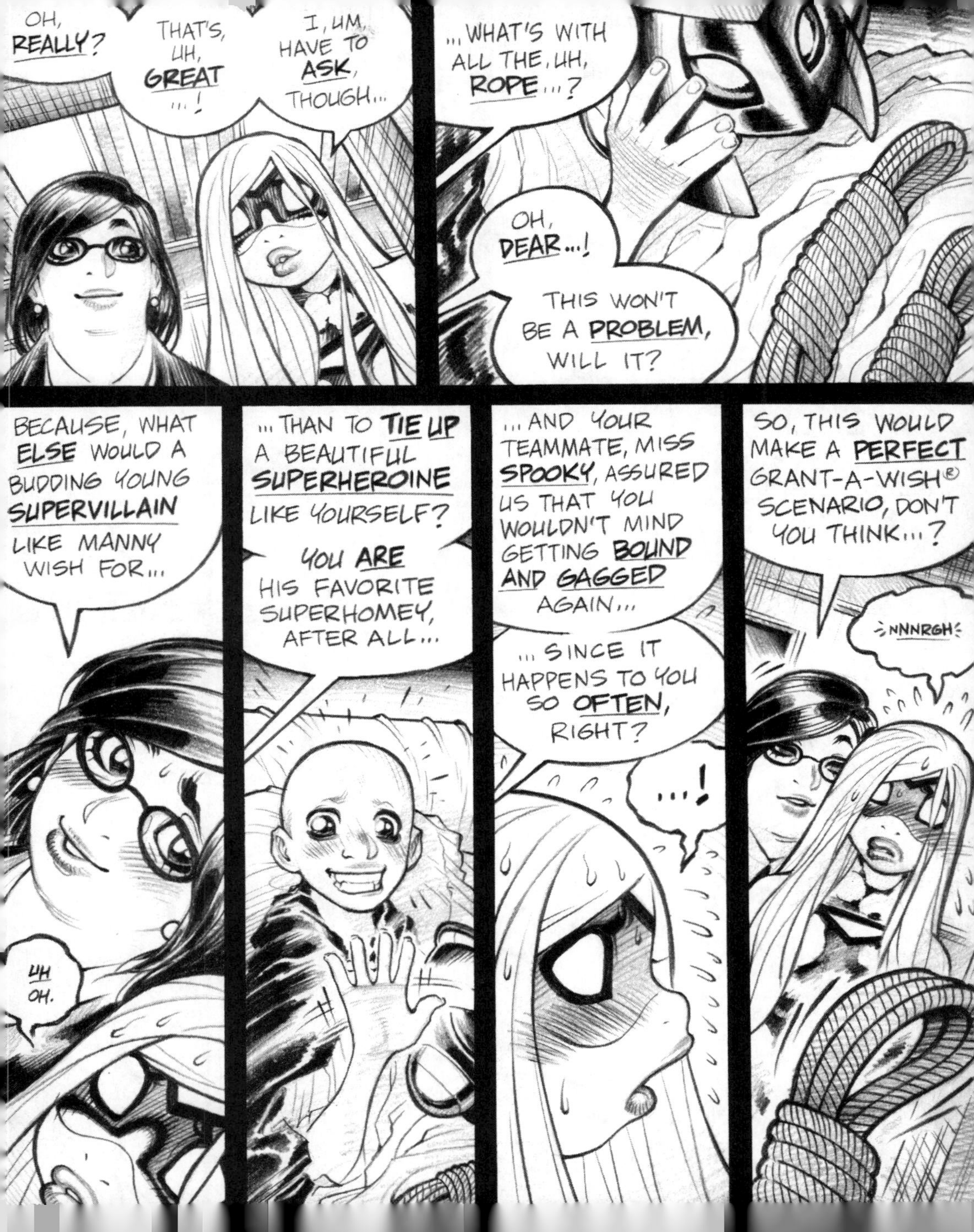
OH, REALLY?
THAT'S, UH, GREAT ...!
I, UM, HAVE TO ASK, THOUGH...
...WHAT'S WITH ALL THE, UH, ROPE...?
OH, DEAR...!
THIS WON'T BE A PROBLEM, WILL IT?
BECAUSE, WHAT ELSE WOULD A BUDDING YOUNG SUPERVILLAIN LIKE MANNY WISH FOR...
UH OH.
...THAN TO TIE UP A BEAUTIFUL SUPERHEROINE LIKE YOURSELF?
YOU ARE HIS FAVORITE SUPERHOMEY, AFTER ALL...
...AND YOUR TEAMMATE, MISS SPOOKY, ASSURED US THAT YOU WOULDN'T MIND GETTING BOUND AND GAGGED AGAIN...
...SINCE IT HAPPENS TO YOU SO OFTEN, RIGHT?
...!
SO, THIS WOULD MAKE A PERFECT GRANT-A-WISH® SCENARIO, DON'T YOU THINK...?
NNNRGH

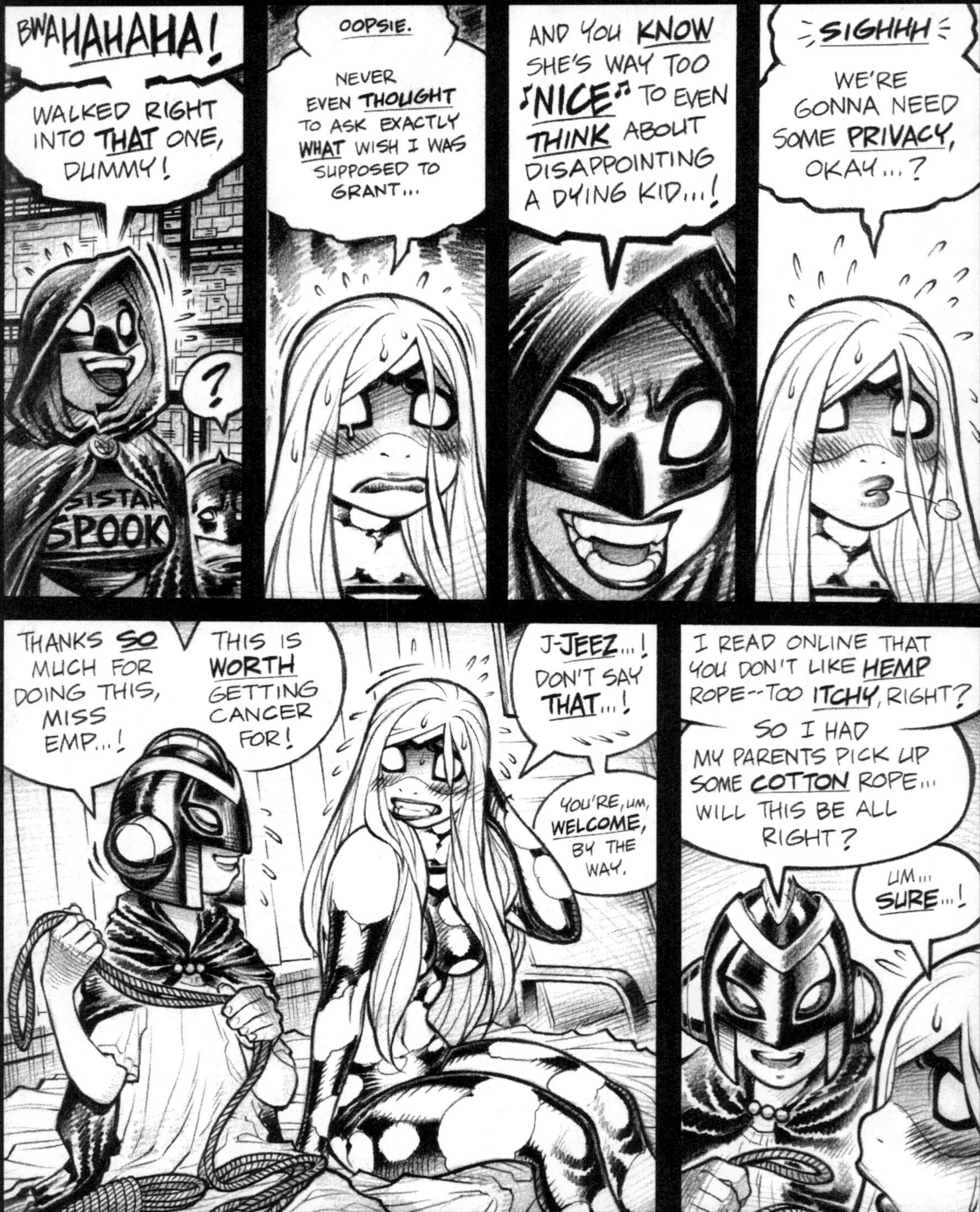
BWAHAHAHA!
WALKED RIGHT INTO THAT ONE, DUMMY!
?
SISTAH SPOOK
OOPSIE.
NEVER EVEN THOUGHT TO ASK EXACTLY WHAT WISH I WAS SUPPOSED TO GRANT...
AND YOU KNOW SHE'S WAY TOO ♪NICE♫ TO EVEN THINK ABOUT DISAPPOINTING A DYING KID...!
SIGHHH
WE'RE GONNA NEED SOME PRIVACY, OKAY...?
THANKS SO MUCH FOR DOING THIS, MISS EMP...!
THIS IS WORTH GETTING CANCER FOR!
J-JEEZ...! DON'T SAY THAT...!
YOU'RE, UM, WELCOME, BY THE WAY.
I READ ONLINE THAT YOU DON'T LIKE HEMP ROPE--TOO ITCHY, RIGHT?
SO I HAD MY PARENTS PICK UP SOME COTTON ROPE... WILL THIS BE ALL RIGHT?
UM... SURE...!

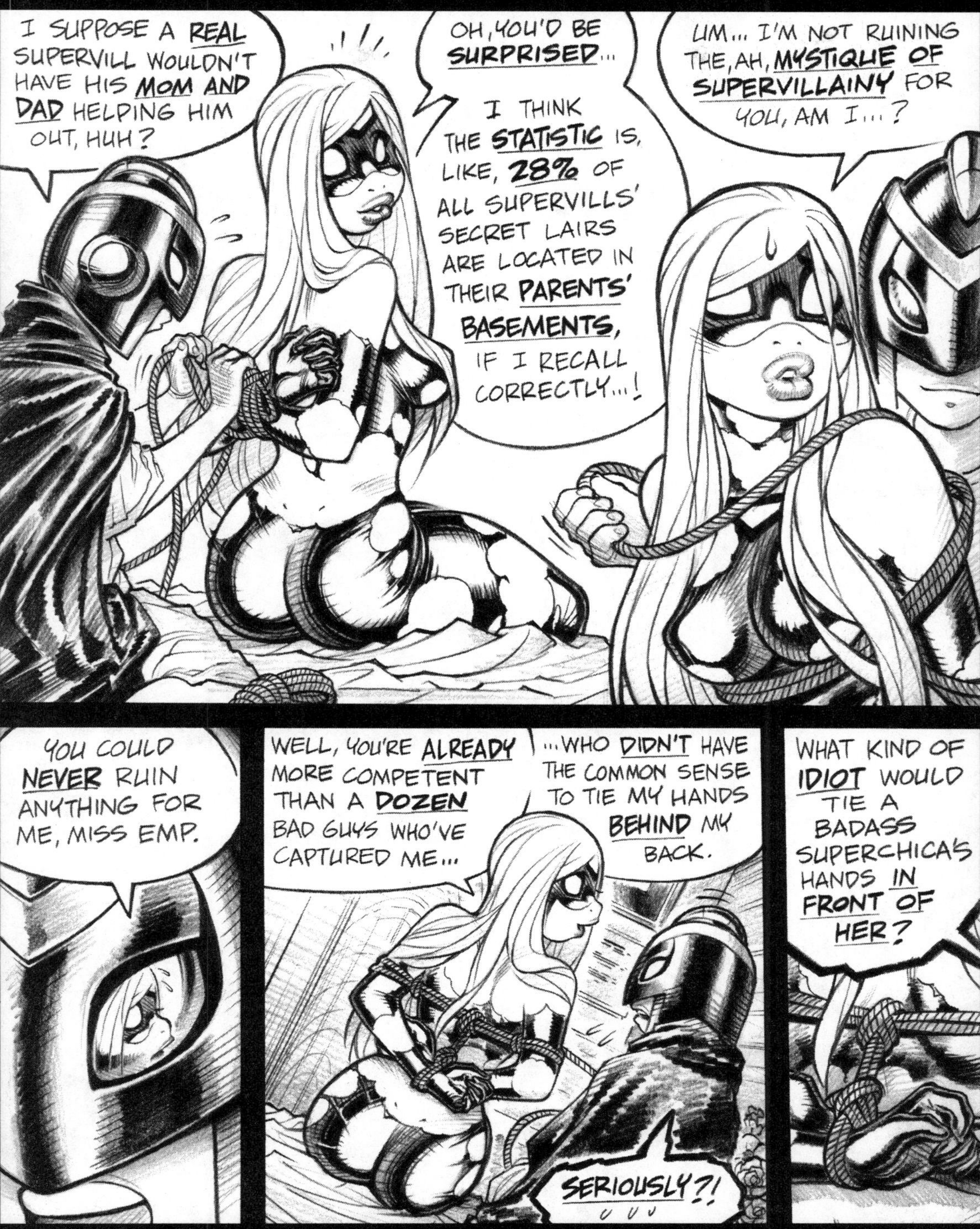
I SUPPOSE A REAL SUPERVILL WOULDN'T HAVE HIS MOM AND DAD HELPING HIM OUT, HUH?
OH, YOU'D BE SURPRISED...
I THINK THE STATISTIC IS, LIKE, 28% OF ALL SUPERVILLS' SECRET LAIRS ARE LOCATED IN THEIR PARENTS' BASEMENTS, IF I RECALL CORRECTLY...!
UM... I'M NOT RUINING THE, AH, MYSTIQUE OF SUPERVILLAINY FOR YOU, AM I...?
YOU COULD NEVER RUIN ANYTHING FOR ME, MISS EMP.
WELL, YOU'RE ALREADY MORE COMPETENT THAN A DOZEN BAD GUYS WHO'VE CAPTURED ME...
...WHO DIDN'T HAVE THE COMMON SENSE TO TIE MY HANDS BEHIND MY BACK.
SERIOUSLY?!
WHAT KIND OF IDIOT WOULD TIE A BADASS SUPERCHICA'S HANDS IN FRONT OF HER?

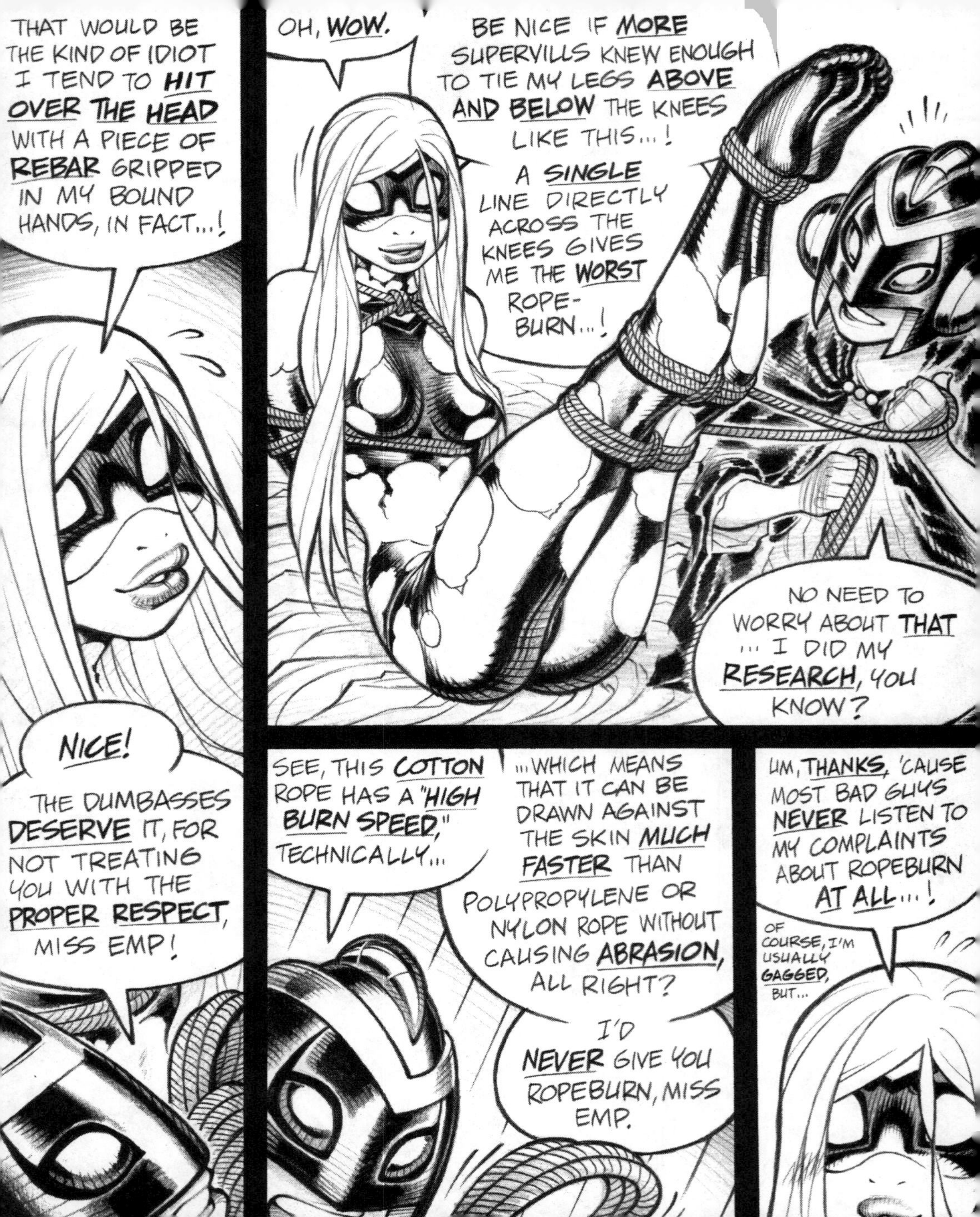
THAT WOULD BE THE KIND OF IDIOT I TEND TO HIT OVER THE HEAD WITH A PIECE OF REBAR GRIPPED IN MY BOUND HANDS, IN FACT...!
NICE!
THE DUMBASSES DESERVE IT, FOR NOT TREATING YOU WITH THE PROPER RESPECT, MISS EMP!
OH, WOW.
BE NICE IF MORE SUPERVILLS KNEW ENOUGH TO TIE MY LEGS ABOVE AND BELOW THE KNEES LIKE THIS...!
A SINGLE LINE DIRECTLY ACROSS THE KNEES GIVES ME THE WORST ROPE-BURN...!
NO NEED TO WORRY ABOUT THAT ... I DID MY RESEARCH, YOU KNOW?
SEE, THIS COTTON ROPE HAS A "HIGH BURN SPEED," TECHNICALLY...
...WHICH MEANS THAT IT CAN BE DRAWN AGAINST THE SKIN MUCH FASTER THAN POLYPROPYLENE OR NYLON ROPE WITHOUT CAUSING ABRASION, ALL RIGHT?
I'D NEVER GIVE YOU ROPEBURN, MISS EMP.
UM, THANKS, 'CAUSE MOST BAD GUYS NEVER LISTEN TO MY COMPLAINTS ABOUT ROPEBURN AT ALL...!
OF COURSE, I'M USUALLY GAGGED, BUT...

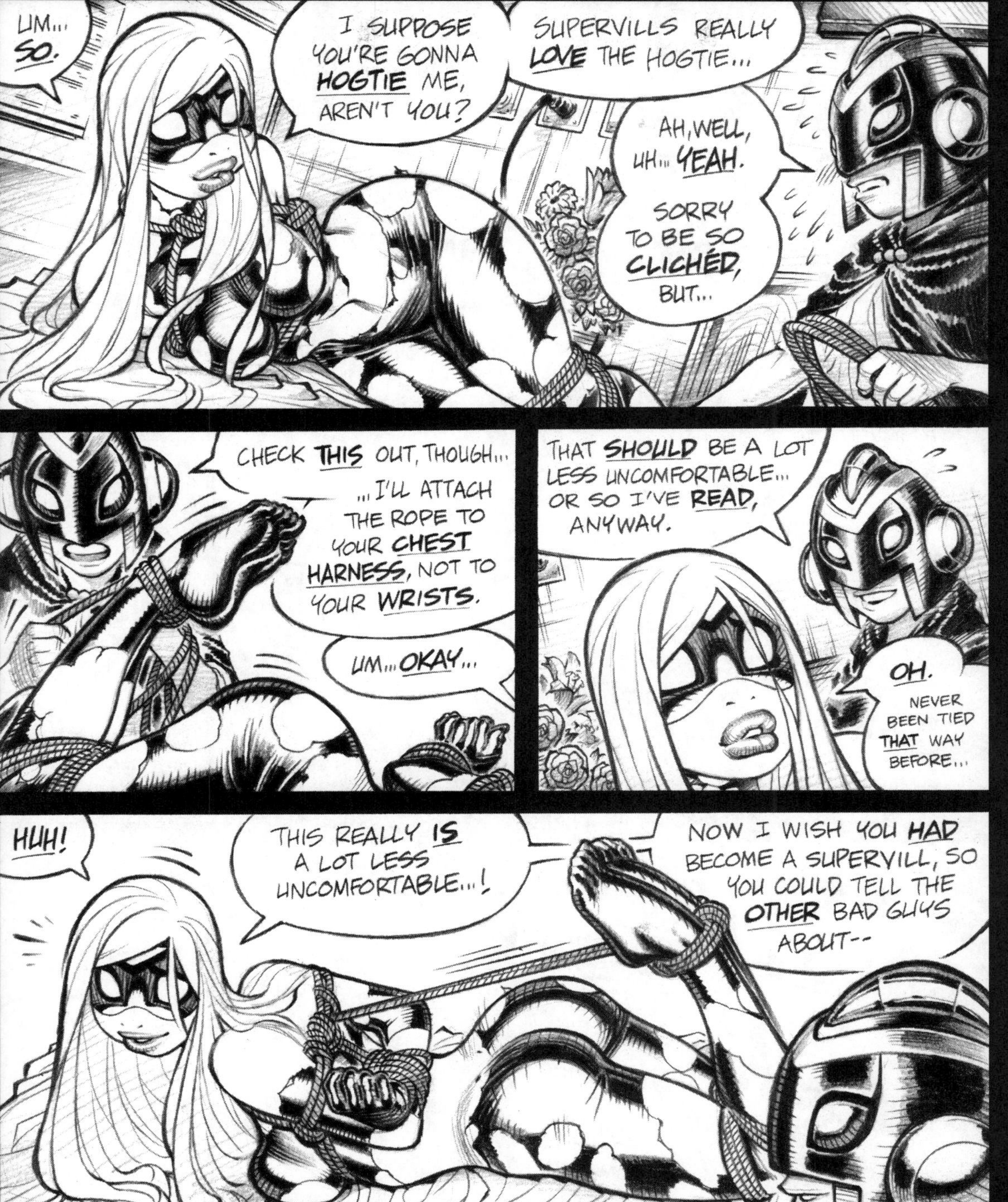
UM... SO.
I SUPPOSE YOU'RE GONNA HOGTIE ME, AREN'T YOU?
SUPERVILLS REALLY LOVE THE HOGTIE...
AH, WELL, UH... YEAH.
SORRY TO BE SO CLICHÉD, BUT...
CHECK THIS OUT, THOUGH...
...I'LL ATTACH THE ROPE TO YOUR CHEST HARNESS, NOT TO YOUR WRISTS.
UM... OKAY...
THAT SHOULD BE A LOT LESS UNCOMFORTABLE... OR SO I'VE READ, ANYWAY.
OH.
NEVER BEEN TIED THAT WAY BEFORE...
HUH!
THIS REALLY IS A LOT LESS UNCOMFORTABLE...!
NOW I WISH YOU HAD BECOME A SUPERVILL, SO YOU COULD TELL THE OTHER BAD GUYS ABOUT--

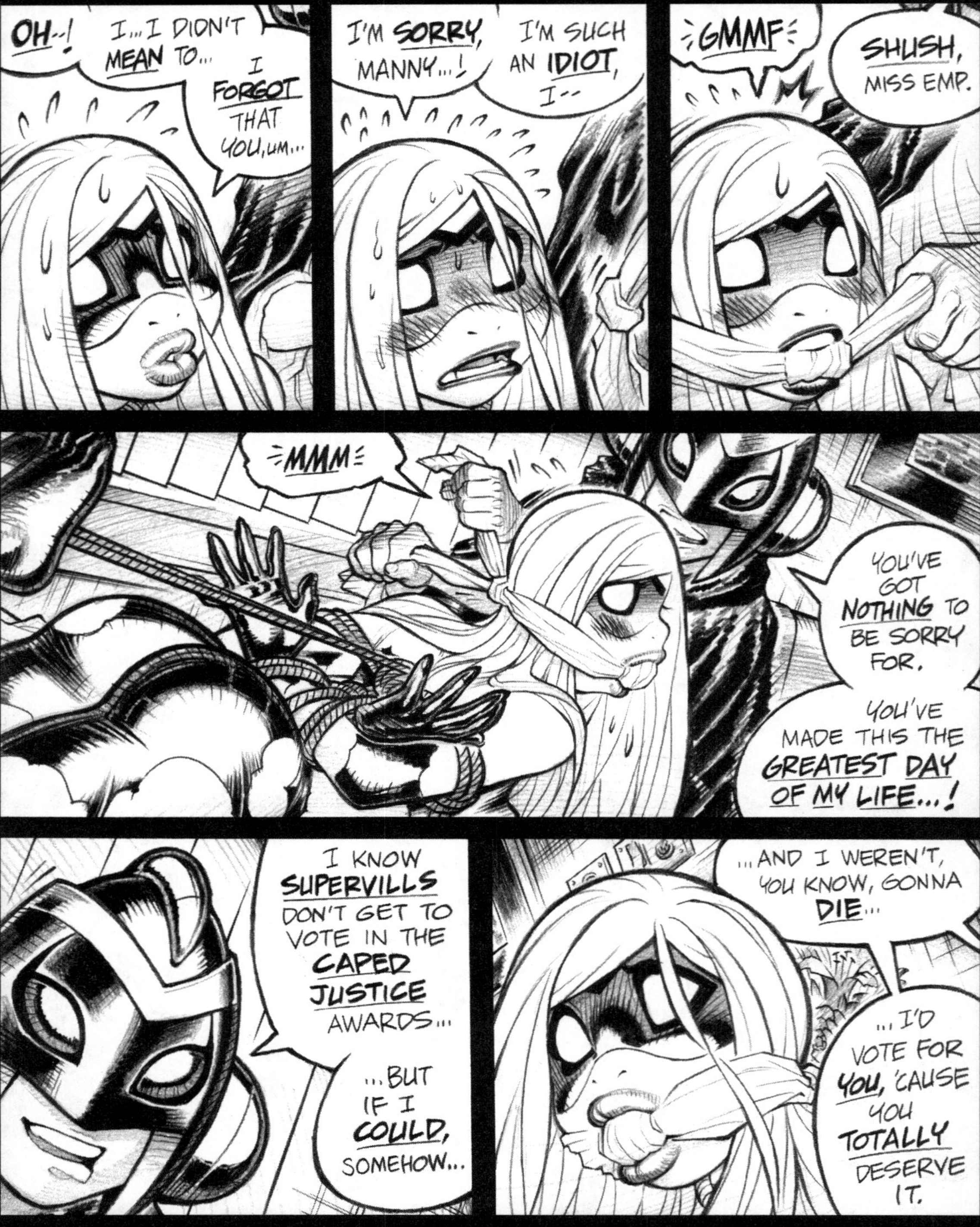
OH--!
I...I DIDN'T MEAN TO...
I FORGOT THAT YOU,UM...
I'M SORRY, MANNY...!
I'M SUCH AN IDIOT, I--
GMMF
SHUSH, MISS EMP.
MMM
YOU'VE GOT NOTHING TO BE SORRY FOR.
YOU'VE MADE THIS THE GREATEST DAY OF MY LIFE...!
I KNOW SUPERVILLS DON'T GET TO VOTE IN THE CAPED JUSTICE AWARDS...
...BUT IF I COULD, SOMEHOW...
...AND I WEREN'T, YOU KNOW, GONNA DIE...
...I'D VOTE FOR YOU, 'CAUSE YOU TOTALLY DESERVE IT.

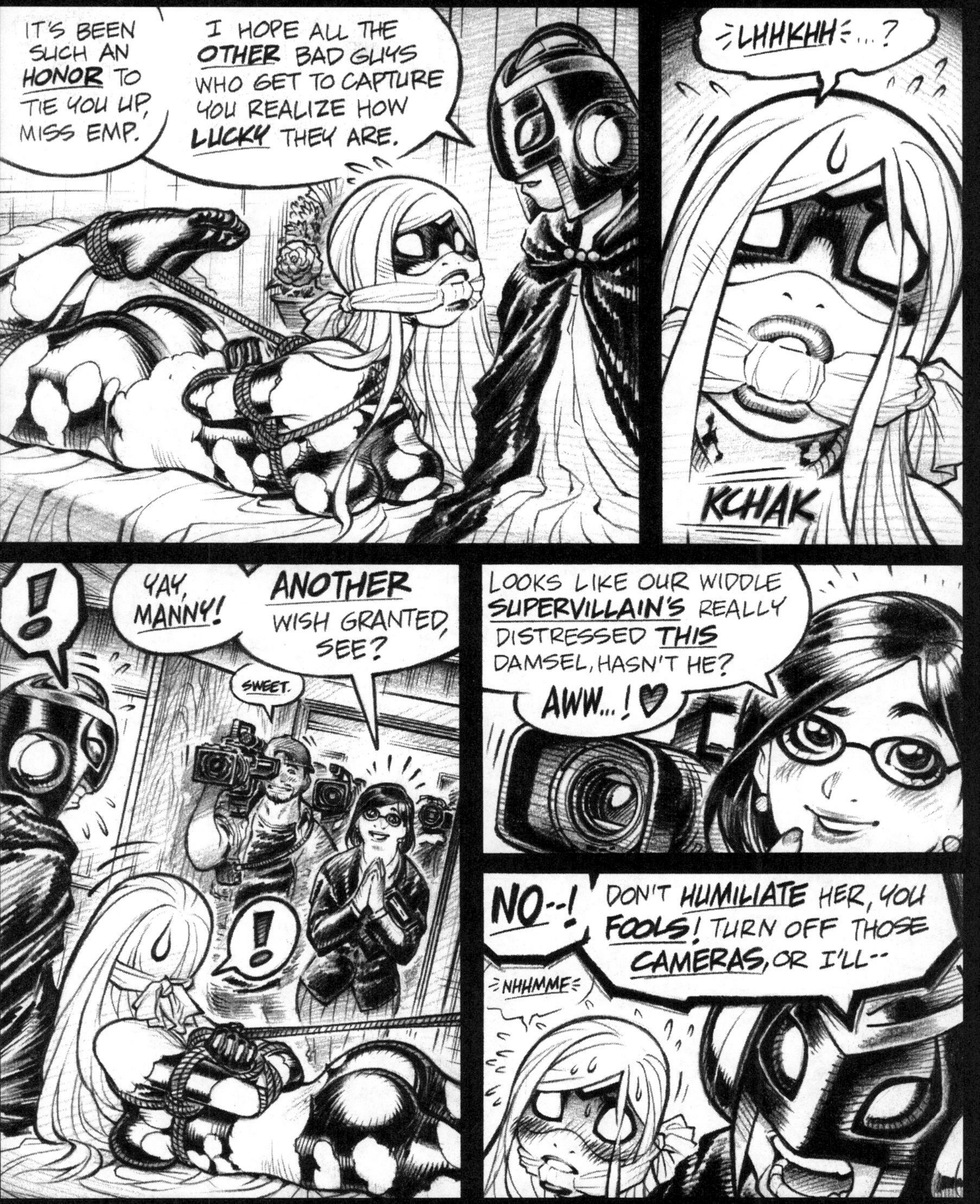
IT'S BEEN SUCH AN HONOR TO TIE YOU UP, MISS EMP.
I HOPE ALL THE OTHER BAD GUYS WHO GET TO CAPTURE YOU REALIZE HOW LUCKY THEY ARE.
LHHKHH...?
KCHAK
!
YAY, MANNY!
ANOTHER WISH GRANTED, SEE?
SWEET.
!
LOOKS LIKE OUR WIDDLE SUPERVILLAIN'S REALLY DISTRESSED THIS DAMSEL, HASN'T HE?
AWW...! ♡
NO--!
DON'T HUMILIATE HER, YOU FOOLS! TURN OFF THOSE CAMERAS, OR I'LL--
NHHMMF

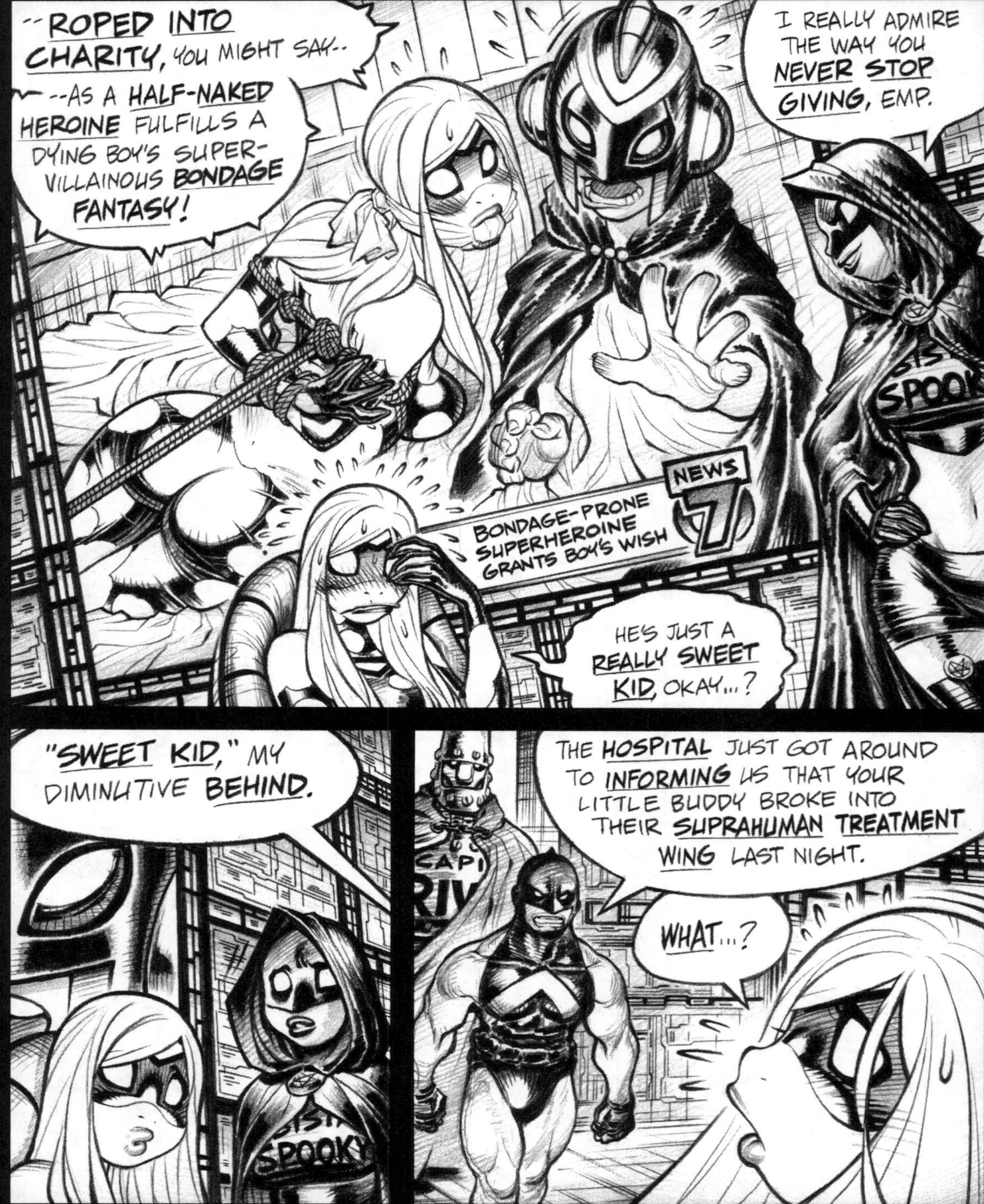
--ROPED INTO CHARITY, YOU MIGHT SAY--
--AS A HALF-NAKED HEROINE FULFILLS A DYING BOY'S SUPER-VILLAINOUS BONDAGE FANTASY!
I REALLY ADMIRE THE WAY YOU NEVER STOP GIVING, EMP.
SPOOK
NEWS 7
BONDAGE-PRONE SUPERHEROINE GRANTS BOY'S WISH
HE'S JUST A REALLY SWEET KID, OKAY...?
"SWEET KID," MY DIMINUTIVE BEHIND.
SPOOKY
THE HOSPITAL JUST GOT AROUND TO INFORMING US THAT YOUR LITTLE BUDDY BROKE INTO THEIR SUPRAHUMAN TREATMENT WING LAST NIGHT.
WHAT...?

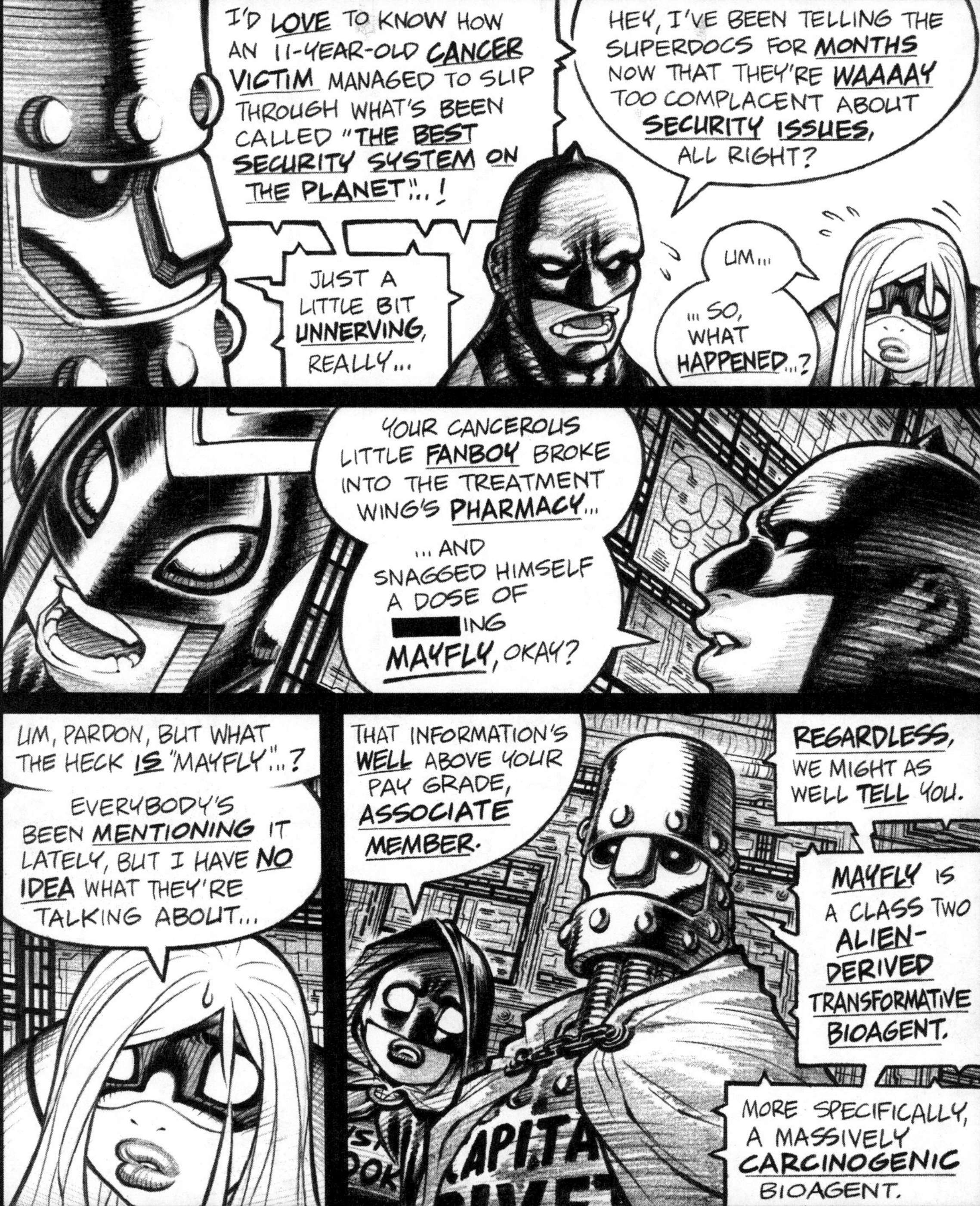
I'D LOVE TO KNOW HOW AN 11-YEAR-OLD CANCER VICTIM MANAGED TO SLIP THROUGH WHAT'S BEEN CALLED "THE BEST SECURITY SYSTEM ON THE PLANET"...!
JUST A LITTLE BIT UNNERVING, REALLY...
HEY, I'VE BEEN TELLING THE SUPERDOCS FOR MONTHS NOW THAT THEY'RE WAAAAY TOO COMPLACENT ABOUT SECURITY ISSUES, ALL RIGHT?
UM...
...SO, WHAT HAPPENED...?
YOUR CANCEROUS LITTLE FANBOY BROKE INTO THE TREATMENT WING'S PHARMACY...
...AND SNAGGED HIMSELF A DOSE OF [redacted]ING MAYFLY, OKAY?
UM, PARDON, BUT WHAT THE HECK IS "MAYFLY"...?
EVERYBODY'S BEEN MENTIONING IT LATELY, BUT I HAVE NO IDEA WHAT THEY'RE TALKING ABOUT...
THAT INFORMATION'S WELL ABOVE YOUR PAY GRADE, ASSOCIATE MEMBER.
REGARDLESS, WE MIGHT AS WELL TELL YOU.
MAYFLY IS A CLASS TWO ALIEN-DERIVED TRANSFORMATIVE BIOAGENT.
MORE SPECIFICALLY, A MASSIVELY CARCINOGENIC BIOAGENT.

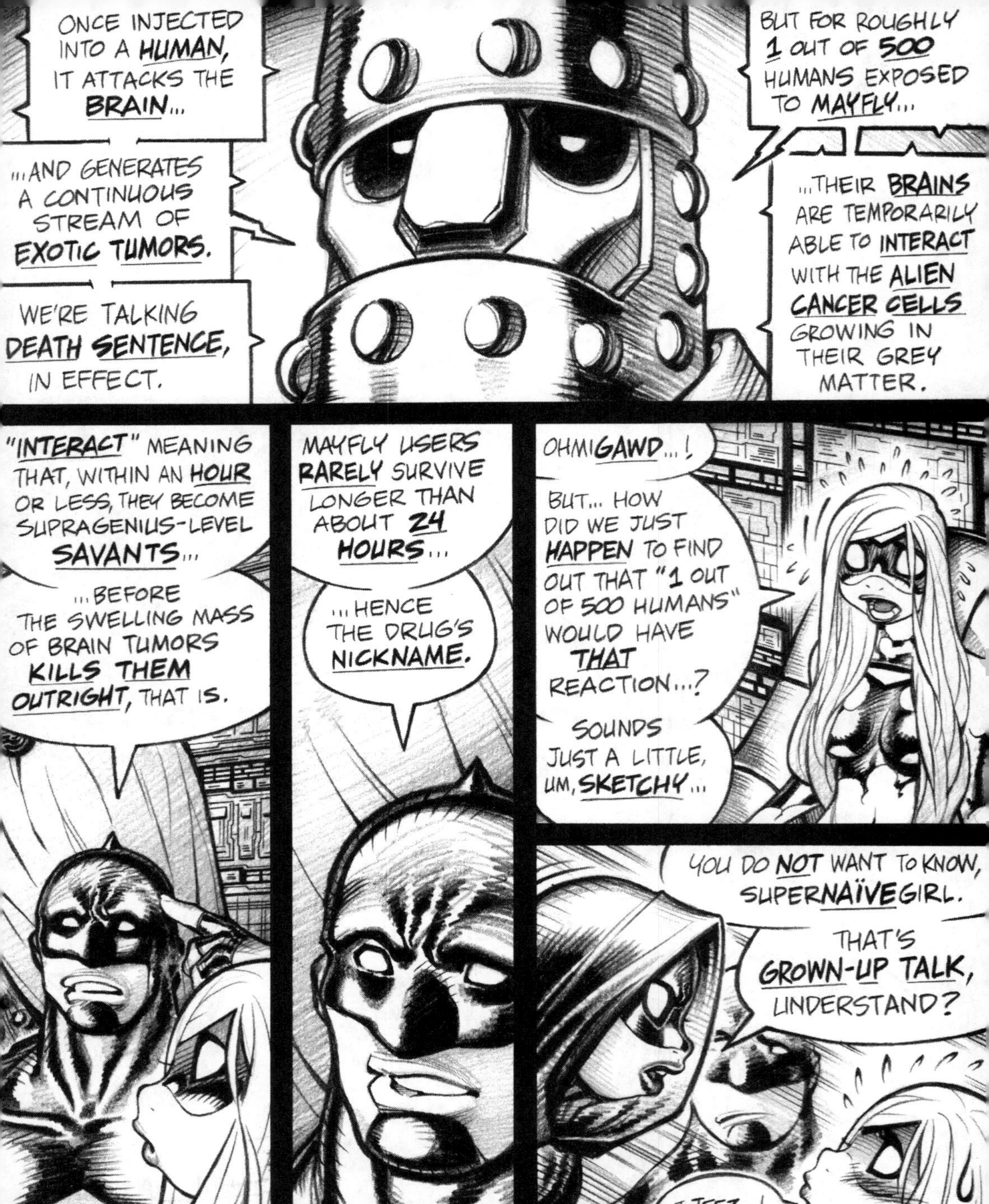
ONCE INJECTED INTO A HUMAN, IT ATTACKS THE BRAIN...
...AND GENERATES A CONTINUOUS STREAM OF EXOTIC TUMORS.
WE'RE TALKING DEATH SENTENCE, IN EFFECT.
BUT FOR ROUGHLY 1 OUT OF 500 HUMANS EXPOSED TO MAYFLY...
...THEIR BRAINS ARE TEMPORARILY ABLE TO INTERACT WITH THE ALIEN CANCER CELLS GROWING IN THEIR GREY MATTER.
"INTERACT" MEANING THAT, WITHIN AN HOUR OR LESS, THEY BECOME SUPRAGENIUS-LEVEL SAVANTS...
...BEFORE THE SWELLING MASS OF BRAIN TUMORS KILLS THEM OUTRIGHT, THAT IS.
MAYFLY USERS RARELY SURVIVE LONGER THAN ABOUT 24 HOURS...
...HENCE THE DRUG'S NICKNAME.
OHMIGAWD...!
BUT... HOW DID WE JUST HAPPEN TO FIND OUT THAT "1 OUT OF 500 HUMANS" WOULD HAVE THAT REACTION...?
SOUNDS JUST A LITTLE, UM, SKETCHY...
YOU DO NOT WANT TO KNOW, SUPERNAÏVEGIRL.
THAT'S GROWN-UP TALK, UNDERSTAND?
J-JEEZ...!

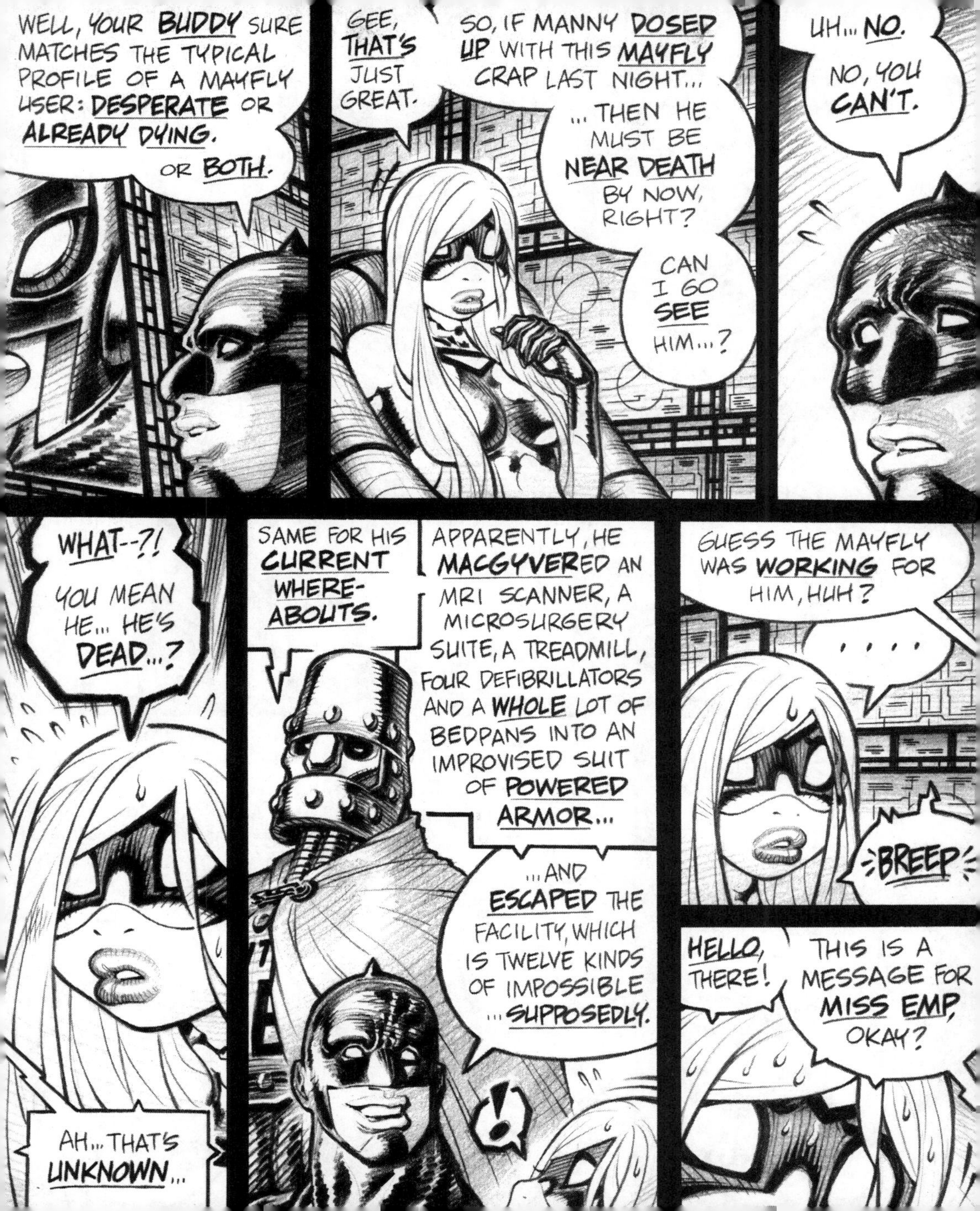
WELL, YOUR BUDDY SURE MATCHES THE TYPICAL PROFILE OF A MAYFLY USER: DESPERATE OR ALREADY DYING.
OR BOTH.
GEE, THAT'S JUST GREAT.
SO, IF MANNY DOSED UP WITH THIS MAYFLY CRAP LAST NIGHT...
...THEN HE MUST BE NEAR DEATH BY NOW, RIGHT?
CAN I GO SEE HIM...?
UH... NO.
NO, YOU CAN'T.
WHAT--?!
YOU MEAN HE... HE'S DEAD...?
AH... THAT'S UNKNOWN...
SAME FOR HIS CURRENT WHERE-ABOUTS.
APPARENTLY, HE MACGYVERED AN MRI SCANNER, A MICROSURGERY SUITE, A TREADMILL, FOUR DEFIBRILLATORS AND A WHOLE LOT OF BEDPANS INTO AN IMPROVISED SUIT OF POWERED ARMOR...
...AND ESCAPED THE FACILITY, WHICH IS TWELVE KINDS OF IMPOSSIBLE ...SUPPOSEDLY.
!
GUESS THE MAYFLY WAS WORKING FOR HIM, HUH?
....
BREEP
HELLO, THERE!
THIS IS A MESSAGE FOR MISS EMP, OKAY?

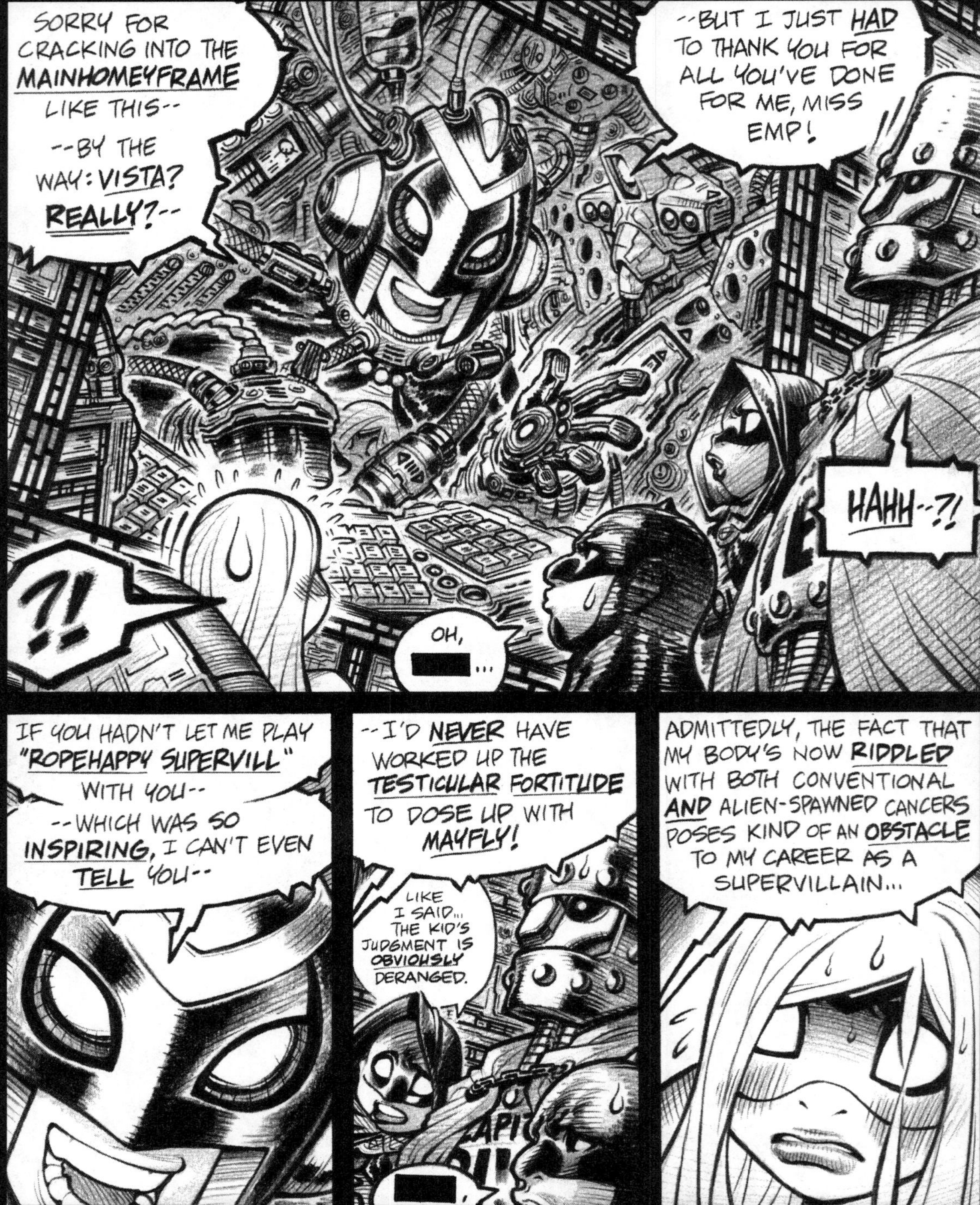

SORRY FOR CRACKING INTO THE MAINHOMEYFRAME LIKE THIS--
--BY THE WAY: VISTA? REALLY?--
--BUT I JUST HAD TO THANK YOU FOR ALL YOU'VE DONE FOR ME, MISS EMP!
?!
OH, [redacted]...
HAHH--?!
IF YOU HADN'T LET ME PLAY "ROPEHAPPY SUPERVILL" WITH YOU--
--WHICH WAS SO INSPIRING, I CAN'T EVEN TELL YOU--
--I'D NEVER HAVE WORKED UP THE TESTICULAR FORTITUDE TO DOSE UP WITH MAYFLY!
LIKE I SAID... THE KID'S JUDGMENT IS OBVIOUSLY DERANGED.
[redacted]
ADMITTEDLY, THE FACT THAT MY BODY'S NOW RIDDLED WITH BOTH CONVENTIONAL AND ALIEN-SPAWNED CANCERS POSES KIND OF AN OBSTACLE TO MY CAREER AS A SUPERVILLAIN...

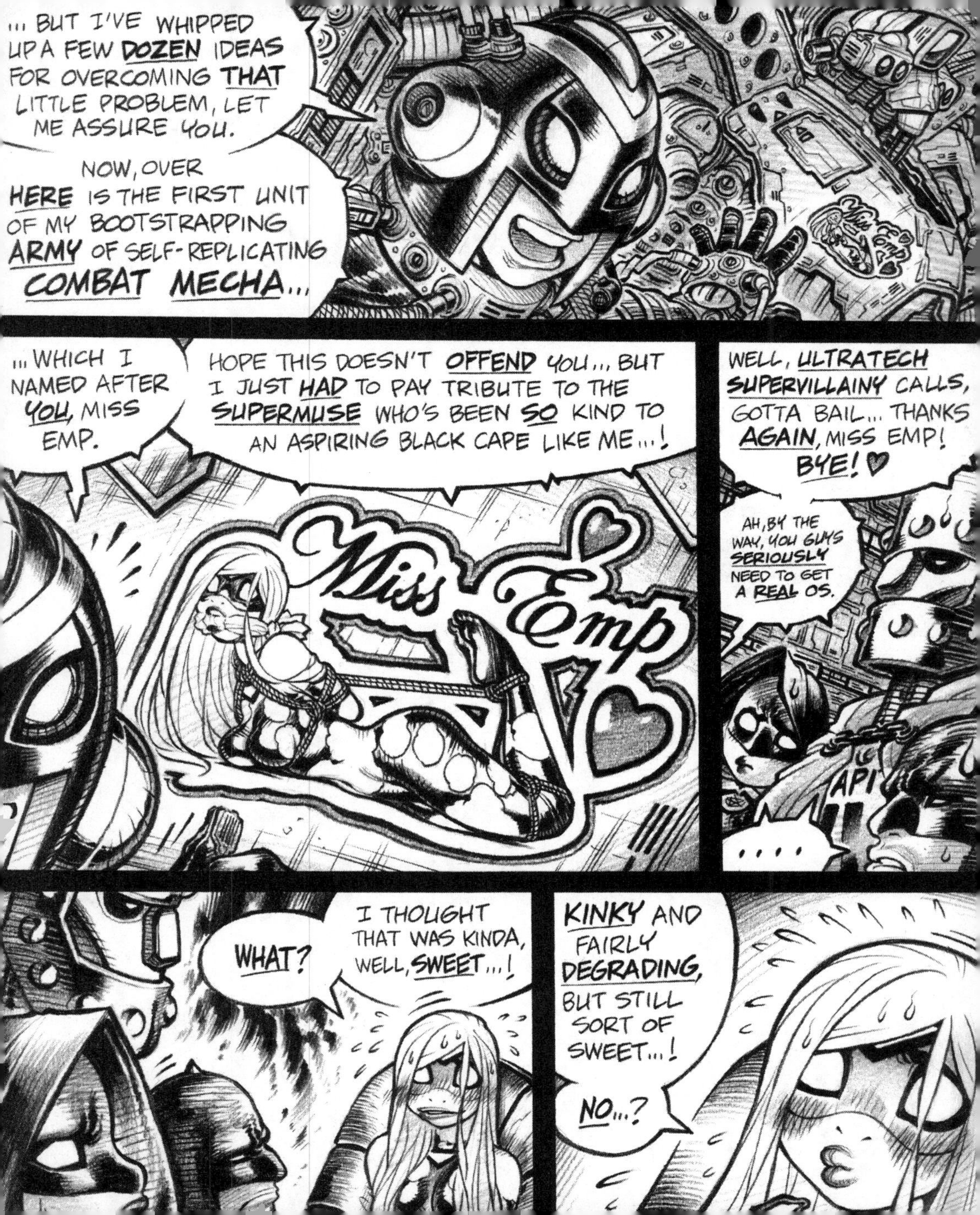

... BUT I'VE WHIPPED UP A FEW DOZEN IDEAS FOR OVERCOMING THAT LITTLE PROBLEM, LET ME ASSURE YOU.
NOW, OVER HERE IS THE FIRST UNIT OF MY BOOTSTRAPPING ARMY OF SELF-REPLICATING COMBAT MECHA...
...WHICH I NAMED AFTER YOU, MISS EMP.
HOPE THIS DOESN'T OFFEND YOU... BUT I JUST HAD TO PAY TRIBUTE TO THE SUPERMUSE WHO'S BEEN SO KIND TO AN ASPIRING BLACK CAPE LIKE ME...!
Miss Emp
WELL, ULTRATECH SUPERVILLAINY CALLS, GOTTA BAIL... THANKS AGAIN, MISS EMP! BYE! ♡
AH, BY THE WAY, YOU GUYS SERIOUSLY NEED TO GET A REAL OS.
API
....
WHAT?
I THOUGHT THAT WAS KINDA, WELL, SWEET...!
KINKY AND FAIRLY DEGRADING, BUT STILL SORT OF SWEET...!
NO...?

Empowered™

Bouncebackalicious

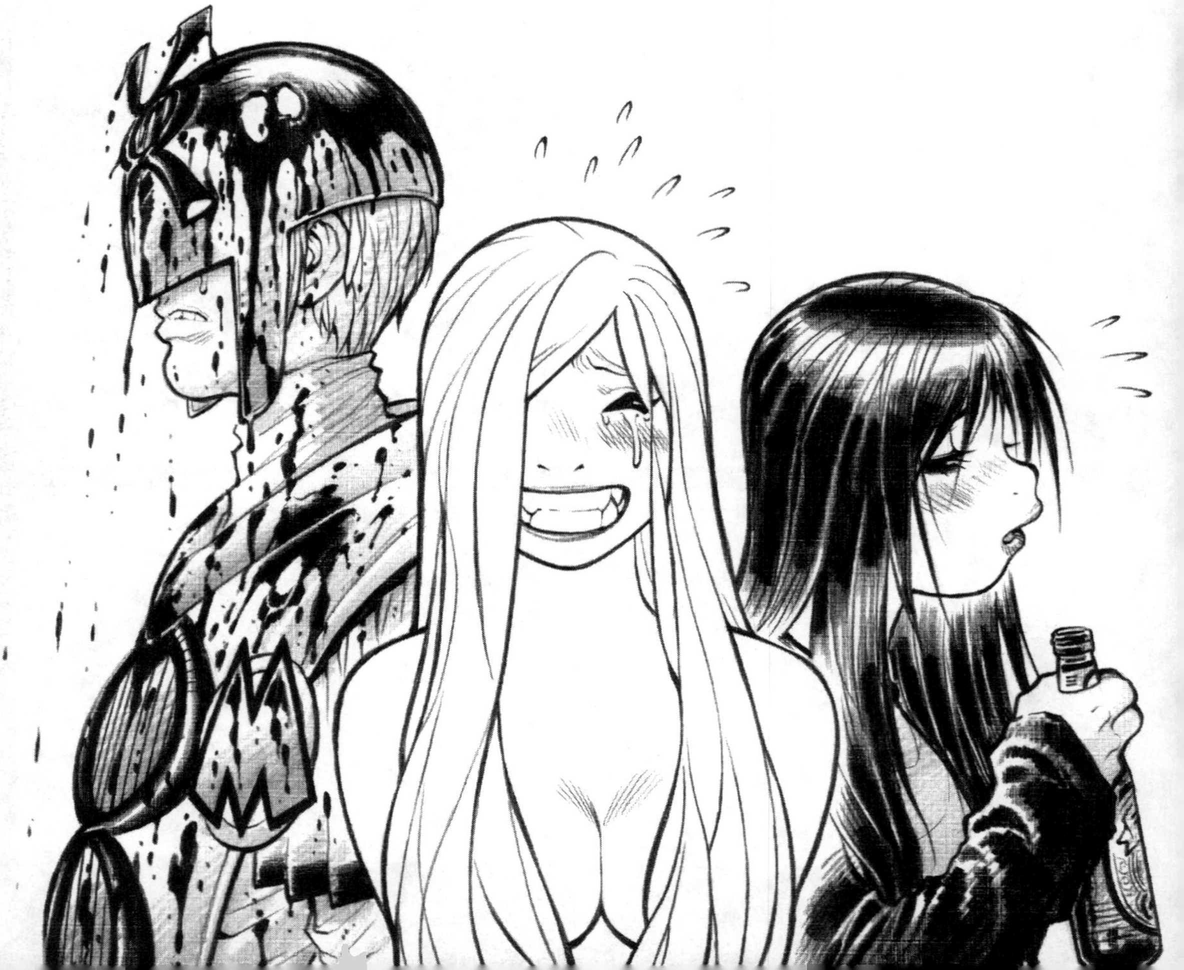

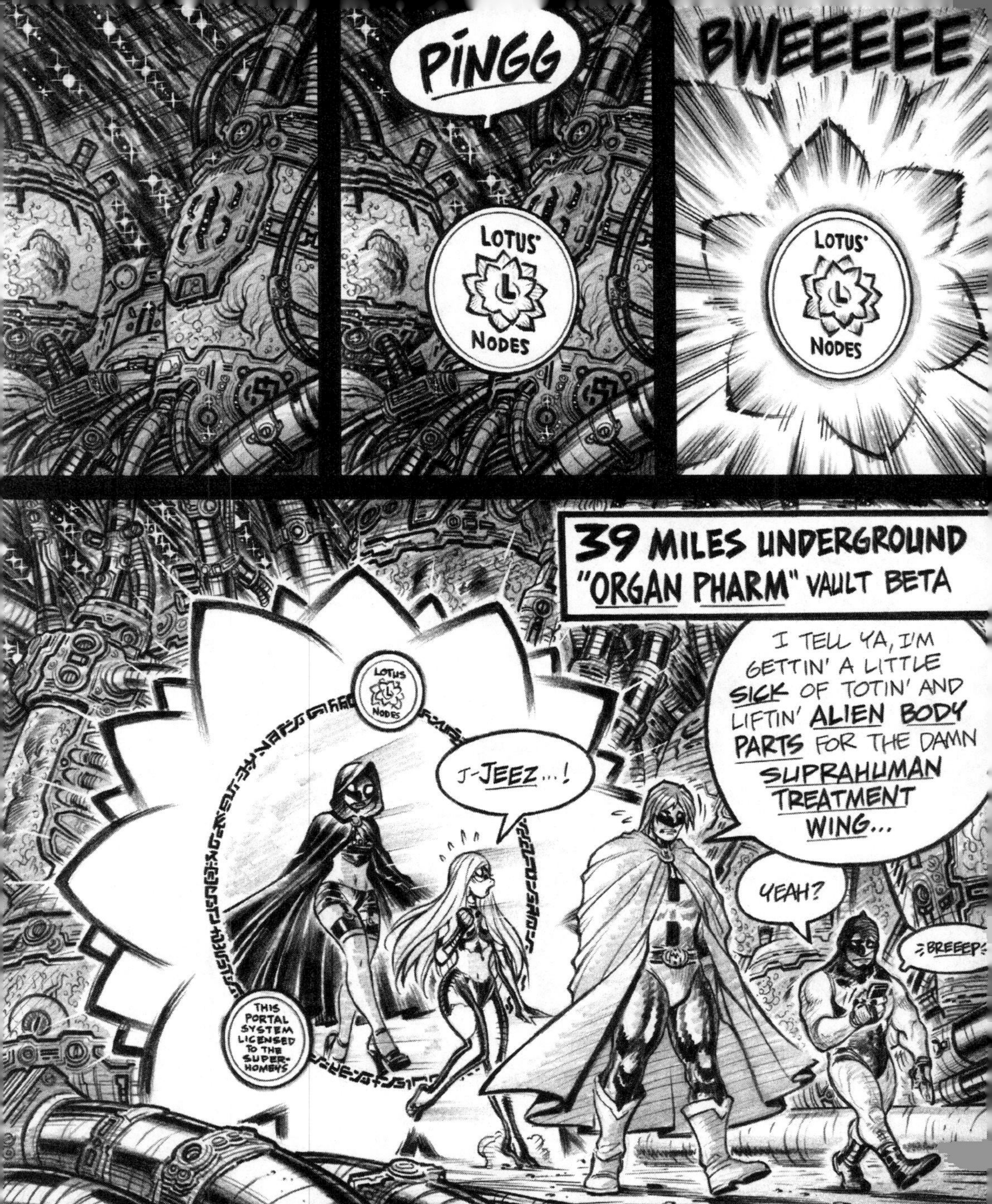
PINGG
LOTUS' L NODES
BWEEEEE
LOTUS' L NODES
39 MILES UNDERGROUND "ORGAN PHARM" VAULT BETA
LOTUS L NODES
J-JEEZ...!
THIS PORTAL SYSTEM LICENSED TO THE SUPER-HOMEYS
I TELL YA, I'M GETTIN' A LITTLE SICK OF TOTIN' AND LIFTIN' ALIEN BODY PARTS FOR THE DAMN SUPRAHUMAN TREATMENT WING...
YEAH?
BREEEP

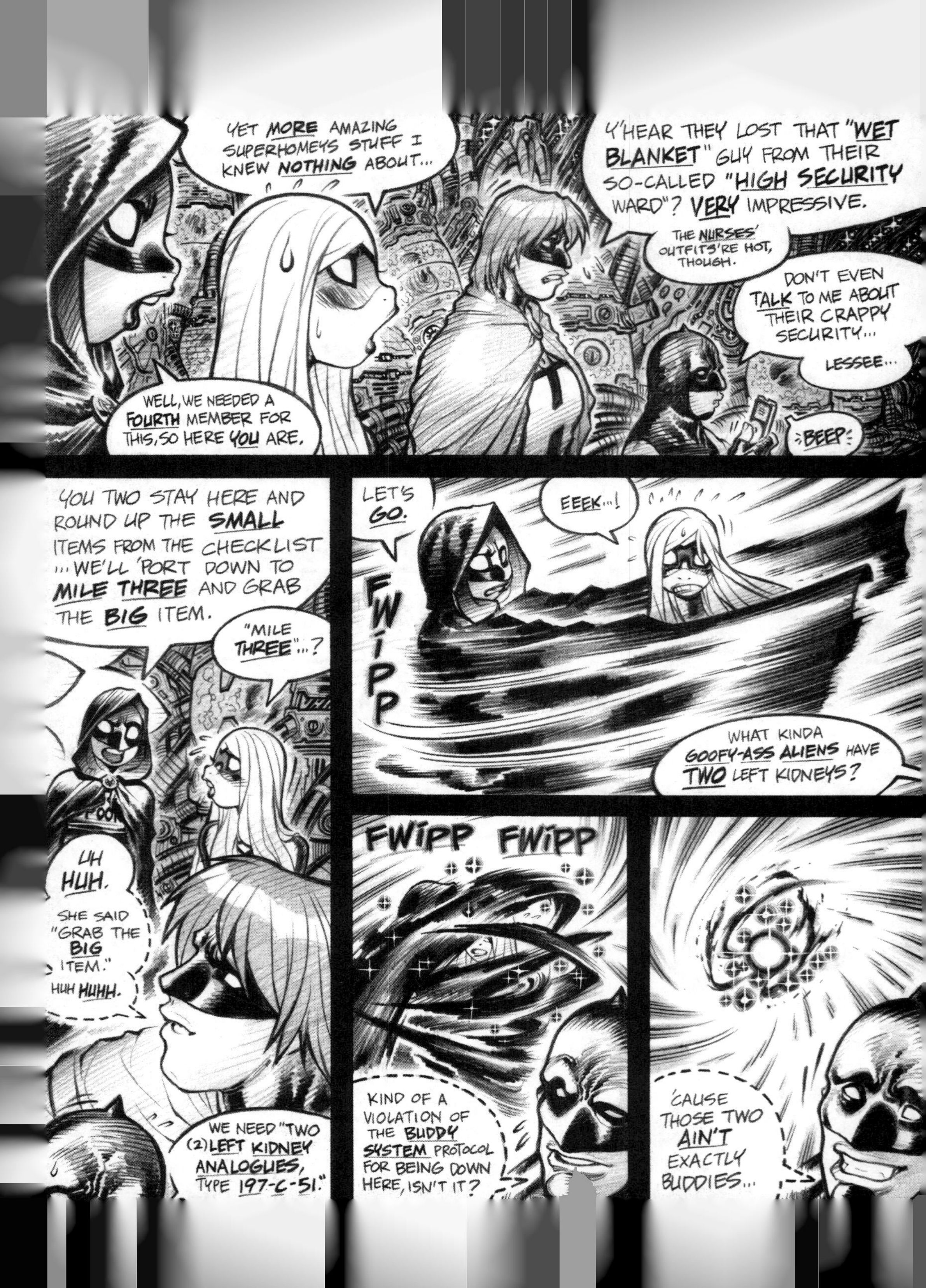
YET MORE AMAZING SUPERHOMEYS STUFF I KNEW NOTHING ABOUT...
WELL, WE NEEDED A FOURTH MEMBER FOR THIS, SO HERE YOU ARE.
Y'HEAR THEY LOST THAT "WET BLANKET" GUY FROM THEIR SO-CALLED "HIGH SECURITY WARD"? VERY IMPRESSIVE.
THE NURSES' OUTFITS'RE HOT, THOUGH.
DON'T EVEN TALK TO ME ABOUT THEIR CRAPPY SECURITY...
LESSEE...
BEEP
YOU TWO STAY HERE AND ROUND UP THE SMALL ITEMS FROM THE CHECKLIST ...WE'LL 'PORT DOWN TO MILE THREE AND GRAB THE BIG ITEM.
"MILE THREE"...?
UH HUH.
SHE SAID "GRAB THE BIG ITEM." HUH HUHH.
WE NEED "TWO (2) LEFT KIDNEY ANALOGUES, TYPE 197-C-51."
LET'S GO.
EEEK...!
FWIPP
WHAT KINDA GOOFY-ASS ALIENS HAVE TWO LEFT KIDNEYS?
FWIPP FWIPP
KIND OF A VIOLATION OF THE BUDDY SYSTEM PROTOCOL FOR BEING DOWN HERE, ISN'T IT?
'CAUSE THOSE TWO AIN'T EXACTLY BUDDIES...

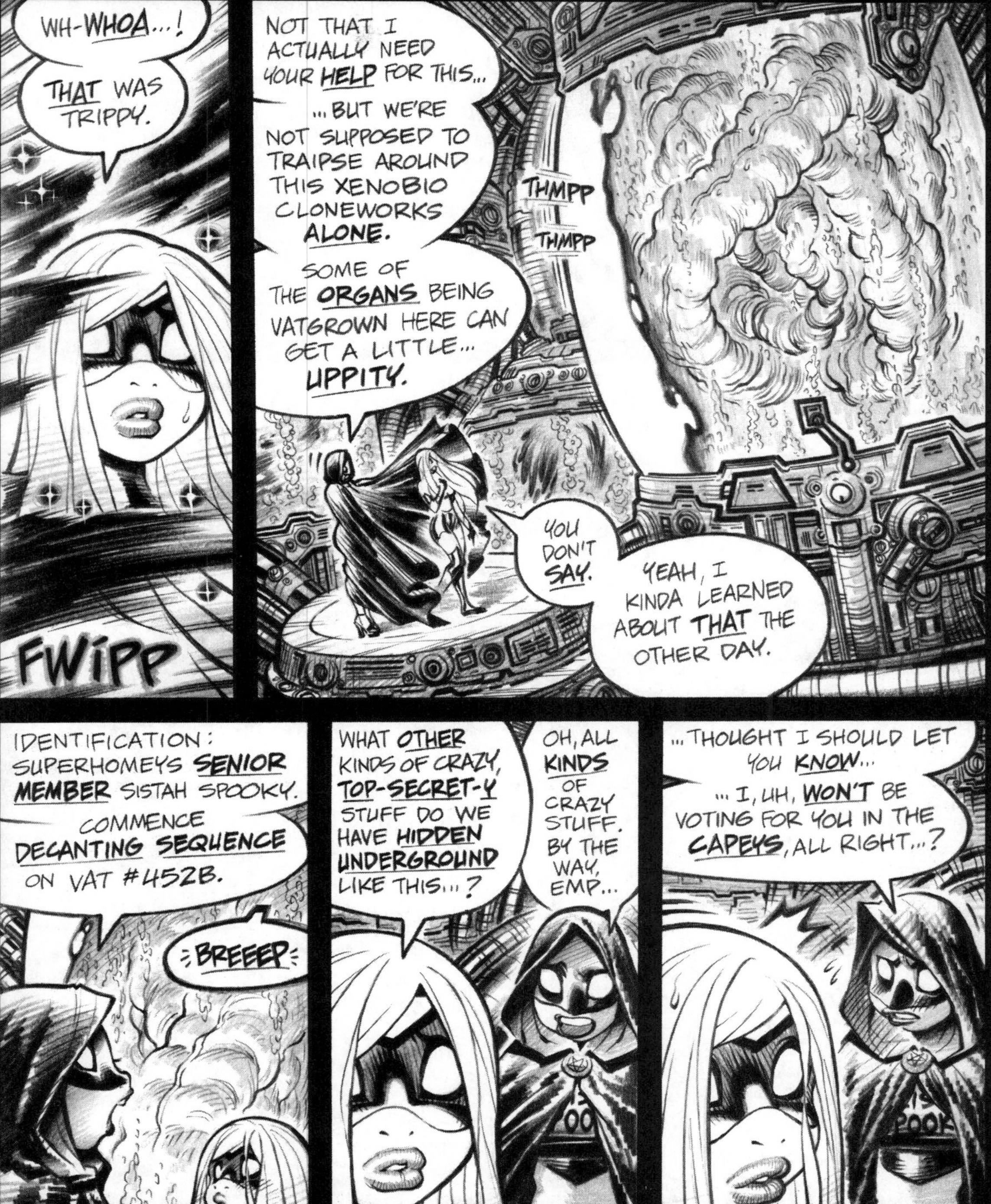
WH-WHOA...!
THAT WAS TRIPPY.
FWIPP
NOT THAT I ACTUALLY NEED YOUR HELP FOR THIS...
...BUT WE'RE NOT SUPPOSED TO TRAIPSE AROUND THIS XENOBIO CLONEWORKS ALONE.
SOME OF THE ORGANS BEING VATGROWN HERE CAN GET A LITTLE... UPPITY.
THMPP
THMPP
YOU DON'T SAY.
YEAH, I KINDA LEARNED ABOUT THAT THE OTHER DAY.
IDENTIFICATION: SUPERHOMEYS SENIOR MEMBER SISTAH SPOOKY.
COMMENCE DECANTING SEQUENCE ON VAT #452B.
BREEEP
WHAT OTHER KINDS OF CRAZY, TOP-SECRET-Y STUFF DO WE HAVE HIDDEN UNDERGROUND LIKE THIS...?
OH, ALL KINDS OF CRAZY STUFF. BY THE WAY, EMP...
...THOUGHT I SHOULD LET YOU KNOW...
...I, UH, WON'T BE VOTING FOR YOU IN THE CAPEYS, ALL RIGHT...?

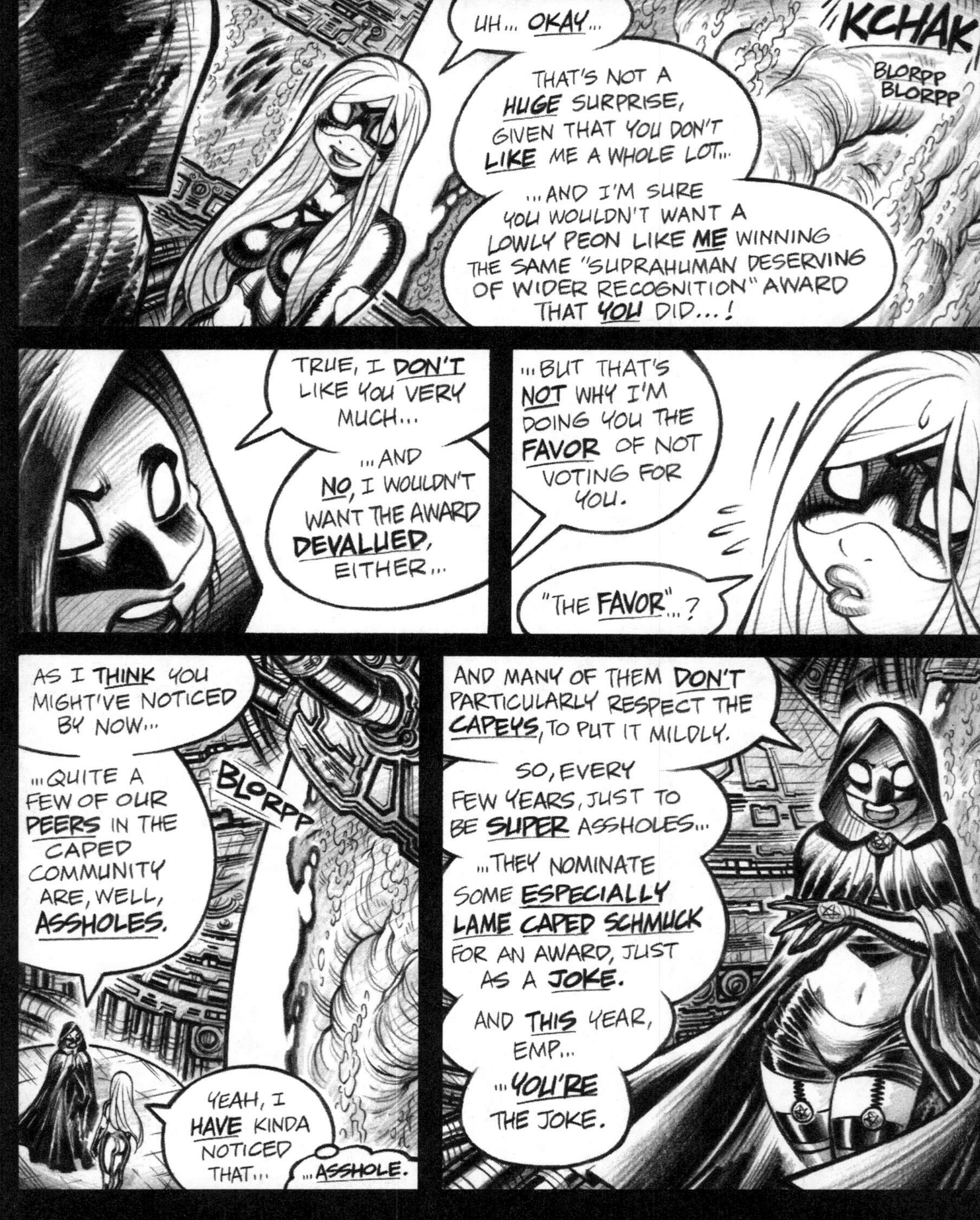
UH... OKAY...
THAT'S NOT A HUGE SURPRISE, GIVEN THAT YOU DON'T LIKE ME A WHOLE LOT...
...AND I'M SURE YOU WOULDN'T WANT A LOWLY PEON LIKE ME WINNING THE SAME "SUPRAHUMAN DESERVING OF WIDER RECOGNITION" AWARD THAT YOU DID...!
KCHAK
BLORPP BLORPP
TRUE, I DON'T LIKE YOU VERY MUCH...
...AND NO, I WOULDN'T WANT THE AWARD DEVALUED, EITHER...
...BUT THAT'S NOT WHY I'M DOING YOU THE FAVOR OF NOT VOTING FOR YOU.
"THE FAVOR"...?
AS I THINK YOU MIGHT'VE NOTICED BY NOW...
...QUITE A FEW OF OUR PEERS IN THE CAPED COMMUNITY ARE, WELL, ASSHOLES.
BLORPP
YEAH, I HAVE KINDA NOTICED THAT...
...ASSHOLE.
AND MANY OF THEM DON'T PARTICULARLY RESPECT THE CAPEYS, TO PUT IT MILDLY.
SO, EVERY FEW YEARS, JUST TO BE SUPER ASSHOLES...
...THEY NOMINATE SOME ESPECIALLY LAME CAPED SCHMUCK FOR AN AWARD, JUST AS A JOKE.
AND THIS YEAR, EMP...
...YOU'RE THE JOKE.

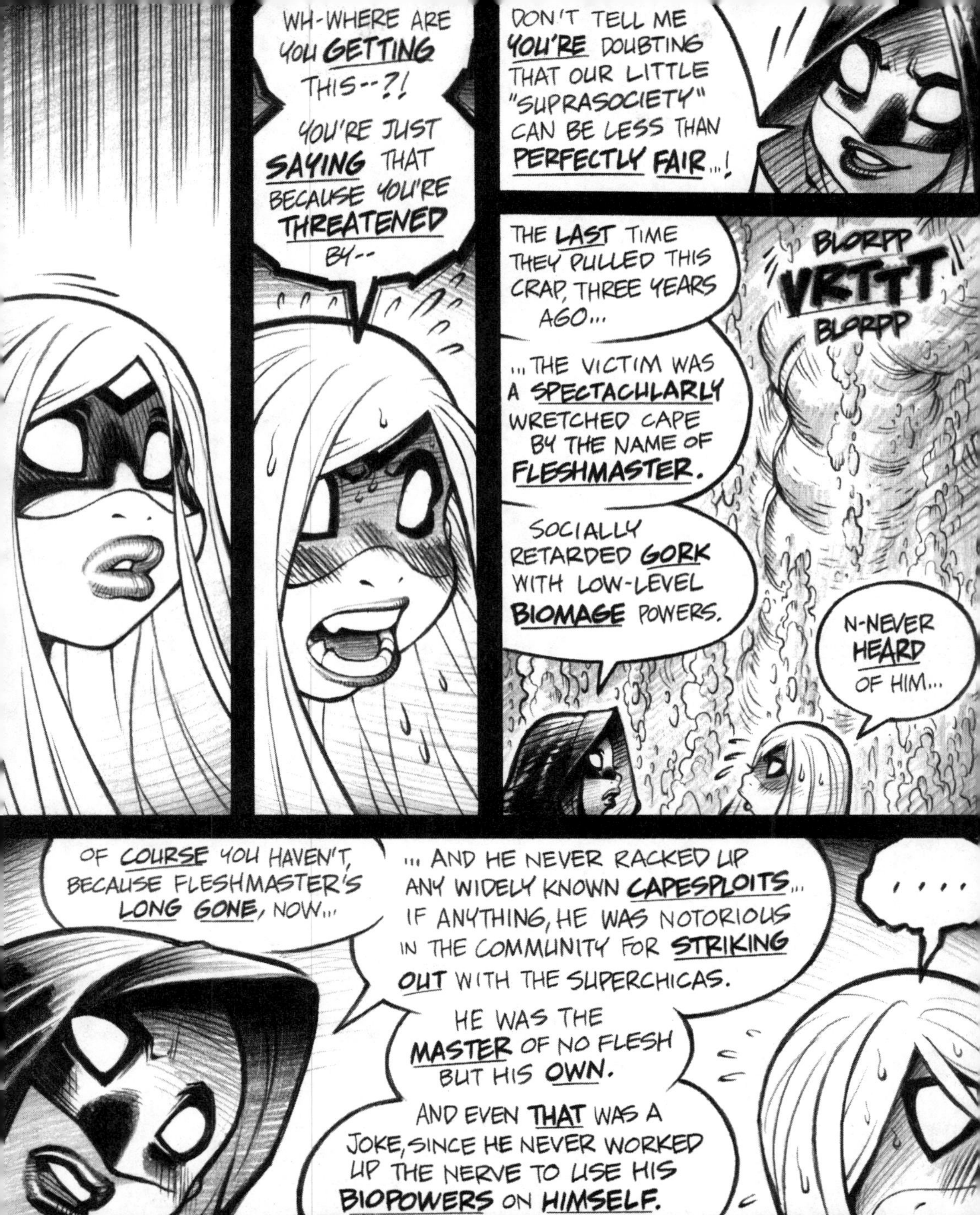

WH-WHERE ARE YOU GETTING THIS--?!
YOU'RE JUST SAYING THAT BECAUSE YOU'RE THREATENED BY--
DON'T TELL ME YOU'RE DOUBTING THAT OUR LITTLE "SUPRASOCIETY" CAN BE LESS THAN PERFECTLY FAIR...!
THE LAST TIME THEY PULLED THIS CRAP, THREE YEARS AGO...
...THE VICTIM WAS A SPECTACULARLY WRETCHED CAPE BY THE NAME OF FLESHMASTER.
SOCIALLY RETARDED GORK WITH LOW-LEVEL BIOMAGE POWERS.
BLORPP
VRTTT
BLORPP
N-NEVER HEARD OF HIM...
OF COURSE YOU HAVEN'T, BECAUSE FLESHMASTER'S LONG GONE, NOW...
...AND HE NEVER RACKED UP ANY WIDELY KNOWN CAPESPLOITS... IF ANYTHING, HE WAS NOTORIOUS IN THE COMMUNITY FOR STRIKING OUT WITH THE SUPERCHICAS.
HE WAS THE MASTER OF NO FLESH BUT HIS OWN.
AND EVEN THAT WAS A JOKE, SINCE HE NEVER WORKED UP THE NERVE TO USE HIS BIOPOWERS ON HIMSELF.
....

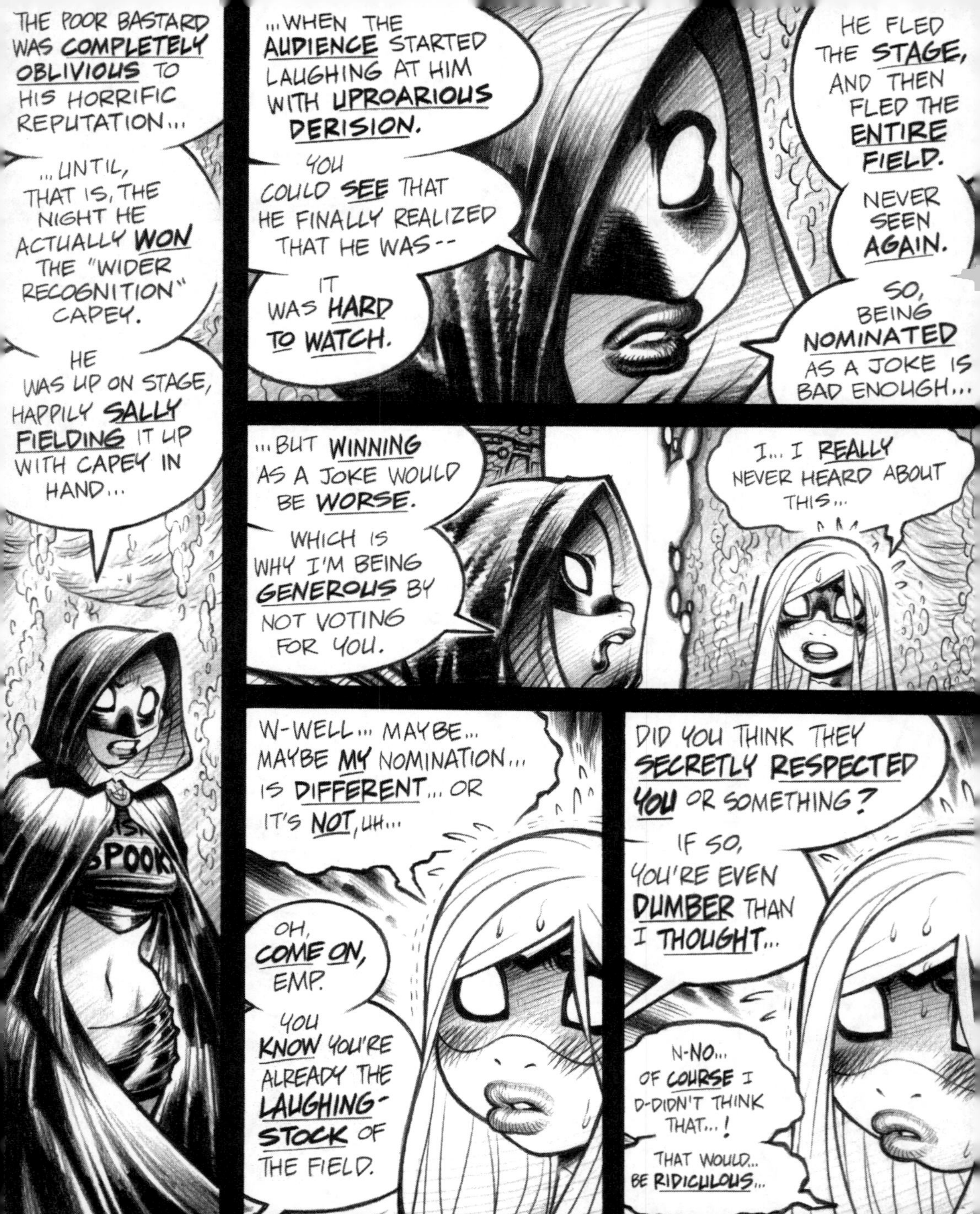
THE POOR BASTARD WAS COMPLETELY OBLIVIOUS TO HIS HORRIFIC REPUTATION...
...UNTIL, THAT IS, THE NIGHT HE ACTUALLY WON THE "WIDER RECOGNITION" CAPEY.
HE WAS UP ON STAGE, HAPPILY SALLY FIELDING IT UP WITH CAPEY IN HAND...
...WHEN THE AUDIENCE STARTED LAUGHING AT HIM WITH UPROARIOUS DERISION.
YOU COULD SEE THAT HE FINALLY REALIZED THAT HE WAS--
IT WAS HARD TO WATCH.
HE FLED THE STAGE, AND THEN FLED THE ENTIRE FIELD.
NEVER SEEN AGAIN.
SO, BEING NOMINATED AS A JOKE IS BAD ENOUGH...
...BUT WINNING AS A JOKE WOULD BE WORSE.
WHICH IS WHY I'M BEING GENEROUS BY NOT VOTING FOR YOU.
I... I REALLY NEVER HEARD ABOUT THIS...
SPOOK
W-WELL... MAYBE... MAYBE MY NOMINATION... IS DIFFERENT... OR IT'S NOT, UH...
OH, COME ON, EMP.
YOU KNOW YOU'RE ALREADY THE LAUGHING-STOCK OF THE FIELD.
DID YOU THINK THEY SECRETLY RESPECTED YOU OR SOMETHING?
IF SO, YOU'RE EVEN DUMBER THAN I THOUGHT...
N-NO... OF COURSE I D-DIDN'T THINK THAT...!
THAT WOULD... BE RIDICULOUS...

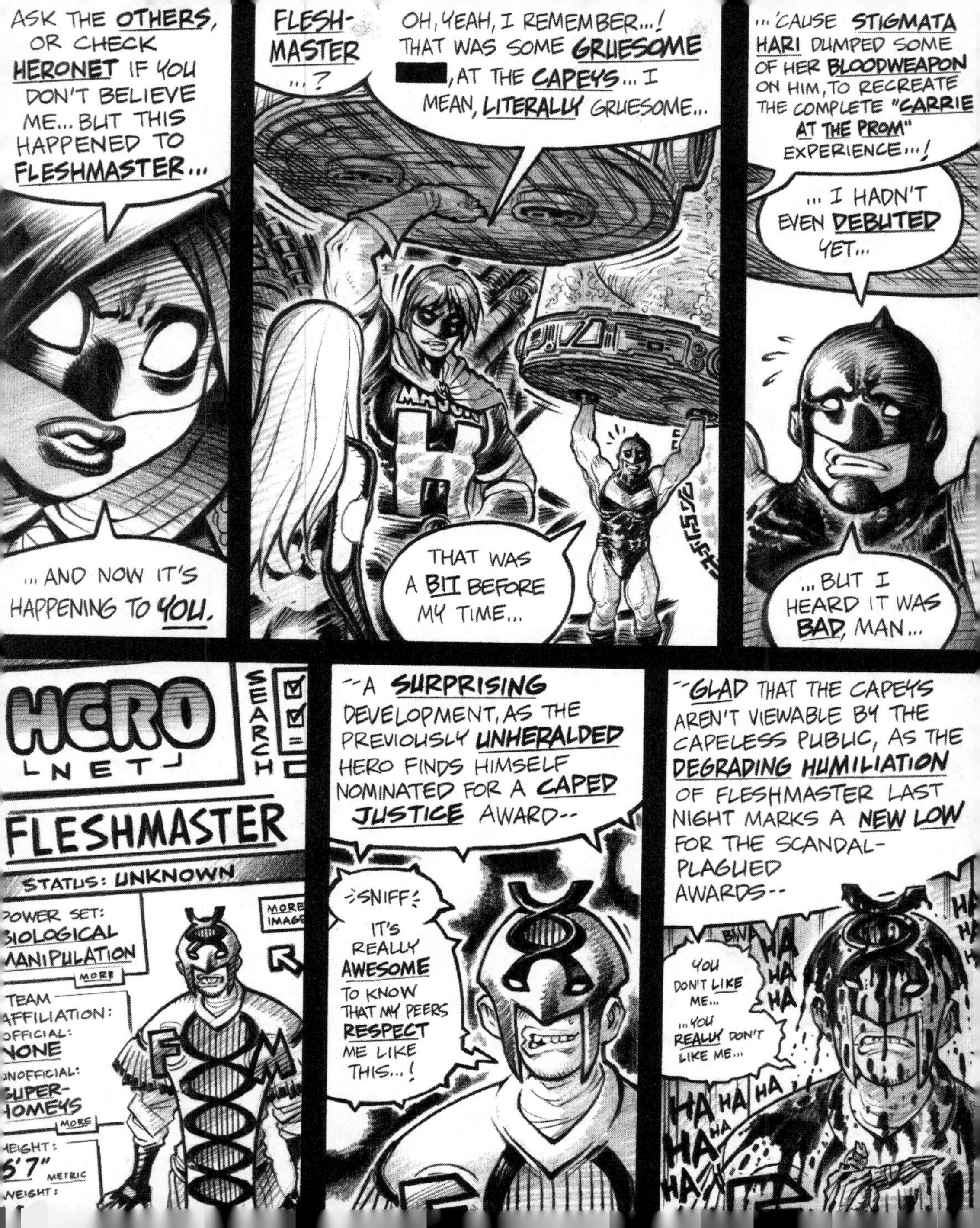
ASK THE OTHERS, OR CHECK HERONET IF YOU DON'T BELIEVE ME... BUT THIS HAPPENED TO FLESHMASTER...
...AND NOW IT'S HAPPENING TO YOU.
FLESH-MASTER ...?
OH, YEAH, I REMEMBER...! THAT WAS SOME GRUESOME [redacted], AT THE CAPEYS... I MEAN, LITERALLY GRUESOME...
THAT WAS A BIT BEFORE MY TIME...
...'CAUSE STIGMATA HARI DUMPED SOME OF HER BLOODWEAPON ON HIM, TO RECREATE THE COMPLETE "CARRIE AT THE PROM" EXPERIENCE...!
...I HADN'T EVEN DEBUTED YET...
...BUT I HEARD IT WAS BAD, MAN...
HERO NET
SEARCH
FLESHMASTER
STATUS: UNKNOWN
POWER SET: BIOLOGICAL MANIPULATION
MORE
MORE IMAGES
TEAM AFFILIATION: OFFICIAL: NONE
UNOFFICIAL: SUPER-HOMEYS
MORE
HEIGHT: 5'7" METRIC
WEIGHT:
--A SURPRISING DEVELOPMENT, AS THE PREVIOUSLY UNHERALDED HERO FINDS HIMSELF NOMINATED FOR A CAPED JUSTICE AWARD--
SNIFF
IT'S REALLY AWESOME TO KNOW THAT MY PEERS RESPECT ME LIKE THIS...!
--GLAD THAT THE CAPEYS AREN'T VIEWABLE BY THE CAPELESS PUBLIC, AS THE DEGRADING HUMILIATION OF FLESHMASTER LAST NIGHT MARKS A NEW LOW FOR THE SCANDAL-PLAGUED AWARDS--
BWA HA HA HA
YOU DON'T LIKE ME... ...YOU REALLY DON'T LIKE ME...
HA HA HA HA HA HA HA

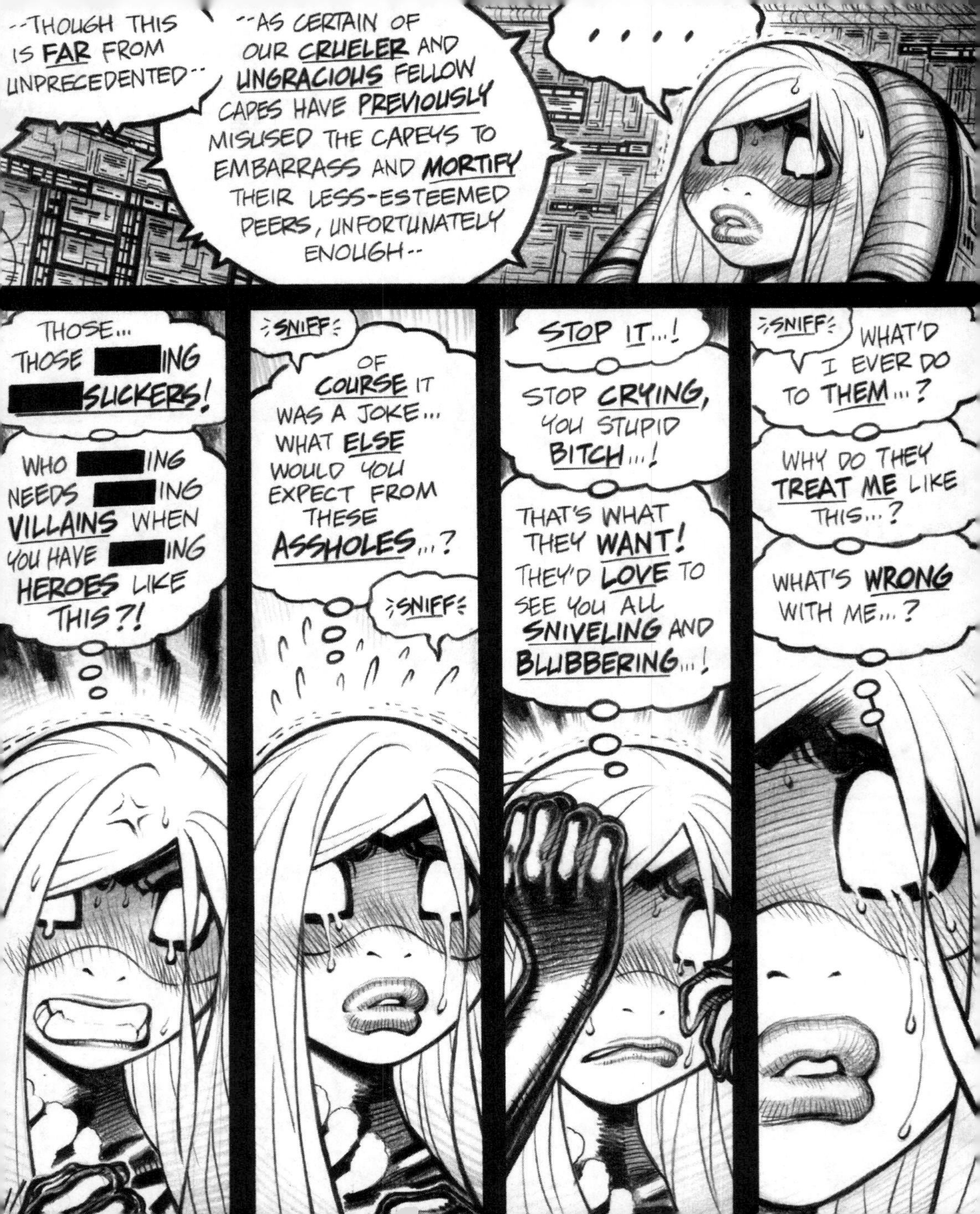
--THOUGH THIS IS FAR FROM UNPRECEDENTED--
--AS CERTAIN OF OUR CRUELER AND UNGRACIOUS FELLOW CAPES HAVE PREVIOUSLY MISUSED THE CAPEYS TO EMBARRASS AND MORTIFY THEIR LESS-ESTEEMED PEERS, UNFORTUNATELY ENOUGH--
....
THOSE... THOSE [redacted]ING [redacted]SLICKERS!
WHO [redacted]ING NEEDS [redacted]ING VILLAINS WHEN YOU HAVE [redacted]ING HEROES LIKE THIS?!
SNIFF
OF COURSE IT WAS A JOKE... WHAT ELSE WOULD YOU EXPECT FROM THESE ASSHOLES...?
SNIFF
STOP IT...!
STOP CRYING, YOU STUPID BITCH...!
THAT'S WHAT THEY WANT! THEY'D LOVE TO SEE YOU ALL SNIVELING AND BLUBBERING...!
SNIFF
WHAT'D I EVER DO TO THEM...?
WHY DO THEY TREAT ME LIKE THIS...?
WHAT'S WRONG WITH ME...?

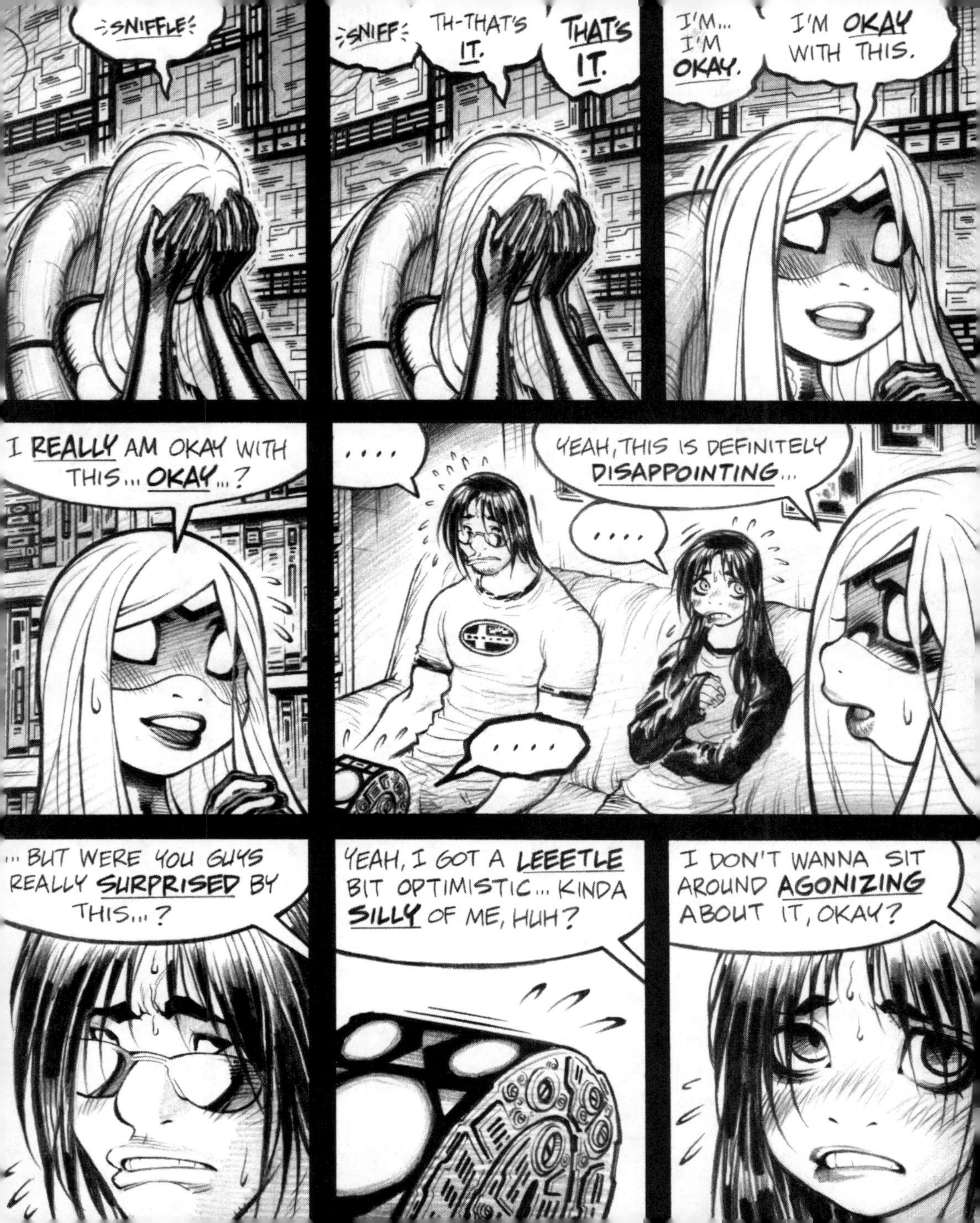
SNIFFLE
SNIFF
TH-THAT'S IT.
THAT'S IT.
I'M... I'M OKAY.
I'M OKAY WITH THIS.
I REALLY AM OKAY WITH THIS... OKAY...?
....
YEAH, THIS IS DEFINITELY DISAPPOINTING...
....
....
...BUT WERE YOU GUYS REALLY SURPRISED BY THIS...?
YEAH, I GOT A LEEETLE BIT OPTIMISTIC... KINDA SILLY OF ME, HUH?
I DON'T WANNA SIT AROUND AGONIZING ABOUT IT, OKAY?

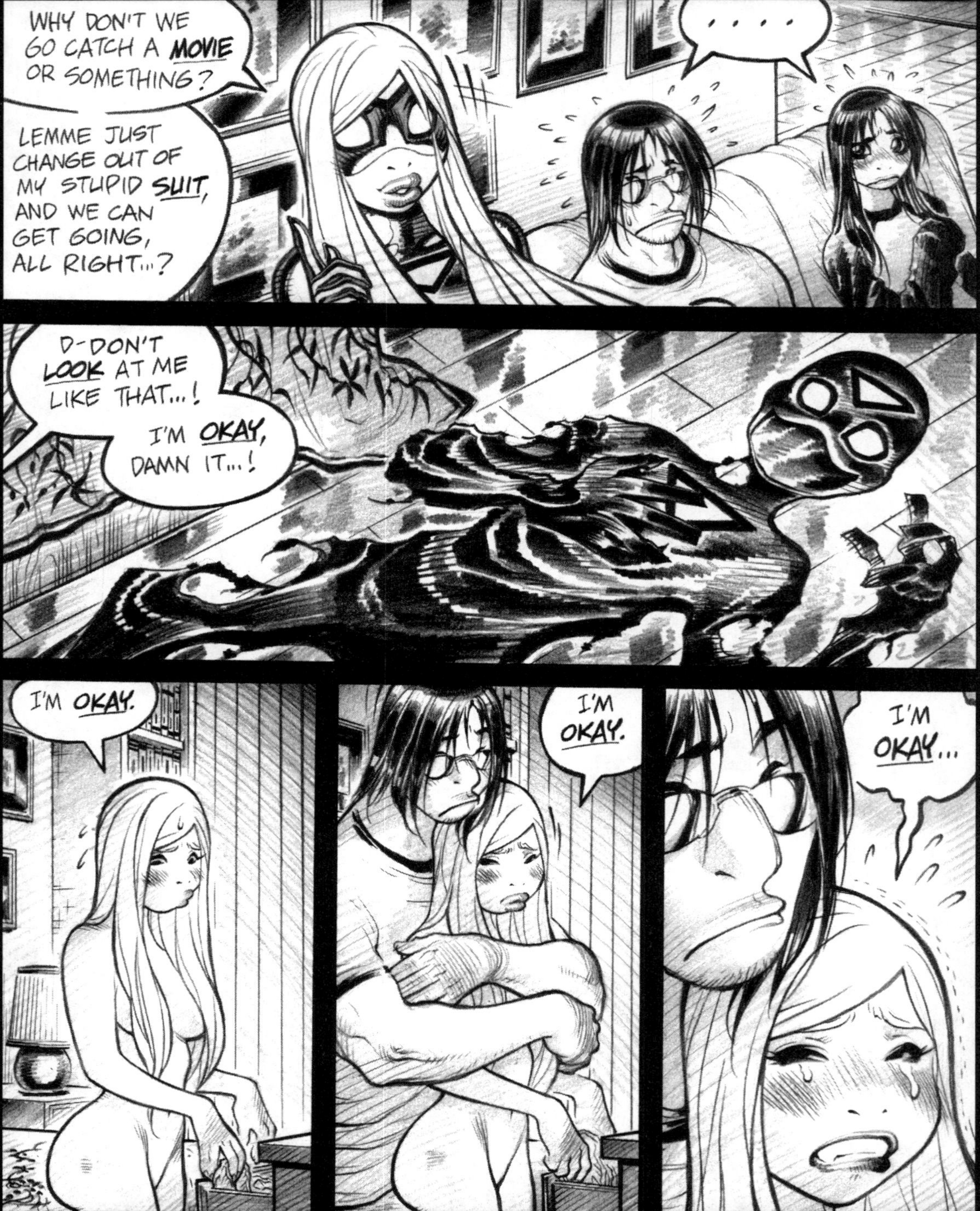
WHY DON'T WE GO CATCH A MOVIE OR SOMETHING?
LEMME JUST CHANGE OUT OF MY STUPID SUIT, AND WE CAN GET GOING, ALL RIGHT...?
. . . .
D-DON'T LOOK AT ME LIKE THAT...!
I'M OKAY, DAMN IT...!
I'M OKAY.
I'M OKAY.
I'M OKAY...

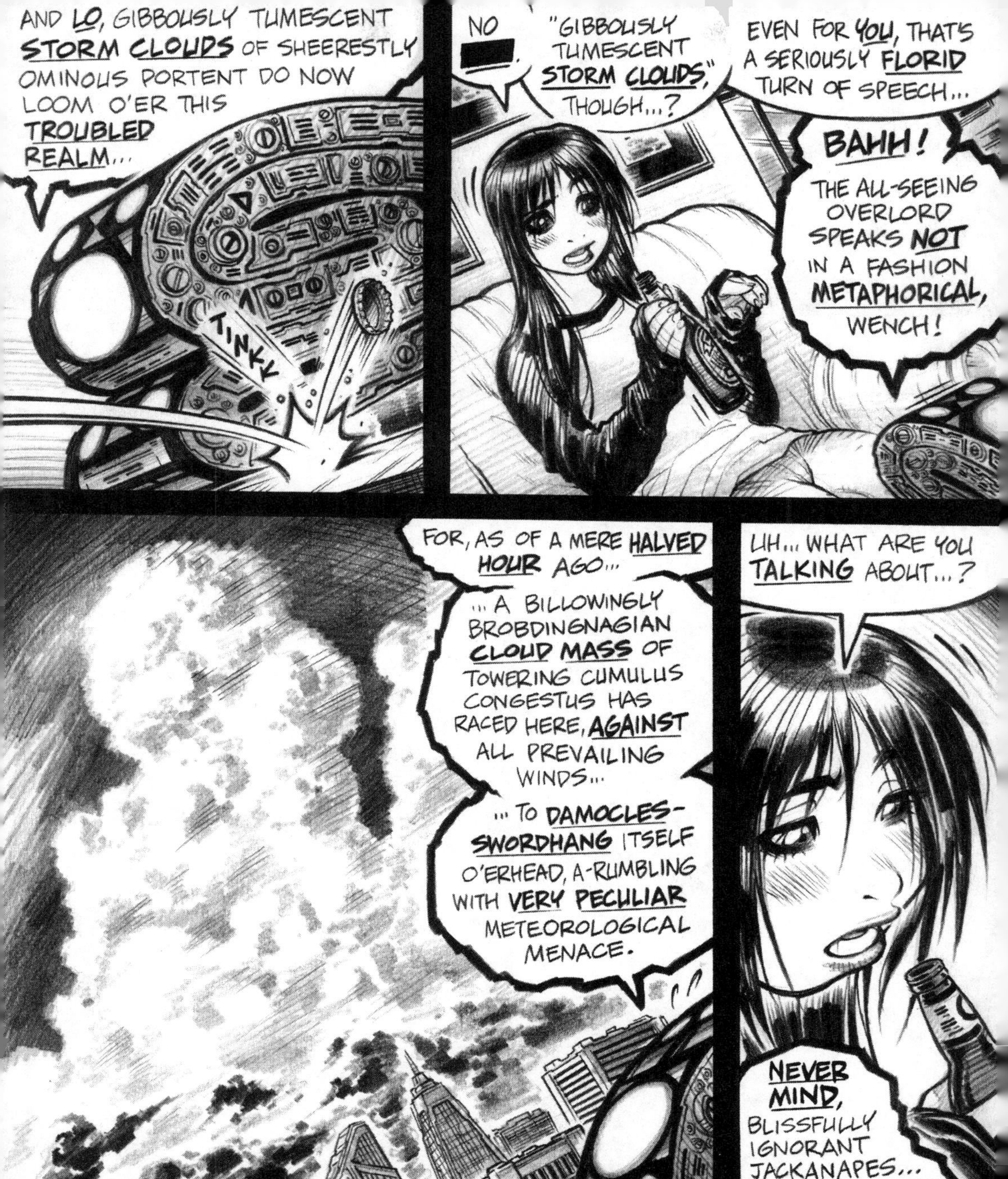
AND LO, GIBBOUSLY TUMESCENT STORM CLOUDS OF SHEERESTLY OMINOUS PORTENT DO NOW LOOM O'ER THIS TROUBLED REALM...
TINKK
NO [redacted].
"GIBBOUSLY TUMESCENT STORM CLOUDS," THOUGH...?
EVEN FOR YOU, THAT'S A SERIOUSLY FLORID TURN OF SPEECH...
BAHH!
THE ALL-SEEING OVERLORD SPEAKS NOT IN A FASHION METAPHORICAL, WENCH!
FOR, AS OF A MERE HALVED HOUR AGO...
...A BILLOWINGLY BROBDINGNAGIAN CLOUD MASS OF TOWERING CUMULUS CONGESTUS HAS RACED HERE, AGAINST ALL PREVAILING WINDS...
...TO DAMOCLES-SWORDHANG ITSELF O'ERHEAD, A-RUMBLING WITH VERY PECULIAR METEOROLOGICAL MENACE.
UH... WHAT ARE YOU TALKING ABOUT...?
NEVER MIND, BLISSFULLY IGNORANT JACKANAPES...
THE IMMORTAL STARBEAST DEIGNS NOT TO WAX SPOILERRIFIC.

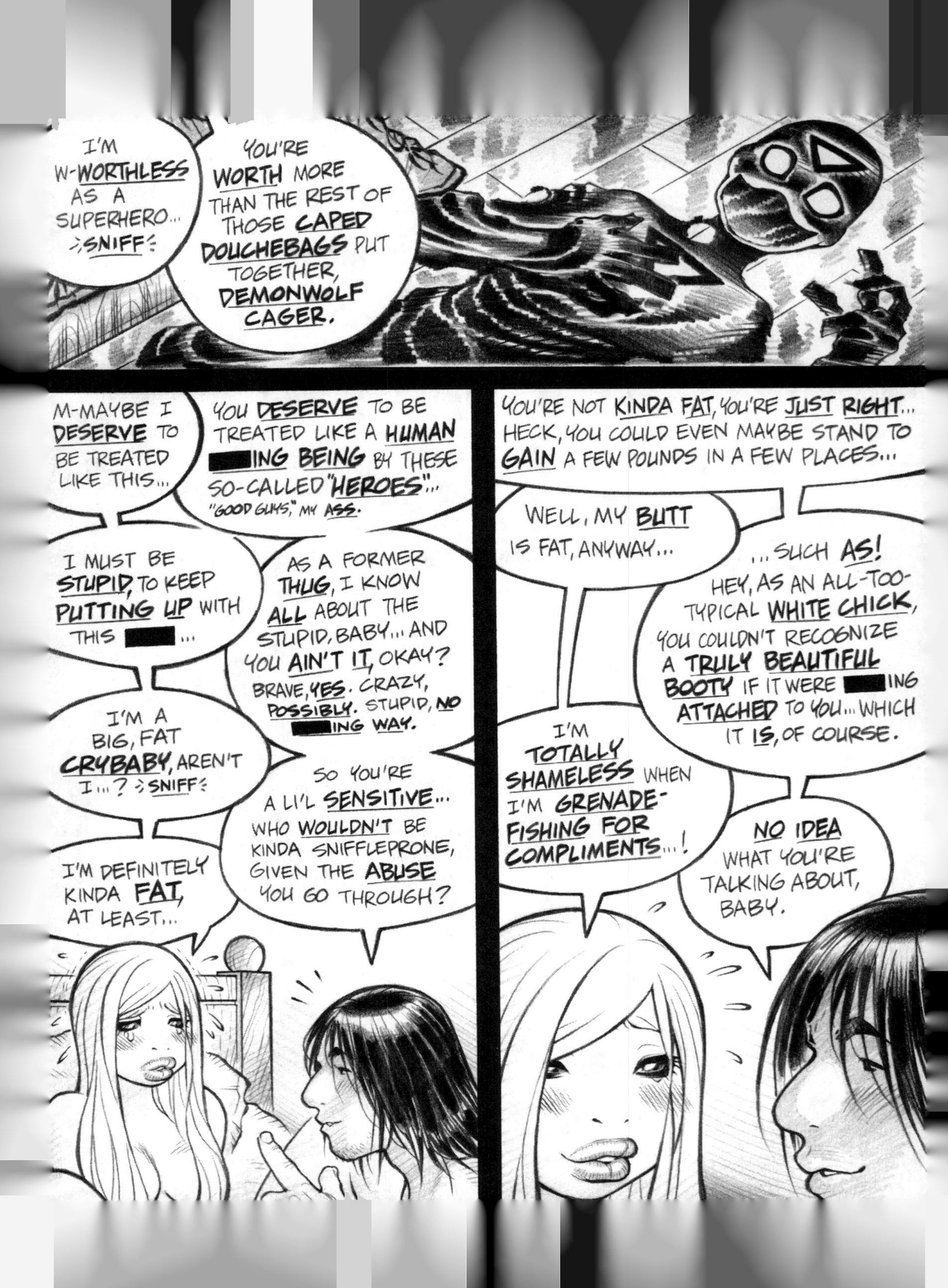
I'M W-WORTHLESS AS A SUPERHERO... SNIFF
YOU'RE WORTH MORE THAN THE REST OF THOSE CAPED DOUCHEBAGS PUT TOGETHER, DEMONWOLF CAGER.
M-MAYBE I DESERVE TO BE TREATED LIKE THIS...
YOU DESERVE TO BE TREATED LIKE A HUMAN [redacted]ING BEING BY THESE SO-CALLED "HEROES"... "GOOD GUYS," MY ASS.
I MUST BE STUPID, TO KEEP PUTTING UP WITH THIS [redacted]...
AS A FORMER THUG, I KNOW ALL ABOUT THE STUPID, BABY... AND YOU AIN'T IT, OKAY? BRAVE, YES. CRAZY, POSSIBLY. STUPID, NO [redacted]ING WAY.
I'M A BIG, FAT CRYBABY, AREN'T I...? SNIFF
SO YOU'RE A LI'L SENSITIVE... WHO WOULDN'T BE KINDA SNIFFLEPRONE, GIVEN THE ABUSE YOU GO THROUGH?
I'M DEFINITELY KINDA FAT, AT LEAST...
YOU'RE NOT KINDA FAT, YOU'RE JUST RIGHT... HECK, YOU COULD EVEN MAYBE STAND TO GAIN A FEW POUNDS IN A FEW PLACES...
WELL, MY BUTT IS FAT, ANYWAY...
...SUCH AS! HEY, AS AN ALL-TOO-TYPICAL WHITE CHICK, YOU COULDN'T RECOGNIZE A TRULY BEAUTIFUL BOOTY IF IT WERE [redacted]ING ATTACHED TO YOU... WHICH IT IS, OF COURSE.
I'M TOTALLY SHAMELESS WHEN I'M GRENADE-FISHING FOR COMPLIMENTS...!
NO IDEA WHAT YOU'RE TALKING ABOUT, BABY.

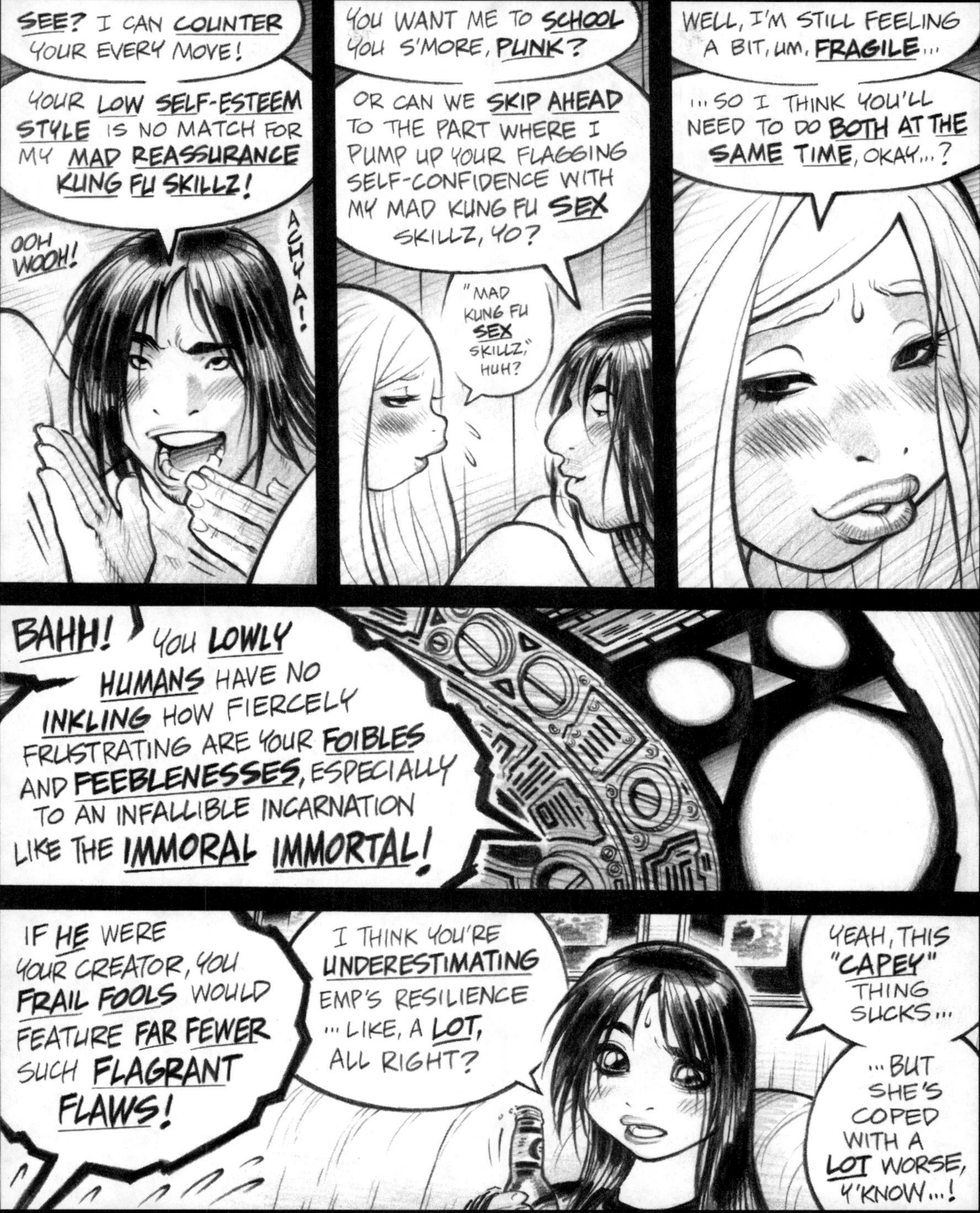
SEE? I CAN COUNTER YOUR EVERY MOVE!
YOUR LOW SELF-ESTEEM STYLE IS NO MATCH FOR MY MAD REASSURANCE KUNG FU SKILLZ!
OOH WOOH!
ACHYA!
YOU WANT ME TO SCHOOL YOU S'MORE, PUNK?
OR CAN WE SKIP AHEAD TO THE PART WHERE I PUMP UP YOUR FLAGGING SELF-CONFIDENCE WITH MY MAD KUNG FU SEX SKILLZ, YO?
"MAD KUNG FU SEX SKILLZ," HUH?
WELL, I'M STILL FEELING A BIT, UM, FRAGILE...
...SO I THINK YOU'LL NEED TO DO BOTH AT THE SAME TIME, OKAY...?
BAHH! YOU LOWLY HUMANS HAVE NO INKLING HOW FIERCELY FRUSTRATING ARE YOUR FOIBLES AND FEEBLENESSES, ESPECIALLY TO AN INFALLIBLE INCARNATION LIKE THE IMMORAL IMMORTAL!
IF HE WERE YOUR CREATOR, YOU FRAIL FOOLS WOULD FEATURE FAR FEWER SUCH FLAGRANT FLAWS!
I THINK YOU'RE UNDERESTIMATING EMP'S RESILIENCE ...LIKE, A LOT, ALL RIGHT?
YEAH, THIS "CAPEY" THING SUCKS...
...BUT SHE'S COPED WITH A LOT WORSE, Y'KNOW...!

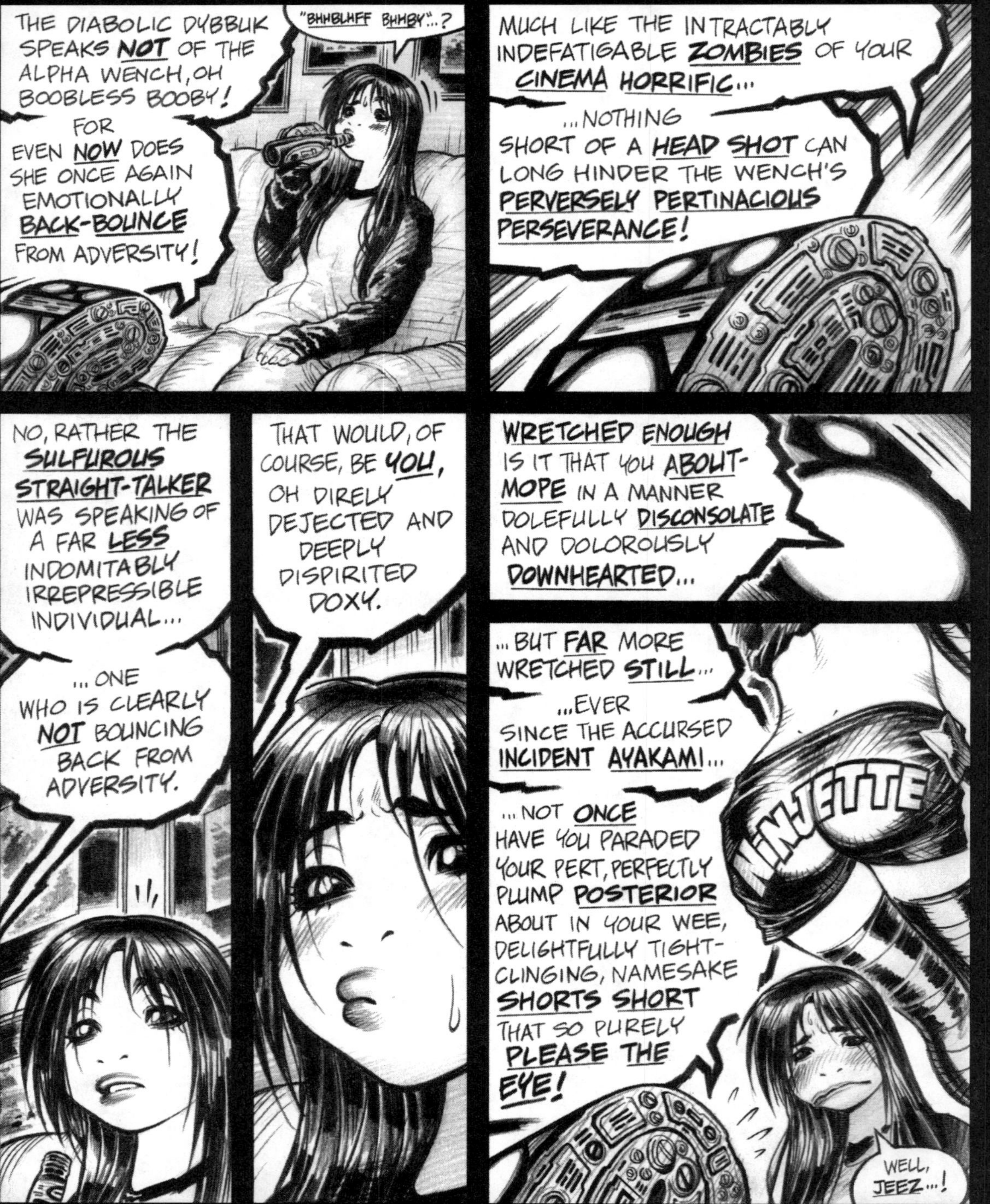
THE DIABOLIC DYBBUK SPEAKS NOT OF THE ALPHA WENCH, OH BOOBLESS BOOBY!
"BHHBLHFF BHHBY"...?
FOR EVEN NOW DOES SHE ONCE AGAIN EMOTIONALLY BACK-BOUNCE FROM ADVERSITY!
MUCH LIKE THE INTRACTABLY INDEFATIGABLE ZOMBIES OF YOUR CINEMA HORRIFIC...
...NOTHING SHORT OF A HEAD SHOT CAN LONG HINDER THE WENCH'S PERVERSELY PERTINACIOUS PERSEVERANCE!
NO, RATHER THE SULFUROUS STRAIGHT-TALKER WAS SPEAKING OF A FAR LESS INDOMITABLY IRREPRESSIBLE INDIVIDUAL...
...ONE WHO IS CLEARLY NOT BOUNCING BACK FROM ADVERSITY.
THAT WOULD, OF COURSE, BE YOU, OH DIRELY DEJECTED AND DEEPLY DISPIRITED DOXY.
WRETCHED ENOUGH IS IT THAT YOU ABOUT-MOPE IN A MANNER DOLEFULLY DISCONSOLATE AND DOLOROUSLY DOWNHEARTED...
...BUT FAR MORE WRETCHED STILL...
...EVER SINCE THE ACCURSED INCIDENT AYAKAMI...
...NOT ONCE HAVE YOU PARADED YOUR PERT, PERFECTLY PLUMP POSTERIOR ABOUT IN YOUR WEE, DELIGHTFULLY TIGHT-CLINGING, NAMESAKE SHORTS SHORT THAT SO PURELY PLEASE THE EYE!
NINJETTE
WELL, JEEZ...!

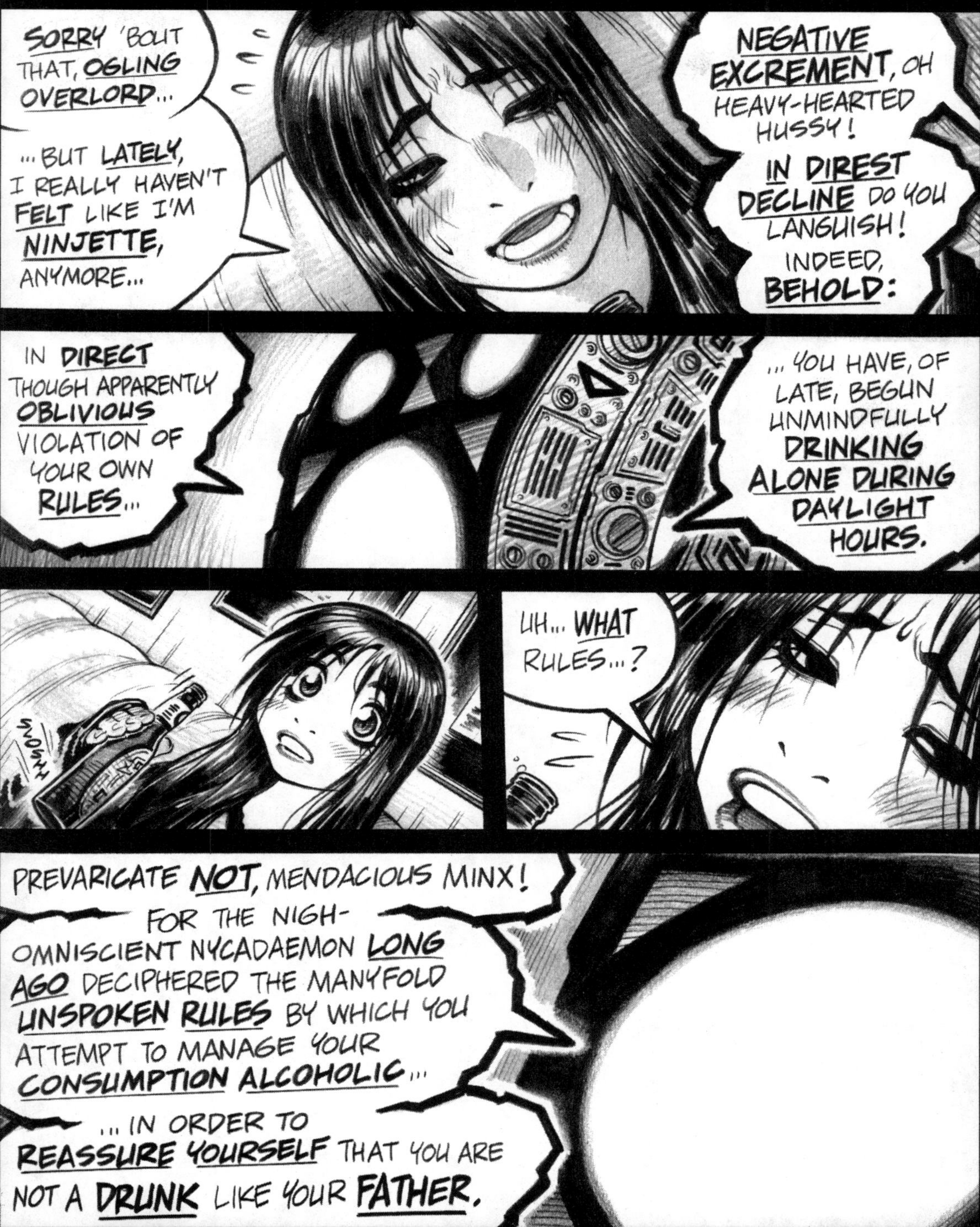
SORRY 'BOUT THAT, OGLING OVERLORD...
...BUT LATELY, I REALLY HAVEN'T FELT LIKE I'M NINJETTE, ANYMORE...
NEGATIVE EXCREMENT, OH HEAVY-HEARTED HUSSY!
IN DIREST DECLINE DO YOU LANGUISH!
INDEED, BEHOLD:
IN DIRECT THOUGH APPARENTLY OBLIVIOUS VIOLATION OF YOUR OWN RULES...
...YOU HAVE, OF LATE, BEGUN UNMINDFULLY DRINKING ALONE DURING DAYLIGHT HOURS.
UH... WHAT RULES...?
PREVARICATE NOT, MENDACIOUS MINX!
FOR THE NIGH-OMNISCIENT NYCADAEMON LONG AGO DECIPHERED THE MANYFOLD UNSPOKEN RULES BY WHICH YOU ATTEMPT TO MANAGE YOUR CONSUMPTION ALCOHOLIC...
...IN ORDER TO REASSURE YOURSELF THAT YOU ARE NOT A DRUNK LIKE YOUR FATHER.

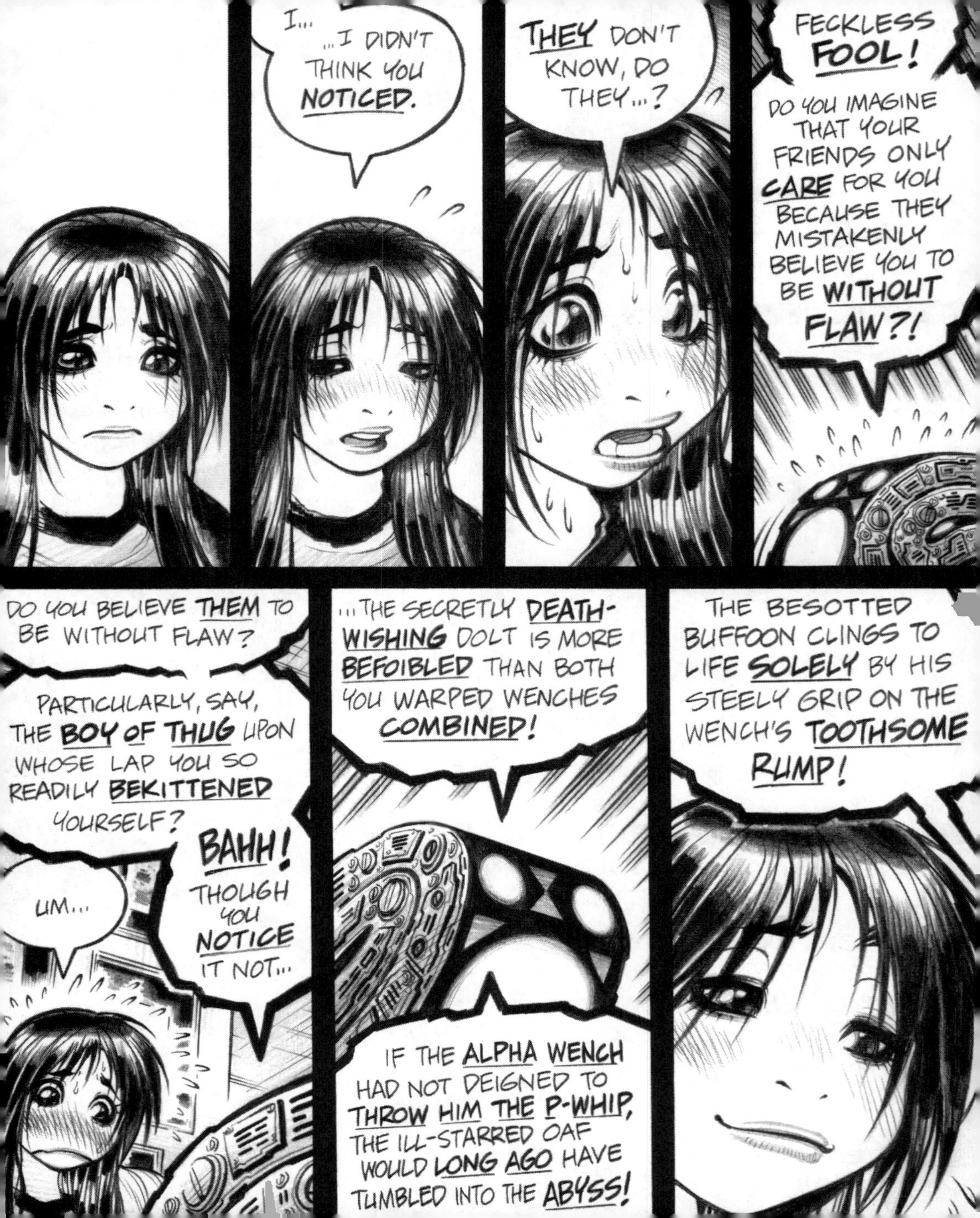
I... ...I DIDN'T THINK YOU NOTICED.
THEY DON'T KNOW, DO THEY...?
FECKLESS FOOL!
DO YOU IMAGINE THAT YOUR FRIENDS ONLY CARE FOR YOU BECAUSE THEY MISTAKENLY BELIEVE YOU TO BE WITHOUT FLAW?!
DO YOU BELIEVE THEM TO BE WITHOUT FLAW?
PARTICULARLY, SAY, THE BOY OF THUG UPON WHOSE LAP YOU SO READILY BEKITTENED YOURSELF?
UM...
BAHH! THOUGH YOU NOTICE IT NOT...
...THE SECRETLY DEATH-WISHING DOLT IS MORE BEFOIBLED THAN BOTH YOU WARPED WENCHES COMBINED!
IF THE ALPHA WENCH HAD NOT DEIGNED TO THROW HIM THE P-WHIP, THE ILL-STARRED OAF WOULD LONG AGO HAVE TUMBLED INTO THE ABYSS!
THE BESOTTED BUFFOON CLINGS TO LIFE SOLELY BY HIS STEELY GRIP ON THE WENCH'S TOOTHSOME RUMP!

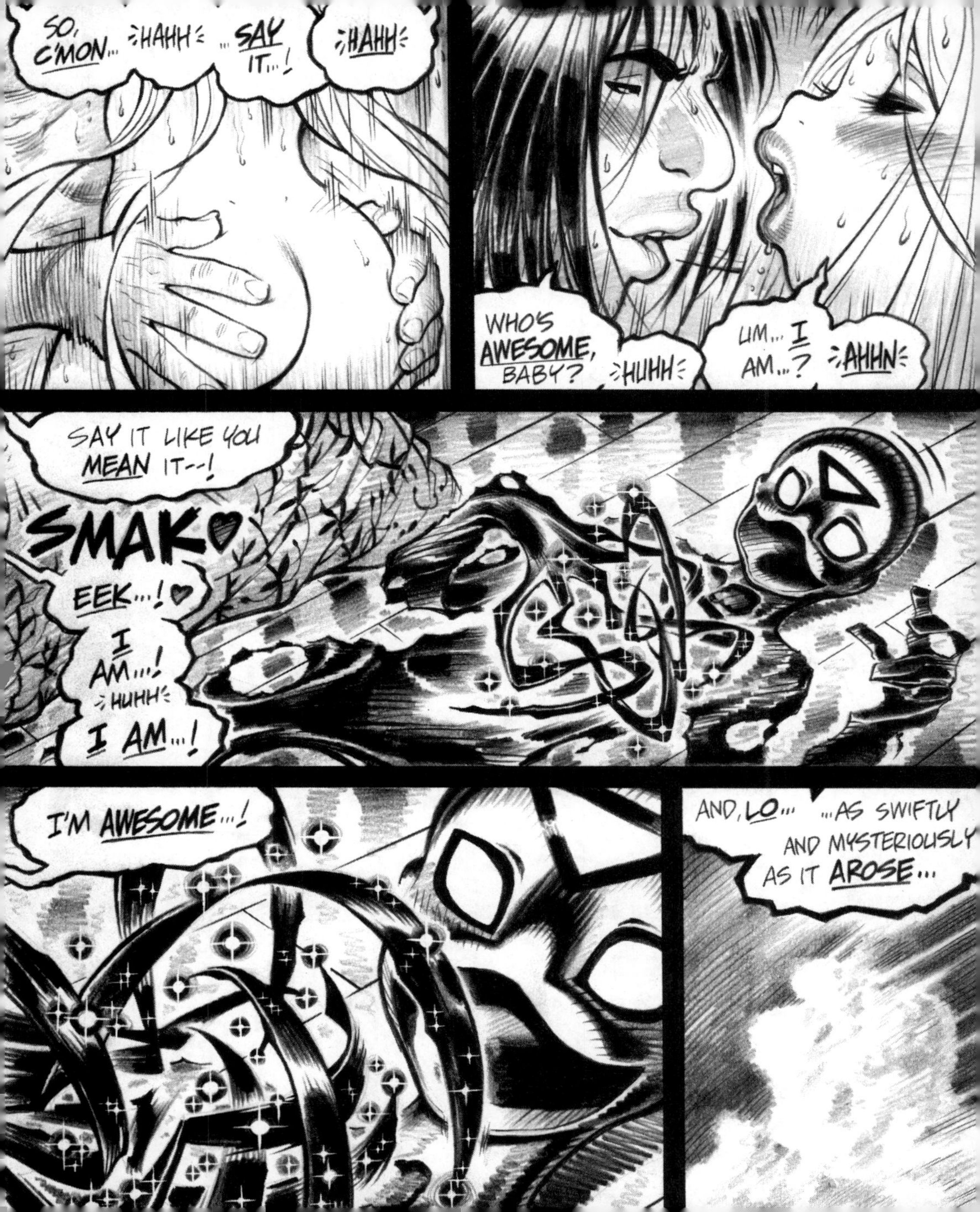
SO, C'MON...
HAHH
...SAY IT...!
HAHH
WHO'S AWESOME, BABY?
HUHH
UM... I AM...?
AHHN
SAY IT LIKE YOU MEAN IT--!
SMAK♥
EEK...!♥
I AM...!
HUHH
I AM...!
I'M AWESOME...!
AND, LO... ...AS SWIFTLY AND MYSTERIOUSLY AS IT AROSE...

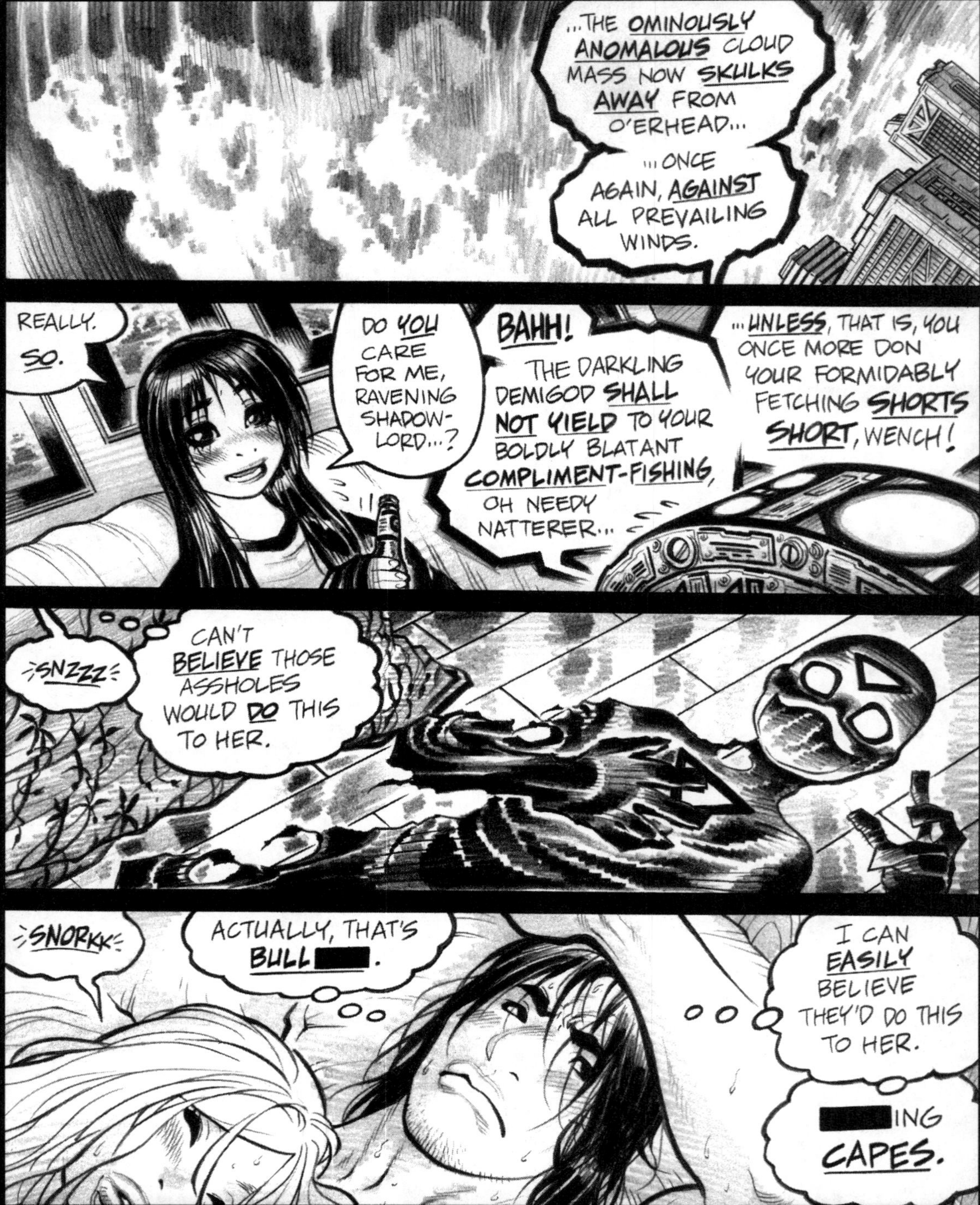
...THE OMINOUSLY ANOMALOUS CLOUD MASS NOW SKULKS AWAY FROM O'ERHEAD...
...ONCE AGAIN, AGAINST ALL PREVAILING WINDS.
REALLY. SO.
DO YOU CARE FOR ME, RAVENING SHADOW-LORD...?
BAHH! THE DARKLING DEMIGOD SHALL NOT YIELD TO YOUR BOLDLY BLATANT COMPLIMENT-FISHING, OH NEEDY NATTERER...
...UNLESS, THAT IS, YOU ONCE MORE DON YOUR FORMIDABLY FETCHING SHORTS SHORT, WENCH!
SNZZZ
CAN'T BELIEVE THOSE ASSHOLES WOULD DO THIS TO HER.
SNORKK
ACTUALLY, THAT'S BULL[redacted].
I CAN EASILY BELIEVE THEY'D DO THIS TO HER.
[redacted]ING CAPES.

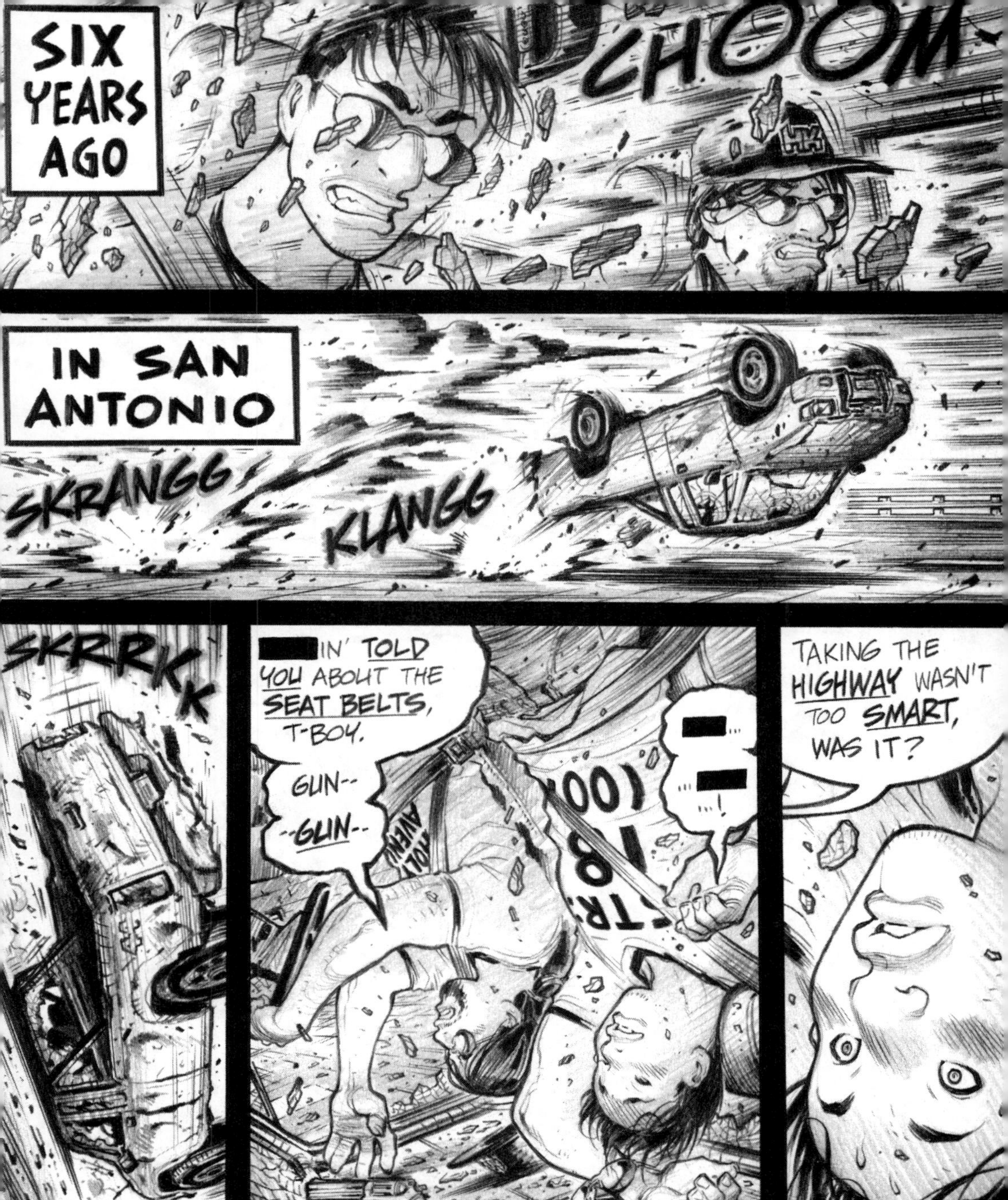
SIX YEARS AGO
CHOOM
IN SAN ANTONIO
SKRANGG
KLANGG
SKRRKK
[redacted]IN' TOLD YOU ABOUT THE SEAT BELTS, T-BOY.
GUN-- --GUN--
[redacted]... [redacted]...!
TAKING THE HIGHWAY WASN'T TOO SMART, WAS IT?

AND I HEARD YOU GUYS WERE SUPPOSED TO BE A **CLEVER** LITTLE BUNCH OF **CAPEKILLING ASSHOLES**, TOO.

WELL, GUESS **WHAT?**

IT'S TIME FOR YOU PUNK-ASS ████ES TO **SAYO** YOUR ████ING **NARA**S.

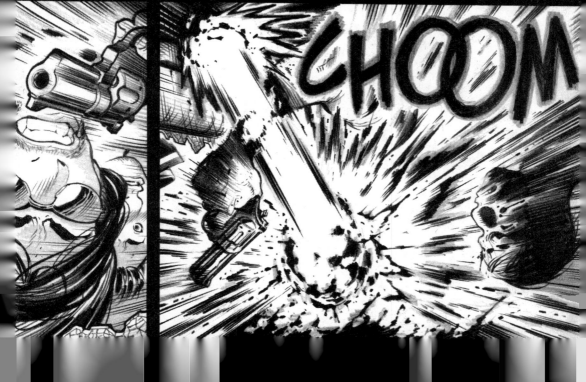

CHOOM

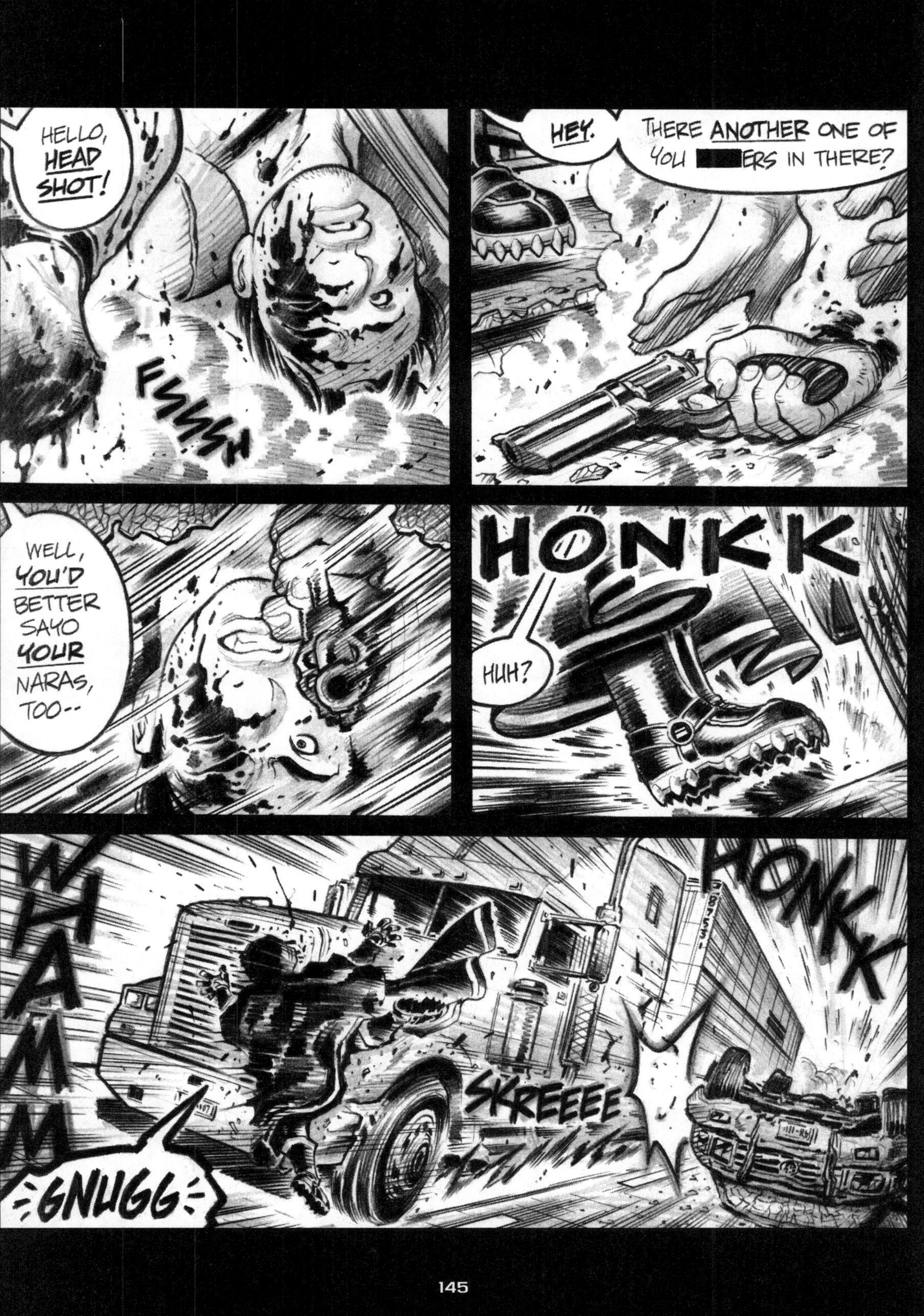
HELLO, HEAD SHOT!
FWSSH
HEY.
THERE ANOTHER ONE OF YOU [redacted]ERS IN THERE?
WELL, YOU'D BETTER SAYO YOUR NARAS, TOO--
HONKK
HUH?
WHAMM
HONKK
SKREEEE
GNUGG

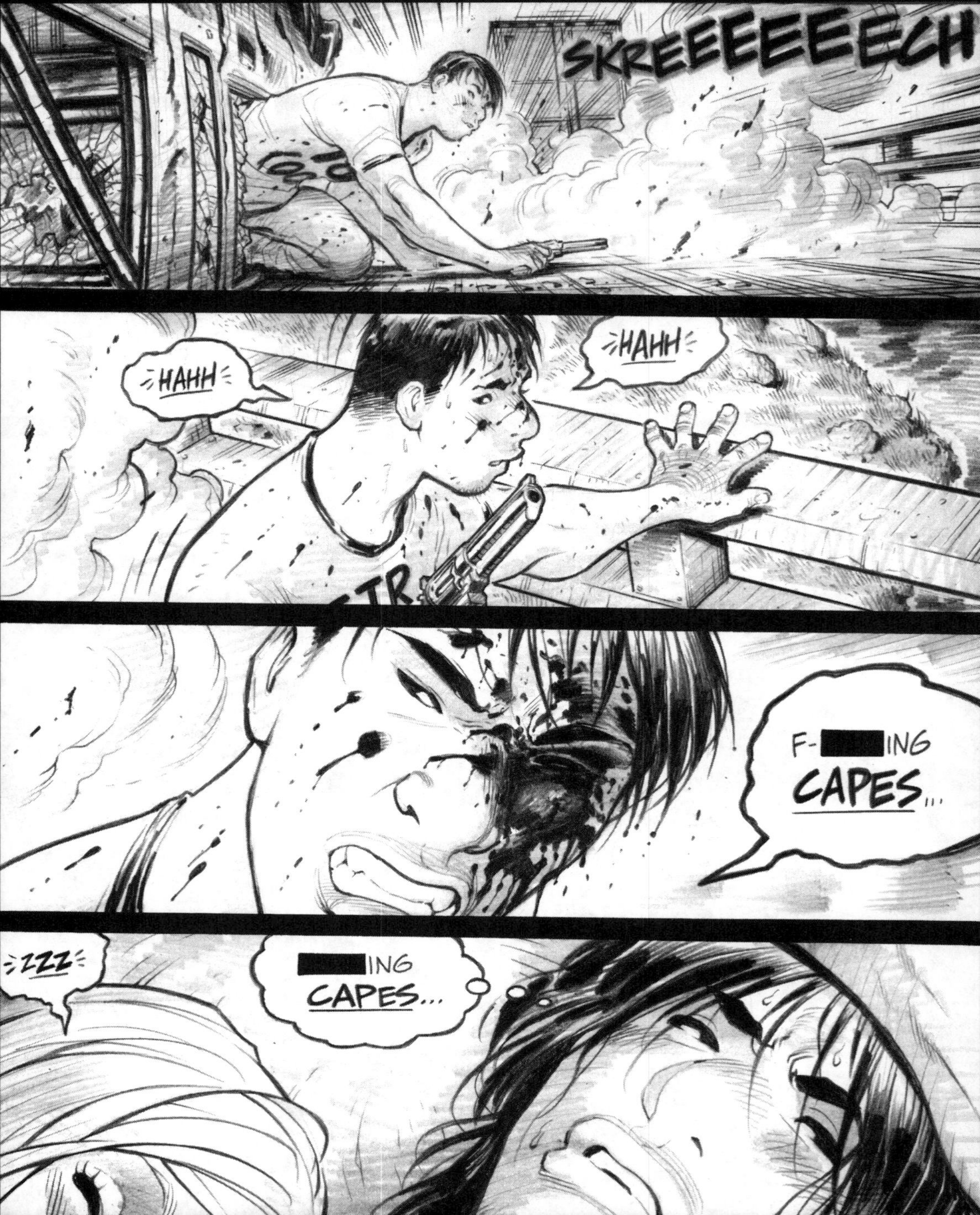
SKREEEEEEECH
HAHH
HAHH
F-[redacted]ING CAPES...
ZZZ
[redacted]ING CAPES...

Proud and Delighted

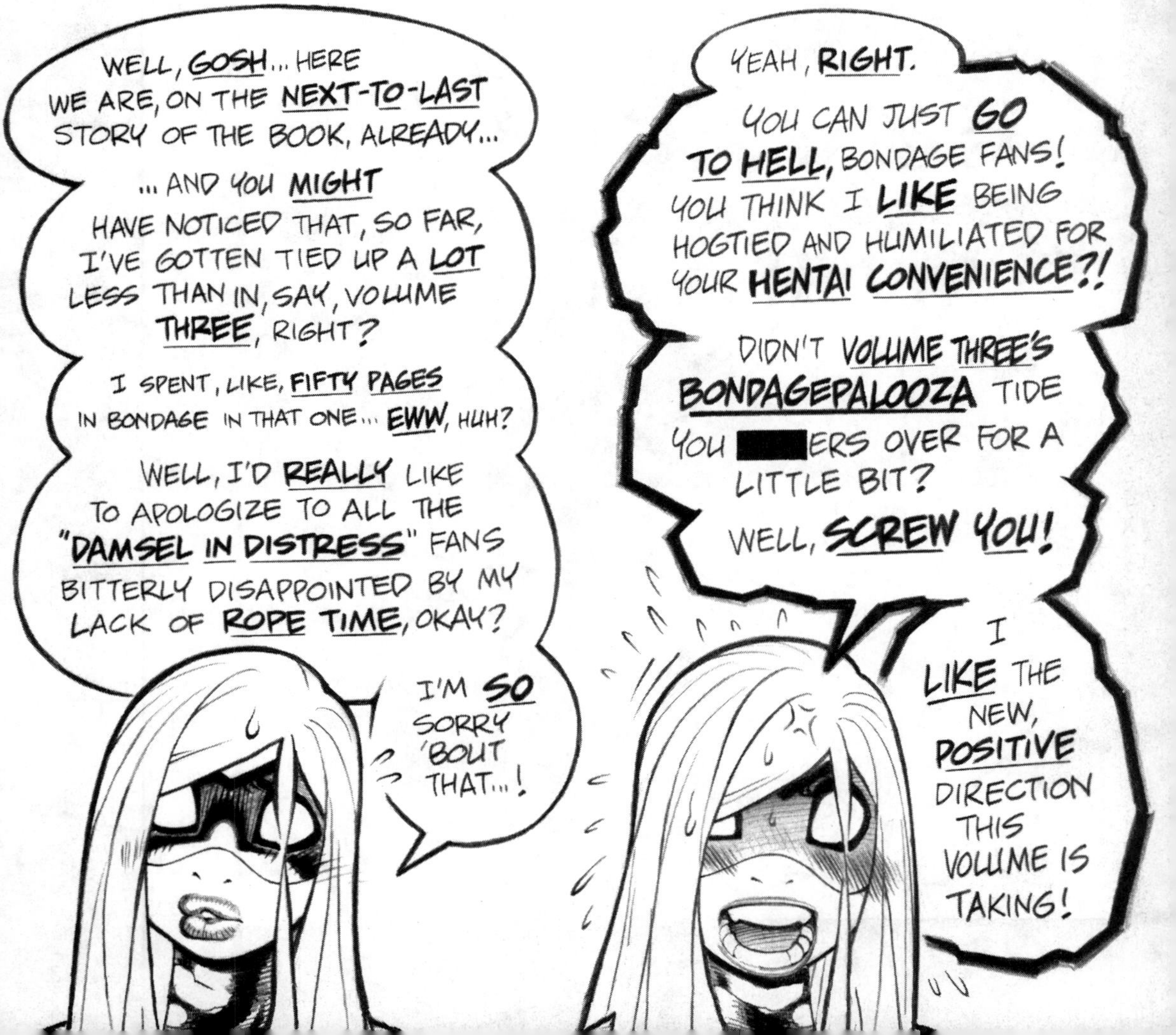
WELL, GOSH... HERE WE ARE, ON THE NEXT-TO-LAST STORY OF THE BOOK, ALREADY...
... AND YOU MIGHT HAVE NOTICED THAT, SO FAR, I'VE GOTTEN TIED UP A LOT LESS THAN IN, SAY, VOLUME THREE, RIGHT?
I SPENT, LIKE, FIFTY PAGES IN BONDAGE IN THAT ONE... EWW, HUH?
WELL, I'D REALLY LIKE TO APOLOGIZE TO ALL THE "DAMSEL IN DISTRESS" FANS BITTERLY DISAPPOINTED BY MY LACK OF ROPE TIME, OKAY?
I'M SO SORRY 'BOUT THAT...!
YEAH, RIGHT.
YOU CAN JUST GO TO HELL, BONDAGE FANS! YOU THINK I LIKE BEING HOGTIED AND HUMILIATED FOR YOUR HENTAI CONVENIENCE?!
DIDN'T VOLUME THREE'S BONDAGEPALOOZA TIDE YOU [redacted]ERS OVER FOR A LITTLE BIT?
WELL, SCREW YOU!
I LIKE THE NEW, POSITIVE DIRECTION THIS VOLUME IS TAKING!

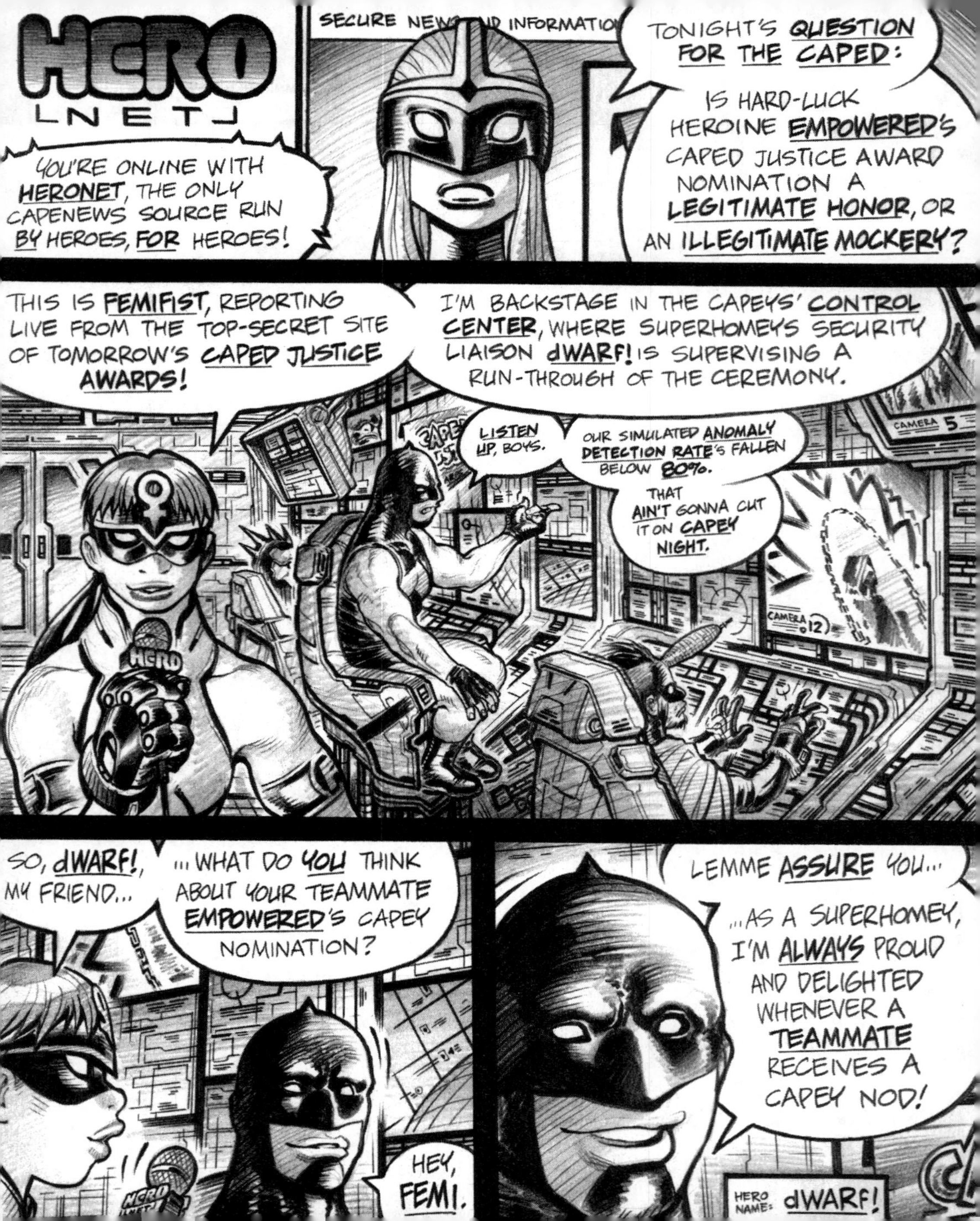
HERO NET
SECURE NEWS AND INFORMATION
YOU'RE ONLINE WITH HERONET, THE ONLY CAPENEWS SOURCE RUN BY HEROES, FOR HEROES!
TONIGHT'S QUESTION FOR THE CAPED:
IS HARD-LUCK HEROINE EMPOWERED'S CAPED JUSTICE AWARD NOMINATION A LEGITIMATE HONOR, OR AN ILLEGITIMATE MOCKERY?
THIS IS FEMIFIST, REPORTING LIVE FROM THE TOP-SECRET SITE OF TOMORROW'S CAPED JUSTICE AWARDS!
I'M BACKSTAGE IN THE CAPEYS' CONTROL CENTER, WHERE SUPERHOMEYS SECURITY LIAISON dWARF! IS SUPERVISING A RUN-THROUGH OF THE CEREMONY.
LISTEN UP, BOYS.
OUR SIMULATED ANOMALY DETECTION RATE'S FALLEN BELOW 80%.
THAT AIN'T GONNA CUT IT ON CAPEY NIGHT.
CAMERA 5
CAMERA 12
HERO
SO, dWARF!, MY FRIEND...
...WHAT DO YOU THINK ABOUT YOUR TEAMMATE EMPOWERED'S CAPEY NOMINATION?
HEY, FEMI.
LEMME ASSURE YOU...
...AS A SUPERHOMEY, I'M ALWAYS PROUD AND DELIGHTED WHENEVER A TEAMMATE RECEIVES A CAPEY NOD!
HERO NAME: dWARF!

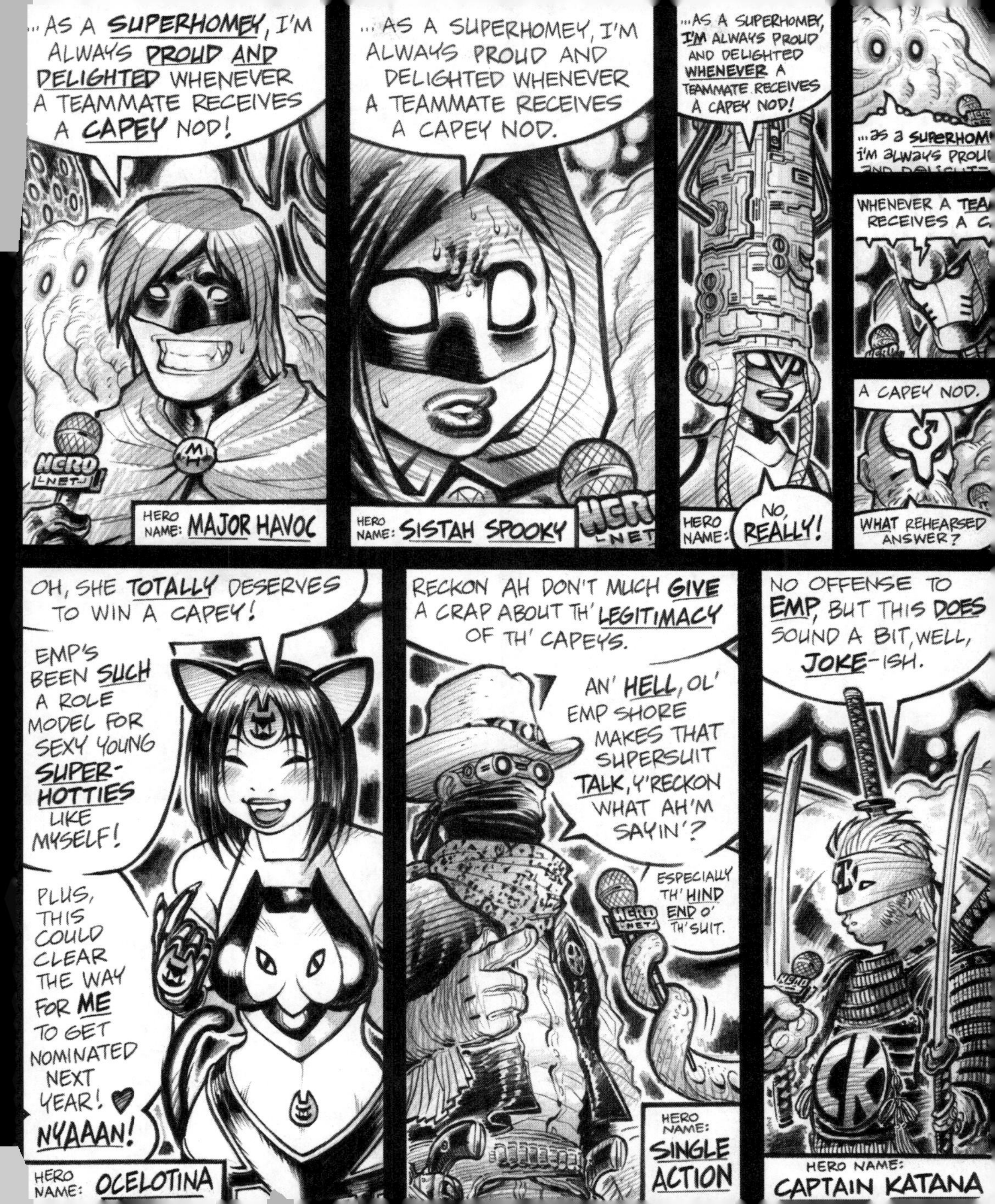
...AS A SUPERHOMEY, I'M ALWAYS PROUD AND DELIGHTED WHENEVER A TEAMMATE RECEIVES A CAPEY NOD!
HERO NAME: MAJOR HAVOC
...AS A SUPERHOMEY, I'M ALWAYS PROUD AND DELIGHTED WHENEVER A TEAMMATE RECEIVES A CAPEY NOD.
HERO NAME: SISTAH SPOOKY
...AS A SUPERHOMEY, I'M ALWAYS PROUD AND DELIGHTED WHENEVER A TEAMMATE RECEIVES A CAPEY NOD!
NO, REALLY!
HERO NAME:
A CAPEY NOD.
WHAT REHEARSED ANSWER?
OH, SHE TOTALLY DESERVES TO WIN A CAPEY!
EMP'S BEEN SUCH A ROLE MODEL FOR SEXY YOUNG SUPER-HOTTIES LIKE MYSELF!
PLUS, THIS COULD CLEAR THE WAY FOR ME TO GET NOMINATED NEXT YEAR! ♥
NYAAAN!
HERO NAME: OCELOTINA
RECKON AH DON'T MUCH GIVE A CRAP ABOUT TH' LEGITIMACY OF TH' CAPEYS.
AN' HELL, OL' EMP SHORE MAKES THAT SUPERSUIT TALK, Y'RECKON WHAT AH'M SAYIN'?
ESPECIALLY TH' HIND END O' TH' SUIT.
HERO NAME: SINGLE ACTION
NO OFFENSE TO EMP, BUT THIS DOES SOUND A BIT, WELL, JOKE-ISH.
HERO NAME: CAPTAIN KATANA

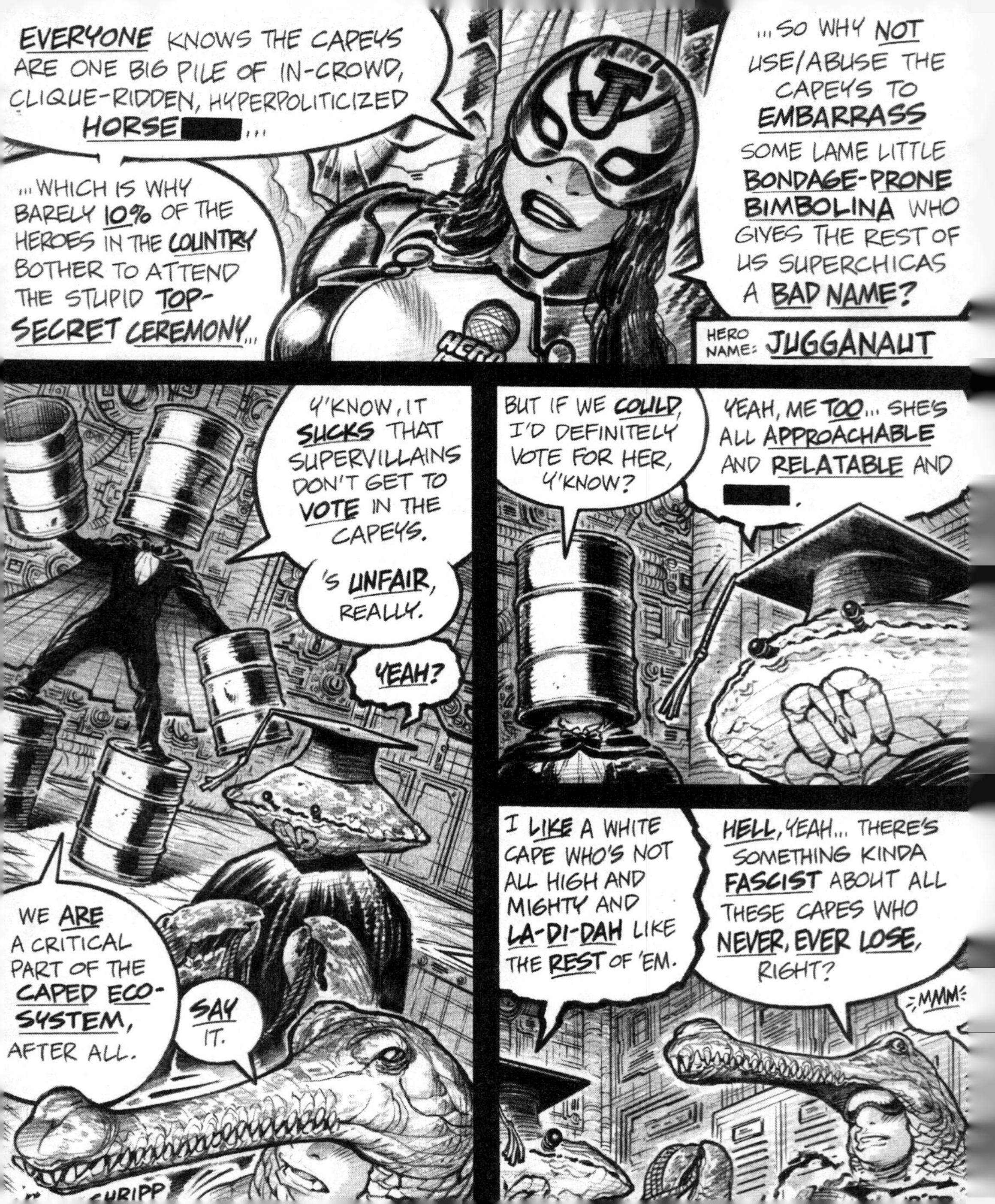
EVERYONE KNOWS THE CAPEYS ARE ONE BIG PILE OF IN-CROWD, CLIQUE-RIDDEN, HYPERPOLITICIZED HORSE[redacted]...
...WHICH IS WHY BARELY 10% OF THE HEROES IN THE COUNTRY BOTHER TO ATTEND THE STUPID TOP-SECRET CEREMONY...
...SO WHY NOT USE/ABUSE THE CAPEYS TO EMBARRASS SOME LAME LITTLE BONDAGE-PRONE BIMBOLINA WHO GIVES THE REST OF US SUPERCHICAS A BAD NAME?
HERO NAME: JUGGANAUT
Y'KNOW, IT SUCKS THAT SUPERVILLAINS DON'T GET TO VOTE IN THE CAPEYS.
'S UNFAIR, REALLY.
YEAH?
WE ARE A CRITICAL PART OF THE CAPED ECO-SYSTEM, AFTER ALL.
SAY IT.
BUT IF WE COULD, I'D DEFINITELY VOTE FOR HER, Y'KNOW?
YEAH, ME TOO... SHE'S ALL APPROACHABLE AND RELATABLE AND [redacted].
I LIKE A WHITE CAPE WHO'S NOT ALL HIGH AND MIGHTY AND LA-DI-DAH LIKE THE REST OF 'EM.
HELL, YEAH... THERE'S SOMETHING KINDA FASCIST ABOUT ALL THESE CAPES WHO NEVER, EVER LOSE, RIGHT?
MMM

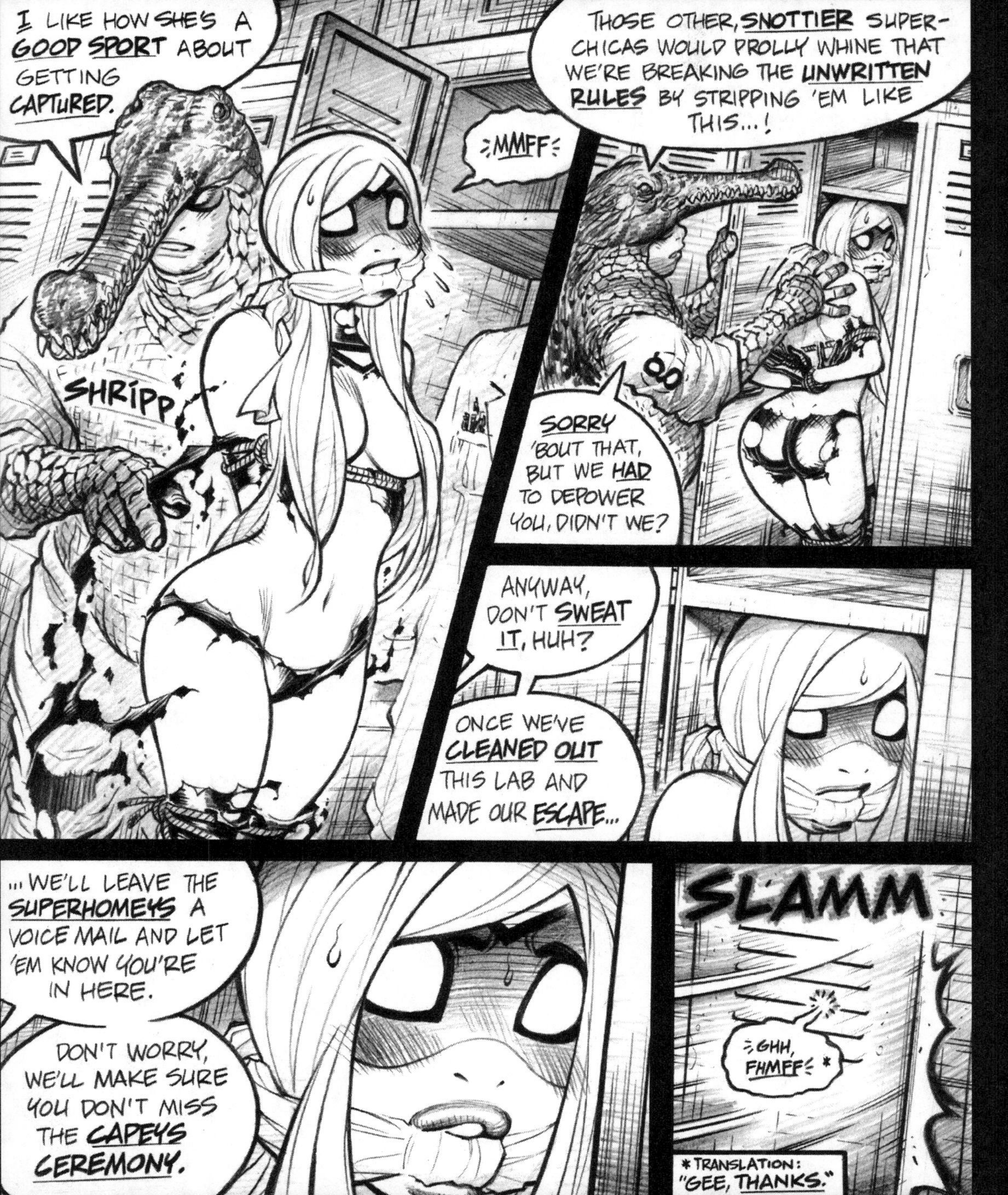
I LIKE HOW SHE'S A GOOD SPORT ABOUT GETTING CAPTURED.
SHRIPP
MMFF
THOSE OTHER, SNOTTIER SUPER-CHICAS WOULD PROLLY WHINE THAT WE'RE BREAKING THE UNWRITTEN RULES BY STRIPPING 'EM LIKE THIS...!
SORRY 'BOUT THAT, BUT WE HAD TO DEPOWER YOU, DIDN'T WE?
ANYWAY, DON'T SWEAT IT, HUH?
ONCE WE'VE CLEANED OUT THIS LAB AND MADE OUR ESCAPE...
...WE'LL LEAVE THE SUPERHOMEYS A VOICE MAIL AND LET 'EM KNOW YOU'RE IN HERE.
DON'T WORRY, WE'LL MAKE SURE YOU DON'T MISS THE CAPEYS CEREMONY.
SLAMM
GHH, FHMFF *
* TRANSLATION: "GEE, THANKS."

empowered™

Because This Is What I Am

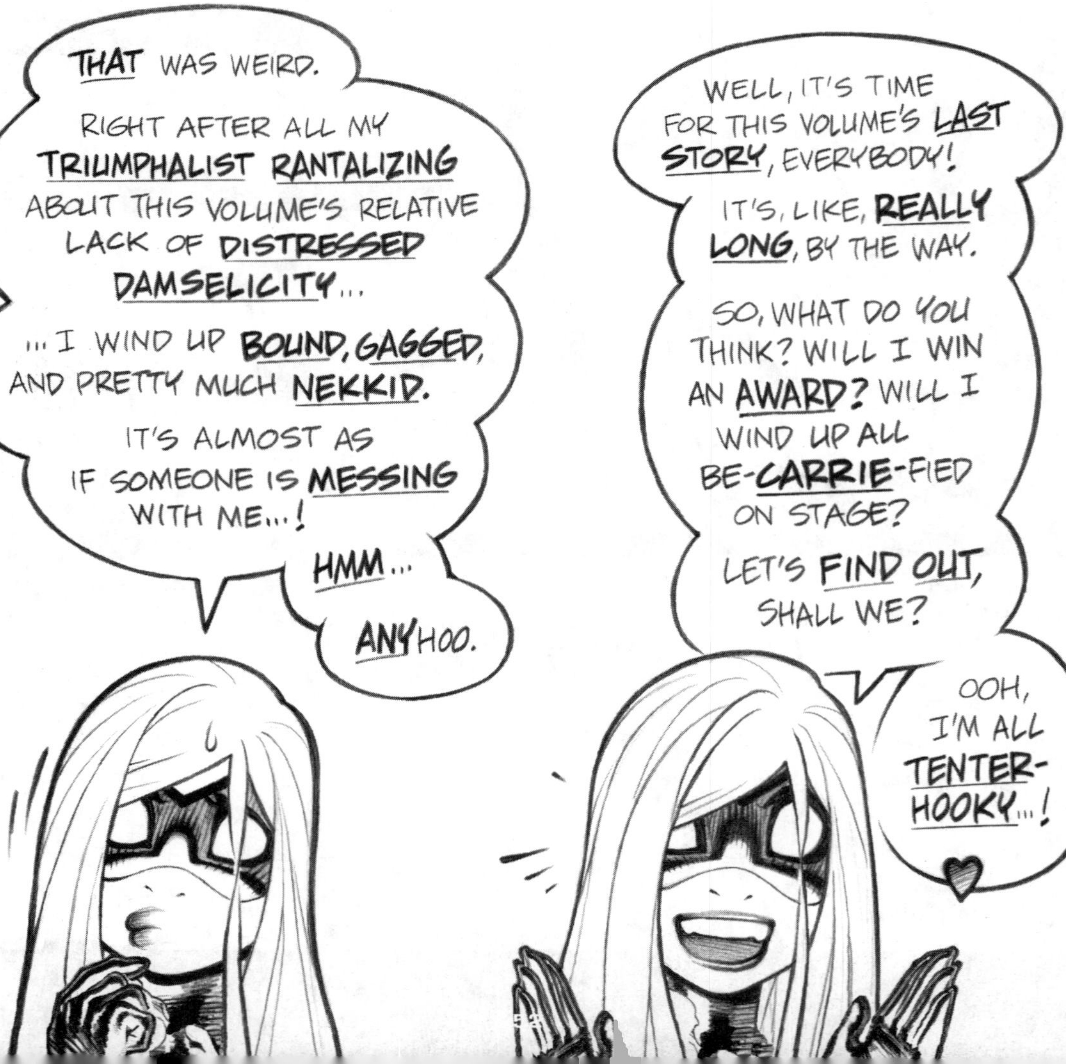

THAT WAS WEIRD.
RIGHT AFTER ALL MY TRIUMPHALIST RANTALIZING ABOUT THIS VOLUME'S RELATIVE LACK OF DISTRESSED DAMSELICITY...
...I WIND UP BOUND, GAGGED, AND PRETTY MUCH NEKKID.
IT'S ALMOST AS IF SOMEONE IS MESSING WITH ME...!
HMM...
ANYHOO.
WELL, IT'S TIME FOR THIS VOLUME'S LAST STORY, EVERYBODY!
IT'S, LIKE, REALLY LONG, BY THE WAY.
SO, WHAT DO YOU THINK? WILL I WIN AN AWARD? WILL I WIND UP ALL BE-CARRIE-FIED ON STAGE?
LET'S FIND OUT, SHALL WE?
OOH, I'M ALL TENTER-HOOKY...!

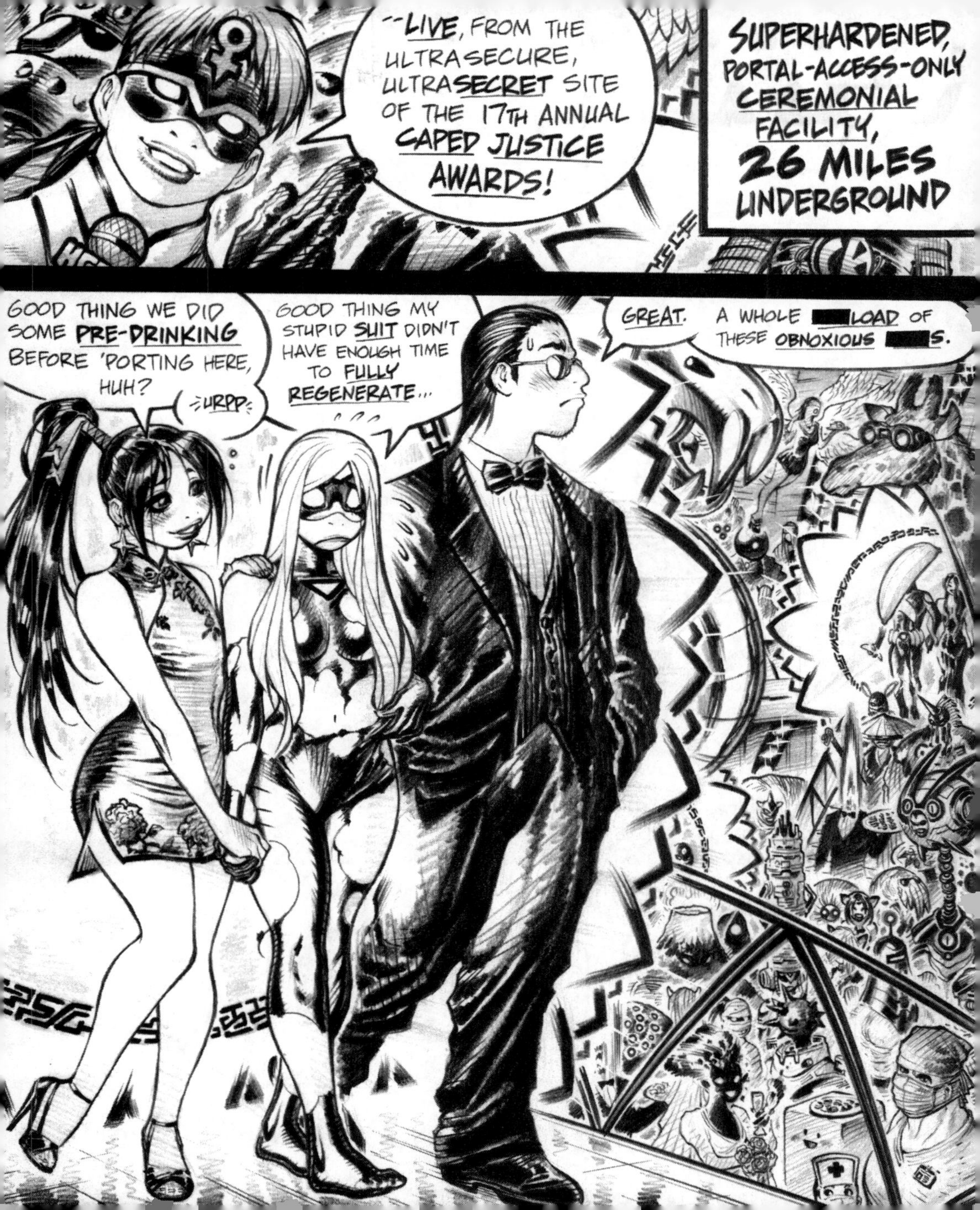
--LIVE, FROM THE ULTRASECURE, ULTRASECRET SITE OF THE 17TH ANNUAL CAPED JUSTICE AWARDS!
SUPERHARDENED, PORTAL-ACCESS-ONLY CEREMONIAL FACILITY, 26 MILES UNDERGROUND
GOOD THING WE DID SOME PRE-DRINKING BEFORE 'PORTING HERE, HUH?
URPP
GOOD THING MY STUPID SUIT DIDN'T HAVE ENOUGH TIME TO FULLY REGENERATE...
GREAT.
A WHOLE [redacted]LOAD OF THESE OBNOXIOUS [redacted]S.

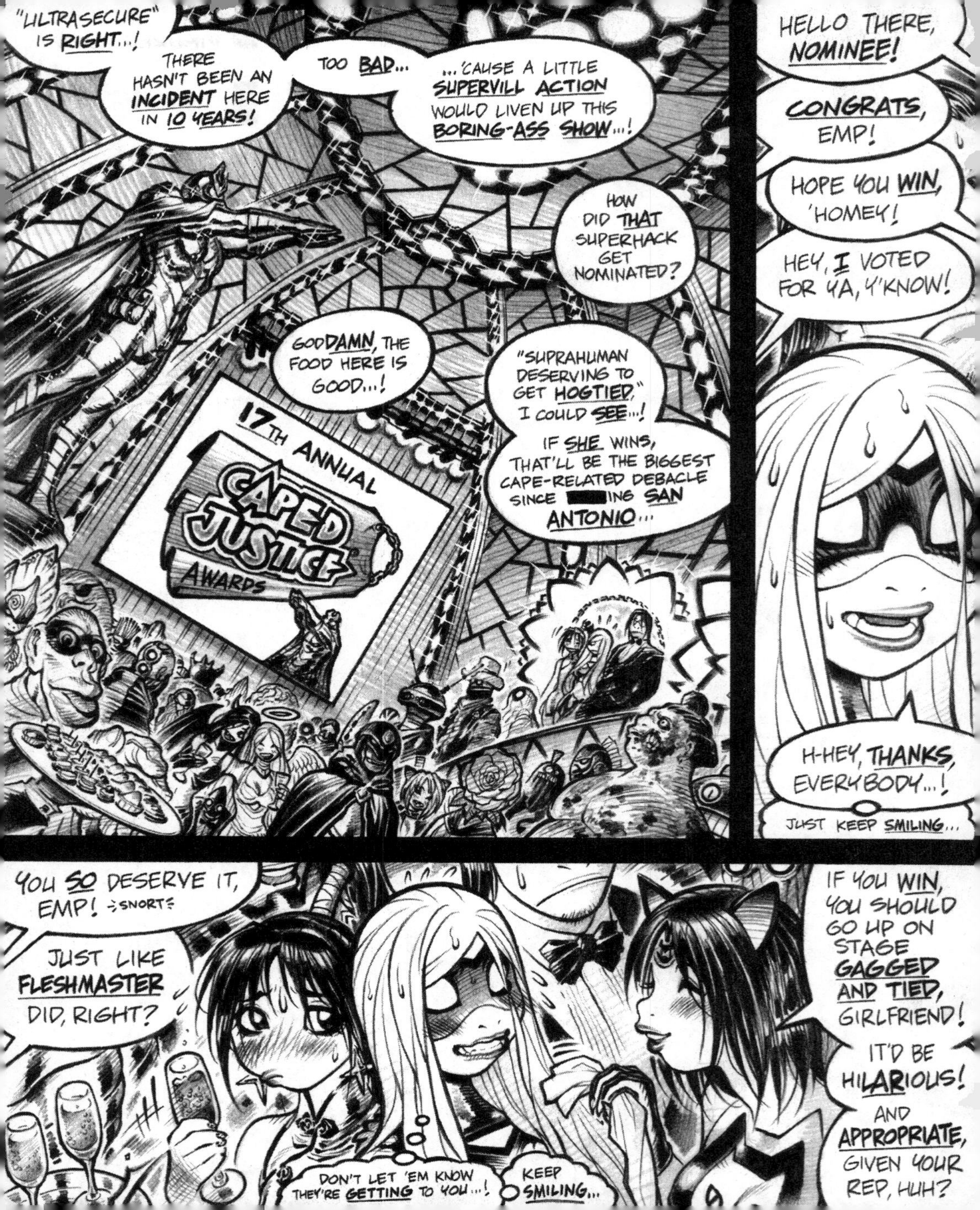
"ULTRASECURE" IS RIGHT...!
THERE HASN'T BEEN AN INCIDENT HERE IN 10 YEARS!
TOO BAD...
...'CAUSE A LITTLE SUPERVILL ACTION WOULD LIVEN UP THIS BORING-ASS SHOW...!
HOW DID THAT SUPERHACK GET NOMINATED?
GODDAMN, THE FOOD HERE IS GOOD...!
17TH ANNUAL CAPED JUSTICE AWARDS
"SUPRAHUMAN DESERVING TO GET HOGTIED," I COULD SEE...!
IF SHE WINS, THAT'LL BE THE BIGGEST CAPE-RELATED DEBACLE SINCE [redacted]ING SAN ANTONIO...
HELLO THERE, NOMINEE!
CONGRATS, EMP!
HOPE YOU WIN, 'HOMEY!
HEY, I VOTED FOR YA, Y'KNOW!
H-HEY, THANKS, EVERYBODY...!
JUST KEEP SMILING...
YOU SO DESERVE IT, EMP! ⁏SNORT⁏
JUST LIKE FLESHMASTER DID, RIGHT?
DON'T LET 'EM KNOW THEY'RE GETTING TO YOU...!
KEEP SMILING...
IF YOU WIN, YOU SHOULD GO UP ON STAGE GAGGED AND TIED, GIRLFRIEND!
IT'D BE HILARIOUS!
AND APPROPRIATE, GIVEN YOUR REP, HUH?

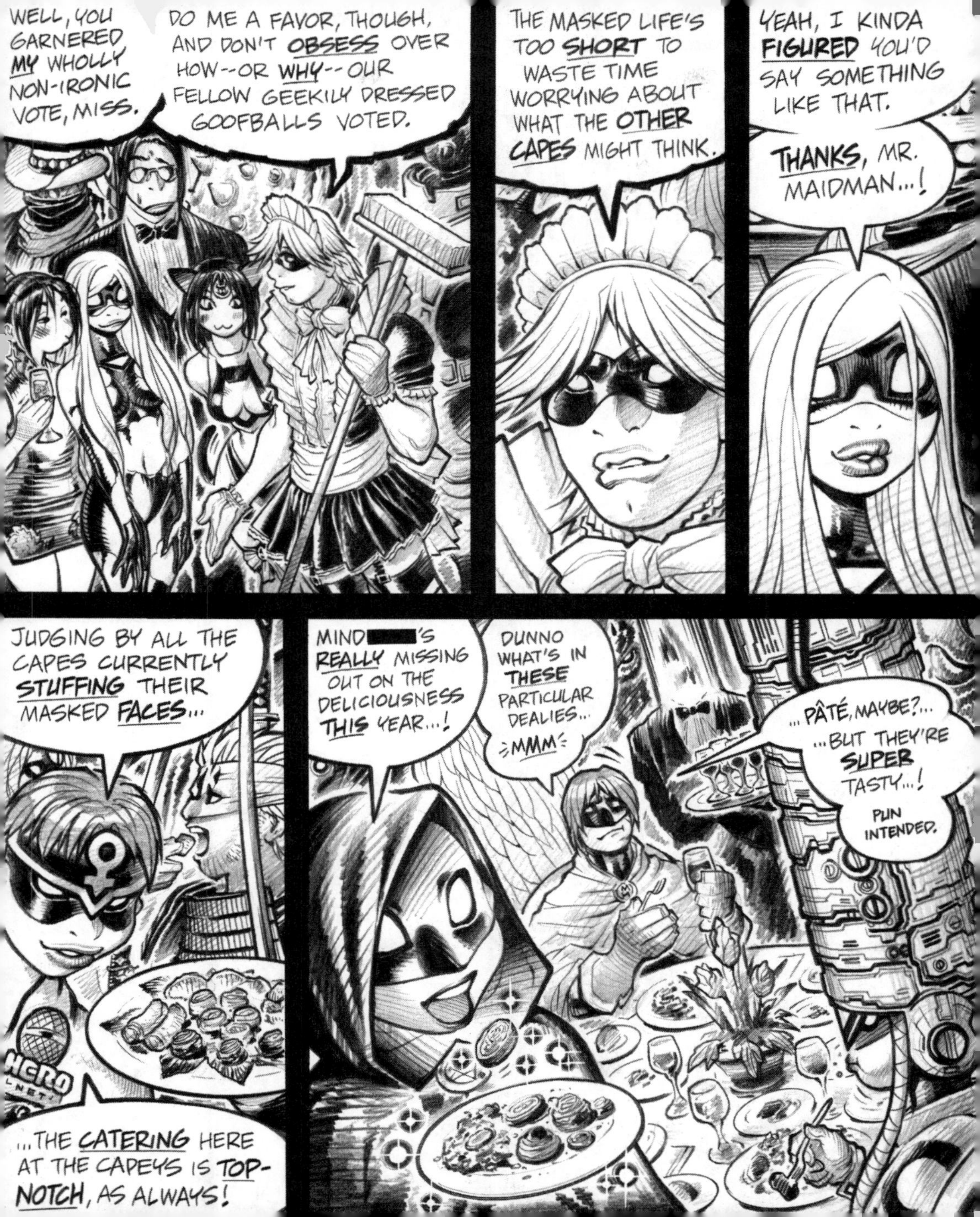

WELL, YOU GARNERED MY WHOLLY NON-IRONIC VOTE, MISS.
DO ME A FAVOR, THOUGH, AND DON'T OBSESS OVER HOW--OR WHY--OUR FELLOW GEEKILY DRESSED GOOFBALLS VOTED.
THE MASKED LIFE'S TOO SHORT TO WASTE TIME WORRYING ABOUT WHAT THE OTHER CAPES MIGHT THINK.
YEAH, I KINDA FIGURED YOU'D SAY SOMETHING LIKE THAT.
THANKS, MR. MAIDMAN...!
JUDGING BY ALL THE CAPES CURRENTLY STUFFING THEIR MASKED FACES...
...THE CATERING HERE AT THE CAPEYS IS TOP-NOTCH, AS ALWAYS!
MIND[redacted]'S REALLY MISSING OUT ON THE DELICIOUSNESS THIS YEAR...!
DUNNO WHAT'S IN THESE PARTICULAR DEALIES...
MMM
...PÂTÉ, MAYBE?...
...BUT THEY'RE SUPER TASTY...!
PUN INTENDED.

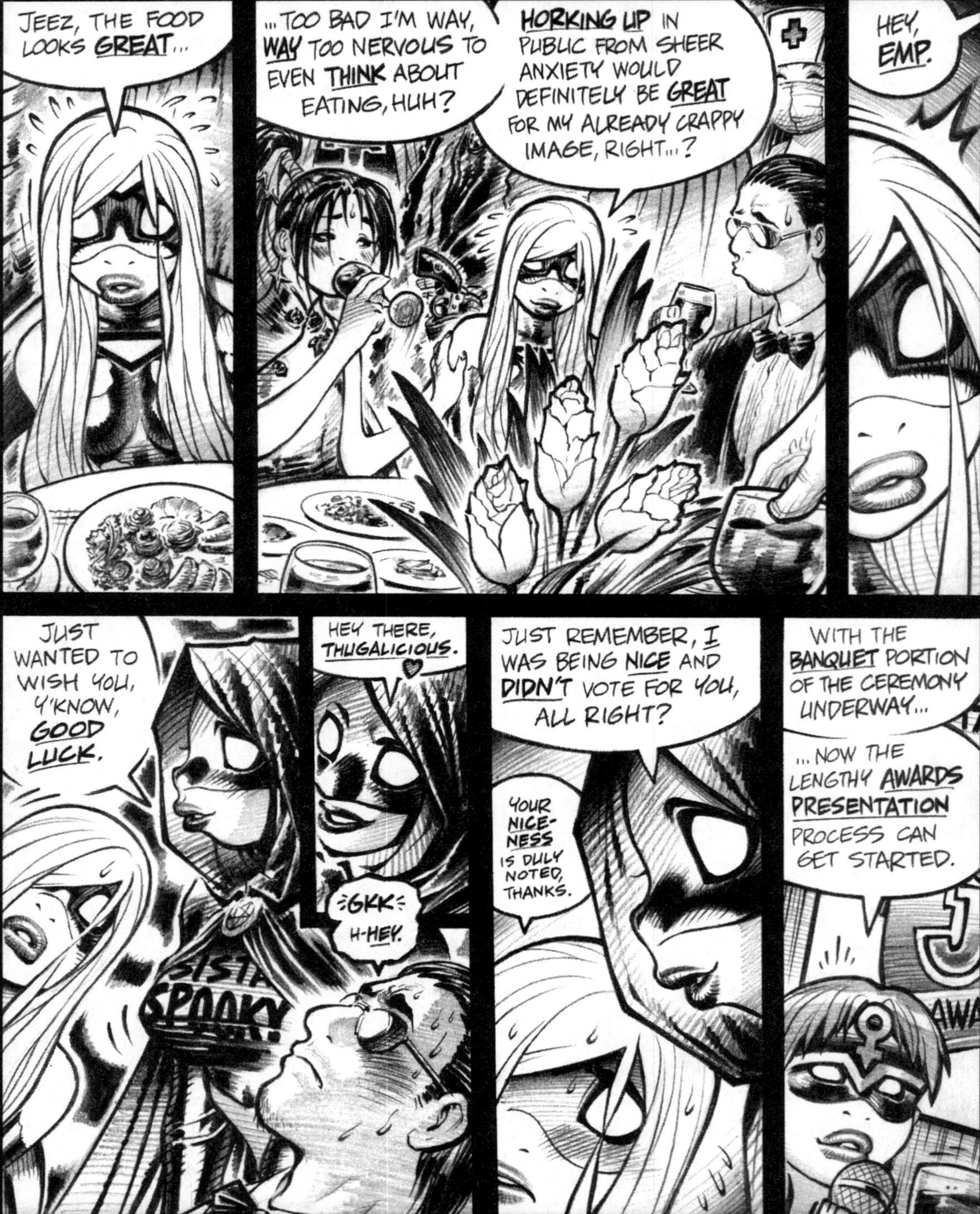
JEEZ, THE FOOD LOOKS GREAT...
...TOO BAD I'M WAY, WAY TOO NERVOUS TO EVEN THINK ABOUT EATING, HUH?
HORKING UP IN PUBLIC FROM SHEER ANXIETY WOULD DEFINITELY BE GREAT FOR MY ALREADY CRAPPY IMAGE, RIGHT...?
HEY, EMP.
JUST WANTED TO WISH YOU, Y'KNOW, GOOD LUCK.
HEY THERE, THUGALICIOUS.
GKK
H-HEY.
SISTA SPOOKY
JUST REMEMBER, I WAS BEING NICE AND DIDN'T VOTE FOR YOU, ALL RIGHT?
YOUR NICE-NESS IS DULY NOTED, THANKS.
WITH THE BANQUET PORTION OF THE CEREMONY UNDERWAY...
...NOW THE LENGTHY AWARDS PRESENTATION PROCESS CAN GET STARTED.

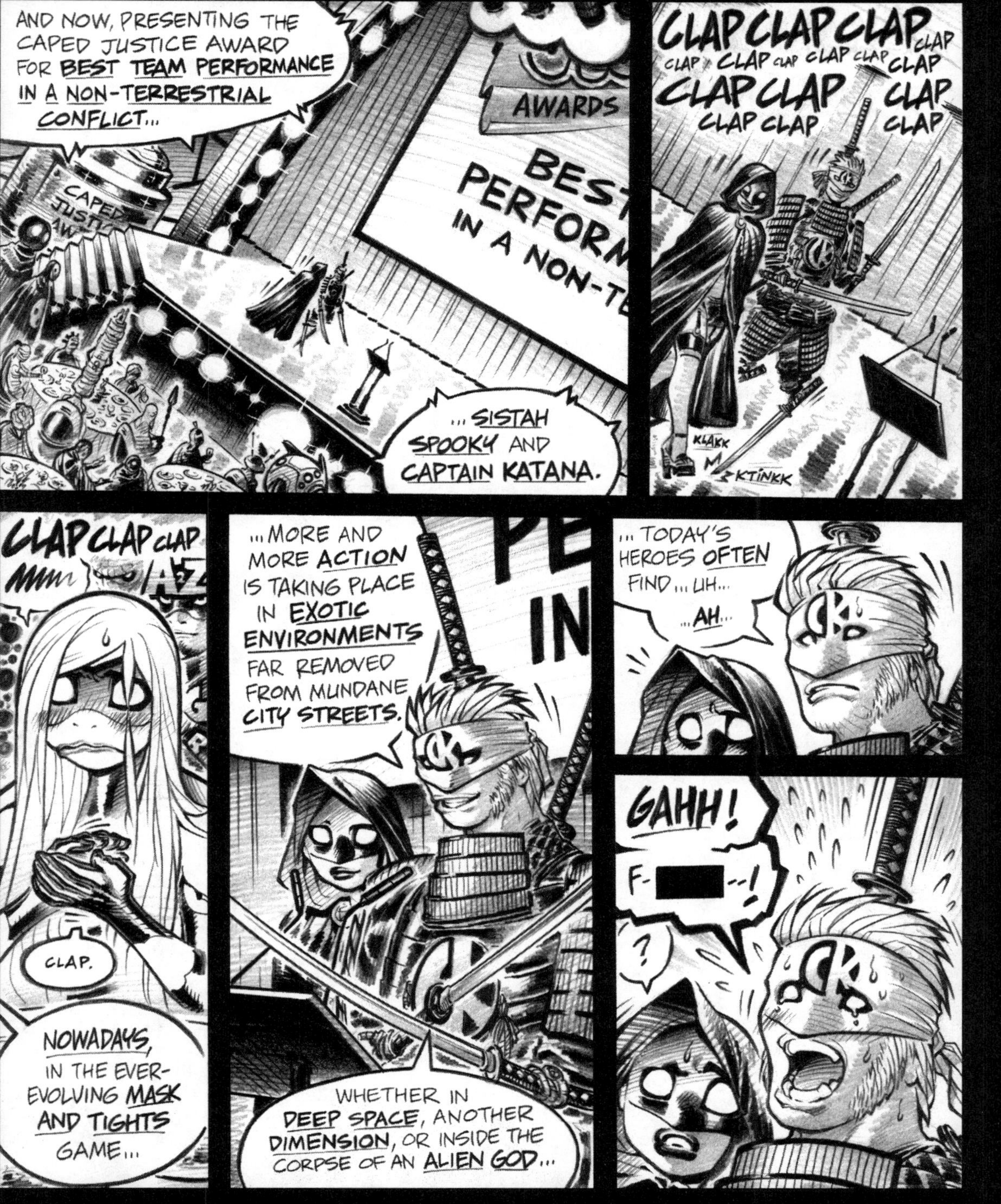
AND NOW, PRESENTING THE CAPED JUSTICE AWARD FOR BEST TEAM PERFORMANCE IN A NON-TERRESTRIAL CONFLICT...
AWARDS
...SISTAH SPOOKY AND CAPTAIN KATANA.
CLAP CLAP CLAP CLAP CLAP CLAP CLAP CLAP CLAP CLAP CLAP CLAP CLAP CLAP CLAP CLAP
KLAKK
KTINKK
CLAP CLAP CLAP
CLAP.
NOWADAYS, IN THE EVER-EVOLVING MASK AND TIGHTS GAME...
...MORE AND MORE ACTION IS TAKING PLACE IN EXOTIC ENVIRONMENTS FAR REMOVED FROM MUNDANE CITY STREETS.
WHETHER IN DEEP SPACE, ANOTHER DIMENSION, OR INSIDE THE CORPSE OF AN ALIEN GOD...
...TODAY'S HEROES OFTEN FIND... UH...
...AH...
GAHH!
F-[redacted]--!
?

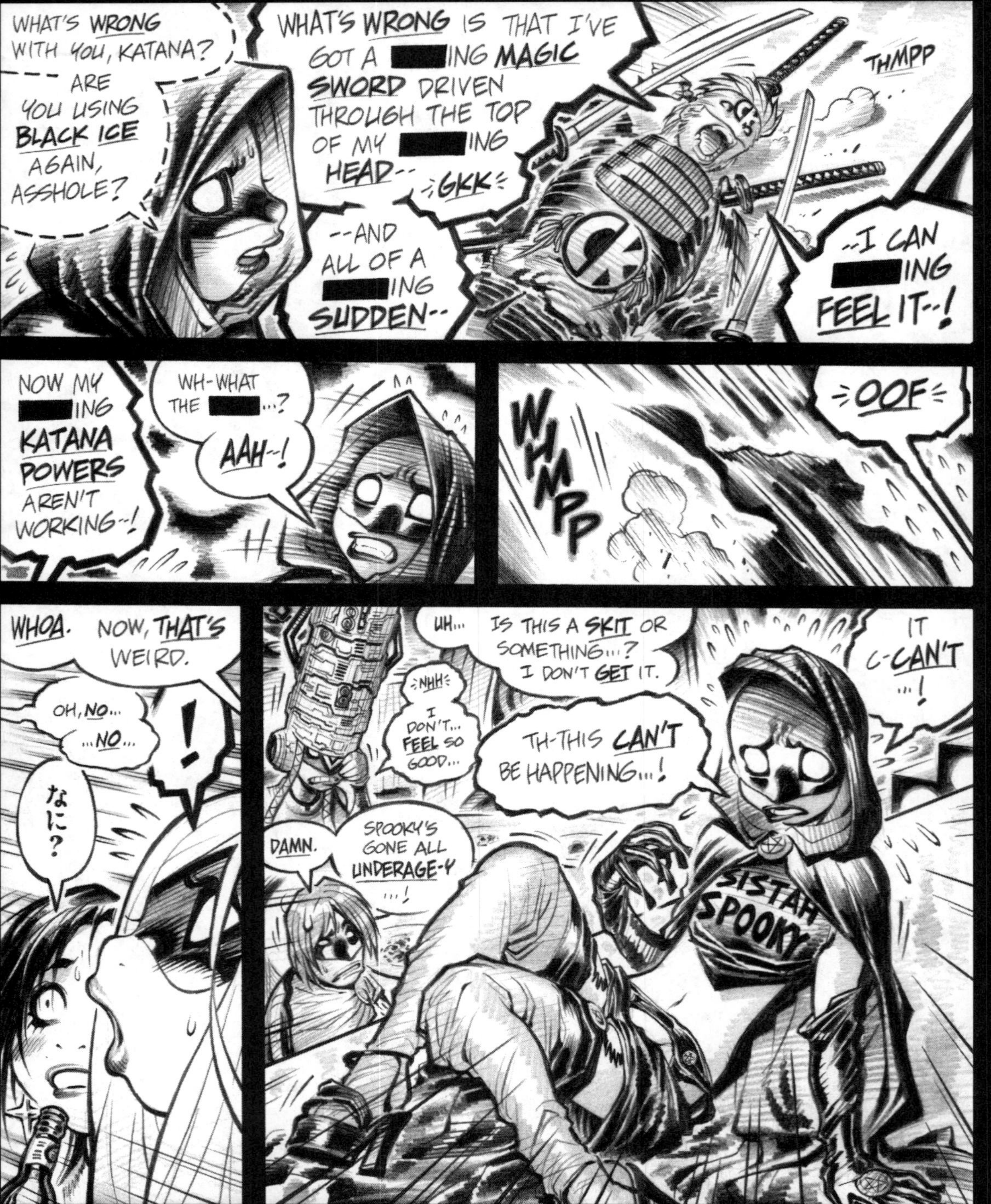
WHAT'S WRONG WITH YOU, KATANA?
ARE YOU USING BLACK ICE AGAIN, ASSHOLE?
WHAT'S WRONG IS THAT I'VE GOT A [redacted]ING MAGIC SWORD DRIVEN THROUGH THE TOP OF MY [redacted]ING HEAD--
GKK
THMPP
--AND ALL OF A [redacted]ING SUDDEN--
--I CAN [redacted]ING FEEL IT--!
NOW MY [redacted]ING KATANA POWERS AREN'T WORKING--!
WH-WHAT THE [redacted]...?
AAH--!
WHMPP
OOF
WHOA.
NOW, THAT'S WEIRD.
OH, NO...
...NO...
!
なに？
UH...
IS THIS A SKIT OR SOMETHING...? I DON'T GET IT.
IT C-CAN'T ...!
NHH
I DON'T... FEEL SO GOOD...
TH-THIS CAN'T BE HAPPENING...!
DAMN.
SPOOKY'S GONE ALL UNDERAGE-Y ...!
SISTAH SPOOKY

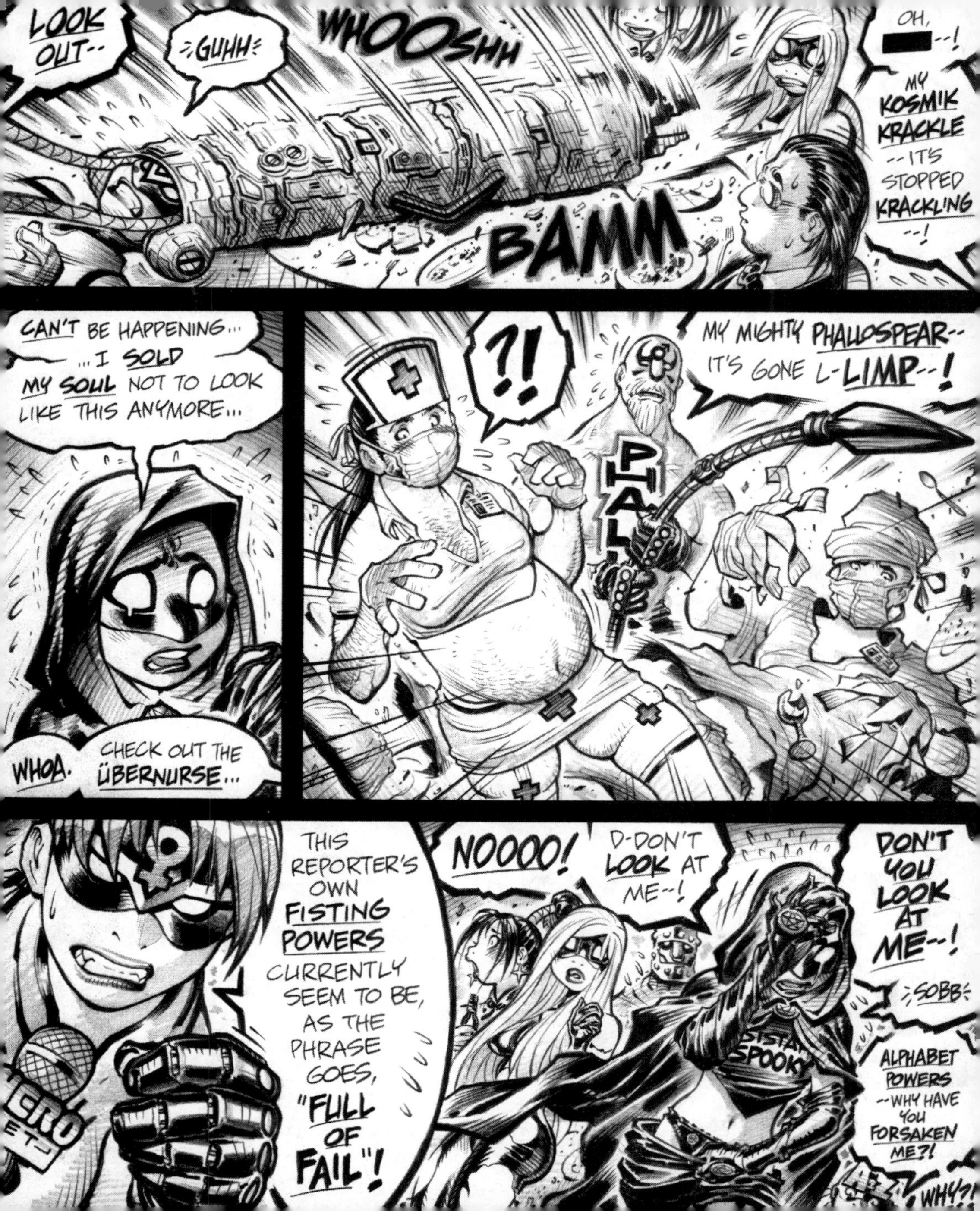
LOOK OUT--
GUHH
WHOOOSHH
BAMM
OH, [redacted]--!
MY KOSMIK KRACKLE --IT'S STOPPED KRACKLING --!
CAN'T BE HAPPENING... ...I SOLD MY SOUL NOT TO LOOK LIKE THIS ANYMORE...
WHOA.
CHECK OUT THE ÜBERNURSE...
?!
MY MIGHTY PHALLOSPEAR-- IT'S GONE L-LIMP--!
PHAL
THIS REPORTER'S OWN FISTING POWERS CURRENTLY SEEM TO BE, AS THE PHRASE GOES, "FULL OF FAIL"!
NOOOO!
D-DON'T LOOK AT ME--!
DON'T YOU LOOK AT ME--!
SOBB
ALPHABET POWERS --WHY HAVE YOU FORSAKEN ME?!
WHY?!

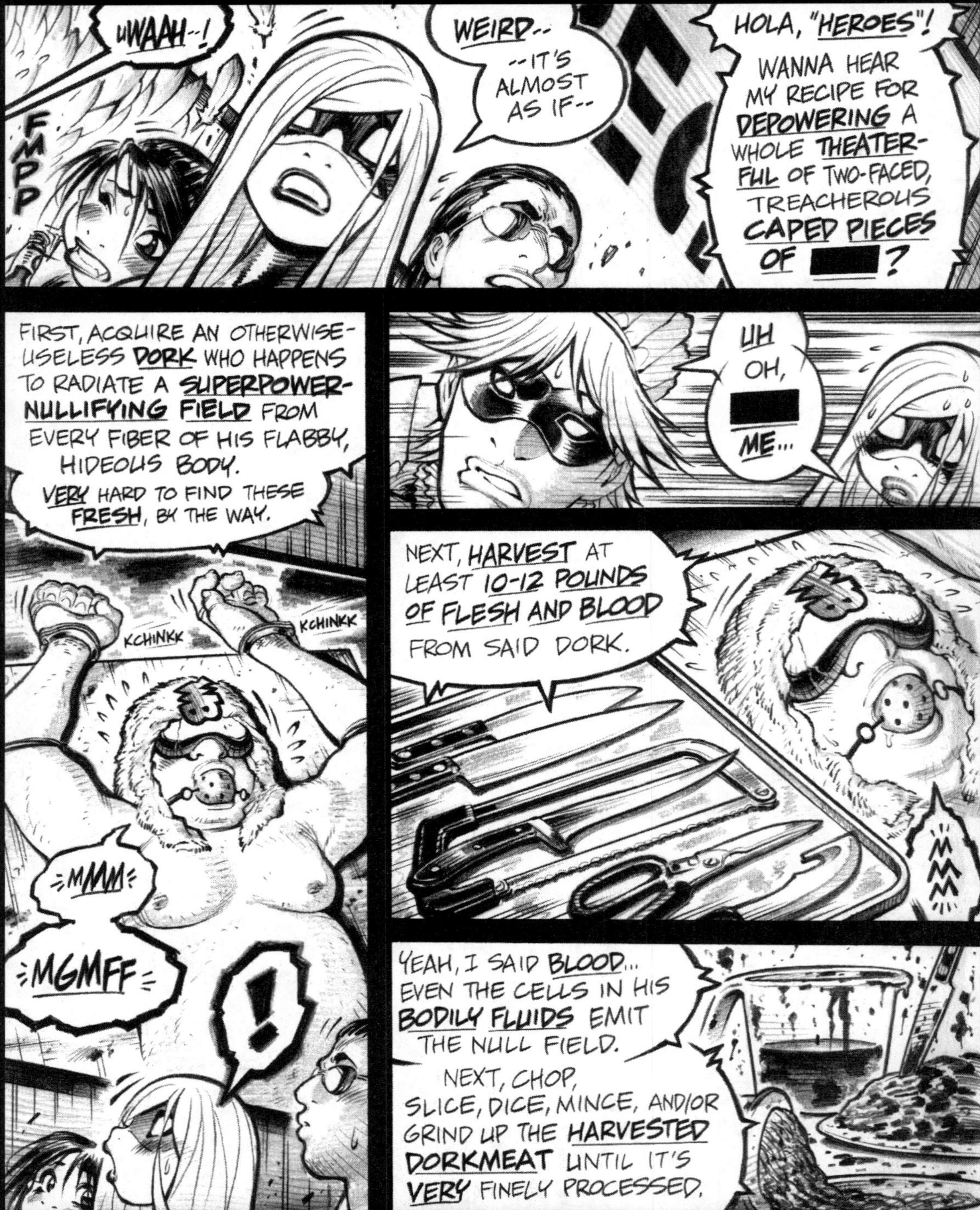
UWAAH--!
FMPP
WEIRD--
--IT'S ALMOST AS IF--
HOLA, "HEROES"!
WANNA HEAR MY RECIPE FOR DEPOWERING A WHOLE THEATER-FUL OF TWO-FACED, TREACHEROUS CAPED PIECES OF [redacted]?
FIRST, ACQUIRE AN OTHERWISE-USELESS DORK WHO HAPPENS TO RADIATE A SUPERPOWER-NULLIFYING FIELD FROM EVERY FIBER OF HIS FLABBY, HIDEOUS BODY.
VERY HARD TO FIND THESE FRESH, BY THE WAY.
KCHINKK
KCHINKK
MMM
MGMFF
!
UH OH, [redacted] ME...
NEXT, HARVEST AT LEAST 10-12 POUNDS OF FLESH AND BLOOD FROM SAID DORK.
MMM
YEAH, I SAID BLOOD... EVEN THE CELLS IN HIS BODILY FLUIDS EMIT THE NULL FIELD.
NEXT, CHOP, SLICE, DICE, MINCE, AND/OR GRIND UP THE HARVESTED DORKMEAT UNTIL IT'S VERY FINELY PROCESSED.

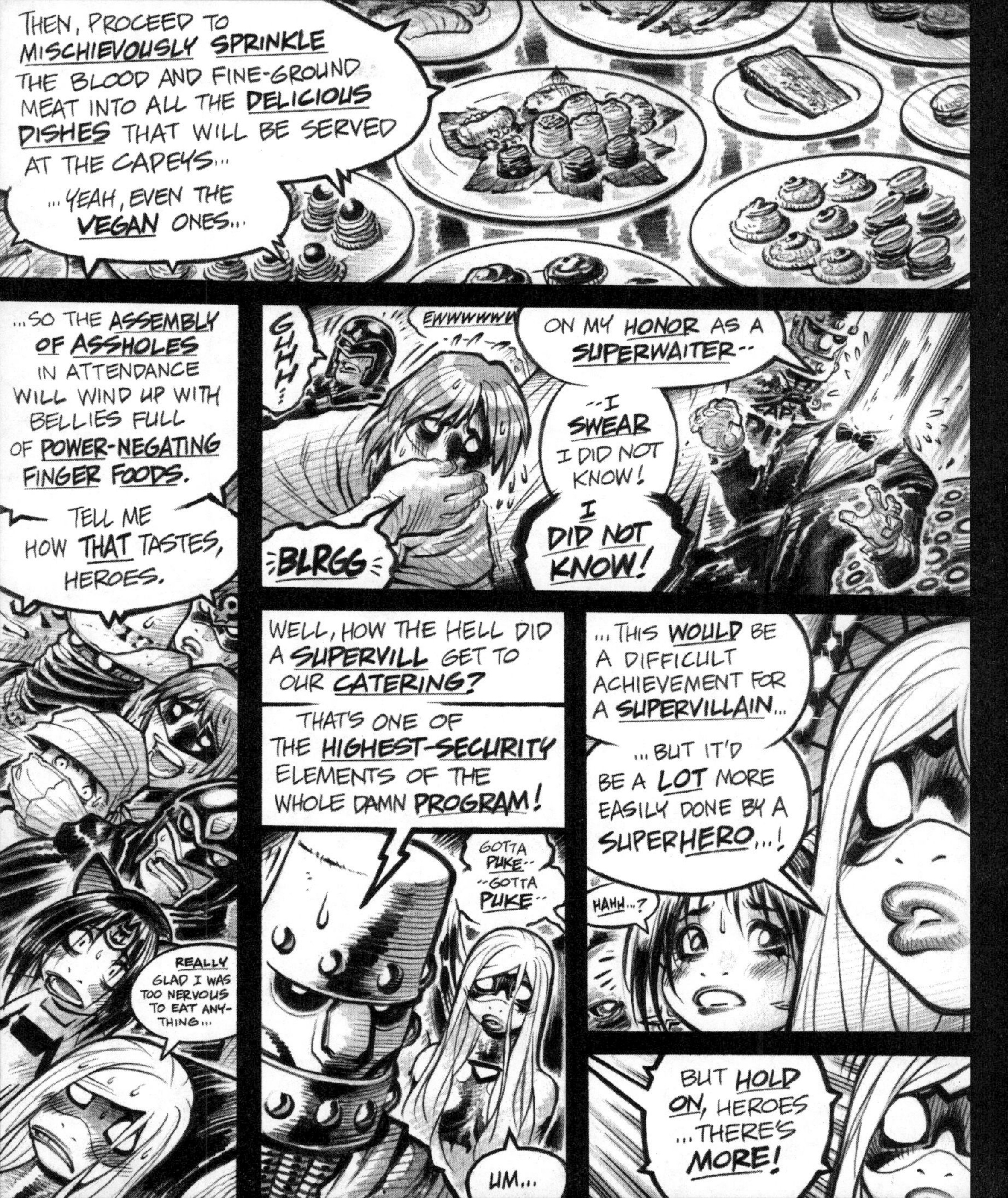

THEN, PROCEED TO MISCHIEVOUSLY SPRINKLE THE BLOOD AND FINE-GROUND MEAT INTO ALL THE DELICIOUS DISHES THAT WILL BE SERVED AT THE CAPEYS...
...YEAH, EVEN THE VEGAN ONES...
...SO THE ASSEMBLY OF ASSHOLES IN ATTENDANCE WILL WIND UP WITH BELLIES FULL OF POWER-NEGATING FINGER FOODS.
TELL ME HOW THAT TASTES, HEROES.
EWWWWWW
BLRGG
ON MY HONOR AS A SUPERWAITER--
--I SWEAR I DID NOT KNOW!
I DID NOT KNOW!
WELL, HOW THE HELL DID A SUPERVILL GET TO OUR CATERING?
THAT'S ONE OF THE HIGHEST-SECURITY ELEMENTS OF THE WHOLE DAMN PROGRAM!
GOTTA PUKE-- --GOTTA PUKE--
REALLY GLAD I WAS TOO NERVOUS TO EAT ANY-THING...
UM...
...THIS WOULD BE A DIFFICULT ACHIEVEMENT FOR A SUPERVILLAIN...
...BUT IT'D BE A LOT MORE EASILY DONE BY A SUPERHERO...!
HAHH...?
BUT HOLD ON, HEROES ...THERE'S MORE!

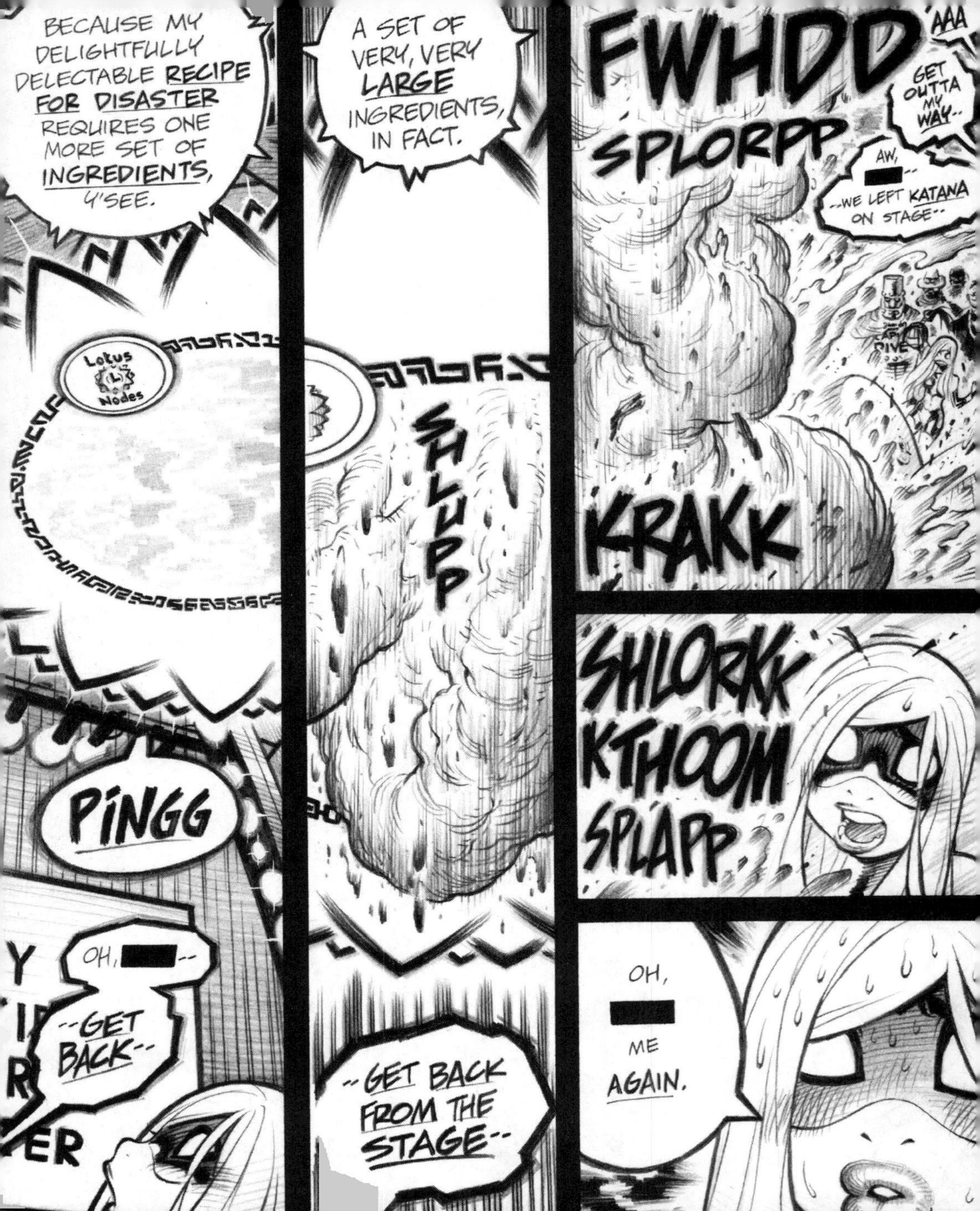
BECAUSE MY DELIGHTFULLY DELECTABLE RECIPE FOR DISASTER REQUIRES ONE MORE SET OF INGREDIENTS, Y'SEE.
Lotus Nodes
PINGG
OH, [redacted]--
--GET BACK--
A SET OF VERY, VERY LARGE INGREDIENTS, IN FACT.
SHLUPP
--GET BACK FROM THE STAGE--
FWHDD
AAA
GET OUTTA MY WAY--
SPLORPP
AW, [redacted]--
--WE LEFT KATANA ON STAGE--
KRAKK
SHLORKK
KTHOOM
SPLAPP
OH, [redacted] ME AGAIN.

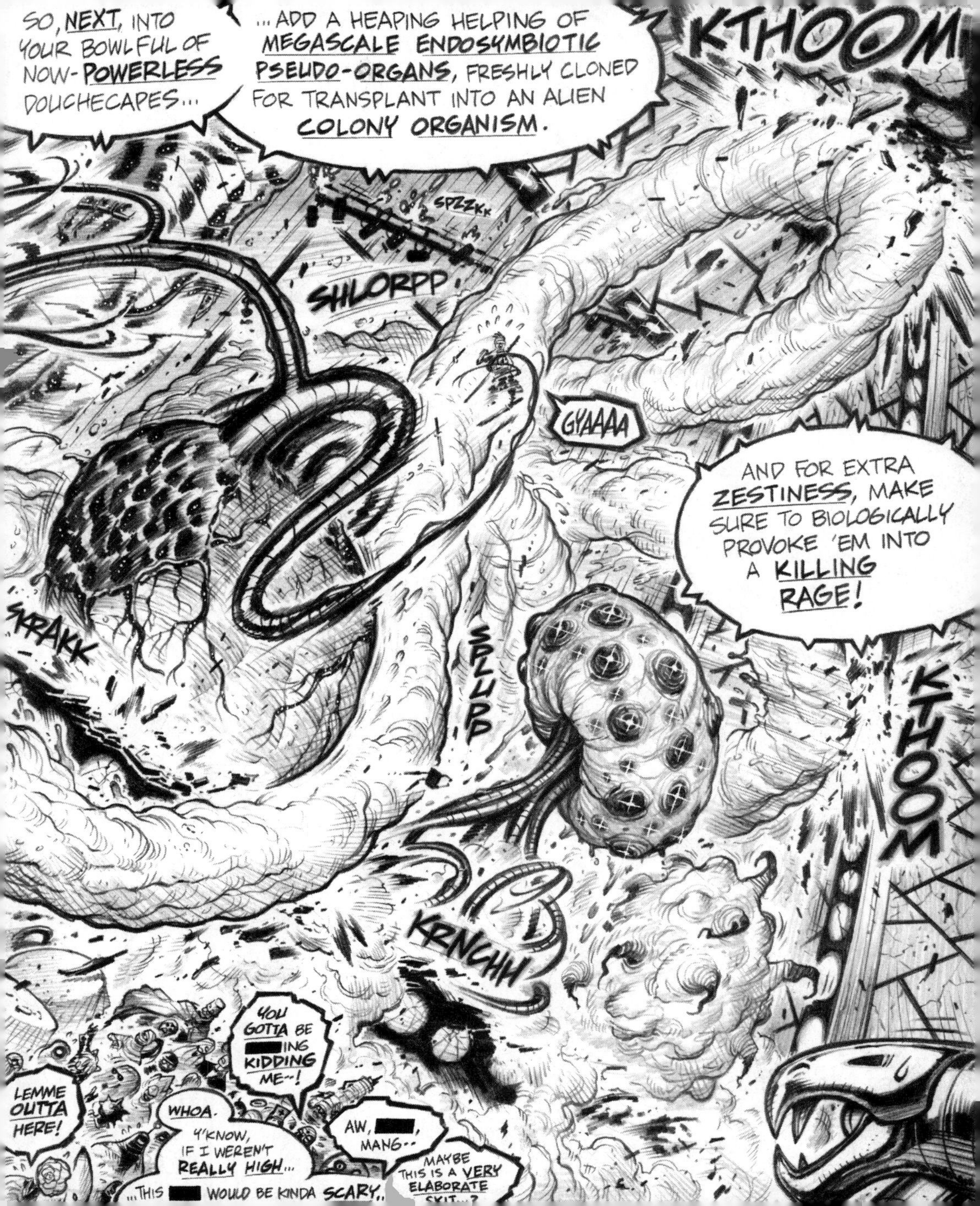

SO, NEXT, INTO YOUR BOWLFUL OF NOW-POWERLESS DOUCHECAPES...
...ADD A HEAPING HELPING OF MEGASCALE ENDOSYMBIOTIC PSEUDO-ORGANS, FRESHLY CLONED FOR TRANSPLANT INTO AN ALIEN COLONY ORGANISM.
KTHOOM
SPZZKK
SHLORPP
GYAAAA
AND FOR EXTRA ZESTINESS, MAKE SURE TO BIOLOGICALLY PROVOKE 'EM INTO A KILLING RAGE!
SKRAKK
SPLURP
KTHOOM
KRNCHH
YOU GOTTA BE [redacted]ING KIDDING ME--!
LEMME OUTTA HERE!
WHOA.
Y'KNOW, IF I WEREN'T REALLY HIGH...
...THIS [redacted] WOULD BE KINDA SCARY..
AW, [redacted], MANG--
MAYBE THIS IS A VERY ELABORATE SKIT...?

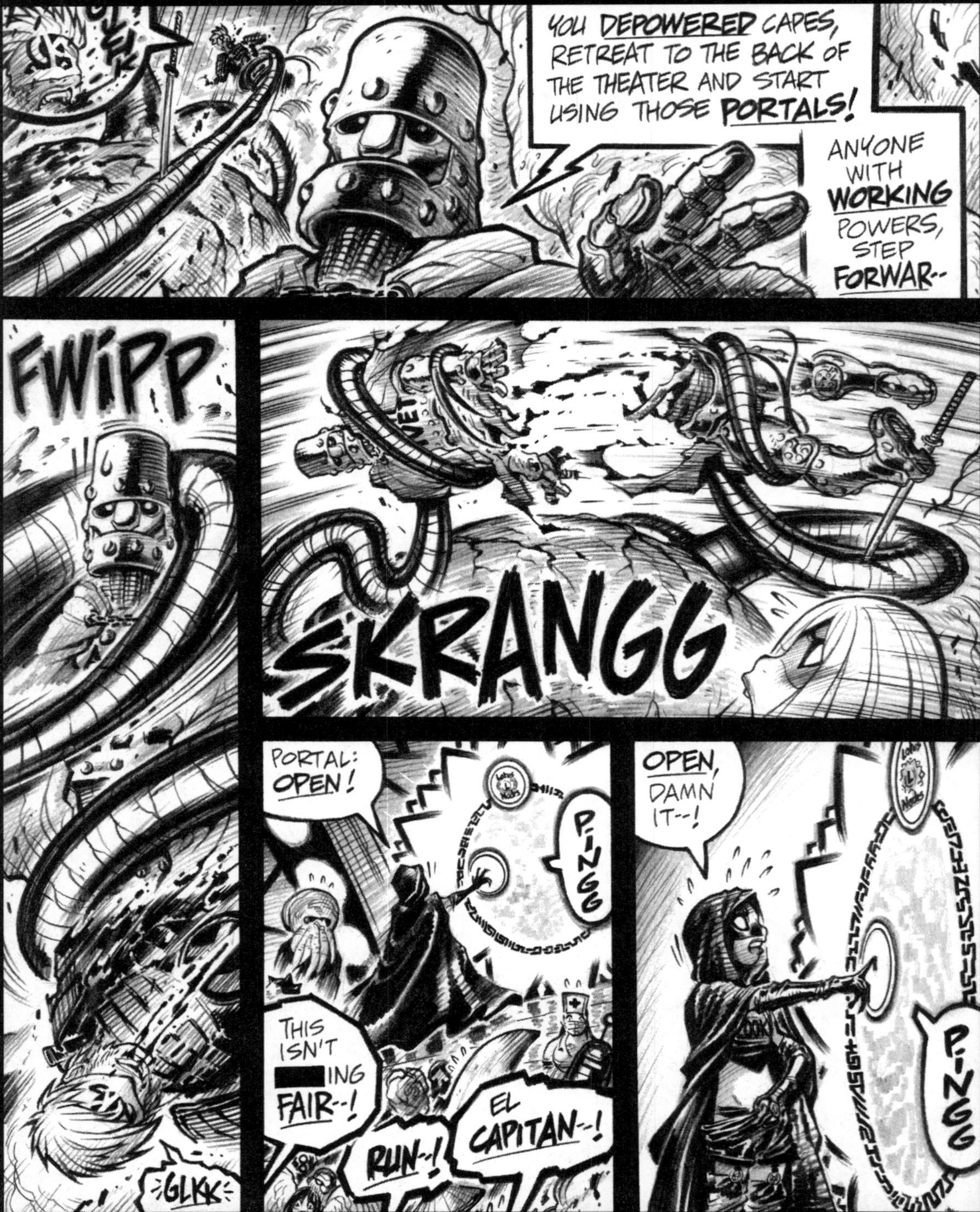

YOU DEPOWERED CAPES, RETREAT TO THE BACK OF THE THEATER AND START USING THOSE PORTALS!
ANYONE WITH WORKING POWERS, STEP FORWAR--
FWIPP
GLKK
SKRANGG
PORTAL: OPEN!
PINGG
THIS ISN'T [redacted]ING FAIR--!
EL CAPITAN--!
RUN--!
OPEN, DAMN IT--!
PINGG

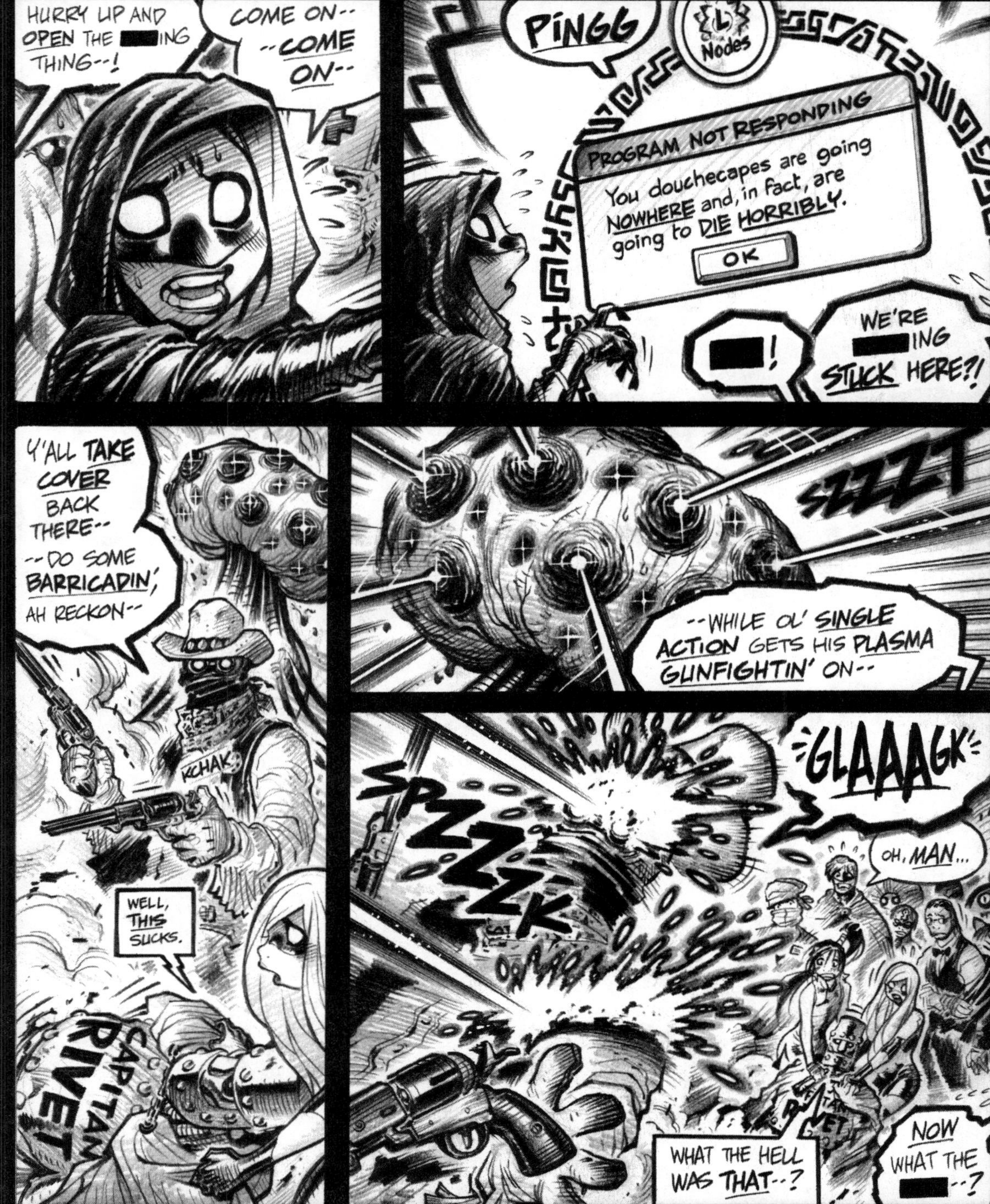
HURRY UP AND OPEN THE [redacted]ING THING--!
COME ON-- --COME ON--
PINGG
Nodes
PROGRAM NOT RESPONDING
You douchecapes are going NOWHERE and, in fact, are going to DIE HORRIBLY.
OK
[redacted]!
WE'RE [redacted]ING STUCK HERE?!
Y'ALL TAKE COVER BACK THERE-- --DO SOME BARRICADIN', AH RECKON--
KCHAK
WELL, THIS SUCKS.
CAPITAN RIVET
SZZZT
--WHILE OL' SINGLE ACTION GETS HIS PLASMA GUNFIGHTIN' ON--
SPZZZK
GLAAAGK
OH, MAN...
WHAT THE HELL WAS THAT--?
NOW WHAT THE [redacted]--?

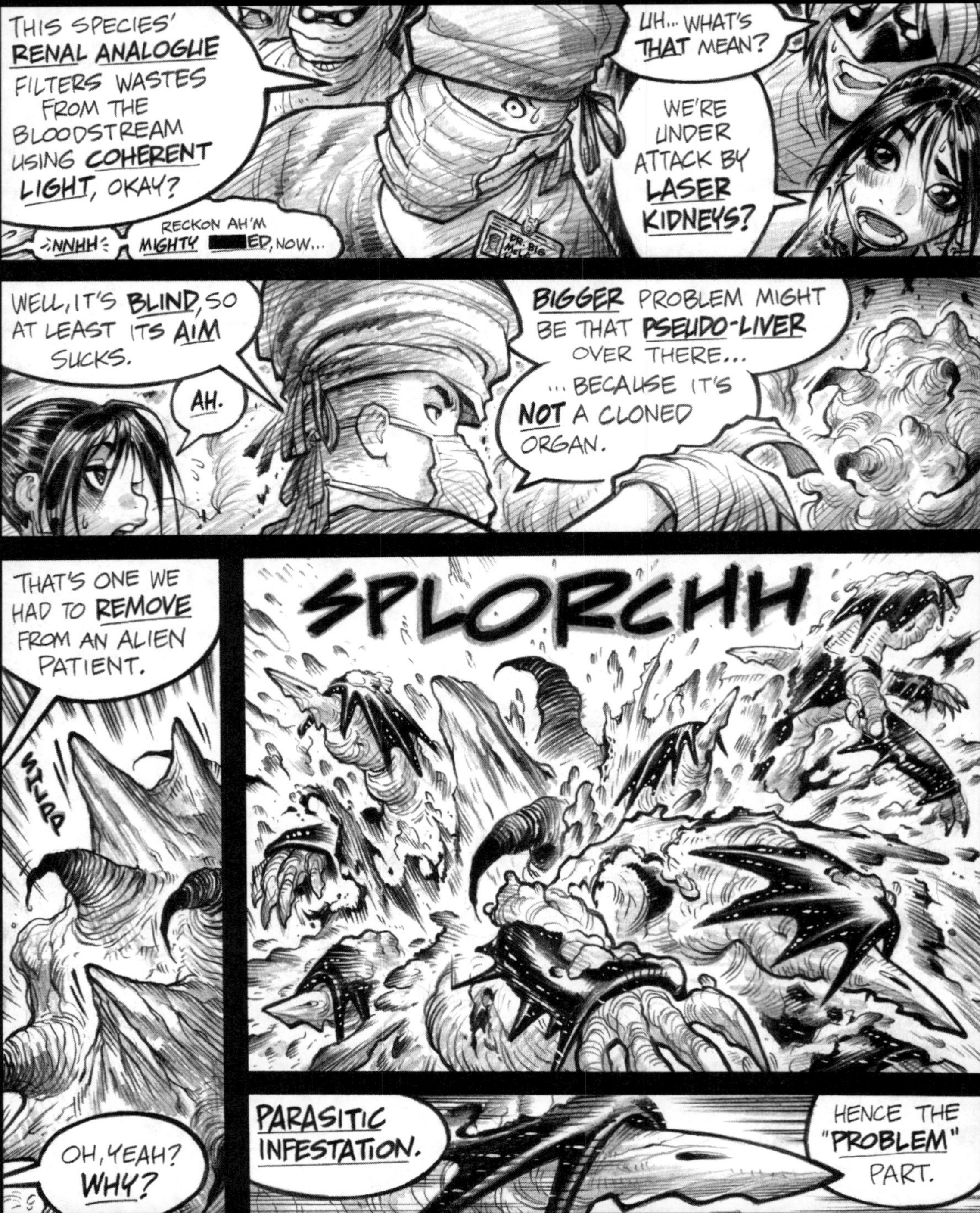
THIS SPECIES' RENAL ANALOGUE FILTERS WASTES FROM THE BLOODSTREAM USING COHERENT LIGHT, OKAY?
UH... WHAT'S THAT MEAN?
WE'RE UNDER ATTACK BY LASER KIDNEYS?
NNHH
RECKON AH'M MIGHTY [redacted]ED, NOW...
WELL, IT'S BLIND, SO AT LEAST ITS AIM SUCKS.
AH.
BIGGER PROBLEM MIGHT BE THAT PSEUDO-LIVER OVER THERE...
... BECAUSE IT'S NOT A CLONED ORGAN.
THAT'S ONE WE HAD TO REMOVE FROM AN ALIEN PATIENT.
SHLPP
SPLORCHH
OH, YEAH? WHY?
PARASITIC INFESTATION.
HENCE THE "PROBLEM" PART.

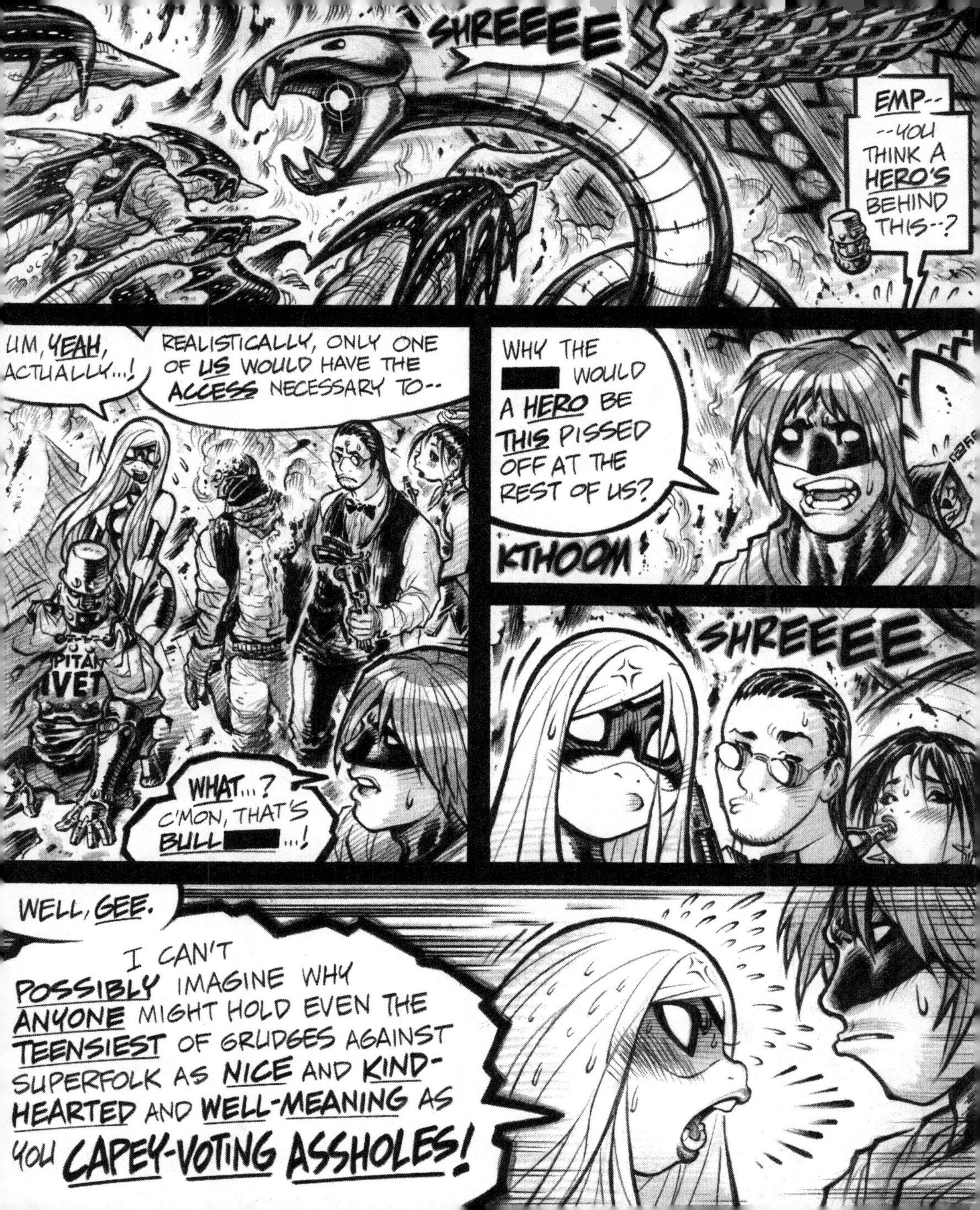
SHREEEEE
EMP-- --YOU THINK A HERO'S BEHIND THIS--?
UM, YEAH, ACTUALLY...!
REALISTICALLY, ONLY ONE OF US WOULD HAVE THE ACCESS NECESSARY TO--
WHAT...? C'MON, THAT'S BULL[redacted]...!
WHY THE [redacted] WOULD A HERO BE THIS PISSED OFF AT THE REST OF US?
KTHOOM
SHREEEE
WELL, GEE.
I CAN'T POSSIBLY IMAGINE WHY ANYONE MIGHT HOLD EVEN THE TEENSIEST OF GRUDGES AGAINST SUPERFOLK AS NICE AND KIND-HEARTED AND WELL-MEANING AS YOU CAPEY-VOTING ASSHOLES!

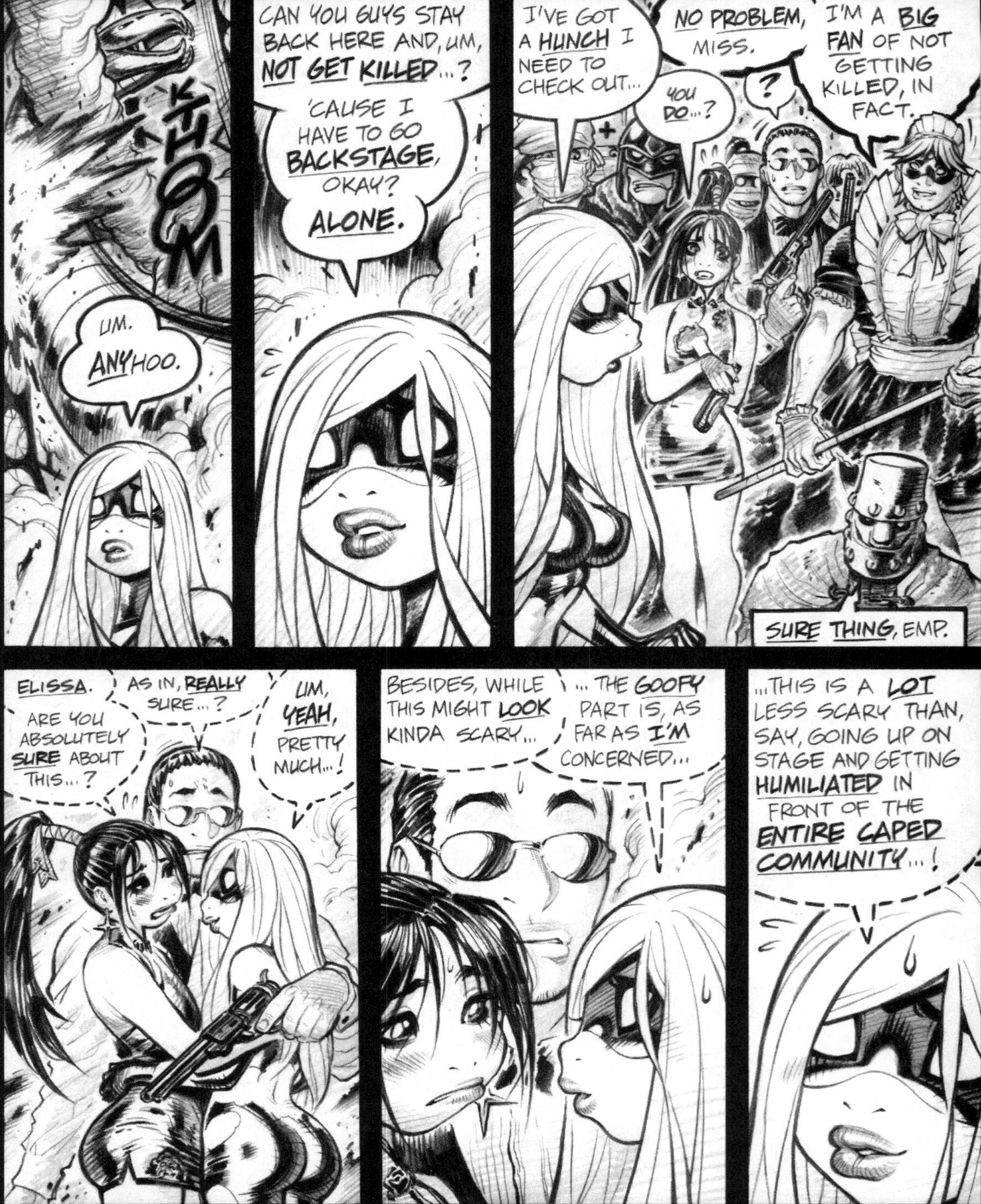

KTHOOM
UM. ANYHOO.
CAN YOU GUYS STAY BACK HERE AND, UM, NOT GET KILLED...?
'CAUSE I HAVE TO GO BACKSTAGE, OKAY? ALONE.
I'VE GOT A HUNCH I NEED TO CHECK OUT...
NO PROBLEM, MISS.
I'M A BIG FAN OF NOT GETTING KILLED, IN FACT.
YOU DO...?
?
SURE THING, EMP.
ELISSA.
ARE YOU ABSOLUTELY SURE ABOUT THIS...?
AS IN, REALLY SURE...?
UM, YEAH, PRETTY MUCH...!
BESIDES, WHILE THIS MIGHT LOOK KINDA SCARY...
...THE GOOFY PART IS, AS FAR AS I'M CONCERNED...
...THIS IS A LOT LESS SCARY THAN, SAY, GOING UP ON STAGE AND GETTING HUMILIATED IN FRONT OF THE ENTIRE CAPED COMMUNITY...!

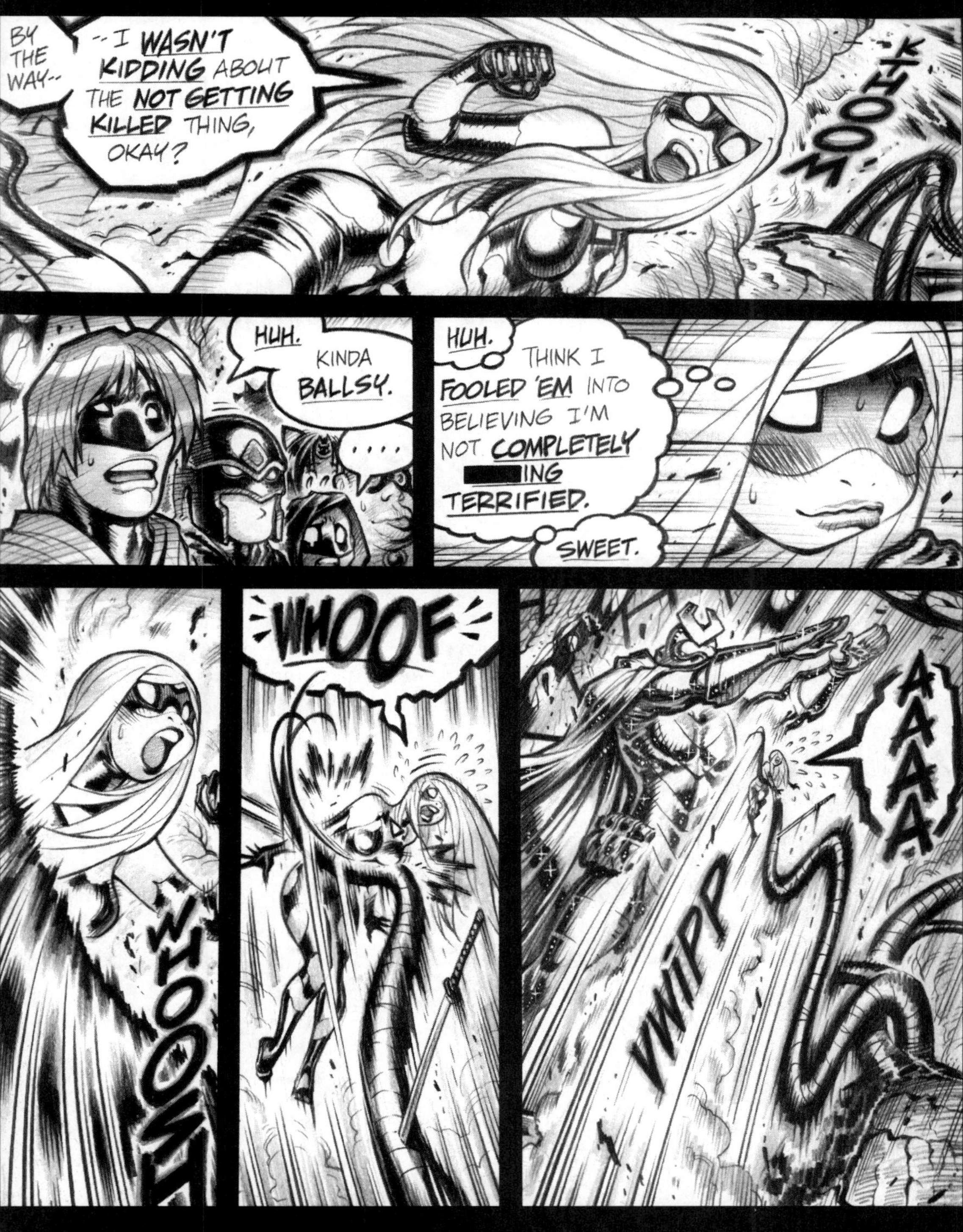
BY THE WAY--
--I WASN'T KIDDING ABOUT THE NOT GETTING KILLED THING, OKAY?
KHOOOM
HUH.
KINDA BALLSY.
....
HUH.
THINK I FOOLED 'EM INTO BELIEVING I'M NOT COMPLETELY [redacted]ING TERRIFIED.
SWEET.
WHOOSH
WHOOF
VWIPP
AAAA

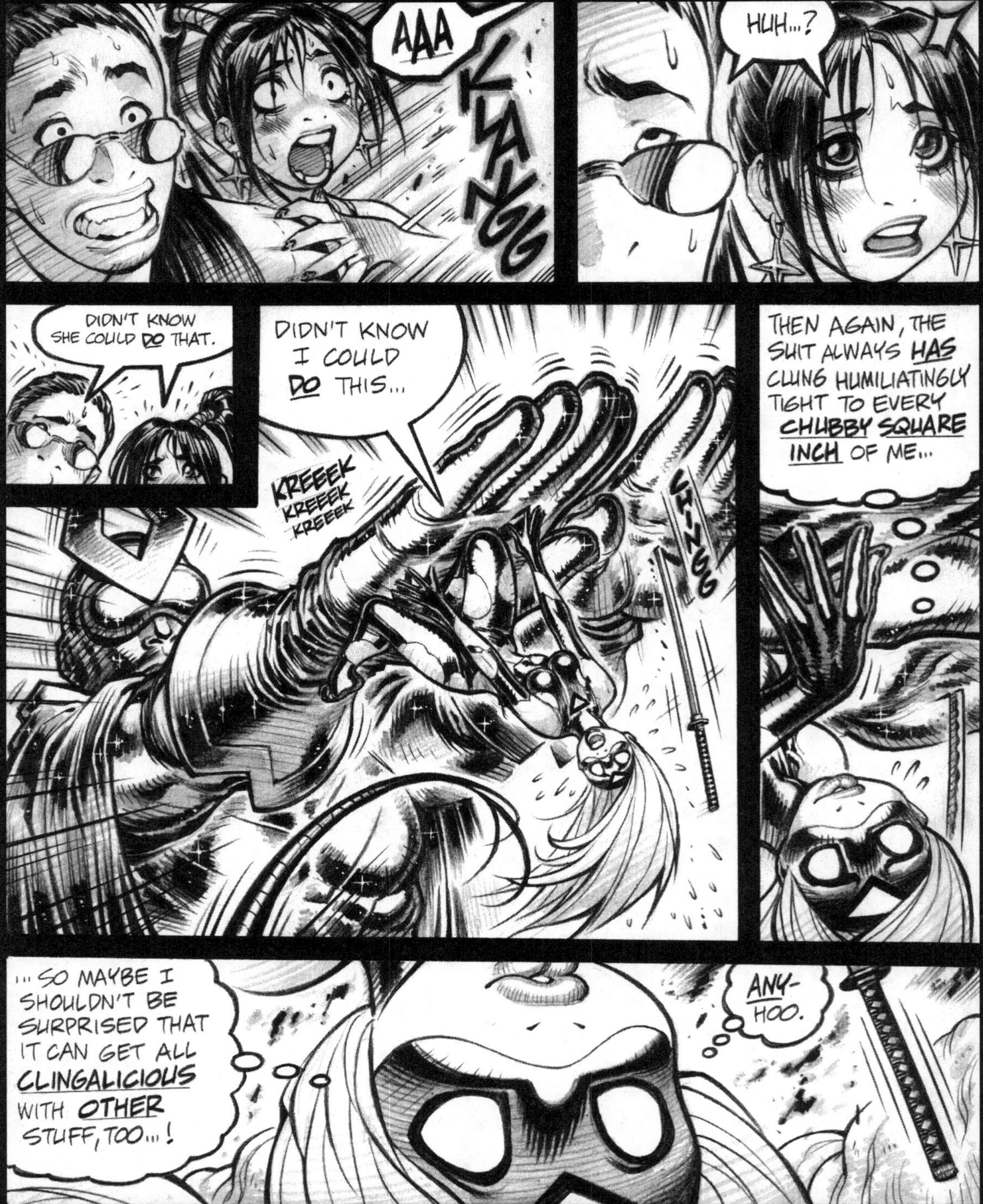

AAA
KLANGG
HUH...?
DIDN'T KNOW SHE COULD DO THAT.
DIDN'T KNOW I COULD DO THIS...
KREEEK KREEEK KREEEK
SHINGG
THEN AGAIN, THE SUIT ALWAYS HAS CLUNG HUMILIATINGLY TIGHT TO EVERY CHUBBY SQUARE INCH OF ME...
...SO MAYBE I SHOULDN'T BE SURPRISED THAT IT CAN GET ALL CLINGALICIOUS WITH OTHER STUFF, TOO...!
ANY-HOO.

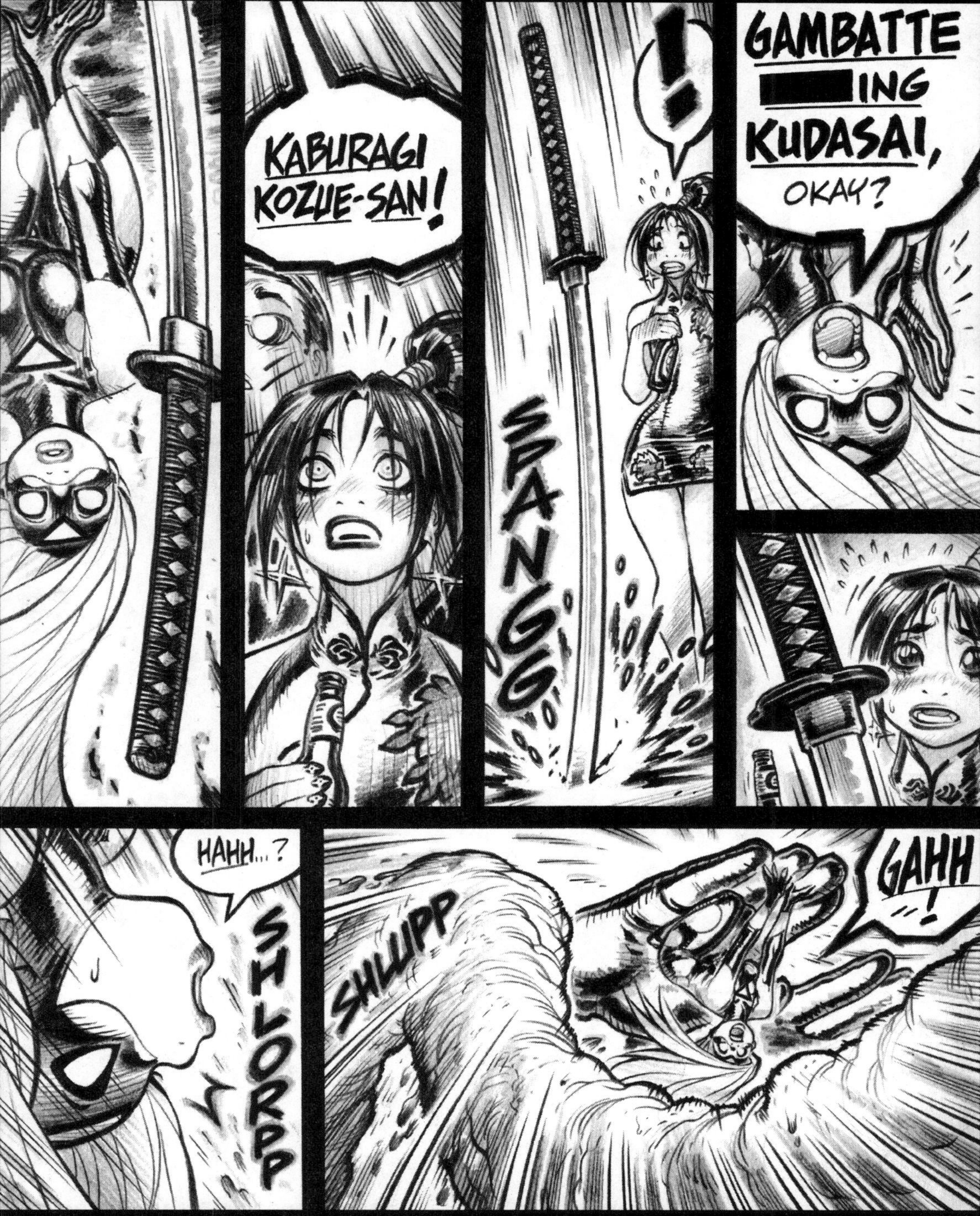
KABURAGI KOZUE-SAN!
!
SPANGG
GAMBATTE [redacted]ING KUDASAI, OKAY?
HAHH...?
SHLORPP
SHLUPP
GAHH!

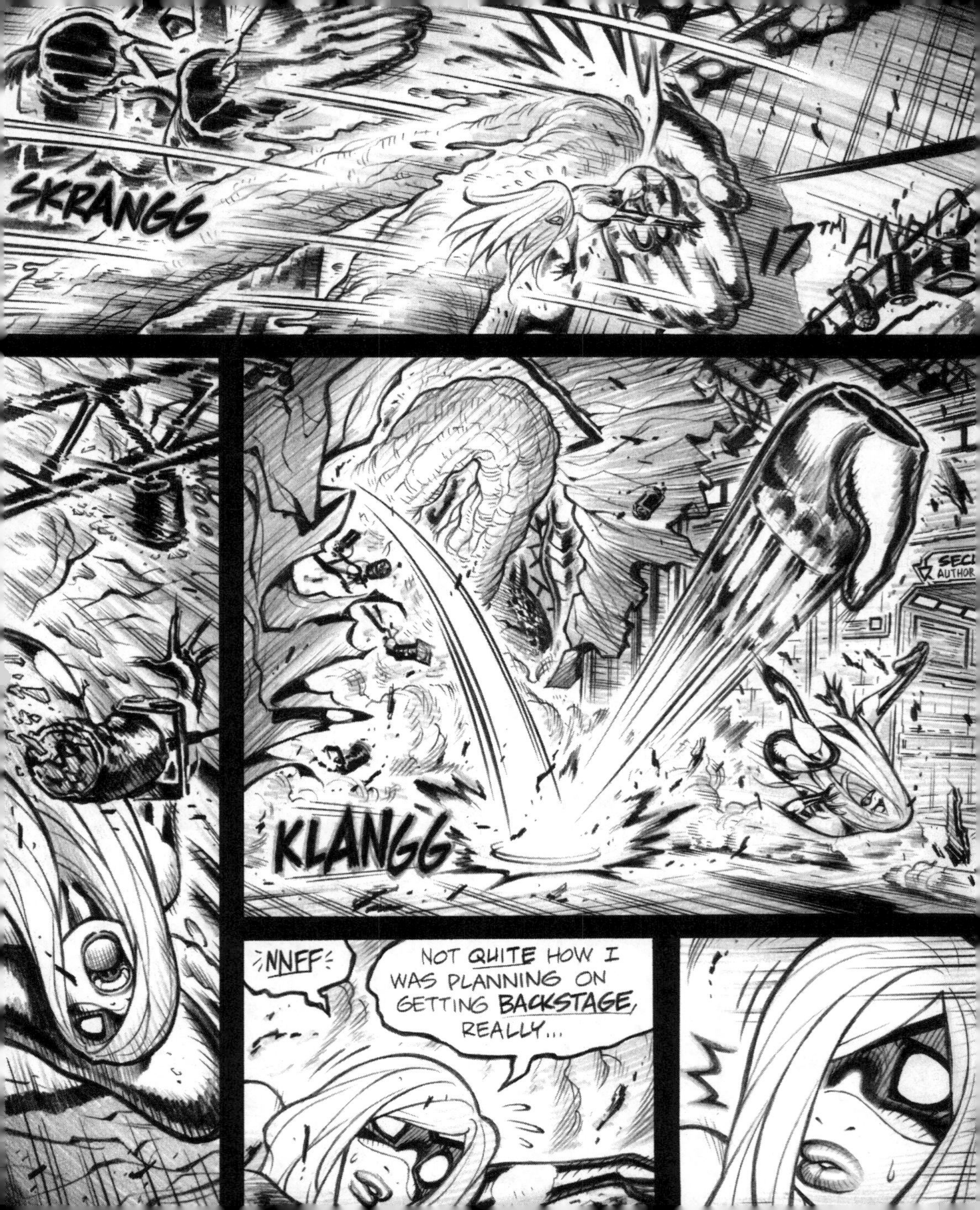
SKRANGG
17TH ANN
KLANGG
SECT AUTHOR
NNFF
NOT QUITE HOW I WAS PLANNING ON GETTING BACKSTAGE, REALLY...

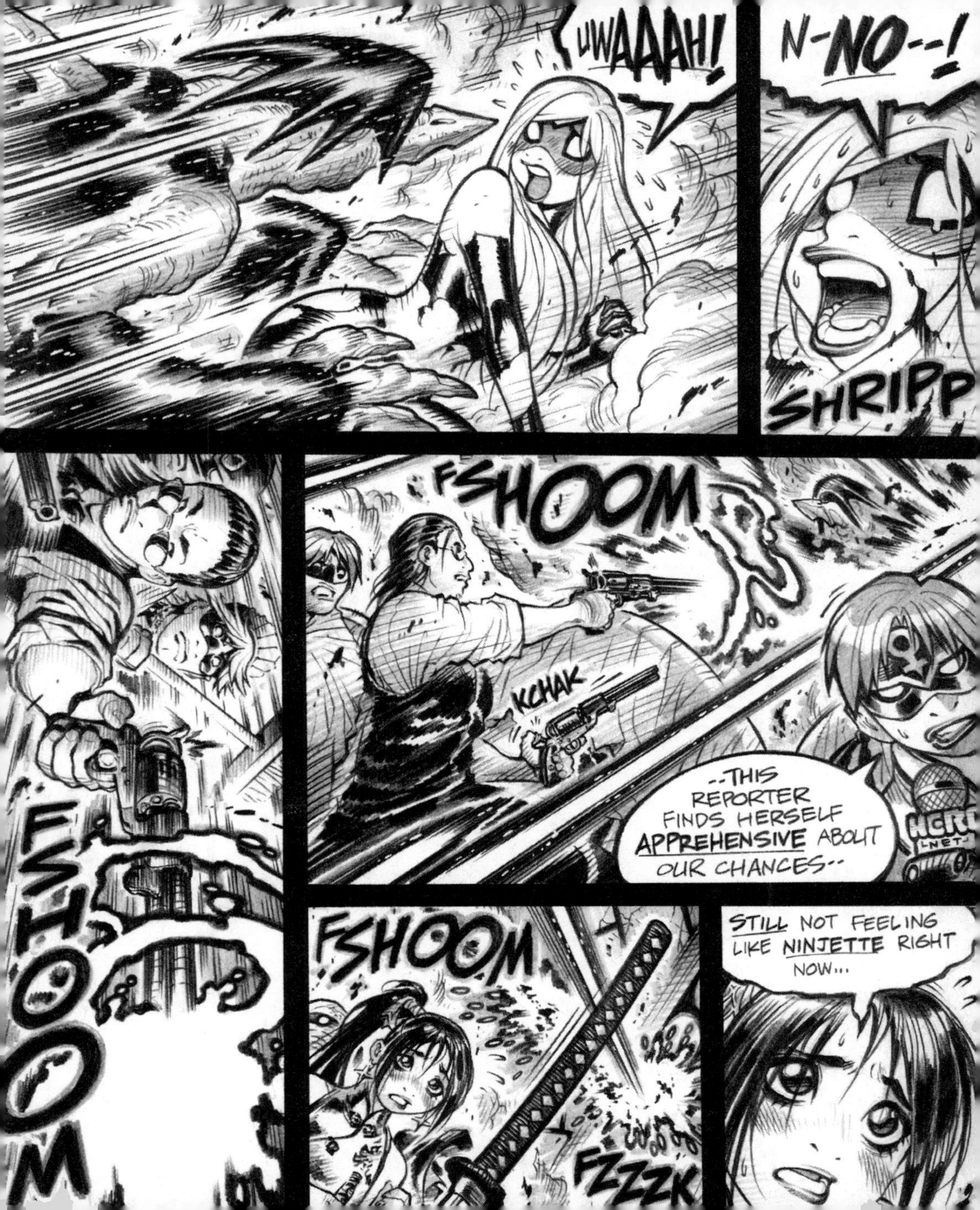
UWAAAH!
N-NO--!
SHRIPP
FSHOOM
FSHOOM
KCHAK
--THIS REPORTER FINDS HERSELF APPREHENSIVE ABOUT OUR CHANCES--
FSHOOM
FZZZK
STILL NOT FEELING LIKE NINJETTE RIGHT NOW...

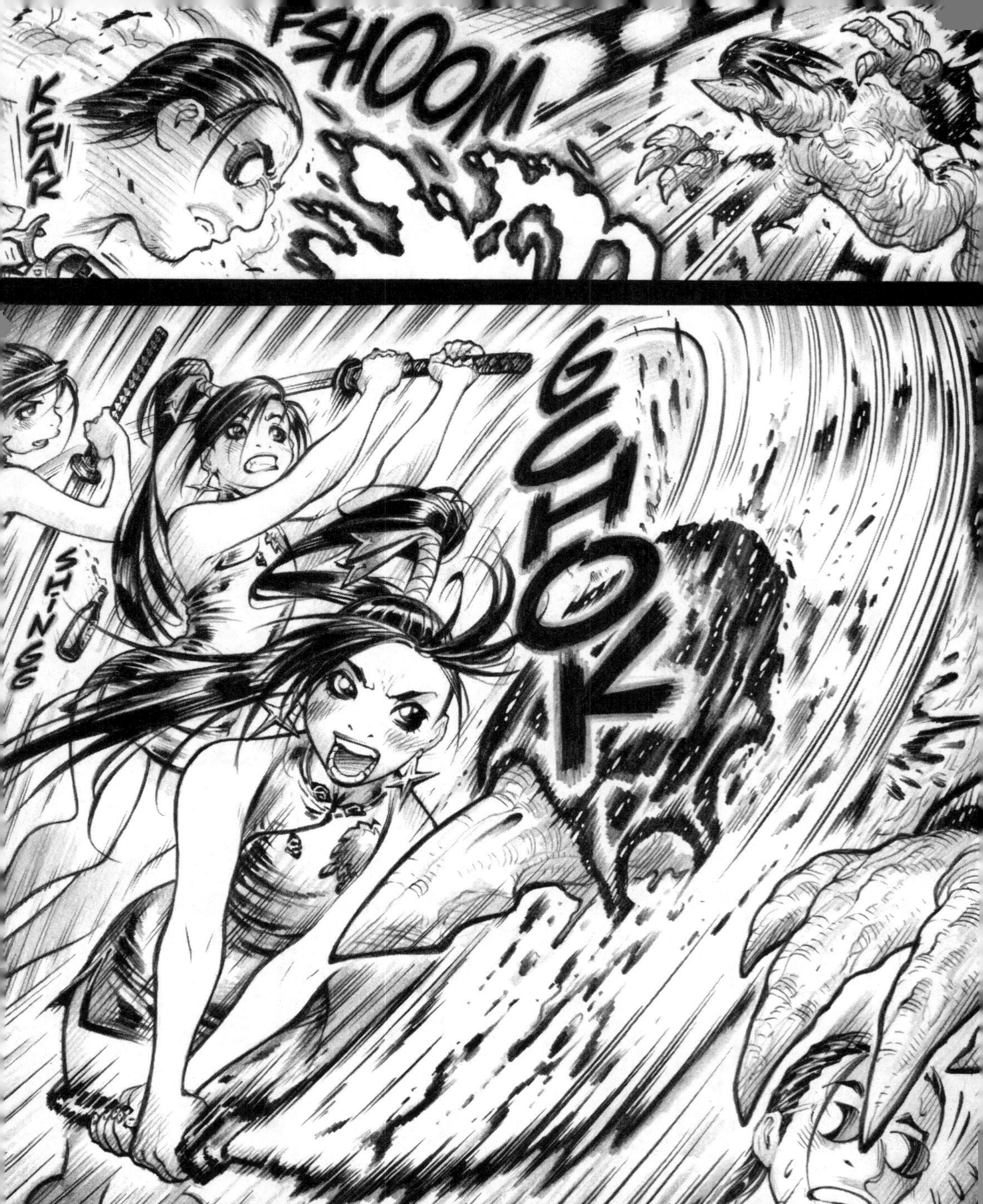
KCHAK
FSHOOM
SHINGG

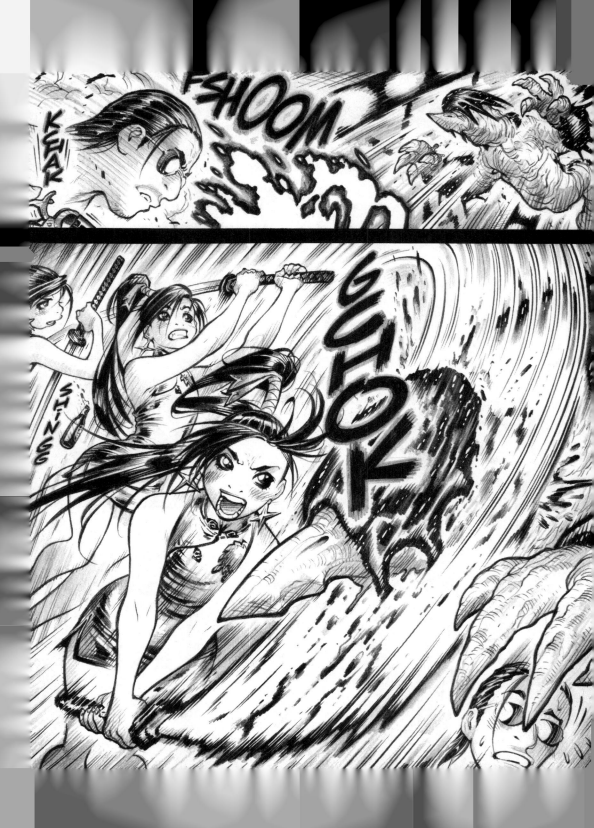

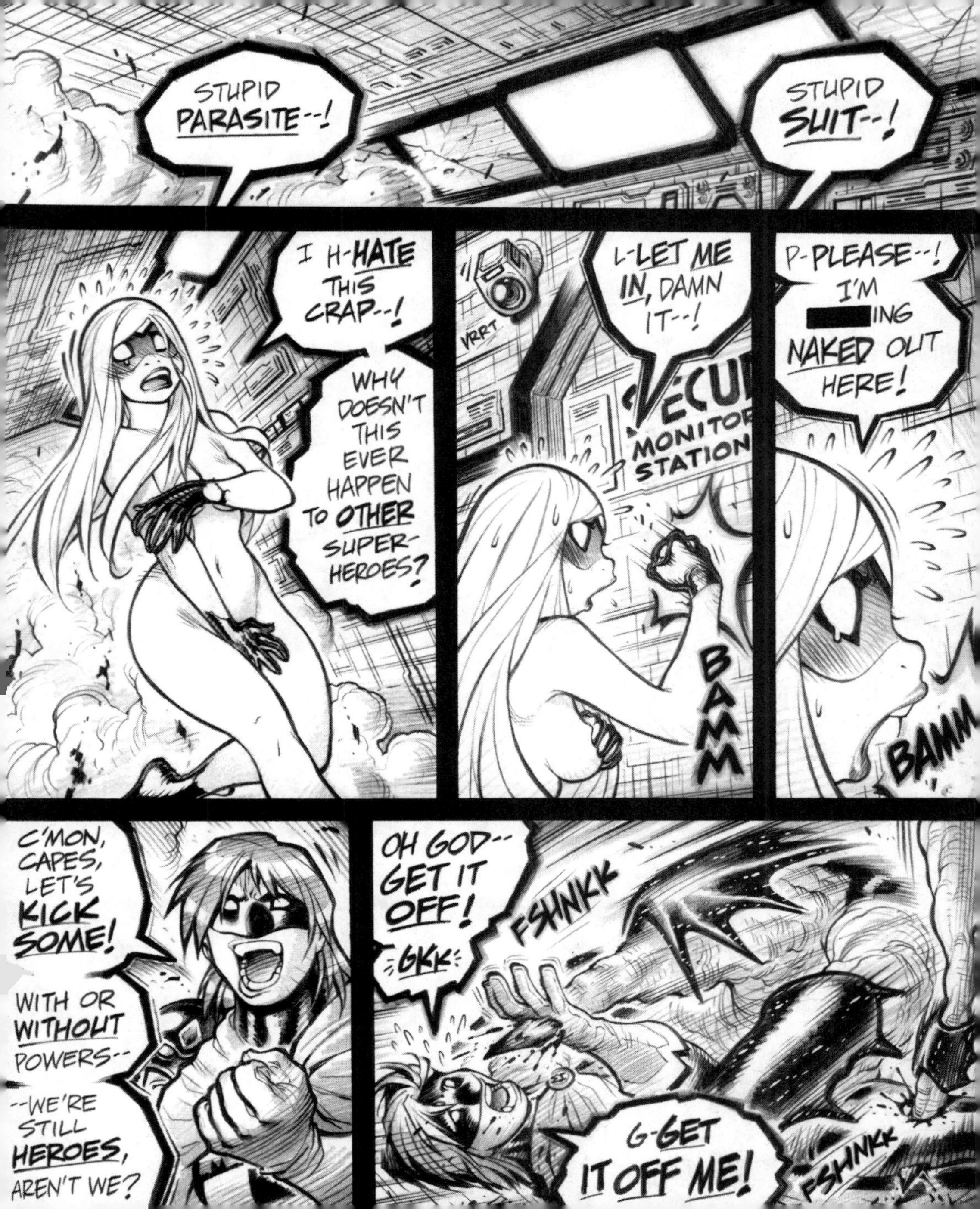
STUPID PARASITE--!
STUPID SUIT--!
I H-HATE THIS CRAP--!
WHY DOESN'T THIS EVER HAPPEN TO OTHER SUPER-HEROES?
VRRT
L-LET ME IN, DAMN IT--!
STATION
BAMM
P-PLEASE--! I'M [redacted]ING NAKED OUT HERE!
BAMM
C'MON, CAPES, LET'S KICK SOME!
WITH OR WITHOUT POWERS--
--WE'RE STILL HEROES, AREN'T WE?
OH GOD-- GET IT OFF!
GKK
FSHNKK
G-GET IT OFF ME!
FSHNKK

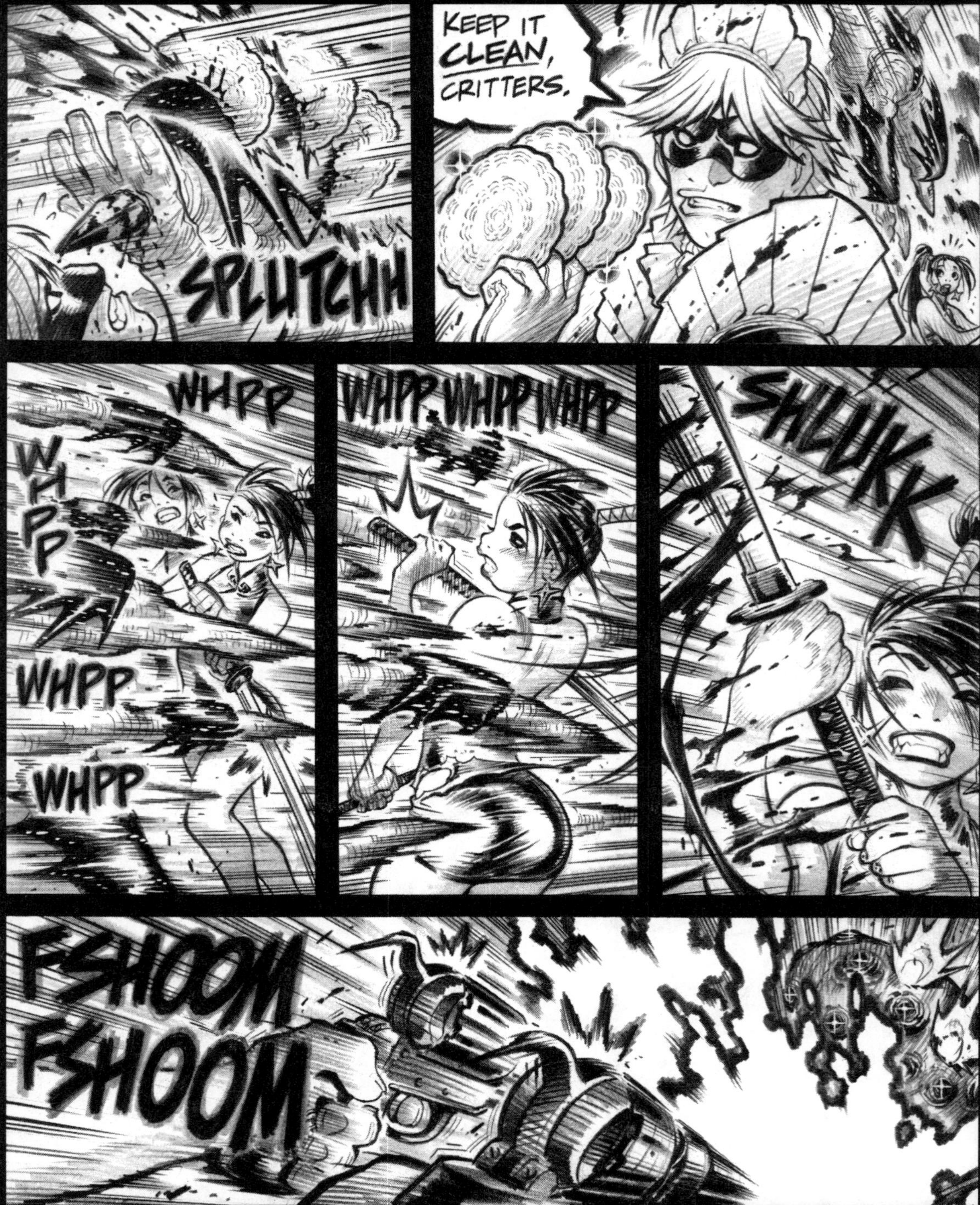
SPLUTCHH
KEEP IT CLEAN, CRITTERS.
WHPP
WHPP
WHPP
WHPP
WHPP WHPP WHPP
SHLUKK
FSHOOM
FSHOOM

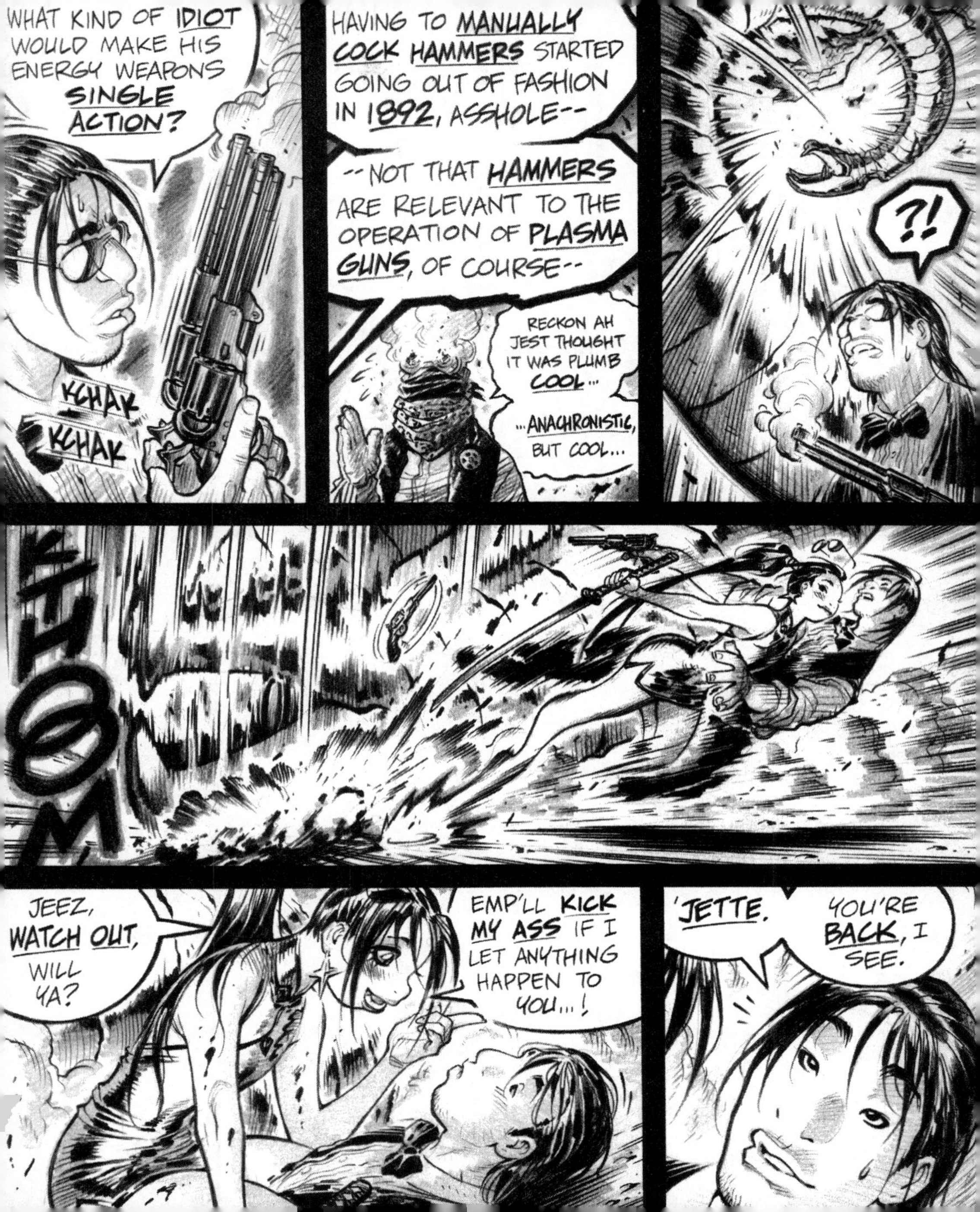
WHAT KIND OF IDIOT WOULD MAKE HIS ENERGY WEAPONS SINGLE ACTION?
KCHAK KCHAK
HAVING TO MANUALLY COCK HAMMERS STARTED GOING OUT OF FASHION IN 1892, ASSHOLE--
--NOT THAT HAMMERS ARE RELEVANT TO THE OPERATION OF PLASMA GUNS, OF COURSE--
RECKON AH JEST THOUGHT IT WAS PLUMB COOL...
...ANACHRONISTIC, BUT COOL...
?!
KHOOM
JEEZ, WATCH OUT, WILL YA?
EMP'LL KICK MY ASS IF I LET ANYTHING HAPPEN TO YOU...!
'JETTE.
YOU'RE BACK, I SEE.

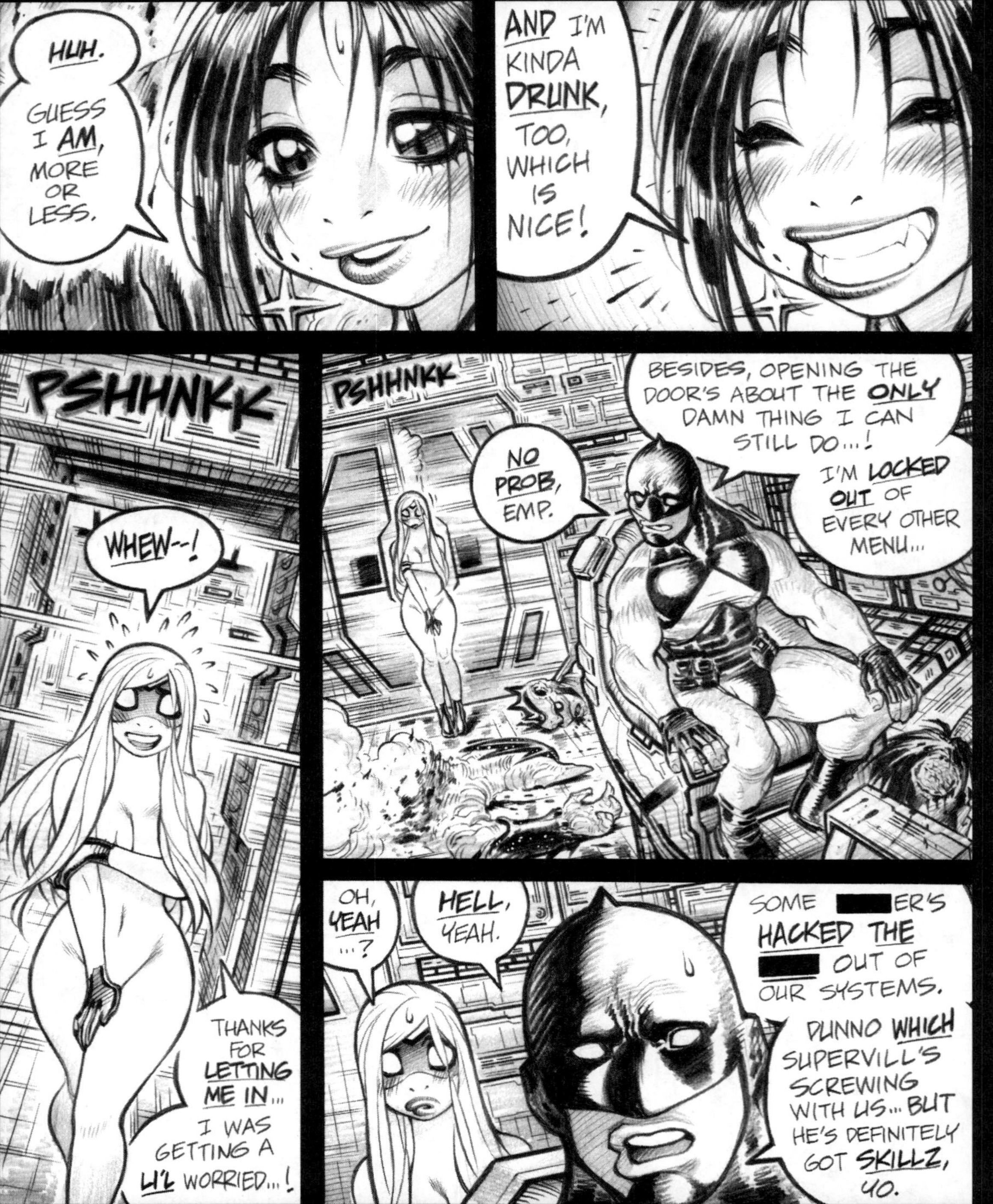
HUH.
GUESS I AM, MORE OR LESS.
AND I'M KINDA DRUNK, TOO, WHICH IS NICE!
PSHHNKK
WHEW--!
THANKS FOR LETTING ME IN...
I WAS GETTING A LI'L WORRIED...!
PSHHNKK
NO PROB, EMP.
BESIDES, OPENING THE DOOR'S ABOUT THE ONLY DAMN THING I CAN STILL DO...!
I'M LOCKED OUT OF EVERY OTHER MENU...
OH, YEAH ...?
HELL, YEAH.
SOME [redacted]ER'S HACKED THE [redacted] OUT OF OUR SYSTEMS.
DUNNO WHICH SUPERVILL'S SCREWING WITH US... BUT HE'S DEFINITELY GOT SKILLZ, YO.

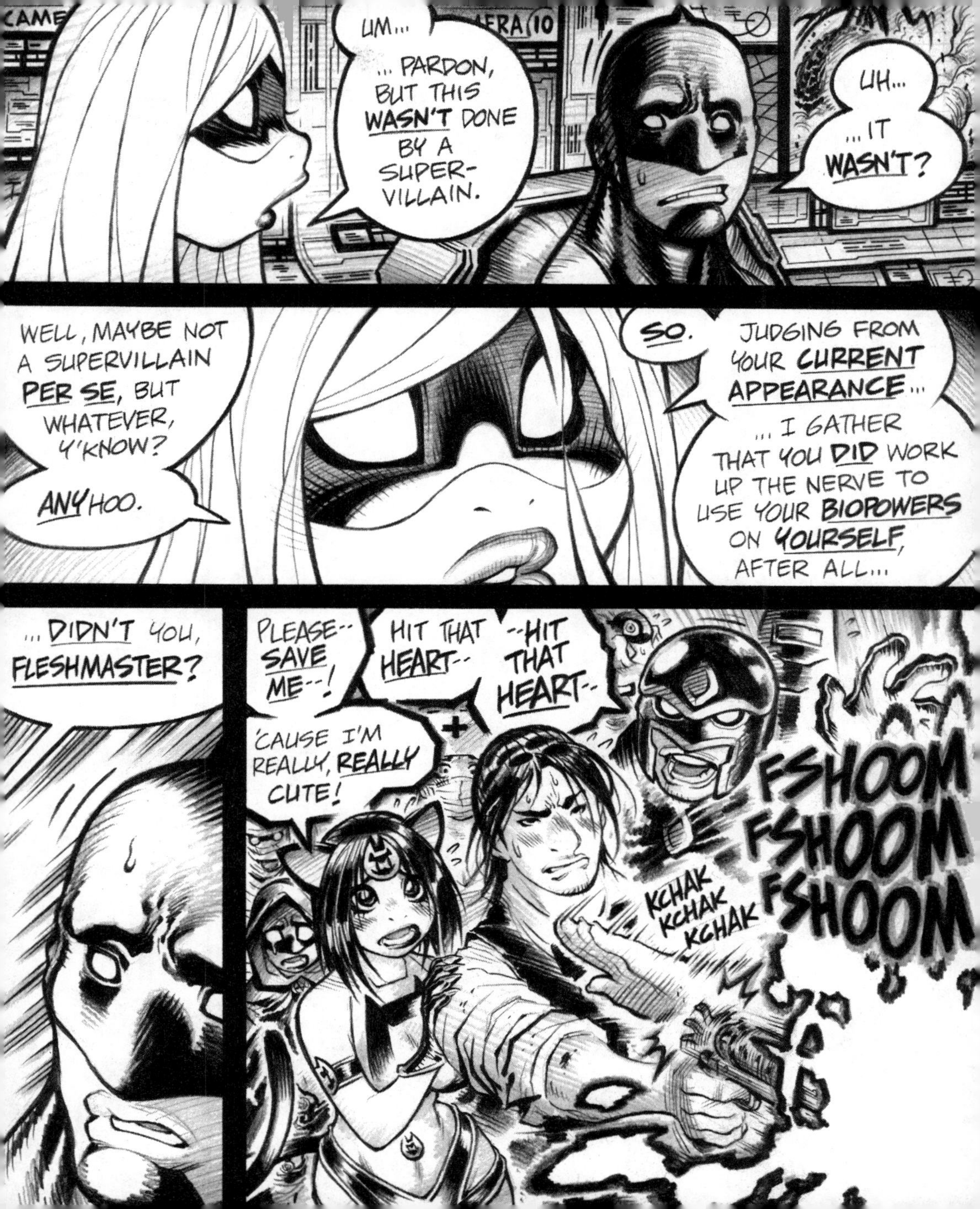
CAMERA 10
UM...
... PARDON, BUT THIS WASN'T DONE BY A SUPER-VILLAIN.
UH...
... IT WASN'T?
WELL, MAYBE NOT A SUPERVILLAIN PER SE, BUT WHATEVER, Y'KNOW?
ANYHOO.
SO.
JUDGING FROM YOUR CURRENT APPEARANCE...
... I GATHER THAT YOU DID WORK UP THE NERVE TO USE YOUR BIOPOWERS ON YOURSELF, AFTER ALL...
... DIDN'T YOU, FLESHMASTER?
PLEASE-- SAVE ME--!
'CAUSE I'M REALLY, REALLY CUTE!
HIT THAT HEART--
--HIT THAT HEART--
KCHAK KCHAK KCHAK
FSHOOM FSHOOM FSHOOM

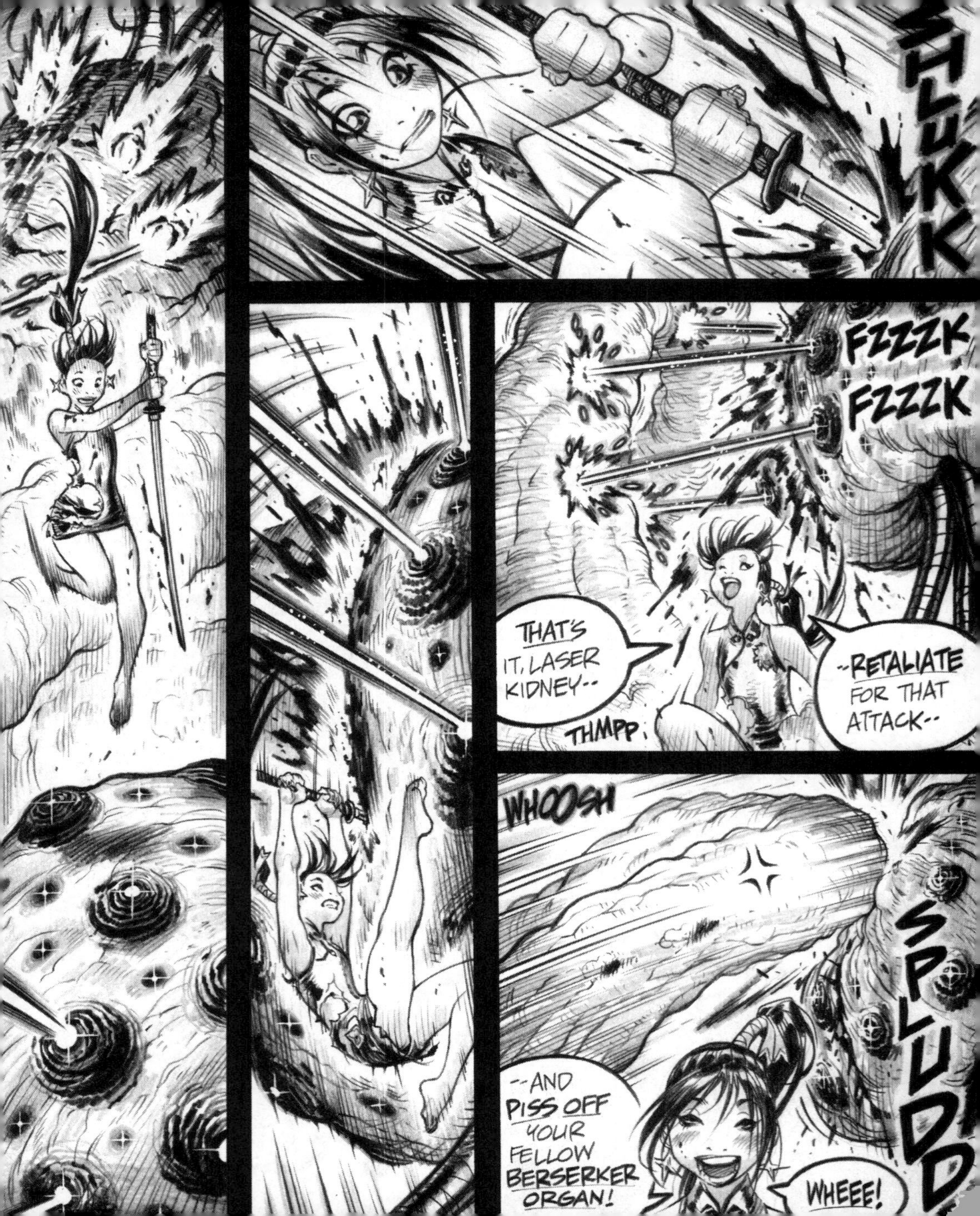
SHLUKK
FZZZK
FZZZK
THAT'S IT, LASER KIDNEY--
THMPP
--RETALIATE FOR THAT ATTACK--
WHOOSH
SPLUDD
--AND PISS OFF YOUR FELLOW BERSERKER ORGAN!
WHEEE!

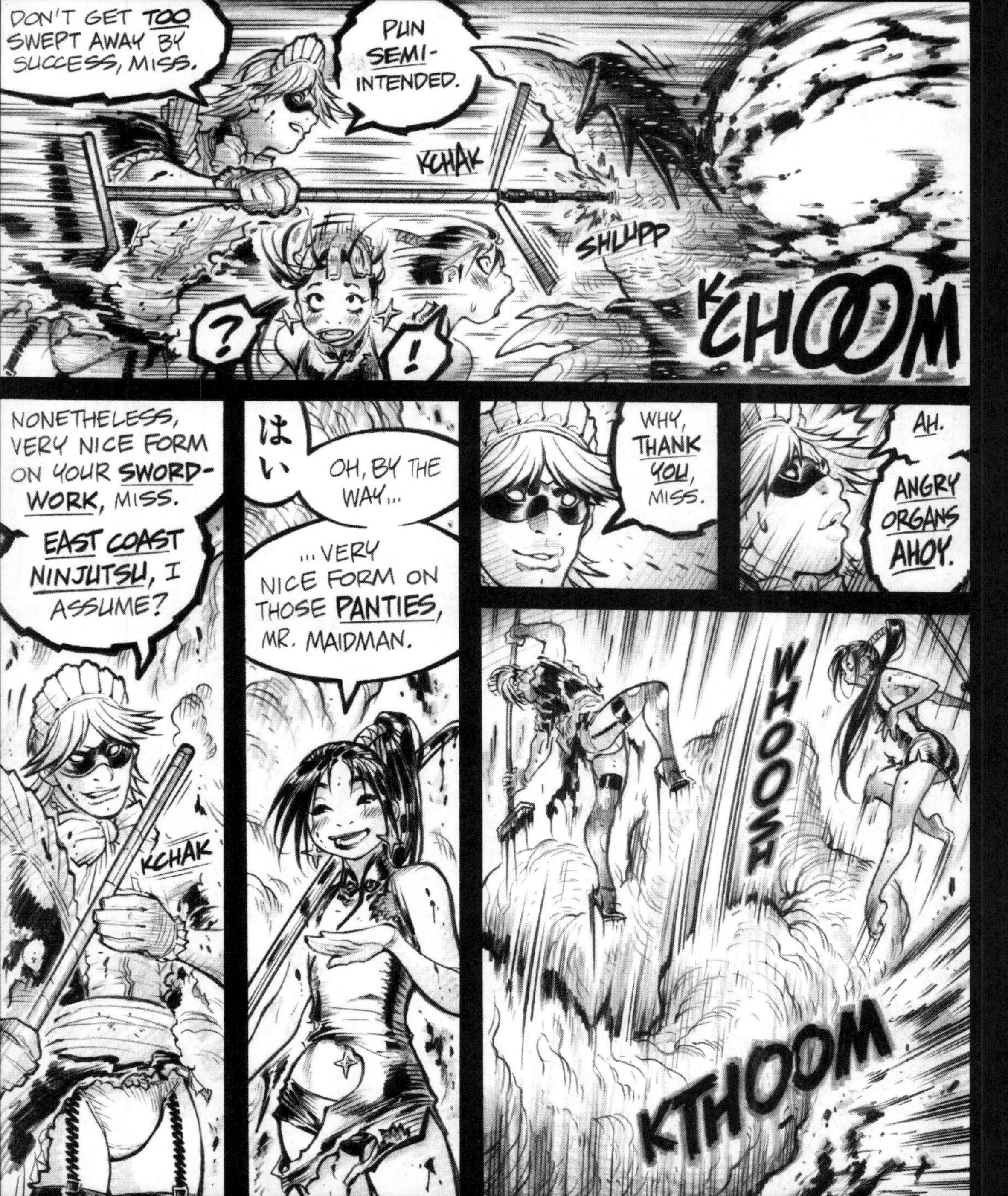
DON'T GET TOO SWEPT AWAY BY SUCCESS, MISS.
PUN SEMI-INTENDED.
KCHAK
SHLUPP
?
!
KCHOOM
NONETHELESS, VERY NICE FORM ON YOUR SWORD-WORK, MISS.
EAST COAST NINJUTSU, I ASSUME?
KCHAK
はい
OH, BY THE WAY...
...VERY NICE FORM ON THOSE PANTIES, MR. MAIDMAN.
WHY, THANK YOU, MISS.
AH.
ANGRY ORGANS AHOY.
WHOOSH
KTHOOM

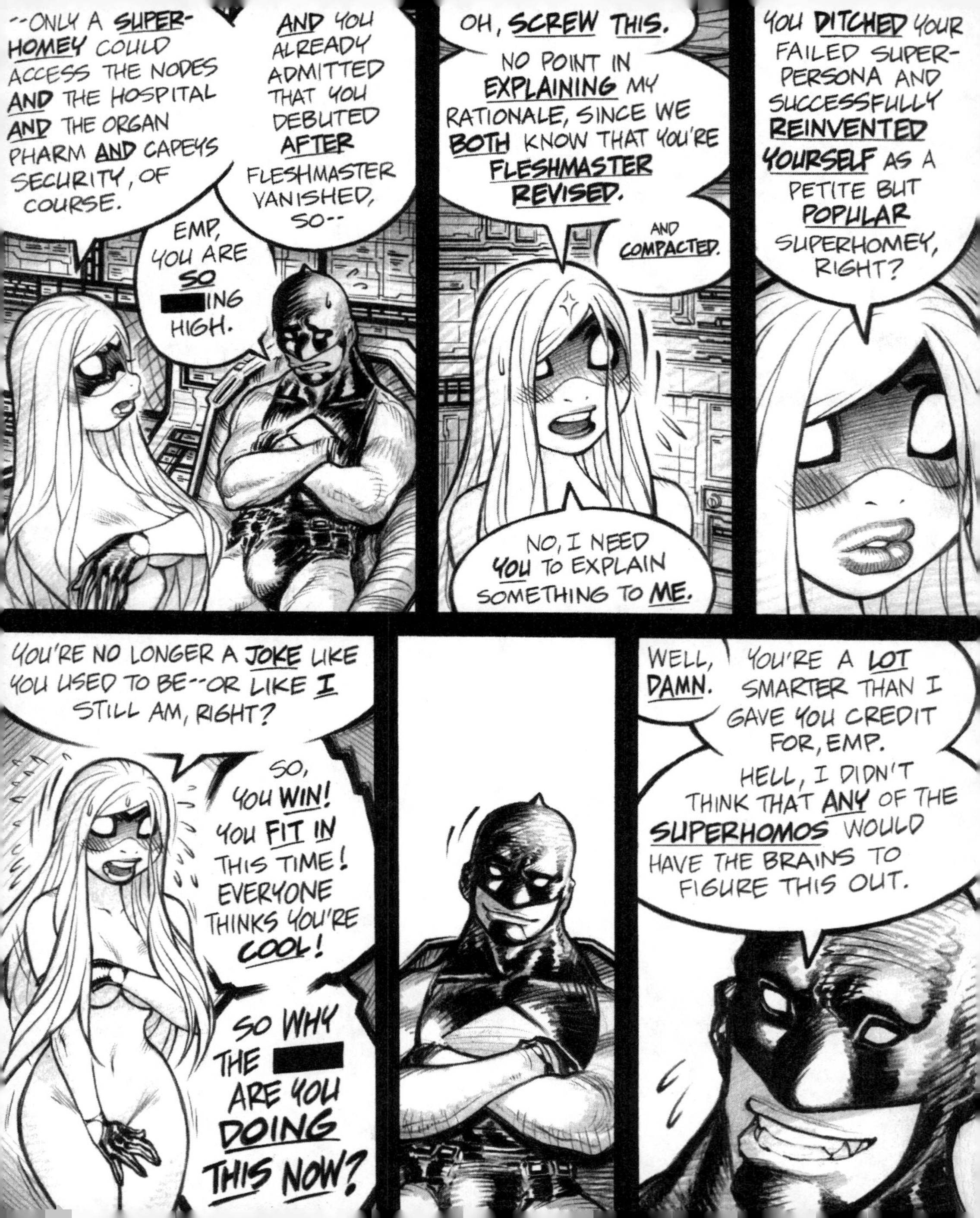
--ONLY A SUPER-HOMEY COULD ACCESS THE NODES AND THE HOSPITAL AND THE ORGAN PHARM AND CAPEYS SECURITY, OF COURSE.
AND YOU ALREADY ADMITTED THAT YOU DEBUTED AFTER FLESHMASTER VANISHED, SO--
EMP, YOU ARE SO [redacted]ING HIGH.
OH, SCREW THIS.
NO POINT IN EXPLAINING MY RATIONALE, SINCE WE BOTH KNOW THAT YOU'RE FLESHMASTER REVISED.
AND COMPACTED.
NO, I NEED YOU TO EXPLAIN SOMETHING TO ME.
YOU DITCHED YOUR FAILED SUPER-PERSONA AND SUCCESSFULLY REINVENTED YOURSELF AS A PETITE BUT POPULAR SUPERHOMEY, RIGHT?
YOU'RE NO LONGER A JOKE LIKE YOU USED TO BE--OR LIKE I STILL AM, RIGHT?
SO, YOU WIN! YOU FIT IN THIS TIME! EVERYONE THINKS YOU'RE COOL!
SO WHY THE [redacted] ARE YOU DOING THIS NOW?
WELL, DAMN.
YOU'RE A LOT SMARTER THAN I GAVE YOU CREDIT FOR, EMP.
HELL, I DIDN'T THINK THAT ANY OF THE SUPERHOMOS WOULD HAVE THE BRAINS TO FIGURE THIS OUT.

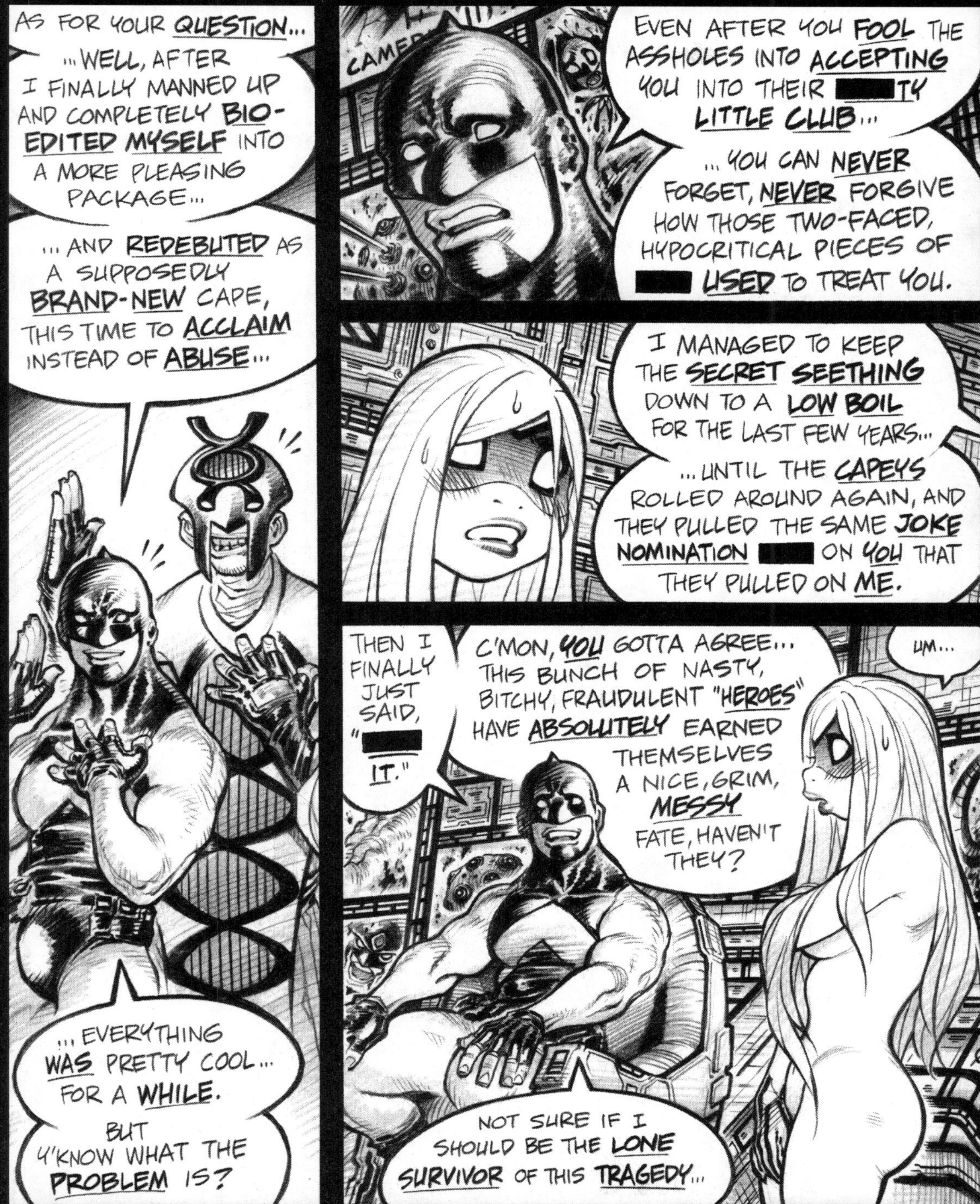
AS FOR YOUR QUESTION...
...WELL, AFTER I FINALLY MANNED UP AND COMPLETELY BIO-EDITED MYSELF INTO A MORE PLEASING PACKAGE...
...AND REDEBUTED AS A SUPPOSEDLY BRAND-NEW CAPE, THIS TIME TO ACCLAIM INSTEAD OF ABUSE...
...EVERYTHING WAS PRETTY COOL... FOR A WHILE.
BUT Y'KNOW WHAT THE PROBLEM IS?
EVEN AFTER YOU FOOL THE ASSHOLES INTO ACCEPTING YOU INTO THEIR [redacted]TY LITTLE CLUB...
...YOU CAN NEVER FORGET, NEVER FORGIVE HOW THOSE TWO-FACED, HYPOCRITICAL PIECES OF [redacted] USED TO TREAT YOU.
I MANAGED TO KEEP THE SECRET SEETHING DOWN TO A LOW BOIL FOR THE LAST FEW YEARS...
...UNTIL THE CAPEYS ROLLED AROUND AGAIN, AND THEY PULLED THE SAME JOKE NOMINATION [redacted] ON YOU THAT THEY PULLED ON ME.
THEN I FINALLY JUST SAID, "[redacted] IT."
C'MON, YOU GOTTA AGREE... THIS BUNCH OF NASTY, BITCHY, FRAUDULENT "HEROES" HAVE ABSOLUTELY EARNED THEMSELVES A NICE, GRIM, MESSY FATE, HAVEN'T THEY?
UM...
NOT SURE IF I SHOULD BE THE LONE SURVIVOR OF THIS TRAGEDY...

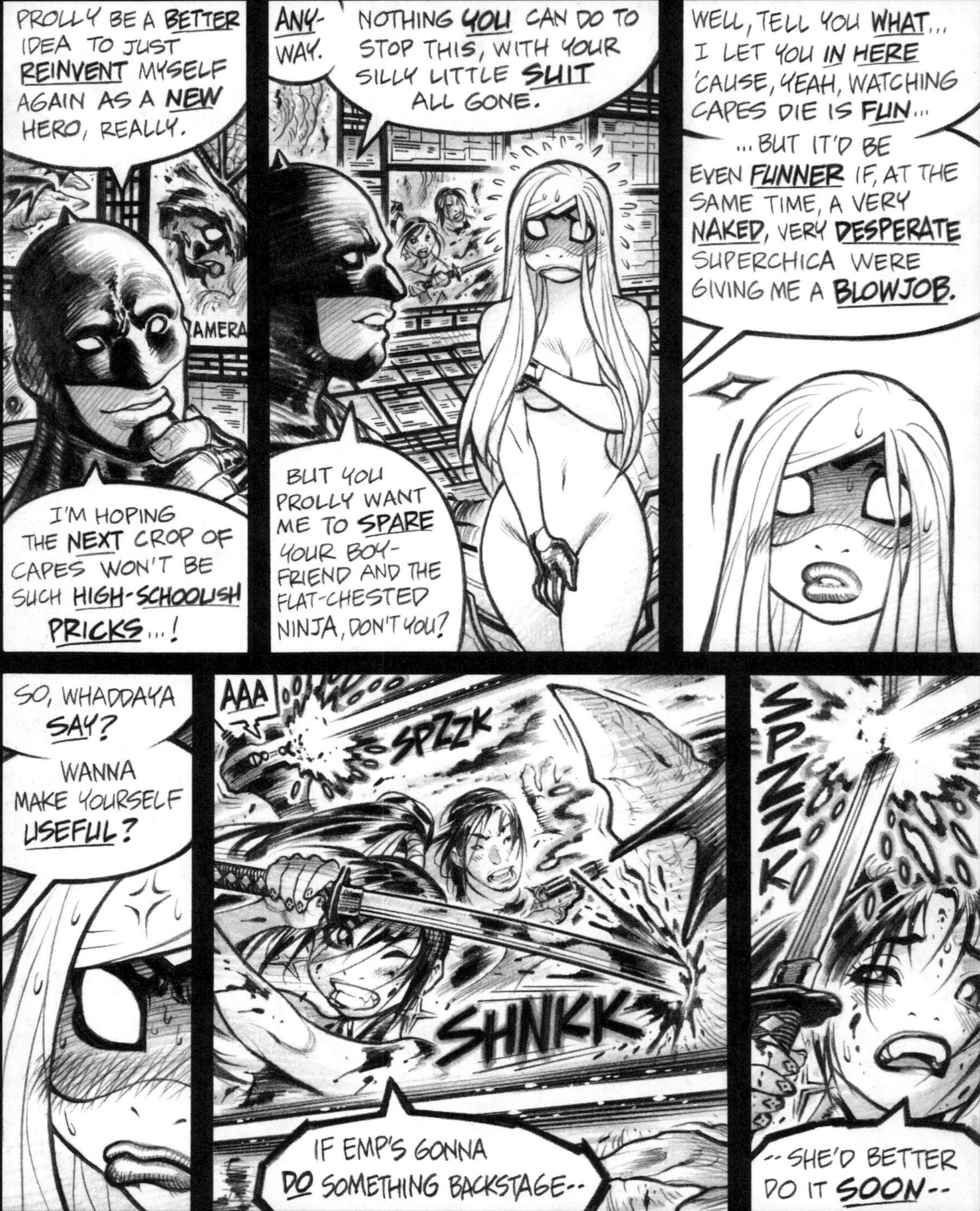
PROLLY BE A BETTER IDEA TO JUST REINVENT MYSELF AGAIN AS A NEW HERO, REALLY.
AMERA
I'M HOPING THE NEXT CROP OF CAPES WON'T BE SUCH HIGH-SCHOOLISH PRICKS...!
ANY-WAY.
NOTHING YOU CAN DO TO STOP THIS, WITH YOUR SILLY LITTLE SUIT ALL GONE.
BUT YOU PROLLY WANT ME TO SPARE YOUR BOY-FRIEND AND THE FLAT-CHESTED NINJA, DON'T YOU?
WELL, TELL YOU WHAT... I LET YOU IN HERE 'CAUSE, YEAH, WATCHING CAPES DIE IS FUN...
...BUT IT'D BE EVEN FUNNER IF, AT THE SAME TIME, A VERY NAKED, VERY DESPERATE SUPERCHICA WERE GIVING ME A BLOWJOB.
SO, WHADDAYA SAY?
WANNA MAKE YOURSELF USEFUL?
AAA
SPZZK
SHNKK
IF EMP'S GONNA DO SOMETHING BACKSTAGE--
SPZZZK
--SHE'D BETTER DO IT SOON--

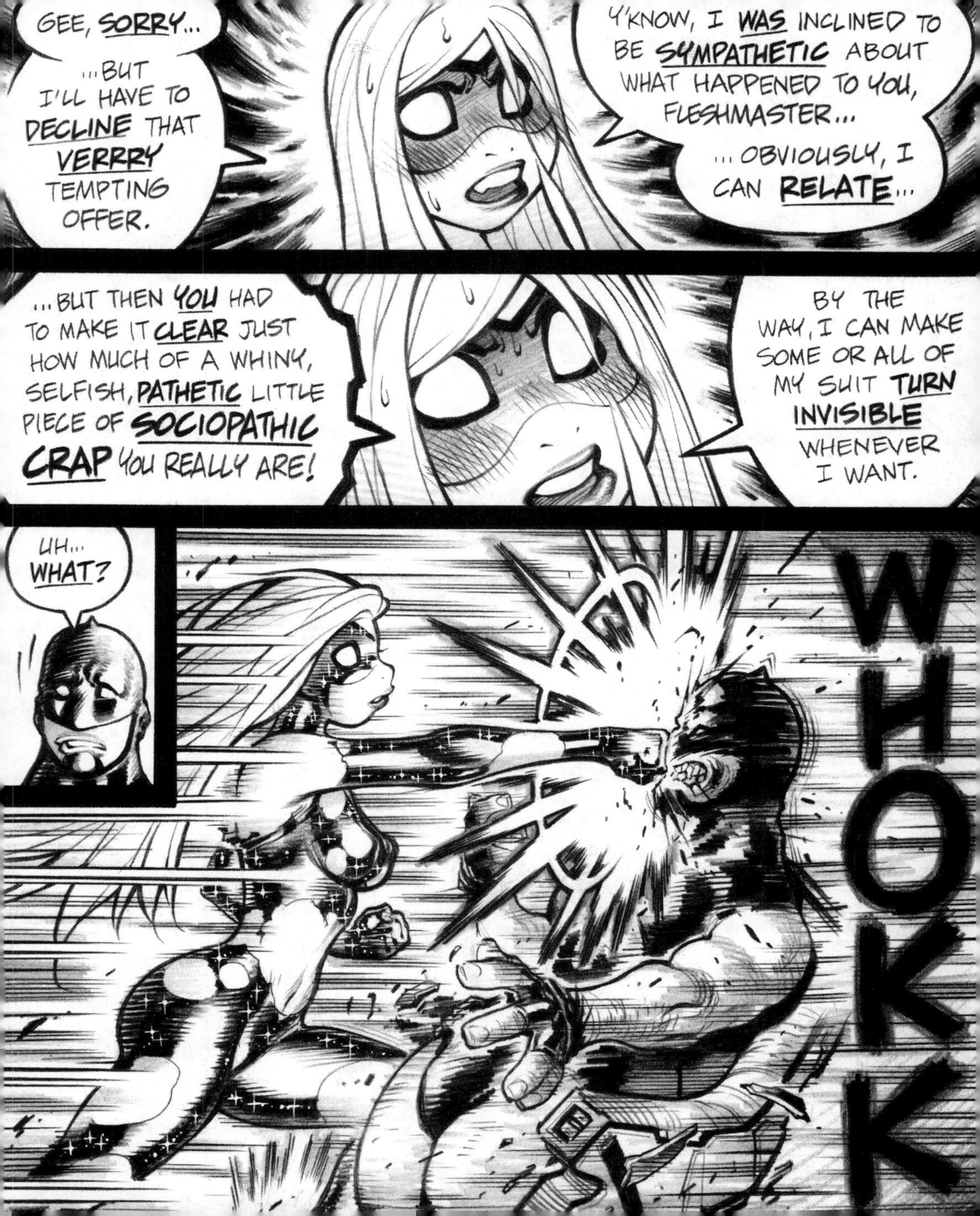
GEE, SORRY...
...BUT I'LL HAVE TO DECLINE THAT VERRRY TEMPTING OFFER.
Y'KNOW, I WAS INCLINED TO BE SYMPATHETIC ABOUT WHAT HAPPENED TO YOU, FLESHMASTER...
...OBVIOUSLY, I CAN RELATE...
...BUT THEN YOU HAD TO MAKE IT CLEAR JUST HOW MUCH OF A WHINY, SELFISH, PATHETIC LITTLE PIECE OF SOCIOPATHIC CRAP YOU REALLY ARE!
BY THE WAY, I CAN MAKE SOME OR ALL OF MY SUIT TURN INVISIBLE WHENEVER I WANT.
UH... WHAT?
WHOKK

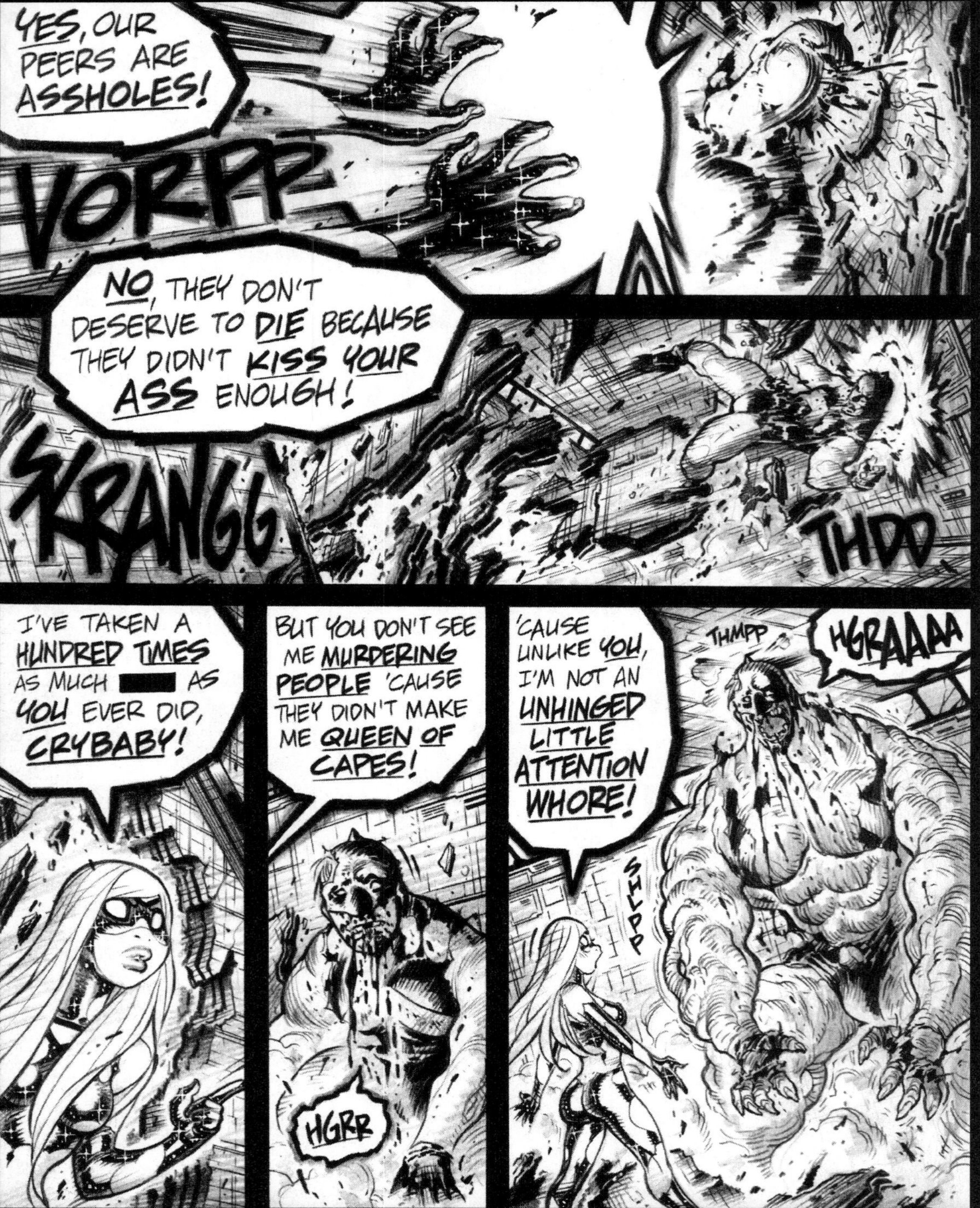
YES, OUR PEERS ARE ASSHOLES!
VORPP
NO, THEY DON'T DESERVE TO DIE BECAUSE THEY DIDN'T KISS YOUR ASS ENOUGH!
SKRANGG
THDD
I'VE TAKEN A HUNDRED TIMES AS MUCH [redacted] AS YOU EVER DID, CRYBABY!
BUT YOU DON'T SEE ME MURDERING PEOPLE 'CAUSE THEY DIDN'T MAKE ME QUEEN OF CAPES!
HGRR
'CAUSE UNLIKE YOU, I'M NOT AN UNHINGED LITTLE ATTENTION WHORE!
THMPP
HGRAAAA
SHLPP

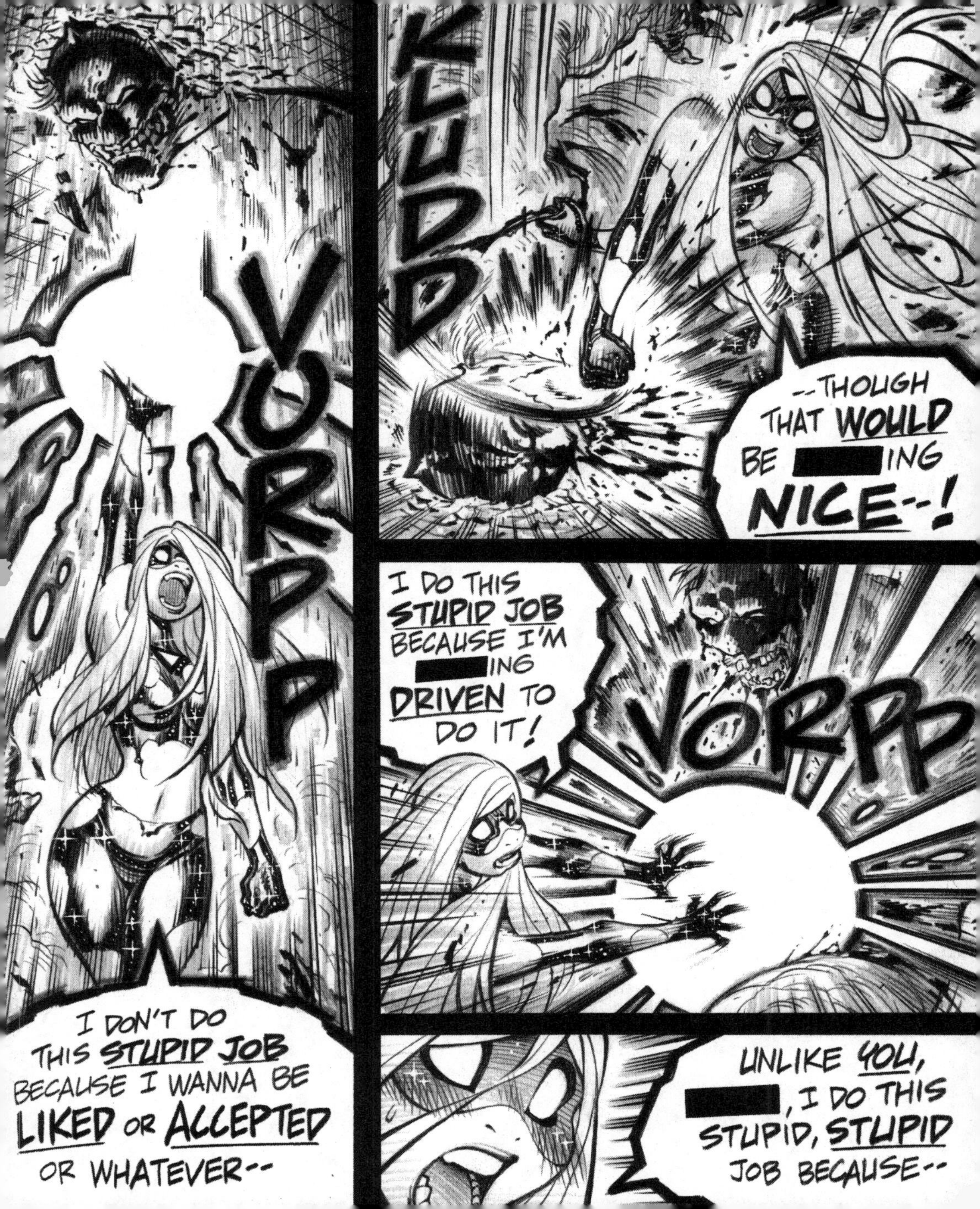
VORPP
I DON'T DO THIS STUPID JOB BECAUSE I WANNA BE LIKED OR ACCEPTED OR WHATEVER--
KLUDD
--THOUGH THAT WOULD BE [redacted]ING NICE--!
I DO THIS STUPID JOB BECAUSE I'M [redacted]ING DRIVEN TO DO IT!
VORPP
UNLIKE YOU, [redacted], I DO THIS STUPID, STUPID JOB BECAUSE--

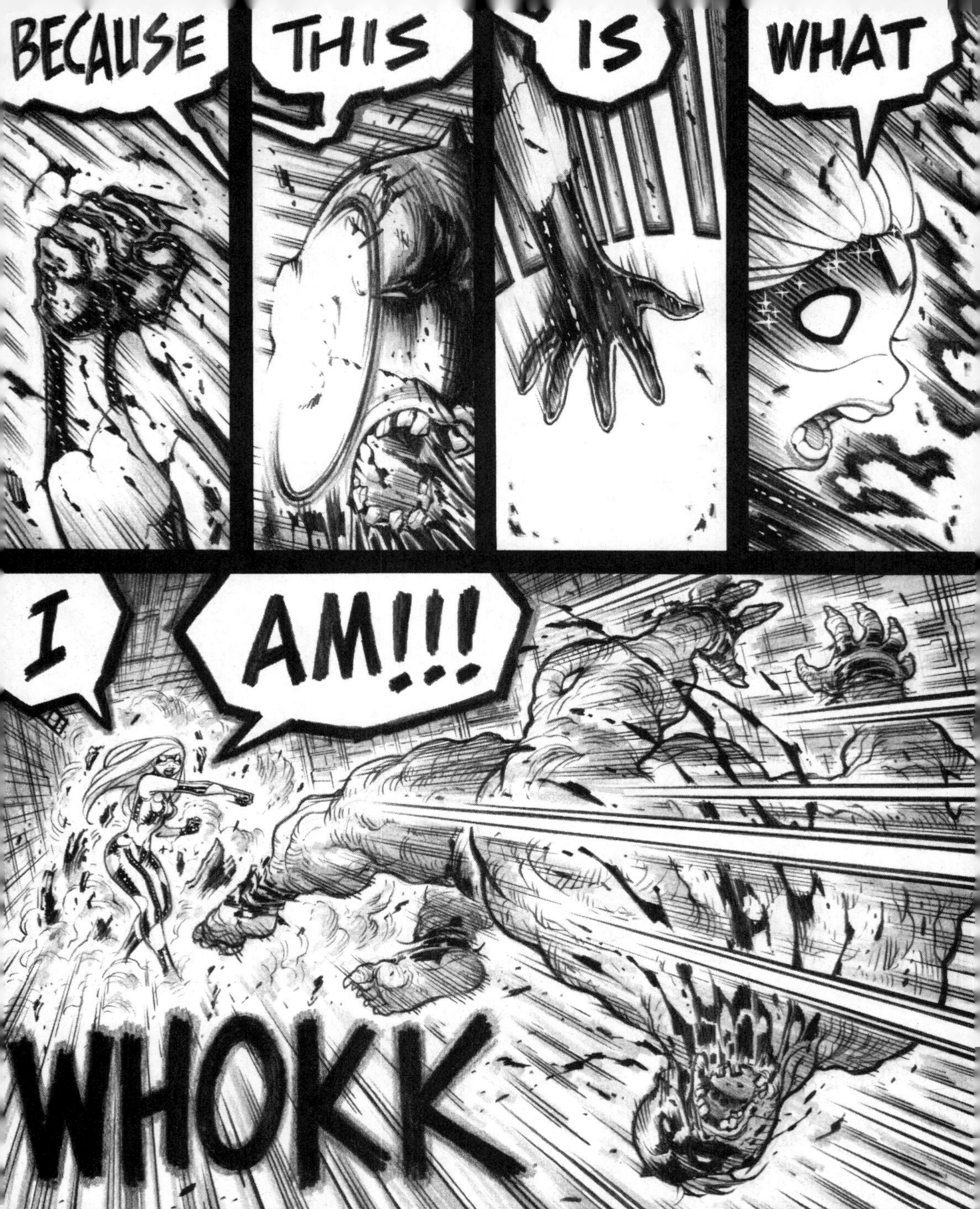
BECAUSE
THIS
IS
WHAT
I
AM!!!
WHOKK

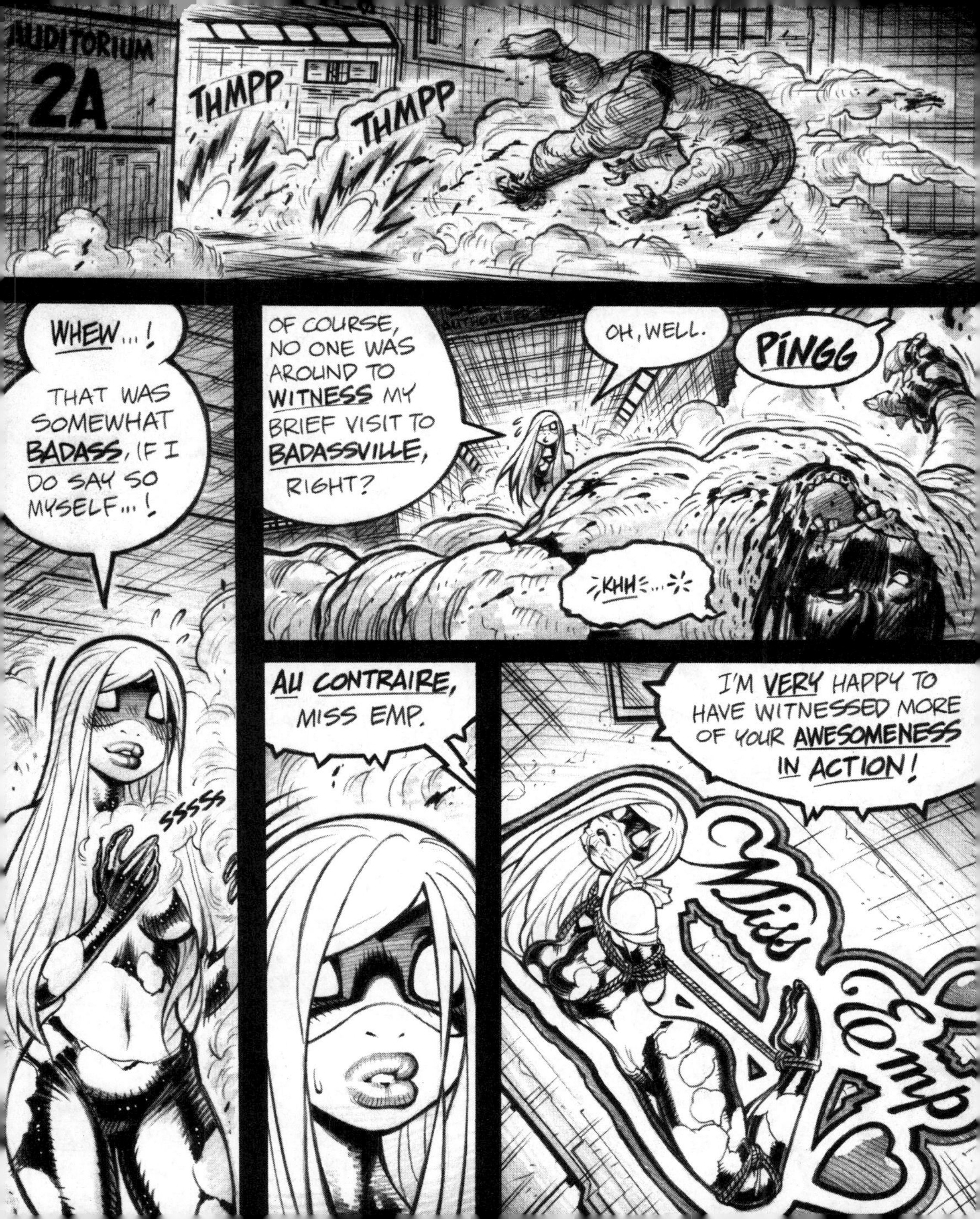
AUDITORIUM
2A
THMPP
THMPP
WHEW...! THAT WAS SOMEWHAT BADASS, IF I DO SAY SO MYSELF...!
OF COURSE, NO ONE WAS AROUND TO WITNESS MY BRIEF VISIT TO BADASSVILLE, RIGHT?
OH, WELL.
PINGG
KHH...
SSSSS
AU CONTRAIRE, MISS EMP.
I'M VERY HAPPY TO HAVE WITNESSED MORE OF YOUR AWESOMENESS IN ACTION!
Miss Emp

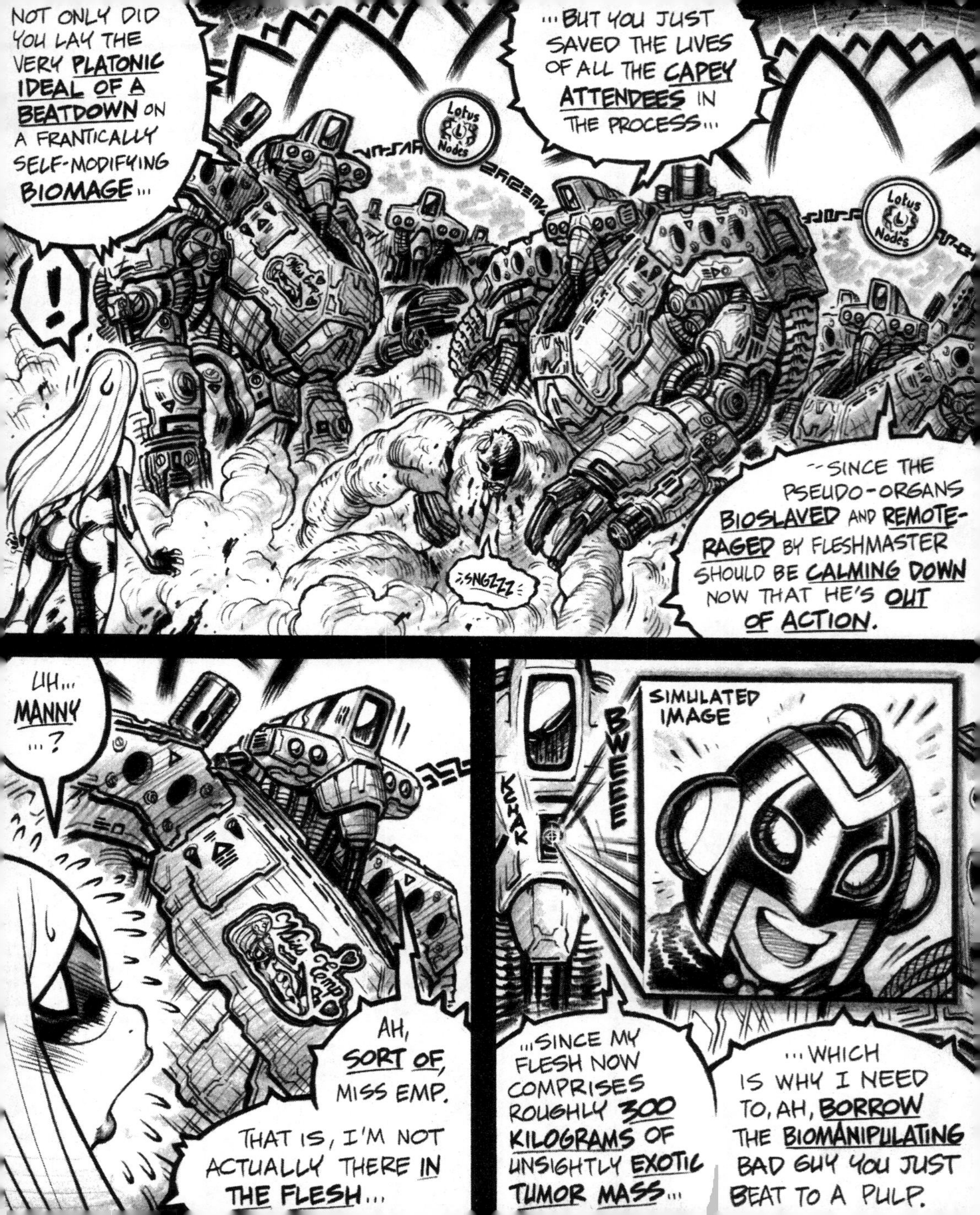
NOT ONLY DID YOU LAY THE VERY PLATONIC IDEAL OF A BEATDOWN ON A FRANTICALLY SELF-MODIFYING BIOMAGE...
...BUT YOU JUST SAVED THE LIVES OF ALL THE CAPEY ATTENDEES IN THE PROCESS...
Lotus Nodes
!
Lotus Nodes
--SINCE THE PSEUDO-ORGANS BIOSLAVED AND REMOTE-RAGED BY FLESHMASTER SHOULD BE CALMING DOWN NOW THAT HE'S OUT OF ACTION.
SNGZZZ
UH... MANNY ...?
AH, SORT OF, MISS EMP.
THAT IS, I'M NOT ACTUALLY THERE IN THE FLESH...
SIMULATED IMAGE
BWEEEE
KCHAK
...SINCE MY FLESH NOW COMPRISES ROUGHLY 300 KILOGRAMS OF UNSIGHTLY EXOTIC TUMOR MASS...
...WHICH IS WHY I NEED TO, AH, BORROW THE BIOMANIPULATING BAD GUY YOU JUST BEAT TO A PULP.

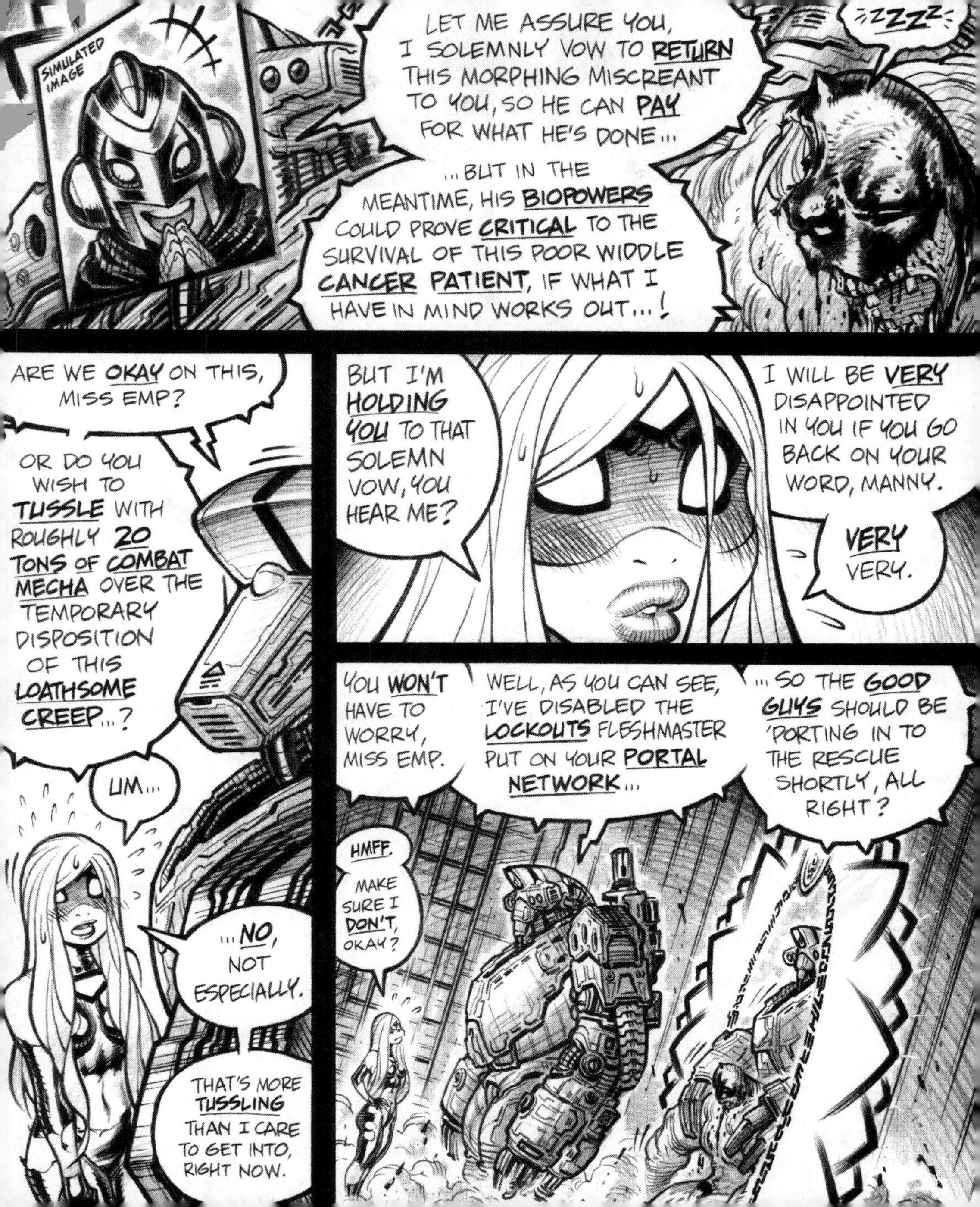
SIMULATED IMAGE
LET ME ASSURE YOU, I SOLEMNLY VOW TO RETURN THIS MORPHING MISCREANT TO YOU, SO HE CAN PAY FOR WHAT HE'S DONE...
...BUT IN THE MEANTIME, HIS BIOPOWERS COULD PROVE CRITICAL TO THE SURVIVAL OF THIS POOR WIDDLE CANCER PATIENT, IF WHAT I HAVE IN MIND WORKS OUT...!
ZZZZ
ARE WE OKAY ON THIS, MISS EMP?
OR DO YOU WISH TO TUSSLE WITH ROUGHLY 20 TONS OF COMBAT MECHA OVER THE TEMPORARY DISPOSITION OF THIS LOATHSOME CREEP...?
UM...
...NO, NOT ESPECIALLY.
THAT'S MORE TUSSLING THAN I CARE TO GET INTO, RIGHT NOW.
BUT I'M HOLDING YOU TO THAT SOLEMN VOW, YOU HEAR ME?
I WILL BE VERY DISAPPOINTED IN YOU IF YOU GO BACK ON YOUR WORD, MANNY.
VERY VERY.
YOU WON'T HAVE TO WORRY, MISS EMP.
WELL, AS YOU CAN SEE, I'VE DISABLED THE LOCKOUTS FLESHMASTER PUT ON YOUR PORTAL NETWORK...
...SO THE GOOD GUYS SHOULD BE 'PORTING IN TO THE RESCUE SHORTLY, ALL RIGHT?
HMFF.
MAKE SURE I DON'T, OKAY?

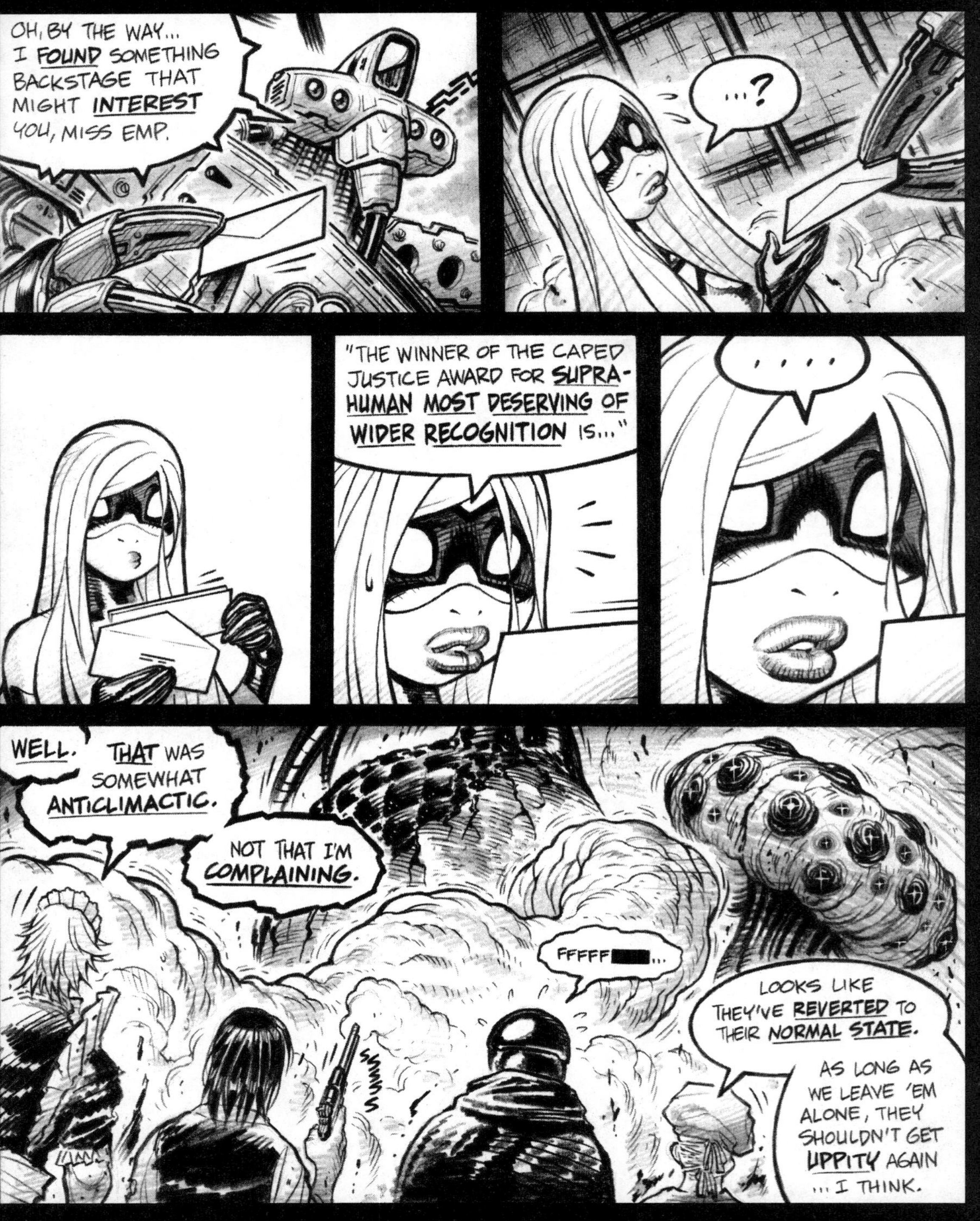
OH, BY THE WAY... I FOUND SOMETHING BACKSTAGE THAT MIGHT INTEREST YOU, MISS EMP.
...?
"THE WINNER OF THE CAPED JUSTICE AWARD FOR SUPRA-HUMAN MOST DESERVING OF WIDER RECOGNITION IS..."
. . . .
WELL. THAT WAS SOMEWHAT ANTICLIMACTIC.
NOT THAT I'M COMPLAINING.
FFFFF[redacted]...
SSSSS
LOOKS LIKE THEY'VE REVERTED TO THEIR NORMAL STATE.
AS LONG AS WE LEAVE 'EM ALONE, THEY SHOULDN'T GET UPPITY AGAIN ... I THINK.

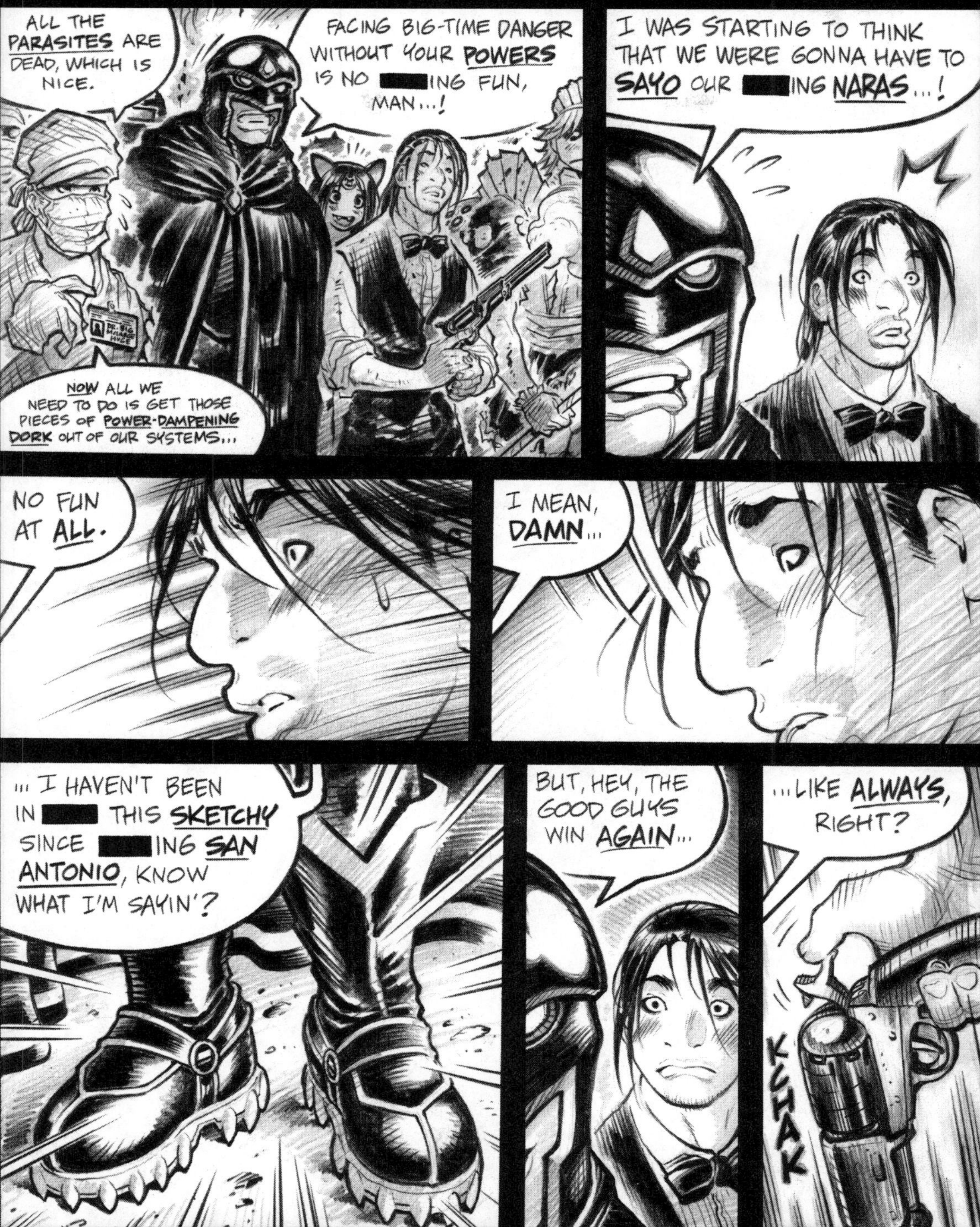
ALL THE PARASITES ARE DEAD, WHICH IS NICE.
FACING BIG-TIME DANGER WITHOUT YOUR POWERS IS NO [redacted]ING FUN, MAN...!
NOW ALL WE NEED TO DO IS GET THOSE PIECES OF POWER-DAMPENING DORK OUT OF OUR SYSTEMS...
I WAS STARTING TO THINK THAT WE WERE GONNA HAVE TO SAYO OUR [redacted]ING NARAS...!
NO FUN AT ALL.
I MEAN, DAMN...
...I HAVEN'T BEEN IN [redacted] THIS SKETCHY SINCE [redacted]ING SAN ANTONIO, KNOW WHAT I'M SAYIN'?
BUT, HEY, THE GOOD GUYS WIN AGAIN...
...LIKE ALWAYS, RIGHT?
KCHAK

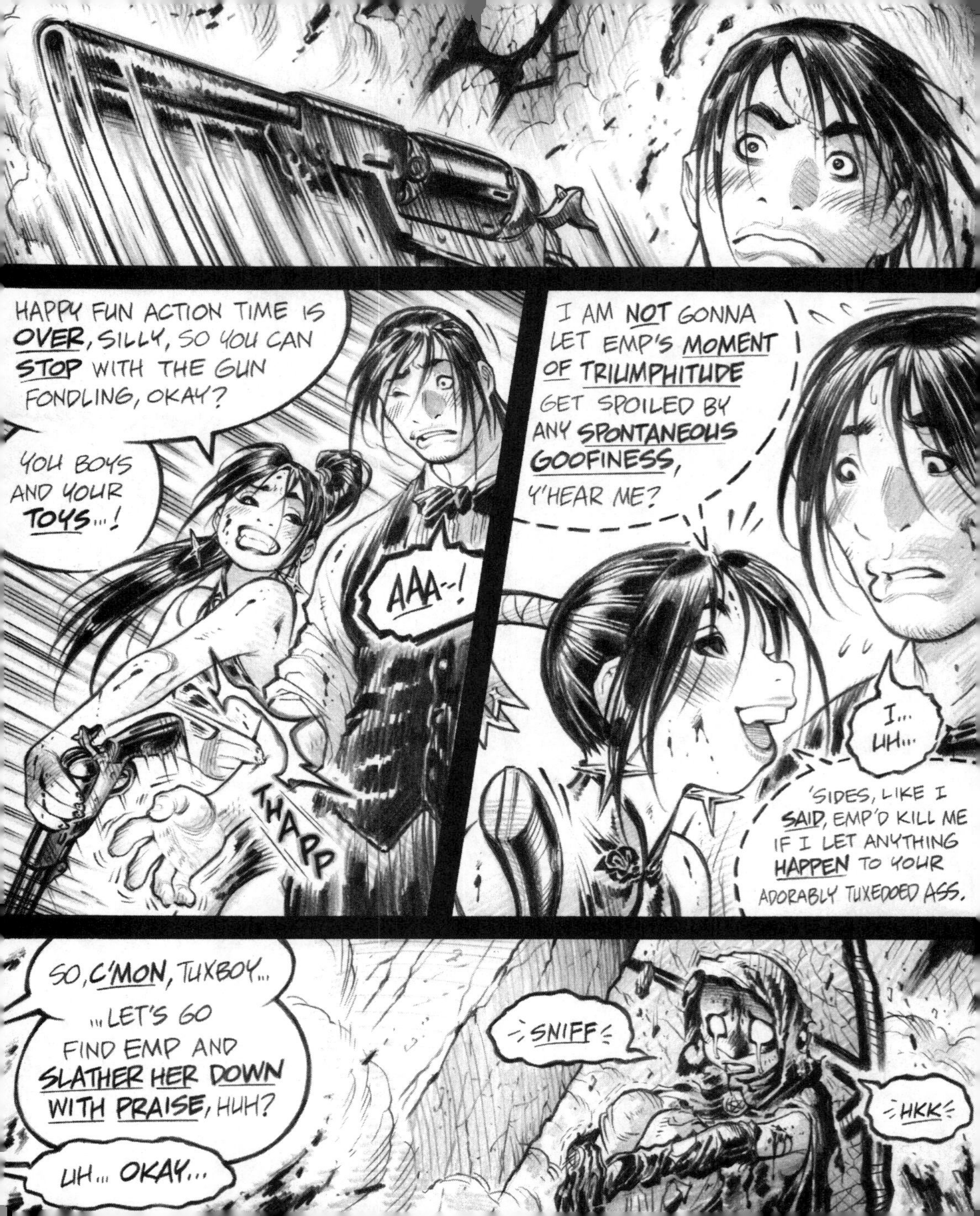
HAPPY FUN ACTION TIME IS OVER, SILLY, SO YOU CAN STOP WITH THE GUN FONDLING, OKAY?
YOU BOYS AND YOUR TOYS...!
AAA--!
THAPP
I AM NOT GONNA LET EMP'S MOMENT OF TRIUMPHITUDE GET SPOILED BY ANY SPONTANEOUS GOOFINESS, Y'HEAR ME?
I... UH...
'SIDES, LIKE I SAID, EMP'D KILL ME IF I LET ANYTHING HAPPEN TO YOUR ADORABLY TUXEDOED ASS.
SO, C'MON, TUXBOY...
...LET'S GO FIND EMP AND SLATHER HER DOWN WITH PRAISE, HUH?
UH... OKAY...
SNIFF
HKK

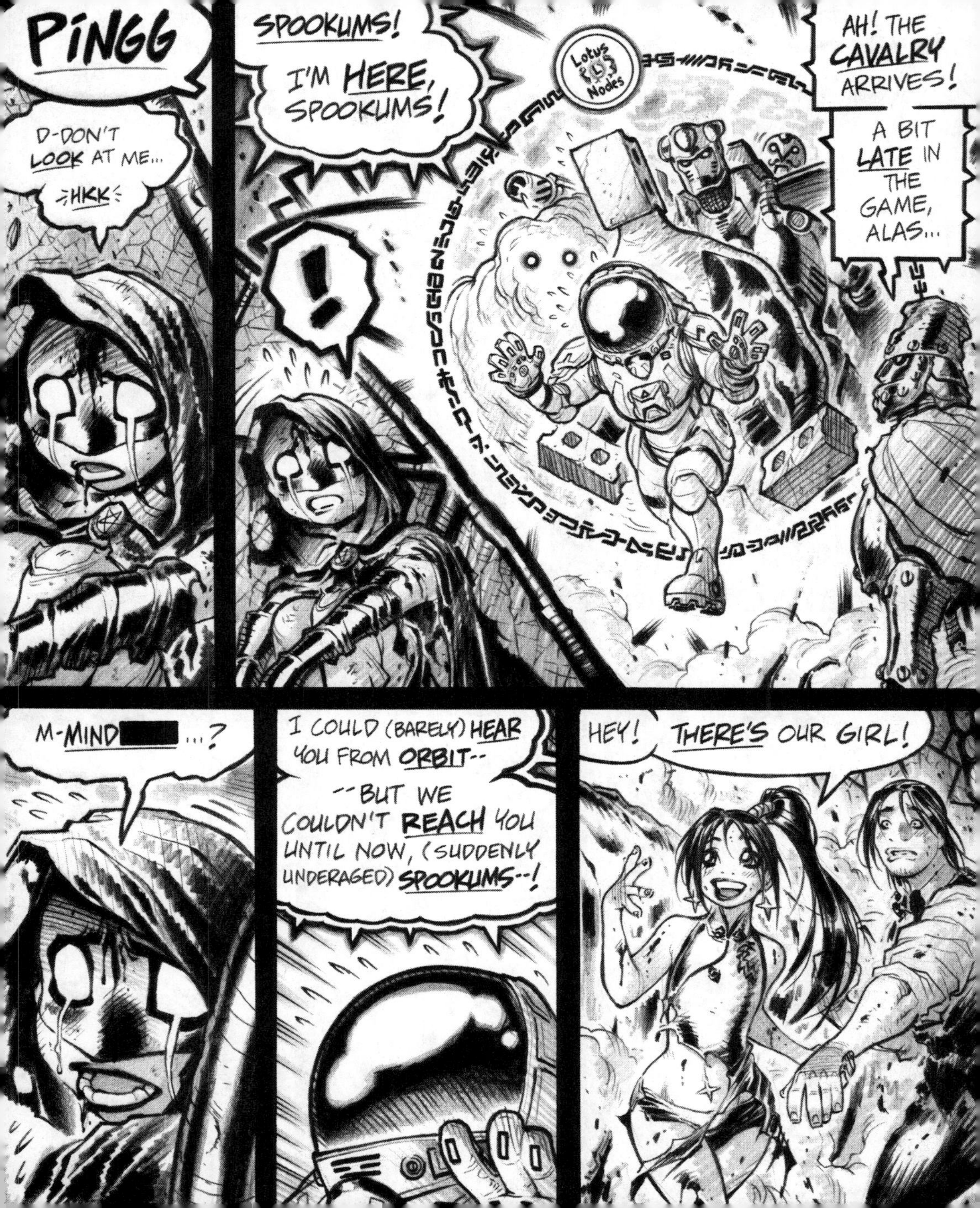
PINGG
D-DON'T LOOK AT ME...
HKK
SPOOKUMS!
I'M HERE, SPOOKUMS!
!
Lotus Nodes
AH! THE CAVALRY ARRIVES!
A BIT LATE IN THE GAME, ALAS...
M-MIND[redacted]...?
I COULD (BARELY) HEAR YOU FROM ORBIT--
--BUT WE COULDN'T REACH YOU UNTIL NOW, (SUDDENLY UNDERAGED) SPOOKUMS--!
HEY!
THERE'S OUR GIRL!

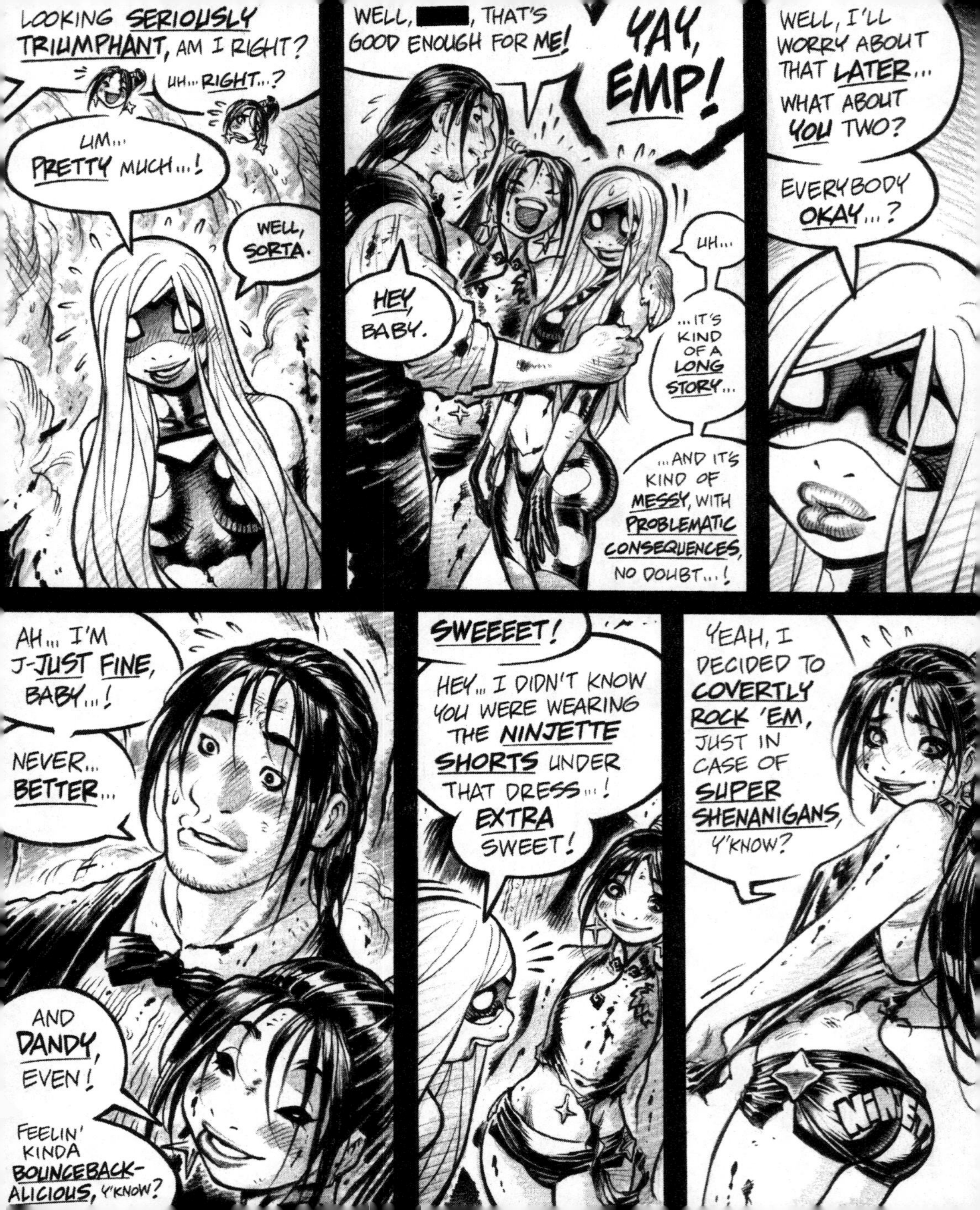
LOOKING SERIOUSLY TRIUMPHANT, AM I RIGHT?
UH... RIGHT...?
UM... PRETTY MUCH...!
WELL, SORTA.
WELL, [redacted], THAT'S GOOD ENOUGH FOR ME!
YAY, EMP!
HEY, BABY.
UH...
...IT'S KIND OF A LONG STORY...
...AND IT'S KIND OF MESSY, WITH PROBLEMATIC CONSEQUENCES, NO DOUBT...!
WELL, I'LL WORRY ABOUT THAT LATER... WHAT ABOUT YOU TWO?
EVERYBODY OKAY...?
AH... I'M J-JUST FINE, BABY...!
NEVER... BETTER...
AND DANDY, EVEN!
FEELIN' KINDA BOUNCEBACK-ALICIOUS, Y'KNOW?
SWEEEET!
HEY... I DIDN'T KNOW YOU WERE WEARING THE NINJETTE SHORTS UNDER THAT DRESS...!
EXTRA SWEET!
YEAH, I DECIDED TO COVERTLY ROCK 'EM, JUST IN CASE OF SUPER SHENANIGANS, Y'KNOW?

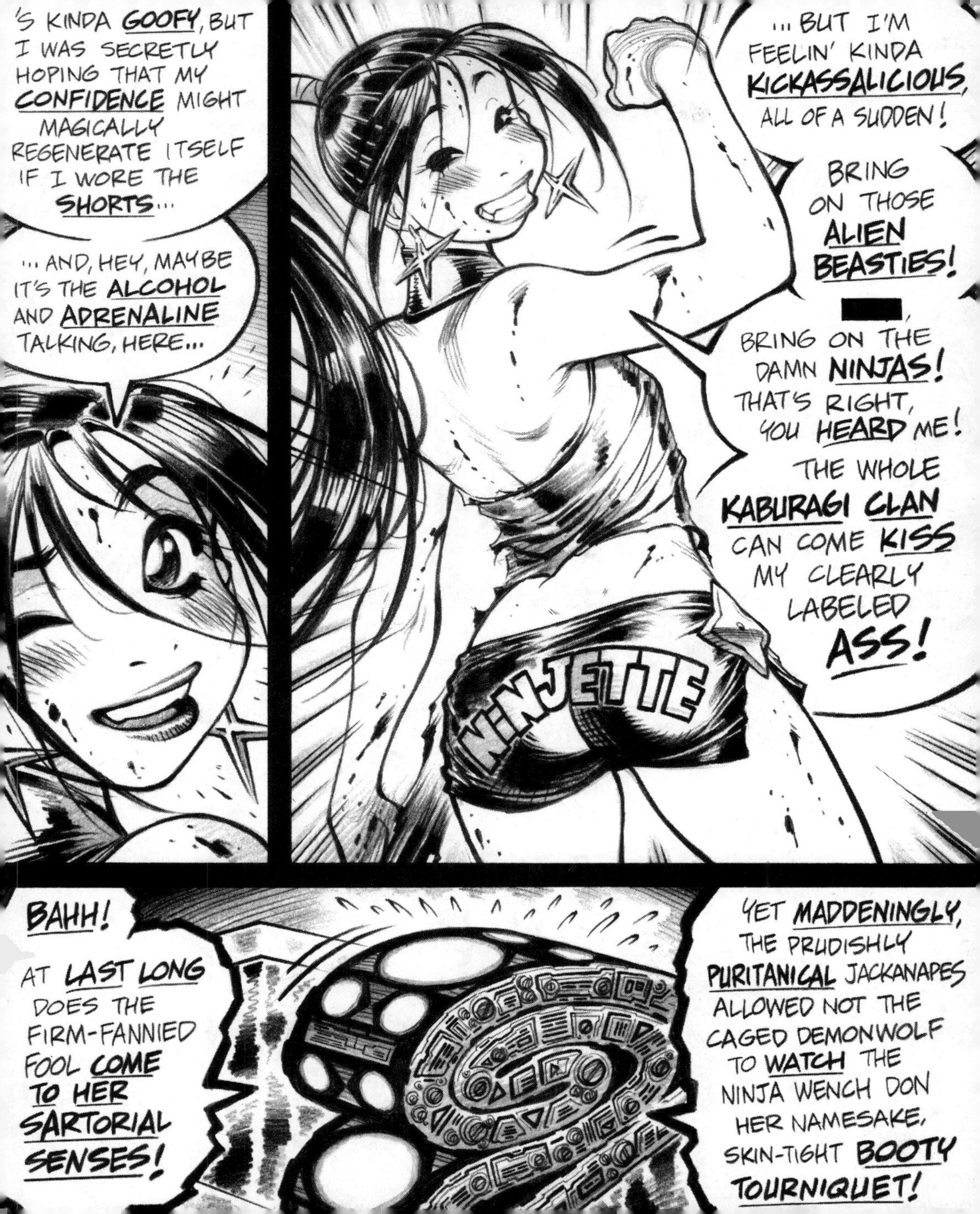
'S KINDA GOOFY, BUT I WAS SECRETLY HOPING THAT MY CONFIDENCE MIGHT MAGICALLY REGENERATE ITSELF IF I WORE THE SHORTS...
...AND, HEY, MAYBE IT'S THE ALCOHOL AND ADRENALINE TALKING, HERE...
...BUT I'M FEELIN' KINDA KICKASSALICIOUS, ALL OF A SUDDEN!
BRING ON THOSE ALIEN BEASTIES!
[redacted], BRING ON THE DAMN NINJAS! THAT'S RIGHT, YOU HEARD ME! THE WHOLE KABURAGI CLAN CAN COME KISS MY CLEARLY LABELED ASS!
NINJETTE
BAHH!
AT LAST LONG DOES THE FIRM-FANNIED FOOL COME TO HER SARTORIAL SENSES!
YET MADDENINGLY, THE PRUDISHLY PURITANICAL JACKANAPES ALLOWED NOT THE CAGED DEMONWOLF TO WATCH THE NINJA WENCH DON HER NAMESAKE, SKIN-TIGHT BOOTY TOURNIQUET!

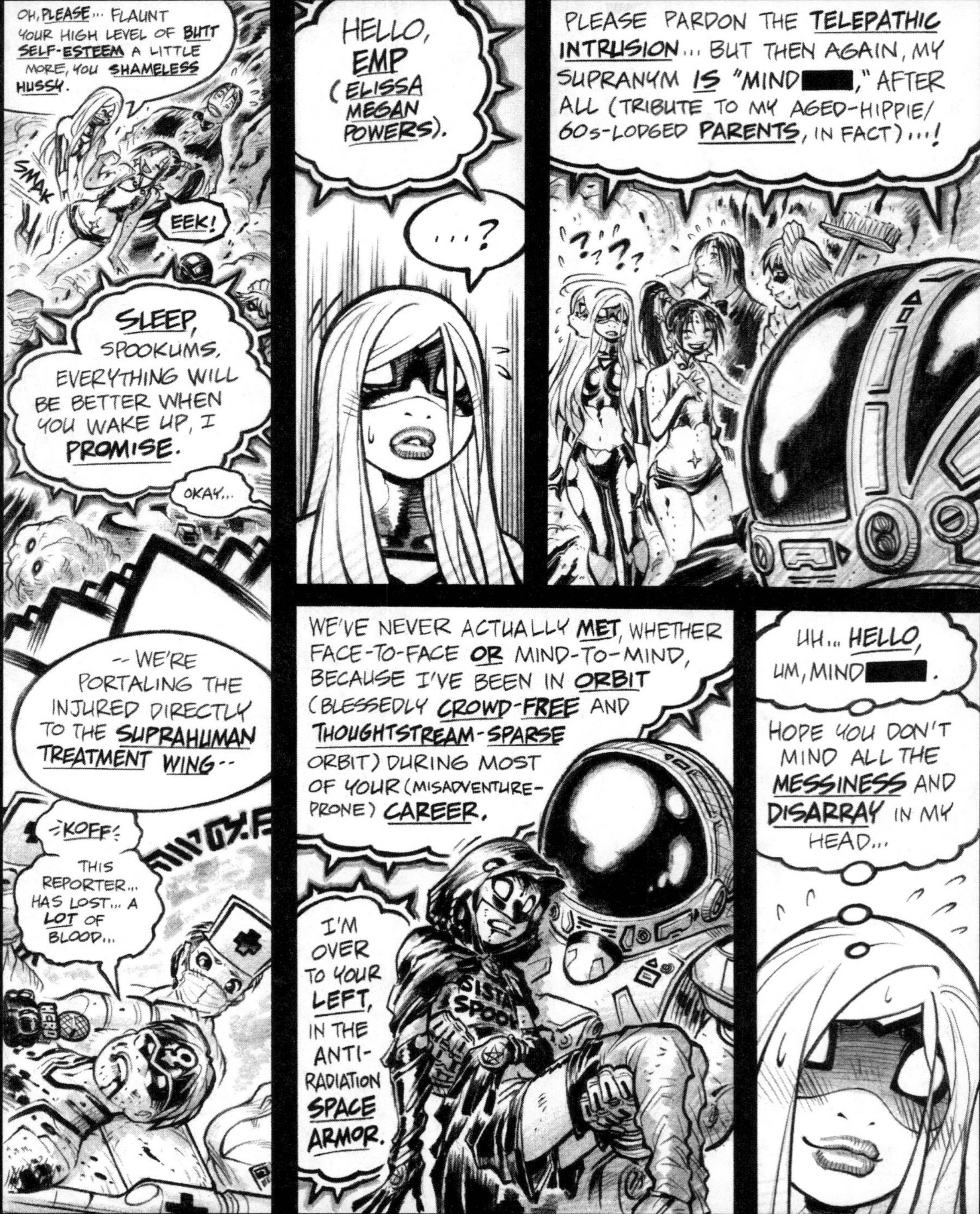
OH, PLEASE... FLAUNT YOUR HIGH LEVEL OF BUTT SELF-ESTEEM A LITTLE MORE, YOU SHAMELESS HUSSY.
SMAK
EEK!
SLEEP, SPOOKUMS. EVERYTHING WILL BE BETTER WHEN YOU WAKE UP, I PROMISE.
OKAY...
HELLO, EMP (ELISSA MEGAN POWERS).
...?
PLEASE PARDON THE TELEPATHIC INTRUSION... BUT THEN AGAIN, MY SUPRANYM IS "MIND[redacted]," AFTER ALL (TRIBUTE TO MY AGED-HIPPIE/ 60s-LODGED PARENTS, IN FACT)...!
?? ??
--WE'RE PORTALING THE INJURED DIRECTLY TO THE SUPRAHUMAN TREATMENT WING--
KOFF
THIS REPORTER... HAS LOST... A LOT OF BLOOD...
WE'VE NEVER ACTUALLY MET, WHETHER FACE-TO-FACE OR MIND-TO-MIND, BECAUSE I'VE BEEN IN ORBIT (BLESSEDLY CROWD-FREE AND THOUGHTSTREAM-SPARSE ORBIT) DURING MOST OF YOUR (MISADVENTURE-PRONE) CAREER.
I'M OVER TO YOUR LEFT, IN THE ANTI-RADIATION SPACE ARMOR.
UH... HELLO, UM, MIND[redacted].
HOPE YOU DON'T MIND ALL THE MESSINESS AND DISARRAY IN MY HEAD...

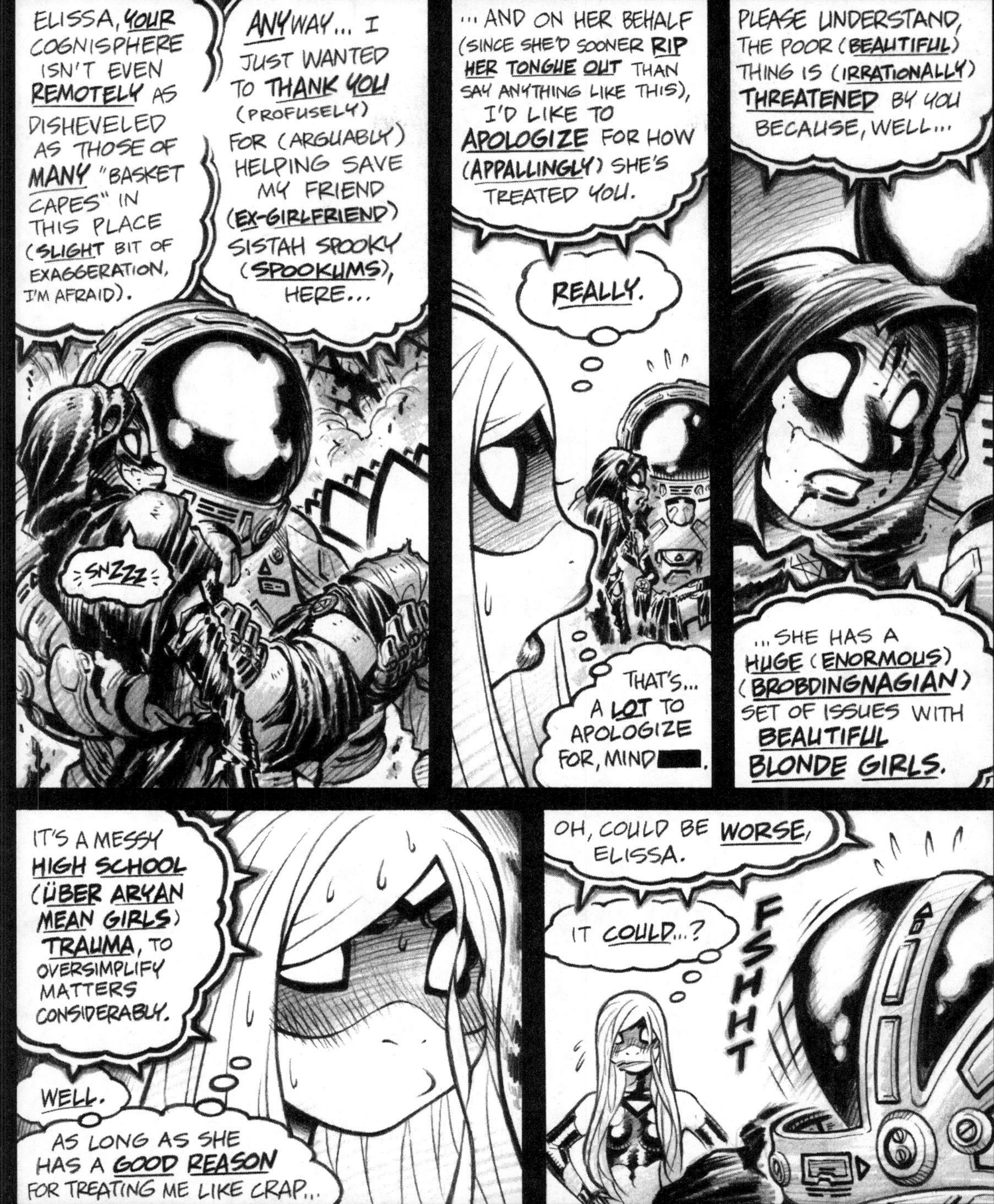
ELISSA, YOUR COGNISPHERE ISN'T EVEN REMOTELY AS DISHEVELED AS THOSE OF MANY "BASKET CAPES" IN THIS PLACE (SLIGHT BIT OF EXAGGERATION, I'M AFRAID).
ANYWAY... I JUST WANTED TO THANK YOU (PROFUSELY) FOR (ARGUABLY) HELPING SAVE MY FRIEND (EX-GIRLFRIEND) SISTAH SPOOKY (SPOOKUMS), HERE...
SNZZZ
...AND ON HER BEHALF (SINCE SHE'D SOONER RIP HER TONGUE OUT THAN SAY ANYTHING LIKE THIS), I'D LIKE TO APOLOGIZE FOR HOW (APPALLINGLY) SHE'S TREATED YOU.
REALLY.
THAT'S... A LOT TO APOLOGIZE FOR, MIND [redacted].
PLEASE UNDERSTAND, THE POOR (BEAUTIFUL) THING IS (IRRATIONALLY) THREATENED BY YOU BECAUSE, WELL...
...SHE HAS A HUGE (ENORMOUS) (BROBDINGNAGIAN) SET OF ISSUES WITH BEAUTIFUL BLONDE GIRLS.
IT'S A MESSY HIGH SCHOOL (ÜBER ARYAN MEAN GIRLS) TRAUMA, TO OVERSIMPLIFY MATTERS CONSIDERABLY.
WELL.
AS LONG AS SHE HAS A GOOD REASON FOR TREATING ME LIKE CRAP...
OH, COULD BE WORSE, ELISSA.
IT COULD...?
FSHHT

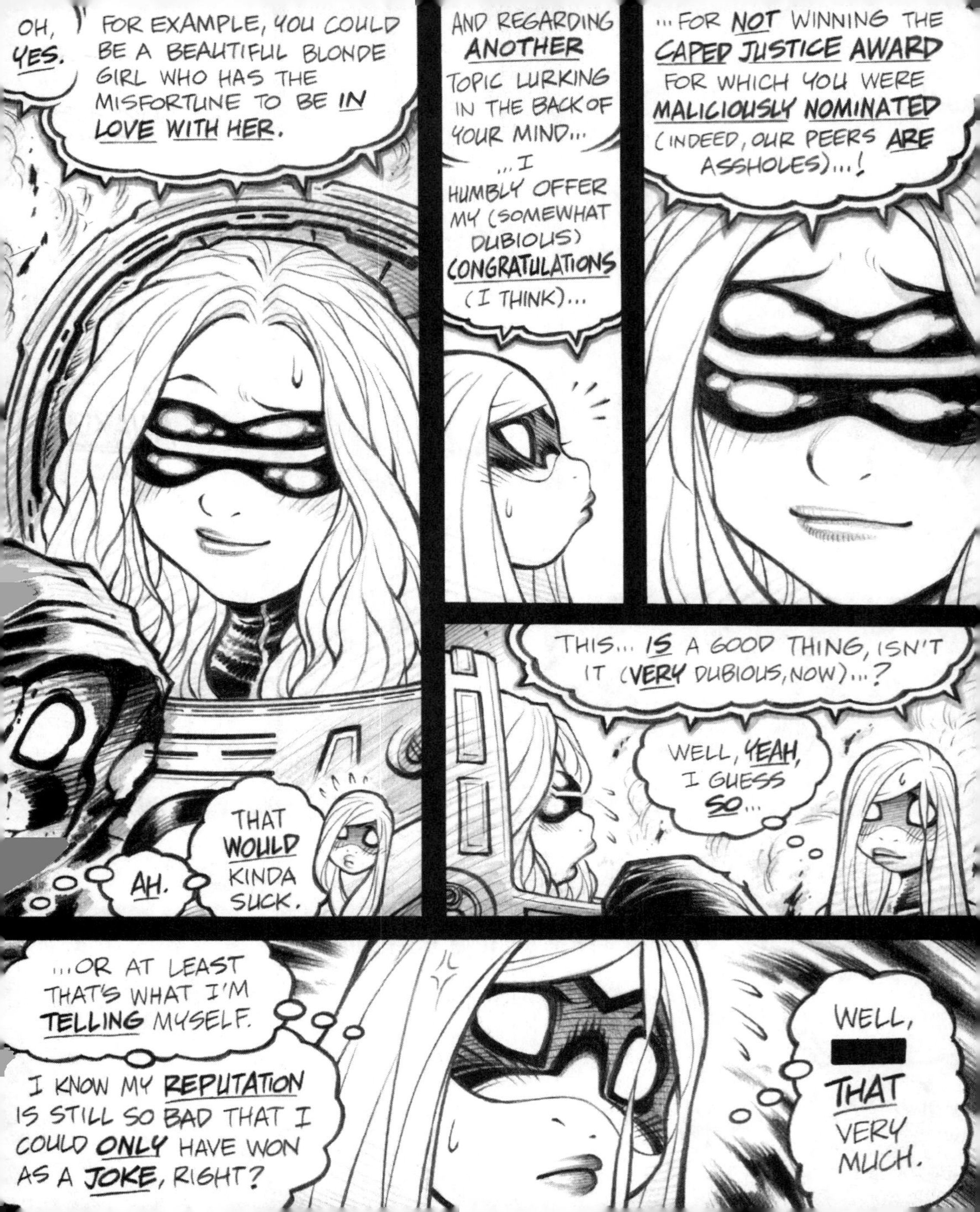

OH, YES.
FOR EXAMPLE, YOU COULD BE A BEAUTIFUL BLONDE GIRL WHO HAS THE MISFORTUNE TO BE IN LOVE WITH HER.
AH.
THAT WOULD KINDA SUCK.
AND REGARDING ANOTHER TOPIC LURKING IN THE BACK OF YOUR MIND... ...I HUMBLY OFFER MY (SOMEWHAT DUBIOUS) CONGRATULATIONS (I THINK)...
...FOR NOT WINNING THE CAPED JUSTICE AWARD FOR WHICH YOU WERE MALICIOUSLY NOMINATED (INDEED, OUR PEERS ARE ASSHOLES)...!
THIS... IS A GOOD THING, ISN'T IT (VERY DUBIOUS, NOW)...?
WELL, YEAH, I GUESS SO...
...OR AT LEAST THAT'S WHAT I'M TELLING MYSELF.
I KNOW MY REPUTATION IS STILL SO BAD THAT I COULD ONLY HAVE WON AS A JOKE, RIGHT?
WELL, [redacted] THAT VERY MUCH.

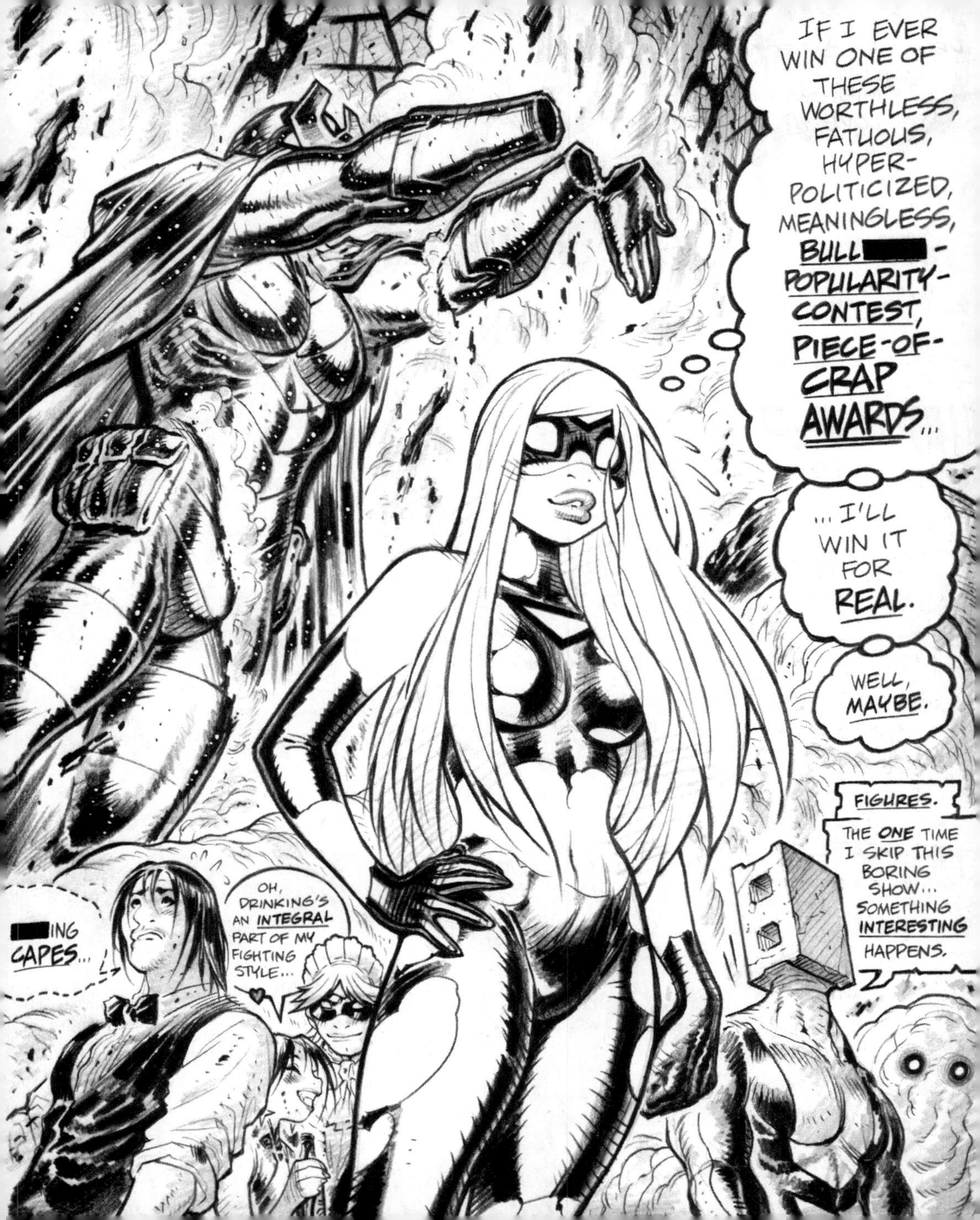
IF I EVER WIN ONE OF THESE WORTHLESS, FATUOUS, HYPER-POLITICIZED, MEANINGLESS, BULL[redacted]-POPULARITY-CONTEST, PIECE-OF-CRAP AWARDS...
...I'LL WIN IT FOR REAL.
WELL, MAYBE.
FIGURES.
THE ONE TIME I SKIP THIS BORING SHOW... SOMETHING INTERESTING HAPPENS.
[redacted]ING CAPES...
OH, DRINKING'S AN INTEGRAL PART OF MY FIGHTING STYLE...

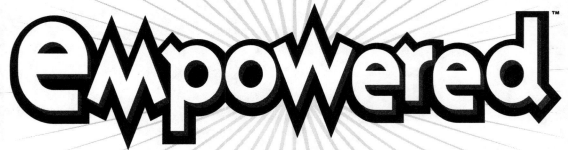

empowered™

Volume 4

WELL, THERE YOU GO.

YOU DIDN'T **REALLY** THINK I'D ACTUALLY **WIN AN AWARD**, DID YOU?

LORD KNOWS THIS GOOFY **BOOK** COULDN'T POSSIBLY WIN AN AWARD, EITHER...

NOT THAT I'M, Y'KNOW, **BITTER** OR ANYTHING.

KNOW **WHAT**?

I THINK I SAW THE OFT-PROMISED **"WERE-GIRAFFE BY NIGHT"** IN THE BACKGROUND OF THAT LAST STORY...!

STILL NO PROGRESS ON THE "EXPLAINING WHY EMP'S **SUPERSUIT** DOESN'T SHOW **CAMEL-TOE**" ISSUE, THOUGH... MAYBE **NEXT** VOLUME, YOU THINK?

The End.

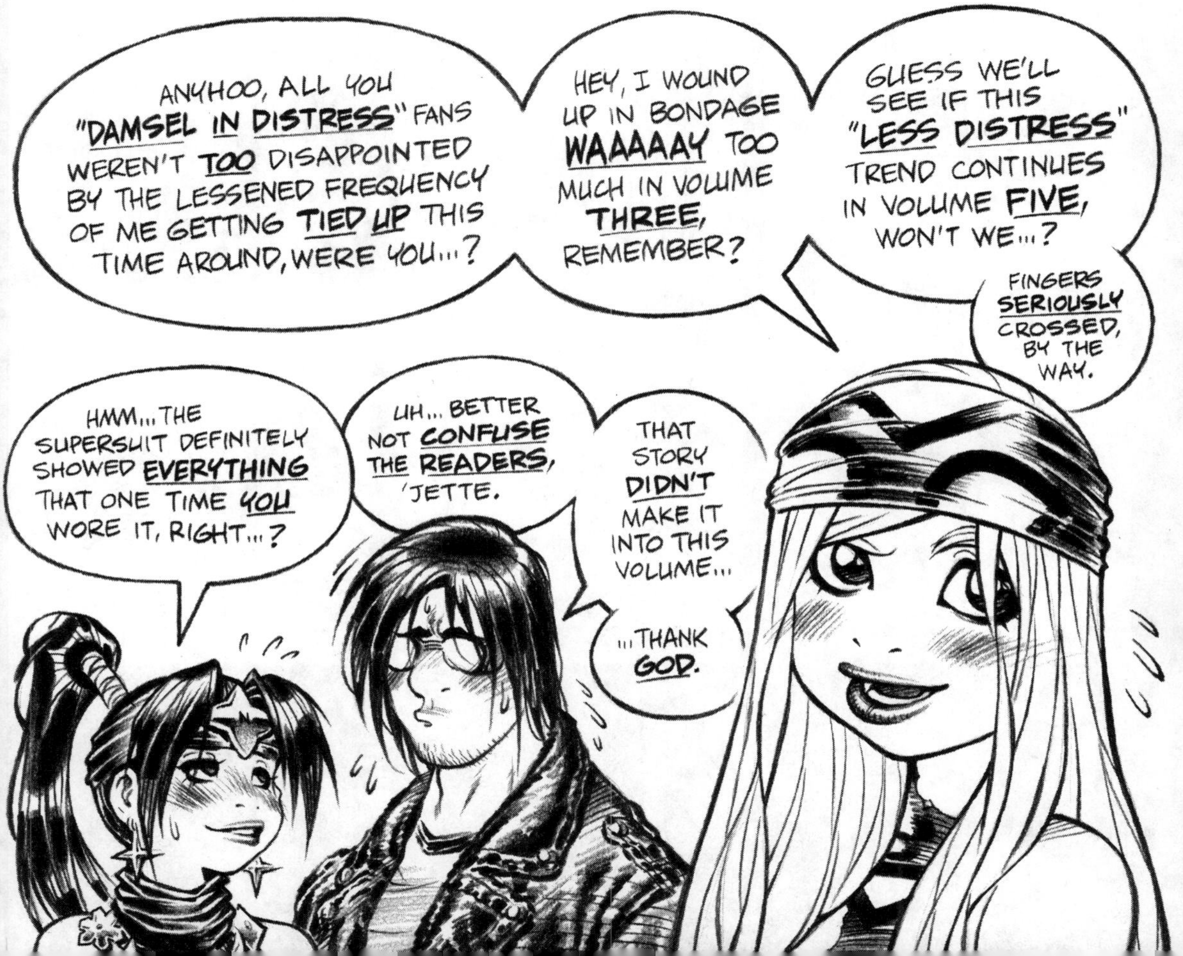
ANYHOO, ALL YOU "DAMSEL IN DISTRESS" FANS WEREN'T TOO DISAPPOINTED BY THE LESSENED FREQUENCY OF ME GETTING TIED UP THIS TIME AROUND, WERE YOU...?
HEY, I WOUND UP IN BONDAGE WAAAAAY TOO MUCH IN VOLUME THREE, REMEMBER?
GUESS WE'LL SEE IF THIS "LESS DISTRESS" TREND CONTINUES IN VOLUME FIVE, WON'T WE...?
FINGERS SERIOUSLY CROSSED, BY THE WAY.
HMM... THE SUPERSUIT DEFINITELY SHOWED EVERYTHING THAT ONE TIME YOU WORE IT, RIGHT...?
UH... BETTER NOT CONFUSE THE READERS, 'JETTE.
THAT STORY DIDN'T MAKE IT INTO THIS VOLUME...
...THANK GOD.

Empowered™ EXTRAS

First off, here's a two-page "interview with Emp" comic I produced for issue 19 of the fine music/pop-culture magazine *Ghettoblaster.* Have to say, I much prefer the idea of my characters being interviewed about a project, as opposed to me being interviewed . . . What can I say, I'm the shy and retiring type.

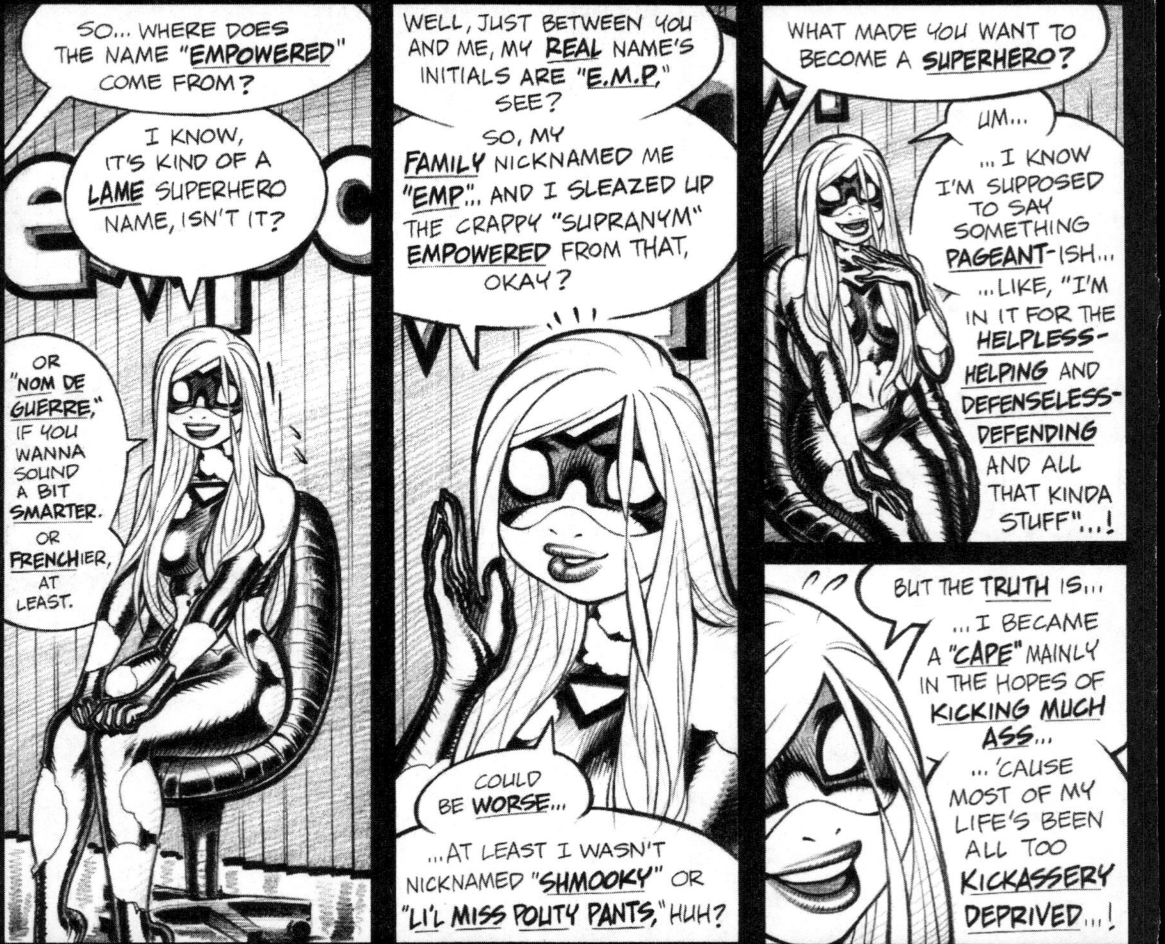
SO... WHERE DOES THE NAME "EMPOWERED" COME FROM?
I KNOW, IT'S KIND OF A LAME SUPERHERO NAME, ISN'T IT?
OR "NOM DE GUERRE," IF YOU WANNA SOUND A BIT SMARTER. OR FRENCHIER, AT LEAST.
WELL, JUST BETWEEN YOU AND ME, MY REAL NAME'S INITIALS ARE "E.M.P.," SEE?
SO, MY FAMILY NICKNAMED ME "EMP"... AND I SLEAZED UP THE CRAPPY "SUPRANYM" EMPOWERED FROM THAT, OKAY?
COULD BE WORSE...
...AT LEAST I WASN'T NICKNAMED "SHMOOKY" OR "LI'L MISS POUTY PANTS," HUH?
WHAT MADE YOU WANT TO BECOME A SUPERHERO?
UM...
...I KNOW I'M SUPPOSED TO SAY SOMETHING PAGEANT-ISH... ...LIKE, "I'M IN IT FOR THE HELPLESS-HELPING AND DEFENSELESS-DEFENDING AND ALL THAT KINDA STUFF"...!
BUT THE TRUTH IS...
...I BECAME A "CAPE" MAINLY IN THE HOPES OF KICKING MUCH ASS...
...'CAUSE MOST OF MY LIFE'S BEEN ALL TOO KICKASSERY DEPRIVED...!

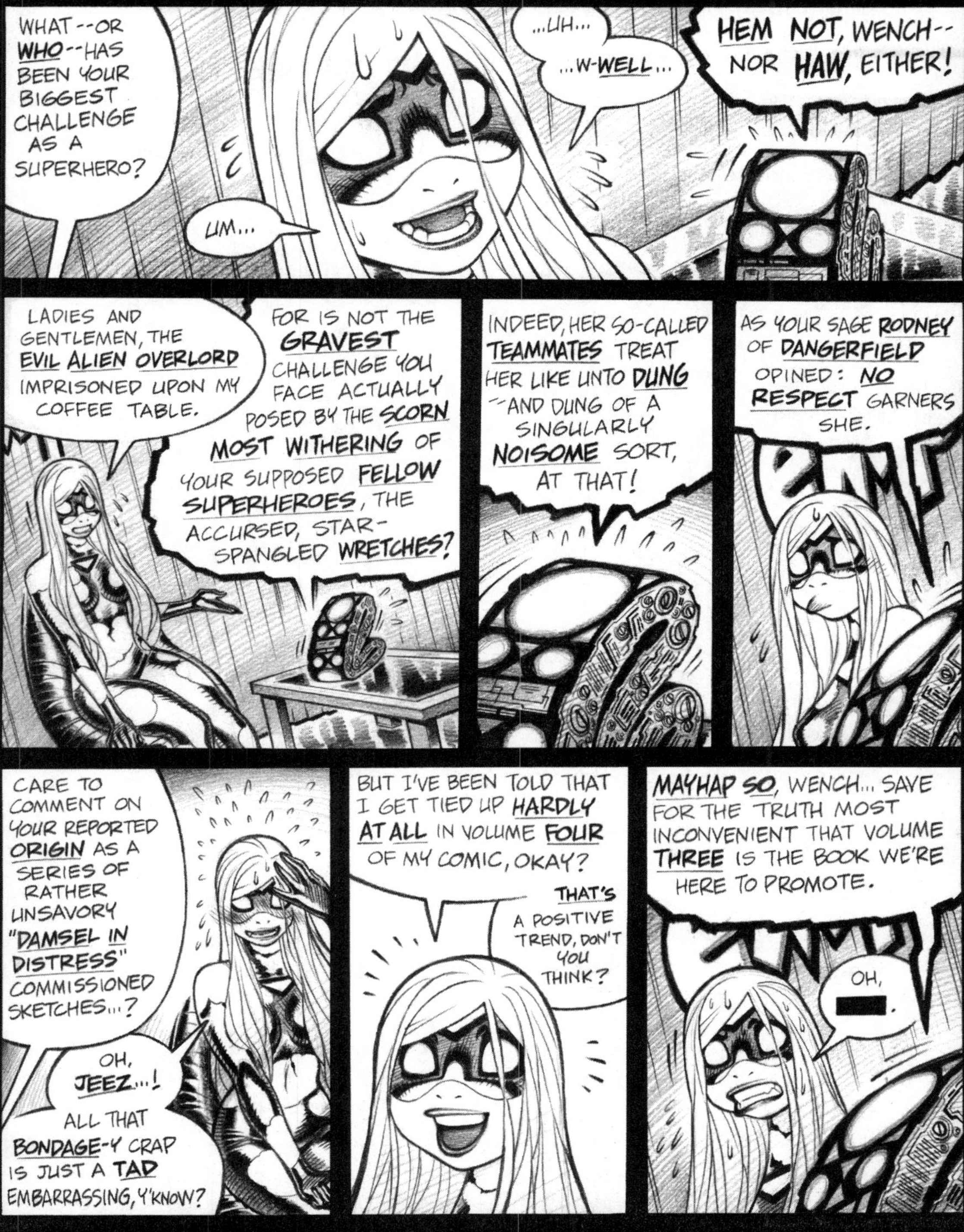
WHAT--OR WHO--HAS BEEN YOUR BIGGEST CHALLENGE AS A SUPERHERO?
UM...
...UH...
...W-WELL...
HEM NOT, WENCH-- NOR HAW, EITHER!
LADIES AND GENTLEMEN, THE EVIL ALIEN OVERLORD IMPRISONED UPON MY COFFEE TABLE.
FOR IS NOT THE GRAVEST CHALLENGE YOU FACE ACTUALLY POSED BY THE SCORN MOST WITHERING OF YOUR SUPPOSED FELLOW SUPERHEROES, THE ACCURSED, STAR-SPANGLED WRETCHES?
INDEED, HER SO-CALLED TEAMMATES TREAT HER LIKE UNTO DUNG --AND DUNG OF A SINGULARLY NOISOME SORT, AT THAT!
AS YOUR SAGE RODNEY OF DANGERFIELD OPINED: NO RESPECT GARNERS SHE.
CARE TO COMMENT ON YOUR REPORTED ORIGIN AS A SERIES OF RATHER UNSAVORY "DAMSEL IN DISTRESS" COMMISSIONED SKETCHES...?
OH, JEEZ...!
ALL THAT BONDAGE-Y CRAP IS JUST A TAD EMBARRASSING, Y'KNOW?
BUT I'VE BEEN TOLD THAT I GET TIED UP HARDLY AT ALL IN VOLUME FOUR OF MY COMIC, OKAY?
THAT'S A POSITIVE TREND, DON'T YOU THINK?
MAYHAP SO, WENCH... SAVE FOR THE TRUTH MOST INCONVENIENT THAT VOLUME THREE IS THE BOOK WE'RE HERE TO PROMOTE.
OH, [redacted].

ALSO BY ADAM WARREN

ADAM WARREN
The DIRTY PAIR
SIM HELL

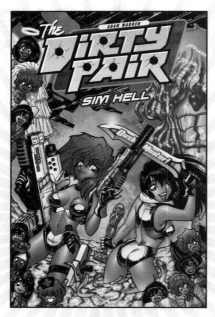

THE DIRTY PAIR: SIM HELL 3RD EDITION TPB
ISBN 978-1-56971-742-4 / $12.95

BUBBLEGUM CRISIS
GRAND MAL
ADAM WARREN

BUBBLEGUM CRISIS: GRAND MAL TPB
ISBN 978-1-56971-120-0 / $14.95

THE DIRTY PAIR–YURI ACTION FIGURE
ITEM #11-149 / $13.99

THE DIRTY PAIR–KEI ACTION FIGURE
ITEM #10-312 / $13.99

AVAILABLE AT YOUR LOCAL COMICS SHOP OR BOOKSTORE

To find a comics shop in your area, call 1-888-266-4226

For more information or to order direct: • On the web: darkhorse.com • E-mail: mailorder@darkhorse.com • Phone: 1-800-862-0052 Mon.-Fri. 9 A.M. to 5 P.M. Pacific Time

EMPOWERED

VOLUME 1
ISBN 978-1-59307-672-6

VOLUME 2
ISBN 978-1-59307-816-4

VOLUME 3
ISBN 978-1-59307-870-6

VOLUME 4
ISBN 978-1-59307-994-9

VOLUME 5
ISBN 978-1-59582-212-3

AVAILABLE AT YOUR LOCAL COMICS SHOP OR BOOKSTORE.
TO FIND A COMICS SHOP IN YOUR AREA, CALL 1-888-266-4226

For more information or to order direct: ·On the web: darkhorse.com
·E-mail: mailorder@darkhorse.com ·Phone: 1-800-862-0052 Mon.–Fri. 9 AM to 5 PM Pacific Time.
*Prices and availability subject to change without notice.

DARK HORSE BOOKS

publisher Mike Richardson • executive vice president Neil Hankerson • chief financial officer Tom Weddle • vice president of publishing Randy Stradley • vice president of business development Michael Martens • vice president of marketing, sales, and licensing Anita Nelson • vice president of product development David Scroggy • vice president of information technology Dale LaFountain • director of purchasing Darlene Vogel • general council Ken Lizzi • editorial director Davey Estrada • senior managing editor Scott Allie • senior books editor Chris Warner • executive editor Diana Schutz • director of design and production Cary Grazzini • art director Lia Ribacchi • director of scheduling Cara Niece

ADAM WARREN was one of the first writer/ artists in the American comics field to integrate the artistic and storytelling techniques of Japanese comics into his work. Yep, he was definitely a manga-influenced pioneer, even going so far as to ride around in a covered wagon and fire his six-shooters in the air while bellowing "Yee-Haw," pioneer-style. Okay, maybe he *didn't* actually go that far.

Off and on since 1988, he's written and drawn an idiosyncratic, English-language comics adaptation of the popular Japanese science-fiction characters known as *The Dirty Pair,* who first appeared in novels by award-winning author Haruka Takachi-ho and were popularized in a varying series of anime incarnations. The six *Dirty Pair* miniseries Adam worked on were known for their purty, purty artwork, future-shockalicious SF concepts, and obnoxiously satirical sense of humor . . . and at least one of which might be available as a trade-paperback collection from Dark Horse (hint, hint).

The rest of Adam's ripped and toned body of comics-related work ranges from forays into the teen-superhero, pop-culture saturation of Wild-storm/DC's *Gen 13*, to a DC prestige-format, far-future iteration of the Teen Titans (*Titans: Scissors, Paper, Stone*), and even a take on old-school anime with a *Bubblegum Crisis* mini-series. More recently, he's created and written the mecha-superteam project *Livewires* for Marvel Comics, along with the miniseries *Iron Man: Hypervelocity.*

Beyond the comics field, he's dabbled in artistic miscellanea such as a dōjinshi "sketchbook" pub-lished in Japan and illustrations for magazines such as *Spin, GamePro, PSM, Wizard,* and *Stuff,* not to mention several (very) short-lived stabs into the fields of video games, CD-cover artwork, and TV animation. Currently, he's engaged in an epic, almost mythic feat of what might (very) loosely be described as "home repair"—indeed, the ordeal is remarkably akin to Hercules cleaning the Augean stables, but, alas, featuring a rather less impressive specimen of bearded manhood.

Adam lives a thrillingly reclusive lifestyle some-where off in the deep woods, where hunting rifles boom, FedEx trucks get stuck in the mud, and grey squirrels the size of Labrador retrievers run up and down the sides of houses all ****ing day long, like the world's loudest and furriest ninja. His hobbies include: pegging himself in the eye with the snapped-off tip from a 3B pencil lead, dosing up with No-Doz®, dosing down with quality microbrews, reading an average of four to eight books per week, bailing over to the local Barnes & Noble to get an average of four to eight more books per week (whilst grinding his teeth at this particular store's repeated, madden-ing failure to stock *Empowered*), working out to *Dance Dance Revolution* for the maximum possible embarrassment value, bitching about the truly critical issues of the day (such as death, taxes, and the tragic state of Tom Brady's anterior cruciate ligament), and damaging what's left of his hearing with an iPod full of songs that are far, far too lame to admit listening to in public. His favorite colors are black and blue, which is almost certainly sym-bolic of something profoundly negative.

Find out more about Adam and his work on **DeviantART** and **MySpace**:
http://adamwarren.deviantart.com
http://www.myspace.com/adamwarrencomics